Merchant Ship Naval Architecture

Merchant Ship Naval Architecture

Shiven Arora

RANDOM

RANDOM PUBLICATIONS
NEW DELHI (INDIA)

Merchant Ship Naval Architecture

ISBN 978-93-5111-403-1

Published in 2014 in India by

RANDOM PUBLICATIONS

4376-A/4B, Gali Murari Lal, Ansari Road
New Delhi-110 002
Phone : +91-11-43580356, +91-11-23289044
e-mail: randomexports@gmail.com, sales@randompublications.com, info@randompublications.com

Type Setting by : Keystoneprintads, Delhi-110051
Digitally Printed at : Replika Press Pvt. Ltd.

Preface

Naval architecture is an engineering discipline dealing with the design, construction, maintenance and operation of marine vessels and structures. Naval architecture involves basic and applied research, design, development, design evaluation and calculations during all stages of the life of a marine vehicle. The preliminary design of the vessel, its detailed design, construction, trials, operation and maintenance, launching and dry-docking are the main activities involved. Ship design calculations are also required for ships being modified (by means of conversion, rebuilding, modernization, or repair). Naval architecture also involves formulation of safety regulations and damage control rules and the approval and certification of ship designs to meet statutory and non-statutory requirements.

Naval architecture is an engineering discipline that deals with design, construction, operations and maintenance of seagoing vessels. Naval architecture plays the primary role in all stages of the life of a marine vessel right from the initial designing with advanced type of design, actual construction, testing, operations, maintenance as well as launching and dry-docking of marine vessels. The role and scope of naval architecture don't end here, as it is also involved in the modification, modernization and repair of old vessels. The discipline also involves in areas dealing with formulation of safety standards, damage control rules and certification of vessel designs.

The naval architect creates the initial overall concept for a new ship, integrates the work of other specialists as the ship design is developed, and is specifically responsible for the hull and superstructure shape, general arrangements, structural design, weights and centers calculations, stability analysis, hydrodynamic performance assessments, propeller and rudder design, and the arrangement and outfit of all living and working spaces, other than machinery spaces. The naval architect's ally, the marine engineer, is responsible for the design of the propulsion plant, the electric plant, and other ship machinery and mechanical systems, including the so-called distributive systems: electric cabling, piping, and ventilation system ducting. The marine engineer also is responsible for ship control systems, including propulsion and electric plant controls and the steering system.

Ships are built for a wide variety of purposes, but all must meet certain fundamental requirements. They must have reserve buoyancy to enable them to carry their designed loads and resist damage, stability to resist environmental forces or damage, and strength to withstand the stresses imposed on their structure by their own weight, cargo, stores, and the sea. The salvage engineer with the basics of surface ship construction, stability, and strength. A ship's hull is a complex geometric form that can be defined accurately by mapping its surface in a three-dimensional orthogonal coordinate system. If a Cartesian coordinate system is used, conventions usually set the Z-axis vertical, the X-axis longitudinal and the Y-axis athwartships. Principal dimensions are measured along these axes. The hull form can be shown in two dimensions by a series of curves formed by the intersection of the hull surface with planes parallel to these axes. The hull form, chosen by the designer, controls the stability and performance characteristics of the ship in its normal environments.

The book will be useful as a reference source for the students, teachers, researchers, policy makers, administrators, engineers and managers of naval ship architecture.

I thank all members of my team who have helped in the preparation of the book. My special thanks go to "Random Publications" who have published the book.

– *Shiven Arora*

Contents

1

Merchant Vessel

A merchant vessel is a ship that transports cargo or passengers. The closely related term commercial vessel is defined by the United States Coast Guard as any vessel (i.e. boat or ship) engaged in commercial trade or that carries passengers for hire. This would exclude pleasure craft that do not carry passengers for hire or warships.

They come in a myriad of sizes and shapes from twenty-foot inflatable dive boats in Hawaii, to 5,000 passenger casino vessels on the Mississippi River, to tugboats plying New York Harbor, to 1,000 foot oil tankers and container ships at major ports, to a passenger carrying submarine in the U.S. Virgin Islands.

Most countries of the world operate fleets of merchant ships. However, due to the high costs of operations, today these fleets are in many cases sailing under the flags of nations that specialize in providing manpower and services at favourable terms. Such flags are known as "flags of convenience". Currently, Liberia and Panama are particularly favoured. Ownership of the vessels can be by any country, however.

The Greek-owned fleet is the largest in the world. Today, the Greek fleet accounts for some 16 per cent of the world's tonnage; this makes it currently the largest single international merchant fleet in the world, albeit not the largest in history.

In English, "Merchant Navy" without further clarification is used to refer to the British Merchant Navy; the United States merchant fleet is known as the United States Merchant Marine.

During wars, merchant ships may be used as auxiliaries to the navies of their respective countries, and are called upon to deliver military personnel and material.

NAME PREFIXES

Merchant ships names are prefixed by which kind of vessel they are:

- MV = Motor Vessel
- SS = Steam Ship

- MT = Motor Tanker or Motor Tug Boat
- MSV = Motor Stand-by Vessel
- MY = Motor Yacht
- RMS = Royal Mail Ship
- RRS = Royal Research Ship
- SV = Sailing Vessel (although these can be sub coded as type of sailing vessel)
- LPG = Gas carrier transporting liquefied petroleum gas
- LNG = Gas carrier transporting liquefied natural gas
- CS = Cable Ship or Cable layer

MERCHANT SHIP CATEGORIES

Merchant ships may be divided into several categories, according to their purpose and/or size.

DRY CARGO SHIPS(M\H)

A cargo ship or freighter is any sort of ship or vessel that carries cargo, goods, and materials from one port to another. Thousands of cargo carriers ply the world's seas and oceans each year; they handle the bulk of international trade. Cargo ships are usually specially designed for the task, often being equipped with cranes and other mechanisms to load and unload, and come in all sizes.

Dry cargo ships today are mainly bulk carriers and container ships. Bulk carriers or bulkers are used for the transportation of homogeneous cargo such as coal, rubber, copra, tin, and wheat. Container ships are used for the carriage of miscellaneous goods.

BULK CARRIERS

A bulk carrier is an ocean-going vessel used to transport bulk cargo items such as iron ore, bauxite, coal, cement, grain and similar cargo. Bulk carriers can be recognized by large box-like hatches on deck, designed to slide outboard or fold fore-and-aft to enable access for loading or discharging cargo. The dimensions of bulk carriers are often determined by the ports and sea routes that they need to serve, and by the maximum width of the Panama Canal.

Most lakes are too small to accommodate bulk carriers, but a large fleet of lake freighters has been plying the Great Lakes and St. Lawrence Seaway of North America for over a century.

CONTAINER SHIPS

Container ships are cargo ships that carry all of their load in truck-size containers, in a technique called containerization. They form a common means of commercial intermodal freight transport.

TANKERS

A tanker is a ship designed to transport liquids in bulk.

Oil tankers for the transport of fluids, such as crude oil, petroleum products, liquefied petroleum gas, liquefied natural gas and chemicals, also vegetable oils, wine and other food - the tanker sector comprises one third of the world tonnage.

Tankers can range in size from several hundred tons, designed for servicing small harbours and coastal settlements, to several hundred thousand tons, with these being designed for long-range haulage. A wide range of products are carried by tankers, including:

- hydrocarbon products such as oil, LPG, and LNG
- Chemicals, such as ammonia, chlorine, and styrene monomer
- fresh water
- wine

Different products require different handling and transport, thus special types of tankers have been built, such as "chemical tankers" and "oil tankers". Gas Carriers such as ""LNG carriers" as they are typically known, are a relatively rare tanker designed to carry liquefied natural gas.

Among oil tankers, supertankers were designed for carrying oil around the Horn of Africa from the Middle East; the FSO Knock Nevis being the largest vessel in the world, a ULCC supertanker formerly known as Jahre Viking (Seawise Giant). It has a deadweight of 565 thousand metric tons and length of about 500 meters. The use of such large ships is in fact very unprofitable, due to the inability to operate them at full cargo capacity; hence, the production of supertankers has currently ceased. Today's largest oil tankers in comparison by gross tonnage are TI Europe, TI Asia, TI Oceania, which are the largest sailing vessels today. But even with their deadweight of 441,585 metric tons, sailing as VLCC most of the time, they do not use more than 70% of their total capacity.

Apart from pipeline transport, supertankers are the only method for transporting large quantities of oil, although such tankers have caused large environmental disasters when sinking close to coastal regions, causing oil spills. See Braer, Erika, Exxon Valdez, Prestige and Torrey Canyon for examples of tankers that have been involved in oil spills.

SPECIALIZED SHIPS

Specialized ships, e.g. for heavy lift goods or refrigerated cargo (Reefer ships), roll-on/roll-off cargo (RoRo) ships for vehicles and wheeled machinery. These ships are not very well developed, except those used as car carriers.

Only this sector of Maritime Industry is well developed. The currently largest roll-on/roll-off cargo (RoRo) ships are Sunbelt Spirit, Liberty (ex-Faust), Phoenix Leader and Aquamarine ACE, each capable of carrying between six and nine thousand units. Another type of specialised ship is the Cable Ship or Cable layer. These are deep-sea vessels designed and used to lay underwater cables for telecommunications, electric power transmission, or other purposes. In addition to cable layer ships, there are cable repairing ships which are tasked with finding and repairing under sea cables that break or for whatever reason became inoperable.

COASTERS

Coasters, smaller ships for any category of cargo which are normally not on ocean-crossing routes, but in coastwise trades. Coasters are shallow-hulled ships used for trade between locations on the same island or continent. Their shallow hulls mean that they can get through reefs where seagoing ships usually cannot (seagoing ships have a very deep hull for supplies and trade etc.).

PASSENGER SHIPS

A passenger ship is a ship whose primary function is to carry passengers. The category does not include cargo vessels which have accommodations for limited numbers of passengers, such as the formerly ubiquitous twelve-passenger freighters in which the transport of passengers is secondary to the carriage of freight.

The type does however include many classes of ships which are designed to transport substantial numbers of passengers as well as freight. Indeed, until recently virtually all ocean liners were able to transport mail, package freight and express, and other cargo in addition to passenger luggage, and were equipped with cargo holds and derricks, kingposts, or other cargo-handling gear for that purpose. Modern cruiseferries have car decks for lorries as well as the passenger's cars. Only in more recent ocean liners and in virtually all cruise ships has this cargo capacity been removed.

CRUISE SHIPS

A cruise ship or a cruise liner is a passenger ship used for pleasure voyages, where the voyage itself and the ship's amenities are considered an essential part of the experience. Cruising has become a major part of the tourism industry, with millions of passengers each year as of 2008. The industry's rapid growth has seen nine or more newly built ships catering to a North American clientele added every year since 1978, as well as others servicing European clientele. Smaller markets such as the Asia-Pacific region are generally serviced by older tonnage displaced by new ships introduced into the high growth areas.

Cruise ships operate on a mostly set roundabout course or round trips (i.e., they tend to return to their originating port) whereas ocean liners are defined by actually doing ocean-crossing voyages, which may not lead back to the same port for years.

FERRIES

A ferry is a form of transportation, usually a boat or ship, but also other forms, carrying (or ferrying) passengers and sometimes their vehicles. Ferries are also used to transport freight (in lorries and sometimes unpowered freight containers) and even railroad cars (in the case of a train ferry). Most ferries operate on regular, frequent, return services. A foot-passenger ferry with many stops, such as in Venice, is sometimes called a waterbus or water taxi.

Ferries form public transport systems of many waterside cities, allowing direct transit between points at a capital cost much lower than bridges or tunnels.

2

Dry Cargo

BARGE

A barge is a flat-bottomed boat, built mainly for river and canal transport of heavy goods. Some barges are not self-propelled and need to be towed or pushed by towboats. Canal barges, towed by draft animals on an adjacent towpath, contended with the railway in the early industrial revolution, but were outcompeted in the carriage of high-value items due to the higher speed, falling costs, and route flexibility of rail.

ETYMOLOGY

Barge is attested from 1300, from Old Frenchbarge, from Vulgar Latinbarga. The word originally could refer to any small boat; the modern meaning arose around 1480. Bark "small ship" is attested from 1420, from Old French barque, from Vulgar Latin barca (400 AD). The more precise meaning "three-masted ship" arose in the 17th century, and often takes the French spelling for disambiguation. Both are probably derived from the Latinbarica, from Greekbaris "Egyptian boat", from Copticbari "small boat", hieroglyphic Egyptian

The long pole used to maneuver or propel a barge have given rise to the saying "I wouldn't touch that [subject/thing] with a barge pole."

TYPES OF BARGES

- Admiral's barge
- Barracks barge (Houseboat)
- Canal motorship
- Car float
- Crane barge
- Dutch barge
- Dry bulk cargo barge

- Hopper barge
- Hotel barge
- Jackup barge
- Lighter and Dumb steel lighter
- Liquid cargo barge
- Log barge
- Norfolk wherry
- Oil barge and Dumb steel oil barge
- Paddle barge
- Pleasure barge
- Power barge
- Row barge
- Royal barge
- Sand barge
- Severn trow
- Spitz barge
- Thames sailing barge
- Tom Pudding
- Vehicular barge

On the Great British canal system, the term 'barge' is used to describe a boat wider than a narrowboat, and the people who move barges are often known as lightermen. In the United States, deckhands perform the labor and are supervised by a leadman or the mate. The captain and pilot steer the towboat, which pushes one or more barges held together with rigging, collectively called 'the tow'. The crew live aboard the towboat as it travels along the inland river system or the intracoastal waterways. These towboats travel between ports and are also called line-haul boats.

Poles are used on barges to fend off the barge as it nears other vessels or a wharf. These are often called 'pike poles'. On shallow canals in the United Kingdom, long punt poles are used to manoeuvre or propel the barge.

MODERN USE

Barges are used today for low-value bulk items, as the cost of hauling goods by barge is very low. Barges are also used for very heavy or bulky items; a typical barge measures 195 by 35 feet (59.4 m × 10.6 m), and can carry up to about 1500 tons of cargo.

As an example, on June 26, 2006, a 565-ton catalytic cracking unit reactor was shipped by barge from the Tulsa Port of Catoosa in Oklahoma to a refinery in Pascagoula, Mississippi. Extremely large objects are normally shipped in sections and assembled onsite, but shipping an assembled unit reduced costs and avoided reliance on construction labor at the delivery site (which in this case was still recovering from Hurricane Katrina). Of the reactor's 700-mile (1,100 km) journey, only about 40 miles were traveled overland, from the final port to the refinery.

Self-propelled barges may be used as such when traveling downstream or upstream in placid waters; they are operated as an unpowered barge, with the assistance of a tugboat, when traveling upstream in faster waters. Canal barges are usually made for the particular canal in which they will operate.

Many barges, primarily Dutch Barges, which were originally designed for carrying cargo along the canals of Europe, are no longer large enough to compete in this industry with larger newer vessels. Many of these barges have been renovated and are now used as luxury Hotel Barges carrying holiday makers along the same canals they once carried grain or coal.

TOWED OR OTHERWISE UNPOWERED BARGES IN THE UNITED STATES

In primitive regions today and in all pre-development (lacking highways or railways) regions worldwide in times before industrial development and highways, barges were the predominant and most efficient means of inland transportation in many regions. This holds true today, for many areas of the world.

In such pre-industrialized, or poorly developed infrastructure regions, many barges are purpose-designed to be powered on waterways by long slender poles — thereby becoming known on American waterways as poleboats as the extensive west of North America was settled using the vast tributary river systems of the Mississippidrainage basin. Poleboats use muscle power of "walkers" along the sides of the craft pushing against a pole against the streambed, canal, or lake bottom to move the vessel where desired. In settling the American west it was generally faster to navigate downriver from Brownsville, Pennsylvania, to the Ohio River confluence with the Mississippi and then pole upriver against the current to St. Louis than to travel overland on the rare primitive dirt roads for many decades after the American revolution.

Once the New York Central and Pennsylvania Railroads reached Chicago, that time dynamic changed, and American poleboats became less common, relegated to smaller rivers and more remote streams. On the Mississippi riverine system today, including that of other sheltered waterways, industrial barge trafficking in bulk raw materials such as coal, coke, timber, iron ore and other minerals is extremely common; in the developed world using huge cargo barges that connect in groups and trains-of-barges in ways that allow cargo volumes and weights that would astonish pioneers of modern barge systems and methods in the Victorian era. Such barges need to be towed by tugboats or pushed by towboats. Canal barges, towed by draft animals on a waterway adjacent towpath were of fundamental importance in the early industrial revolution, whose major early engineering projects were efforts to build viaducts, aqueducts and especially canals to fuel and feed raw materials to nascent factories in the early industrial takeoff and take their goods to ports and cities for distribution.

The barge and canal system contended favorably with the railways in the early industrial revolution before around the 1850s–1960s — for example, the Erie Canal in New York State is credited by economic historians with giving the growth boost needed for New York City to eclipse Philadelphia as America's largest port and city — but such canal systems with their locks, need for maintenance and dredging, pumps and sanitary issues were eventually outcompeted in the carriage of high-value items by the railways due to the higher speed, falling costs, and route flexibility of rail transport.

Barge and canal systems were nonetheless of great, perhaps even primary, economic importance until after World War I in Europe, particularly in the more developed nations of the Low Countries, France, Germany, Poland, and especially Great Britain which more or less made the system characteristically its own.

BULK CARRIER

A bulk carrier,bulk freighter, or bulker is a merchant ship specially designed to transport unpackaged bulk cargo, such as grains, coal, ore, and cement in its cargo holds. Since the first specialized bulk carrier was built in 1852, economic forces have fuelled the development of these ships, causing them to grow in size and sophistication. Today's bulkers are specially designed to maximize capacity, safety, efficiency, and to be able to withstand the rigours of their work.

Today, bulkers make up 15% - 17% of the world's merchant fleets and range in size from single-hold mini-bulkers to mammoth ore ships able to carry 400,000 metric tons of deadweight (DWT). A number of specialized designs exist: some can unload their own cargo, some depend on port facilities for unloading, and some even package the cargo as it is loaded. Over half of all bulkers have Greek, Japanese, or Chinese owners and more than a quarter are registered in Panama. Korea is the largest single builder of bulkers, and 82% of these ships were built in Asia.

A bulk carrier's crew participates in the loading and unloading of cargo, navigating the ship, and keeping its machinery and equipment properly maintained. Loading and unloading the cargo is difficult, dangerous, and can take up to 120 hours on larger ships. Crews can range in size from three people on the smallest ships to over 30 on the largest. Bulk cargo can be very dense, corrosive, or abrasive. This can present safety problems: cargo shifting, spontaneous combustion, and cargo saturation can threaten a ship. The use of ships that are old and have corrosion problems has been linked to a spate of bulker sinkings in the 1990s, as have the bulker's large hatchways, important for efficient cargo handling. New international regulations have since been introduced to improve ship design and inspection, and to streamline the process of abandoning ship.

DEFINITION

There are various ways to define the term bulk carrier. As of 1999, the International Convention for the Safety of Life at Sea defines a bulk carrier as "a ship constructed with a single deck, top side tanks and hopper side tanks in cargo spaces and intended to primarily carry dry cargo in bulk; an ore carrier; or a combination carrier." However, most classification societies use a broader definition where a bulker is any ship that carries dry unpackaged goods.Multipurpose cargo ships can carry bulk cargo, but can also carry other cargoes and are not specifically designed for bulk carriage. The term "dry bulk carrier" is used to distinguish bulkers from bulk liquid carriers such as oil, chemical, or liquefied petroleum gas carriers. Very small bulkers are almost indistinguishable from general cargo ships, and they are often classified based more on the ship's use than its design.

A number of abbreviations are used to describe bulkers. "OBO" describes a bulker which carries a combination of ore, bulk, and oil, and "O/O" is used for combination oil and ore carriers. The terms "VLOC," "VLBC," "ULOC," and "ULBC" for very large and ultra large ore and bulk carriers were adapted from the supertanker designations very large crude carrier and ultra large crude carrier.

HISTORY

Before specialized bulk carriers existed, shippers had two methods to move bulk goods by ship. In the first method, longshoremen loaded the cargo into sacks, stacked the sacks onto pallets, and put the pallets into the cargo hold with a crane. The second method required the shipper to charter an entire ship and spend time and money to build plywood bins into the holds. Then, to guide the cargo through the small hatches, wooden feeders and shifting boards had to be constructed. These methods were slow and labor intensive. As with the container ship, the problem of efficient loading and unloading has driven the evolution of the bulk carrier.

Specialized bulk carriers began to appear as steam-powered ships became more popular. The first steam ship recognized as a bulk carrier was the British coal carrier SS John Bowes in 1852. She featured a metal hull, a steam engine, and a ballasting system which used seawater instead of sandbags. These features helped her succeed in the competitive British coal market. The first self-unloader was the lake freighterHennepin in 1902 on the Great Lakes. This greatly decreased the unloading time of bulkers by using conveyor belt to move the cargo. The first bulkers with diesel propulsion began to appear in 1911.

Before World War II, the international shipping demand for bulk products was low—about 25 million tons for metal ores—and most of this trade was coastal. However, on the Great Lakes, bulkers hauled vast amounts of ore from the northern mines to the steel mills. In 1929, 73 million tons of iron ore was transported on the Lakes, and an almost equal amount of coal, limestone, and other products were also moved. Two defining characteristics of bulkers were already emerging: the double bottom, which was adopted in 1890, and the triangular structure of the ballast tanks, which was introduced in 1905. After World War II, an international bulk trade began to develop among industrialized nations, particularly between the European countries, the United States and Japan.

Due to the economics of this trade, ocean bulkers became larger and more specialized. In this period, Great Lakes freighters increased in size, to maximize economies of scale, and self-unloaders became more common to cut turnaround time. The thousand-footers of the Great Lakes fleets, built in the 1970s, were among the longest ships afloat and in 1979, a record 214 million ton of bulk cargo were moved on the Great Lakes.

CATEGORIES

Size categories

Bulkers are segregated into six major size categories: small, handysize, handymax, panamax, capesize, and very large. Very large bulk and ore carriers fall into the capesize category but are often considered separately.

Categories as per Regions

Categories occur in regional trade, such as Kamsarmax,Seawaymax, Setouchmax, Dunkirkmax, and Newcastlemax also appear in regional trade.

- "Kamsarmax": Maximum length over all 229 meters refers to a new type of ships, larger than panamax, that are suitable for berthing at the Port of Kamsar (Republic of Guinea), where the major loading terminal of bauxite is restricted to vessels not more than 229 meters.
- "Newastlemax": Maximum beam 47 meters. Refers to the largest vessel able to enter the port of Newcastle, Australia at about 185,000 DWT
- "Setouchmax": About 203,000 DWT, being the largest vessels able to navigate the Setouch Sea, Japan
- "Seawaymax": LOA 226 m max/ 7.92 m draft/ 28,502 DWT max.

Refers to the largest vessel that can pass through the canal locks of the St Lawrence Seaway (Great lakes, Canada)

- "Malaccamax": LOA 330 m/ 20 m draft/ 300,000 DWT, Refers to the largest vessel that can pass through the Straits of Malacca.
- "Dunkirkmax": Maximum allowable beam = 45 m/ LOA 289 m. max (175,000 DWT approx) for the eastern harbour lock in the Port of Dunkirk (France)

Mini-bulkers are prevalent in the category of small vessels with a capacity of under 10,000 DWT. Mini-bulkers carry from 500 to 2,500 tons, have a single hold, and are designed for river transport. They are often built to be able to pass under bridges and have small crews of three to eight people.

Handysize and Handymax ships are general purpose in nature. These two segments represent 71% of all bulk carriers over 10,000 DWT and also have the highest rate of growth. This is partly due to new regulations coming into effect which put greater constraints on the building of larger vessels. Handymax ships are typically 150–200 m in length and 52,000 – 58,000 DWT with five cargo holds and four cranes. These ships are also general purpose in nature.

The size of a Panamax vessel is limited by the Panama canal's lock chambers, which can accommodate ships with a beam of up to 32.31 m, a length overall of up to 294.13 m, and a draft of up to 12.04 m.

Capesize ships are too large to traverse the Panama canal and must round Cape Horn to travel between the Pacific and Atlantic oceans. Earlier, capesize ships could not traverse the Suez and needed to go around the Cape of Good Hope. Recent deepening of the Suez canal to 66 ft (20 m) permits most capesize ships to pass through it.

Capesize bulkers are specialized: 93% of their cargo is iron ore and coal. Some ships on the Great Lakes Waterway exceed Panamax dimensions but they are limited to use on the Great Lakes as they cannot pass through the smaller St. Lawrence Seaway to the ocean. Very large ore carriers and very large bulk carriers are a subset of the capesize category reserved for vessels over 200,000 DWT. Carriers of this size are almost always designed to carry iron ore.

FLEET CHARACTERISTICS

The world's bulk transport has reached immense proportions: in 2005, 1.7 billion metric tons of coal, iron ore, grain, bauxite, and phosphate was transported by ship.

Today, the world's bulker fleet includes 6,225 ships of over 10,000 DWT, and represent 40% of all ships in terms of tonnage and 39.4% in terms of vessels. Including smaller ships, bulkers have a total combined capacity of almost 346 million DWT.

Combined carriers are a very small portion of the fleet, representing less than 3% of this capacity. The lake freighters of the Great Lakes, with 98 ships of 3.2 million total DWT, despite forming a small fraction of the total fleet by tonnage and only operating 10 months a year, carried a tenth of the world's bulk cargo because of the short trip distance and fast turnarounds.

As of 2005, the average bulker was just over 13 years old. About 41% of all bulkers were less than ten years old, 33% were over twenty years old, and the remaining 26% were between ten and twenty years of age. All of the 98 bulkers registered in the Great Lakes trade are over 20 years old and the oldest still sailing in 2009 was 106 years old.

FLAG STATES

As of 2005, the United States Maritime Administration counted 6,225 bulkers of 10,000 DWT or greater worldwide. More bulkers are registered in Panama, with 1,703 ships, than any four other flag states combined. In terms of the number of bulk carriers registered, the top five flag states also include Hong Kong with 492 ships, Malta (435), Cyprus (373), and China (371). Panama also dominates bulker registration in terms of deadweight tonnage. Positions two through five are held by Hong Kong, Greece, Malta, and Cyprus.

LARGEST FLEETS

Greece, Japan, and China are the top three owners of bulk carriers, with 1,326, 1,041, and 979 vessels respectively. These three nations account for over 53% of the world's fleet.

Several companies have large private bulker fleets. The multinational company Gearbulk Holding Ltd. has over 70 bulkers.The Fednav Group in Canada operates a fleet of over 80 bulkers, including two designed to work in Arctic ice.Croatia's Atlantska Plovidba d.d. has a fleet of 14 bulkers. The H. Vogemann Group in Hamburg, Germany operates a fleet of 19 bulkers.Portline in Portugal, owns 10 bulkers.Dampskibsselskabet Torm in Denmark and Elcano in Spain also own notable bulker fleets. Other companies specialize in mini-bulker operations: England's Stephenson Clarke Shipping Limited owns a fleet of eight mini-bulkers and five small Handysize bulkers, and Cornships Management and Agency Inc. in Turkey owns a fleet of seven mini-bulkers.

BUILDERS

Asian companies dominate the construction of bulk carriers. Of the world's 6,225 bulkers, almost 62% were built in Japan by shipyards such as Oshima Shipbuilding and Sanoyas Hishino Meisho. South Korea, with notable shipyards Daewoo and Hyundai Heavy Industries, ranked second among builders, with 643 ships. The People's Republic of China, with large shipyards such as Dalian, Chengxi, and Shanghai Waigaoqiao, ranked third, with 509 ships.Taiwan, with shipyards such as China Shipbuilding Corporation, ranked fourth, accounting for 129 ships. Shipyards in these top four countries built over 82% of the bulkers afloat.

FREIGHT CHARGES

Several factors affect the cost to move a bulk cargo by ship. The bulk freight market is very volatile, and it fluctuates, along with the type of cargo, the ship's size, and the route traveled all affect the final price. Moving a capesize load of coal from South America to Europe cost anywhere from $15 to $25 per ton in 2005. Hauling a panamax-sized load of aggregate materials from the Gulf of Mexico to Japan that year could cost as little as $40 per ton to as much as $70 per ton.

Some shippers choose instead to charter a ship, paying a daily rate instead of a set price per ton. In 2005, the average daily rate for a Handymax ship varied between $18,000 – $30,000. A Panamax ship could be chartered for $20,000 – $50,000 per day, and a Capesize for $40,000 – $70,000 per day.

SHIP BREAKING

Generally, ships are removed from the fleet go through a process known as ship breaking or scrapping.Ship-owners and buyers negotiate scrap prices based on factors such as the ship's empty weight (called light ton displacement or LDT) and prices in the scrap metal market. In 1998, almost 700 ships were scrapped in places like Alang, India and Chittagong, Bangladesh.

This is often done by 'beaching' the ship on open sand, then cutting it apart by hand with gas torches, a dangerous operation that results in injuries and fatalities, as well as exposure to toxic materials such as asbestos, lead, and various chemicals. Half a million deadweight tons of worth of bulk carriers were scrapped in 2004, accounting for 4.7% of the year's scrapping. That year, bulkers fetched particularly high scrap prices, between $340 and $350 per LDT.

OPERATION

Crew

The crew on a bulker typically consists of 20 to 30 people, though smaller ships can be handled by 8. The crew includes the captain or master, the deck department, the engineering department, and the steward's department. The practice of taking passengers aboard cargo ships, once almost universal, is very rare today and almost non-existent on bulkers.

During the 1990s, bulkers were involved in an alarming number of shipwrecks. This led ship-owners to commission a study seeking to explain the effect of various factors on the crew's effectiveness and competence. The study showed that crew performance aboard bulk carriers was the lowest of all groups studied. Among bulker crews, the best performance was found aboard younger and larger ships. Crews on better-maintained ships performed better, as did crews on ships where fewer languages were spoken.

Fewer deck officers are employed on bulkers than on similarly sized ships of other types. A mini-bulker carries two to three deck officers, while larger Handysize and Capesize bulkers carry four.Liquid natural gas tankers of the same size have an additional deck officer and unlicensed mariner.

Voyages

A bulker's voyages are determined by market forces; routes and cargoes often vary. A ship may engage in the grain trade during the harvest season and later move on to carry other cargoes or work on a different route. Aboard a coastal carrier in the tramp trade, the crew will often not know the next port of call until the cargo is fully loaded.

Because bulk cargo is so difficult to discharge, bulkers spend more time in port than other ships. A study of mini-bulkers found that it takes, on average, twice as much time to unload a ship as it does to load it. A mini-bulker spends 55 hours at a time in port, compared to 35 hours for a lumber carrier of similar size. This time in port increases to 74 hours for Handymax and 120 hours for Panamax vessels. Compared with the 12-hour turnarounds common for container ships, 15-hour turnarounds for car carriers, and 26-hour turnarounds for large tankers, bulker crews have more opportunities to spend time ashore.

Loading and unloading

Loading and unloading a bulker is time-consuming and dangerous. The process is planned by the ship's captain, often with assistance from the chief mate. International regulations require that the captain and terminal master agree on a detailed plan before operations begin.Deck officers and stevedores oversee the operations. Occasionally loading errors are made that cause a ship to capsize or break in half at the pier.

The loading method used depends on both the cargo and the equipment available on the ship and on the dock. In the least advanced ports, cargo can be loaded with shovels or bags poured from the hatch cover. This system is being replaced with faster, less labor-intensive methods.Double-articulation cranes, which can load at a rate of 1,000 tons per hour, represent a widely used method, and the use of shore-based gantry cranes, reaching 2,000 tons per hour, is growing.

A crane's discharge rate is limited by the bucket's capacity (from 6 to 40 tons) and by the speed at which the crane can take a load, deposit it at the terminal, and to return to take the next. For modern gantry cranes, the total time of the grab-deposit-return cycle is about 50 seconds. Conveyor belts offer a very efficient method of loading, with standard loading rates varying between 100 and 700 tons per hour, although the most advanced ports can offer rates of 16,000 tons per hour. Start-up and shutdown procedures with conveyor belts, though, are complicated and require time to carry out. Self-discharging ships use conveyor belts with load rates of around 1,000 tons per hour.

Once the cargo is discharged, the crew begins to clean the holds. This is particularly important if the next cargo is of a different type. The immense size of cargo holds and the tendency of cargoes to be physically irritating add to the difficulty of cleaning the holds. When the holds are clean, the process of loading begins.

It is crucial to keep the cargo level during loading in order to maintain stability. As the hold is filled, machines such as excavators and bulldozers are often used to keep the cargo in check. Leveling is particularly important when the hold is only partly full, since cargo is more likely to shift. Extra precautions are taken, such as adding longitudinal divisions and securing wood atop the cargo. If a hold is full, a technique called tomming is used, which involves digging out a 6 feet (2 m) hole below the hatch cover and filling it with bagged cargo or weights.

ARCHITECTURE

A bulk carrier's design is largely defined by the cargo it will carry. The cargo's density, also known as its stowage factor, is the key factor. Densities for common bulk cargoes vary from 0.6 tons per cubic meter for light grains to 3 tons per cubic meter for iron ore.

The overall cargo weight is the limiting factor in the design of an ore carrier, since the cargo is so dense. Coal carriers, on the other hand, are limited by overall volume, since most bulkers can be completely filled with coal before reaching their maximum draft.

For a given tonnage, the second factor which governs the ship's dimensions is the size of the ports and waterways it will travel to. For example, a vessel that will pass the Panama Canal will be limited in its beam and draft. For most designs, the ratio of length-to-width ranges between 5 and 7, with an average of 6.2. The ratio of length-to-height will be between 11 and 12.

Machinery

The engine room on a bulker is usually near the stern, under the superstructure. Larger bulkers, from Handymax up, usually have a single two-stroke low-speed crossheaddiesel engine directly coupled to a fixed-pitch propeller. Electricity is produced by auxiliary generators and/or an alternator coupled to the propeller shaft. On the smaller bulkers, one or two four-stroke diesels are used to turn either a fixed or controllable pitch propeller via a reduction gearbox, which may also incorporate an output for an alternator. The average design ship speed for bulkers of Handysize and above is 13.5–15 knots (25.0–28 km/h; 15.5–17 mph). The propeller speed is relatively low, at about 90 revolutions per minute, although it depends on the size of the propeller.

As a result of the 1973 oil crisis, the 1979 energy crisis, and the resulting rise in oil prices, experimental designs using coal to fuel ships were tested in the late 1970s and early 1980s. The Australian National Lines (ANL) constructed two 74,700-ton coal-burner ships called the River Boyne and River Embely. along with two constructed by TNT called TNT Capricornia and TNT Capentaria and renamed Fitzroy River and Endeavor River. These ships were financially effective for the duration of their lives, and their steam engines were able to generate a shaft-power of 19,000 horsepower (14,000 kW). This strategy gave an interesting advantage to carriers of bauxite and similar fuel cargoes, but suffered from poor engine yield compared to higher maintenance cost and efficient modern diesels, maintenance problems due to the supply of ungraded coal, and high initial costs.

Hatches

A hatch or hatchway is the opening at the top of a cargo hold. The mechanical devices which allow hatches to be opened and closed are called hatch covers. In general, hatch covers are between 45% and 60% of the ship's breadth, or beam, and 57% to 67% of the length of the holds. To efficiently load and unload cargo, hatches must be large, but large hatches present structural problems. Hull stress is concentrated around the edges of the hatches, and these areas must be reinforced. Often, hatch areas are reinforced by locally increasing the scantlings or by adding structural members called stiffeners. Both of these options have the undesired effect of adding weight to the ship.

As recently as the 1950s, hatches had wooden covers that would be broken apart and rebuilt by hand, rather than opened and closed. Newer vessels have hydraulic-operated metal hatch covers that can often be operated by one person. Hatch covers can slide forwards, backwards, or to the side, lift up or fold up. It is essential that the hatch covers be watertight: unsealed hatches lead to accidental cargo hold flooding, which has caused many bulkers to sink.

Regulations regarding hatch covers have evolved since the investigation following the loss of the MV Derbyshire. The Load Line Conference of 1966 imposed a requirement that hatch covers be able to withstand load of 1.74 tons/m^2 due to sea water, and a minimum scantling of 6 mm for the tops of the hatch covers. The International Association of Classification Societies then increased this strength standard by creating its Unified Requirement S21 in 1998. This standard requires that the pressure due to sea water be calculated as a function of freeboard and speed, especially for hatch covers located on the forward portion of the ship.

Hull

Bulkers are designed to be easy to build and to store cargo efficiently. To facilitate construction, bulkers are built with a single hull curvature. Also, while a bulbous bow allows a ship to move more efficiently through the water, designers lean towards simple vertical bows on larger ships. Full hulls, with large block coefficients, are almost universal, and as a result, bulkers are inherently slow. This is offset by their efficiency. Comparing a ship's carrying capacity in terms of deadweight tonnage to its weight when empty is one way to measure its efficiency. A small Handymax ship can carry five times its weight. In larger designs, this efficiency is even more pronounced: Capesize vessels can carry over eight times their weight.

Bulkers have a cross-section typical of most merchant ships. The upper and lower corners of the hold are used as ballast tanks, as is the double bottom area. The corner tanks are reinforced and serve another purpose besides controlling the ship's trim. Designers choose the angle of the corner tanks to be less than that of the angle of repose of the anticipated cargoes. This greatly reduces side-to-side movement, or "shifting," of cargo which can endanger the ship.

The double bottoms are also subject to design constraints. The primary concern is that they be high enough to allow the passage of pipes and cables. These areas must also be roomy enough to allow people safe access to perform surveys and maintenance. On the other hand, concerns of excess weight and wasted volume keep the double bottoms very tight spaces.

Bulker hulls are made of steel, usually mild steel. Some manufacturers have preferred high-tensile steel recently in order to reduce the tare weight. However, the use of high-tensile steel for longitudinal and transverse reinforcements can reduce the hull's rigidity and resistance to corrosion. Forged steel is used for some ship parts, such as the propeller shaft support. Transverse partitions are made of corrugated iron, reinforced at the bottom and at connections. The construction of bulker hulls using a concrete-steel sandwich has been investigated.

Double hulls have become popular in the past ten years. Designing a vessel with double sides adds primarily to its breadth, since bulkers are already required to have double bottoms. One of the advantages of the double hull is to make room to place all the structural elements in the sides, removing them from the holds. This increases the volume of the holds, and simplifies their structure which helps in loading, unloading, and cleaning. Double sides also improve a ship's capacity for ballasting, which is useful when carrying light goods: the ship may have to increase its draft for stability or seakeeping reasons, which is done by adding ballast water.

A recent design, called Hy-Con, seeks to combine the strengths of single-hull and double-hull construction. Short for Hybrid Configuration, this design doubles the forward-most and rear-most holds and leaves the others single-hulled. This approach increases the ship's solidity at key points, while reducing the overall tare weight.

Since the adoption of double hull has been more of an economic than a purely architectural decision, some argue that double-sided ships receive less comprehensive surveys and suffer more from hidden corrosion. In spite of opposition, double hulls became a requirement for Panamax and Capesize vessels in 2005.

Freighters are in continual danger of "breaking their backs" and thus longitudinal strength is a primary architectural concern. A naval architect uses the correlation between longitudinal strength and a set of hull thicknesses called scantlings to manage problems of longitudinal strength and stresses. A ship's hull is composed of individual parts called members. The set of dimensions of these members is called the ship's scantlings. Naval architects calculate the stresses a ship can be expected to be subjected to, add in safety factors, and then can calculate the required scantlings.

These analyses are conducted when traveling empty, loading and unloading, when partially and fully loaded, and under conditions of temporary overloading. Places subject to the largest stresses are studied carefully, such as hold-bottoms, hatch-covers, bulkheads between holds, and the bottoms of ballast tanks. Great Lakes bulkers also must be designed to withstand springing, or developing resonance with the waves, which can cause fatigue fractures.

Since 1 April 2006, the International Association of Classification Societies has adopted the Common Structural Rules. The rules apply to bulkers more than 90 meters in length and require that scantlings' calculations take into account items such as the effect of corrosion, the harsh conditions often found in the North Atlantic, and dynamic stresses during loading. The rules also establish margins for corrosion, from 0.5 to 0.9 mm.

SAFETY

The 1980s and 1990s were a very unsafe time for bulk carriers. Many bulkers sank during this time, 99 were lost between 1990 and 1997 alone. Most of these sinkings were sudden and quick, making it impossible for the crew to escape: more than 650 sailors were lost during this same period. Due partly to the sinking of the MV Derbyshire, a series of international safety resolutions regarding bulkers were adopted during the 1990s.

Stability problems

Cargo shifting poses a great danger for bulkers. The problem is even more pronounced with grain cargoes, since grain settles during a voyage and creates extra space between the top of the cargo and the top of the hold. Cargo is then free to move from one side of the ship to the other as the ship rolls. This can cause the ship to list, which, in turn, causes more cargo to shift. This kind of chain reaction can capsize a bulker very quickly.

The 1960 SOLAS Convention sought to control this sort of problem. These regulations required the upper ballast tanks designed in a manner to prevent shifting. They also required cargoes to be leveled, or trimmed, using excavators in the holds. The practice of trimming reduces the amount of the cargo's surface area in contact with air which has a useful side-effect: reducing the chances of spontaneous combustion in cargoes such as coal, iron, and metal shavings.

Another sort of risk that can affect dry cargoes, is absorption of ambient moisture. When very fine concretes and aggregates mix with water, the mud created at the bottom of the hold shifts easily and can produce a free surface effect. The only way to control these risks is by good ventilation practices and careful monitoring for the presence of water.

Structural problems

In 1990 alone, 20 bulk carriers sank, taking with them 94 crewmen. In 1991, 24 bulkers sank, killing 154. This level of loss focused attention on the safety aspects of bulk carriers, and a great deal was learned. The American Bureau of Shipping concluded that the losses were "directly traceable to failure of the cargo hold structure" and Lloyd's Register of Shipping added that the hull sides could not withstand "the combination of local corrosion, fatigue cracking and operational damage."

The accident studies showed a clear pattern:

1. Sea water enters the forward hatch, due to a large wave, a poor seal, corrosion, etc.
2. The extra water weight in hold number one compromises the partition to hold number two,
3. Water enters hold number two and alters the trim so much that more water enters the holds
4. With two holds rapidly filling with water, the bow submerges and the ship quickly sinks, leaving little time for the crew to react.

Previous practices had required ships to withstand the flooding of a single forward hold, but did not guard against situations where two holds would flood.

The case where two after (rear) holds are flooded is no better, because the engine room is quickly flooded, leaving the ship without propulsion. If two holds in the middle of the ship are flooded, the stress on the hull can become so great that the ship snaps in two.

Other contributing factors were identified:

- Most shipwrecks involved ships over 20 years in age. A glut of ships of this age occurred in the 1980s, caused by an overestimate of the growth of international trade. Rather than replace them prematurely, shipping companies were compelled on cost grounds to keep their aging vessels in service.

- Corrosion, due to a lack of maintenance, affected the seals of the hatch covers and the strength of the bulkheads which separate holds. The corrosion is difficult to detect due do the immense size of the surfaces involved.
- Advanced methods of loading were not foreseen when the ships were designed. While the new processes are more efficient, loading is more difficult to control (it can take over an hour just to halt the operation), occasionally resulting in overloading the ship. These unexpected shocks, over time, can damage the hull's structural integrity.
- Recent use of high-tensile steel allows building a structure with less material and weight while retaining similar strength. However, because it is thinner than regular steel, HT steel can corrode though more easily, plus it can develop metal fatigue in choppy seas.
- According to Lloyd's Register, a principal cause of sinkings was the attitude of ship-owners, who sent ships with known problems to sea.

The new rules adopted in the 1997 annexes to the SOLAS convention focused on problems such as reinforcing bulkheads and the longitudinal frame, more stringent inspections (with a particular focus on corrosion) and routine in-port inspections. The 1997 additions also required bulkers with restrictions (for instance, forbidden from carrying certain types of cargoes) to mark their hulls with large, easy-to-see triangles.

Crew safety

Since December 2004, Panamax and Capesize bulkers have been required to carry free-fall lifeboats located on the stern, behind the deckhouse. This arrangement allows the crew to abandon ship quickly in case of a catastrophic emergency. One argument against the use of free-fall lifeboats is that the evacuees require "some degree of physical mobility, even fitness" to enter and launch the boat. Also, injuries have occurred during launches, for example, in the case of incorrectly secured safety belts.

In December 2002, Chapter XII of the SOLAS convention was amended to require the installation of high-level water alarms and monitoring systems on all bulkers. This safety measure quickly alerts watch standers on the bridge and in the engine room in case of flooding in the holds. In cases of catastrophic flooding, these detectors could speed the process of abandoning ship.

LAKE FREIGHTER

Lake freighters, or Lakers, are bulk carrier vessels that ply the Great Lakes.

These vessels are traditionally called boats, although classified as ships. Lakers carry bulk cargoes of materials such as limestone, iron ore, grain, coal or salt from the mines and fields to the populous industrial areas down the lakes. The 63 commercial ports handled 173 million tons of cargo in 2006. Because of winter ice on the lakes, the navigation season is not usually year-round. The Soo Locks and Welland Canal close from mid-January to late March, when most boats are laid up for maintenance. Crewmembers spend these months ashore.

Depending on their application, lakers may also be referred to by their type, such as oreboats (primarily for iron ore), straight deckers (no self-unloading gear), bulkers (carry bulk cargo), sternenders (all cabins aft), self unloaders (with self unloading gear), longboats (due to their slender appearance), or lakeboats, among others.

In the mid-20th century, 300 lakers worked the Lakes, but by the early 21st century there were fewer than 140 active lakers. One of the best known was the SS Edmund Fitzgerald, the most recent and largest major vessel to be wrecked on the Lakes.

LAKERS VS. SALTIES

By way of the Saint Lawrence Seaway, smaller lakers have access to the ocean, and some ocean-going vessels have access to the Lakes. Visiting ocean-going vessels are called "salties."

Due to their additional beam, very large salties are never seen inland of the Saint Lawrence Seaway. Because the smallest of the Soo Locks is larger than any Seaway lock, salties that can pass through the Seaway may travel anywhere in the Great Lakes. Similarly, the largest lakers are confined to the Upper Lakes (Superior, Michigan, Huron, Erie) because they are too large to use the Seaway locks, beginning at the Welland Canal that bypasses the Niagara River. Because of their deeper draft and the lower buoyancy of fresh water, salties may accept partial loads on the Great Lakes, "topping off" upon exiting the Seaway.

CARGO

Average yearly cargoes — 2002-2007 (million tons)	
Iron ore	60.0
Coal	41.3
Limestone	37.7
Grain	12.0
Salt	8.8
Cement	5.2
Potash	0.6
Total	164.6

Lakers are generally bulk carriers; that is, they carry cargoes of rock, ore, salt or grain in large contiguous holds, not packed in containers. The earlier ships required rail cars unloading on ore docks and unloading machinery at the receiving docks, but modern Lakers are self unloaders, allowing them to unload faster and in more ports.

The most common cargoes on the Great Lakes are taconite (a type of iron ore), limestone, grain, salt, coal, cement, gypsum, sand, slag and potash. Much of the cargo supplies the steel mills of the auto industry, centered around the Great Lakes because of the ease of transport. Other destinations include coal-fired power plants, highway department salt domes and stone docks, where limestone is unloaded for the construction industry. US-flag freighters carried the largest portion of the trade, accounting for two-thirds of all cargo by weight. US boats carried most of the iron, limestone and cement while Canadian boats carried most of the potash and almost all of the salt and grain moved on the lakes.

Destination harbors, boat sizes and legal restrictions greatly affect the pattern of haulage. US boats hauled almost all of the iron ore on the lakes (79%) - from US mines to US mills on large US ships. This reflects the requirement of the Jones Act, as well as the industry using large volumes of material while being concentrated in a few large harbor locations. Salt and Canadian grain can be hauled to numerous smaller ports of either country on smaller, mostly Canadian, boats which can also enter the St. Lawrence Seaway with the Canadian ports of Montreal and Quebec City.

SIZE

The largest vessels on the lake are the 1000-footers (300 m). These vessels are between 1000 and 1013.5 feet (305 and 309 m) long, 105 feet (32 m) wide and of 56 feet (17 m) hull depth. They can carry as much 78,850 long tons of bulk cargo although their loading is dependent on lake water levels especially in the channels and ports.

A dozen of these giant ships were built, all constructed between 1976 and 1981, and all remain in service today. The most powerful of these, the Edwin H. Gott, carries two Enterprise DMRV-16-4 diesel engines driving twin propellers and is rated at 19,500 brake horsepower, making the Gott the most powerful lake boat on the seaway. (14.5 MW).

This allows a top speed of 16.7 mph (27 km/h). The MV Paul R. Tregurtha is the largest boat on the lakes, at 1013'6" and 68,000 gross ton capacity. The Stewart J. Cort, which is not only the first 1000-footer to be put into service on the Lakes, but also the only one built in the traditional wheelhouse-forward Great Lakes style (although all accommodations are forward, and the stern deckhouse is occupied by self unloading equipment and the engines), is another notable vessel. The Cort started life in Mississippi, and was sailed as a much smaller vessel consisting of only the bow and stern sections (appropriately nicknamed "Stubby"), to Erie, Pennsylvania, where she was cut in half and an additional 800+ feet of hull were added. Another interesting 1000-footer is the Presque Isle, an integrated tug and barge combination. The Presque Isle is the largest tug/ barge composite in the world.

All of the 1000-footers are US vessels. The Canadian fleet needs to travel to and from its major cities along the St. Lawrence Seaway, so the standard length for the Canadian vessels is around 730 feet (Seawaymax-size). The reason for this standard length is the Welland Canal, which bypasses Niagara Falls. The locks here are only about 800 feet (240 m) long, and for safety reasons, the vessels must be at most 730 feet (220 m). Because of the Jones Act, Canadian ships cannot carry ore from American mines to American mills. This ore is the usual cargo of the largest ships.

More common are lake boats in the 600 and 700 foot (183 and 213 m) classes, due to the limitations of the Welland Canal. These vessels vary greatly in configuration and cargo capacity, being capable of hauling between 10,000 and 40,000 tons per trip depending on the individual boat. These smaller boats can serve smaller harbors around the Lakes which have irregular need for their services. The latest major vessel built for bulk cargoes on the lakes is the articulated tug/barge combo Ken Boothe Sr./Lakes Contender. The 740' barge Lakes Contender and the 135' tug Ken Boothe Sr. entered service in 2012.

DESIGN

Because these vessels must traverse the locks of the Great Lakes Waterway, they all have features in common, and their appearance differs from similarly sized ocean-going freighters. For instance, they are narrower and generally longer. An early variation of the type (designed by Alexander McDougall and built from 1887 through 1898) was the "whaleback" design, which featured significant tumblehome in the sides of the hull and a rounded bow, looking rather like the back of a whale.

Where the superstructure of an ordinary freighter used to have the bridge in the center of the vessel, lake freighters typically have the bridge and associated superstructure on the bow. Traditionally they had a second island, over the engine room in the stern. These dual cabined boats were constructed between 1869 and 1974. The R. J. Hackett premiered the style and the second Algosoo was the final vessel designed this way. More recently built lakers, like the CSL Niagara, have a single large superstructure island at the stern.

Vessel speeds are not as important on the Lakes as on the ocean. Ports are often closer together than in ocean trade, so cargo capacity is more important than speed. Lake vessels are designed with the greatest box coefficient to maximize the vessel's size in the many locks within the Great Lakes/St Lawrence Seaway system. Therefore, ship designers have favored bluff bows over streamlined bows. After World War II, several ocean freighters and tankers were transported to the Great Lakes and converted to bulk carriers as a way to acquire ships cheaply. Several of them served well in the role and continue to sail today (American Victory (fmr. Middletown), Lee A. Tregurtha, and a few others).

Another distinguishing feature of Lake vessels versus Ocean vessels is the cargo hatch configuration. On the Lake vessels, the hatches are traditionally spaced 24 feet (7.8m) apart. This configuration was needed to match the hatches to the loading facilities. At the turn of the 19th century, most ore loading facilities had loading chutes spaced every 12 feet (3.8m). The ship designers used this pattern for their hatch configuration. This pattern continues today, even with modern Lake vessels. A lake vessel has many more hatches than an ocean vessel of equal length.

The largest deep lock at the Soo is the Poe Lock which is 1,200 feet (370 m) long and 110 feet (34 m) wide. Because of size restrictions, thirty vessels on the lakes can only pass between Lake Superior and Lake Huron using the Poe lock although none approaches the lock's size. Many lakers are restricted to the Lakes, being unable to navigate the St Lawrence Seaway whose locks allow a maximum vessel size of 740 feet (226 m) in length or 78 feet (24 m) in breadth. The shallow draft imposed by the rivers (typically dredged to about 28 feet (8.5m) by the United States Army Corps of Engineers) restricts the cargo capacity of Lakers, but that is partially recovered by their extra length and box design.

Since Great Lakes waves never achieve the great length or period of ocean waves, particularly compared to the waves' height, ships are in less danger of being suspended between two waves and breaking, so the ratio between the ship's length, beam and its depth can be a bit larger than that of an ocean-going ship. The Lake vessels generally have a 10:1 length to beam ratio, whereas ocean vessels are typically 7:1. The dimension of locks is the determining factor in Lake vessel construction.

LIFESPAN

Since the freshwater lakes are less corrosive to ships than the salt water of the oceans, many of the Lakers remain in service for long periods and the fleet has a much higher average age than the ocean-going fleet. The average lifespan of a laker is 40–50 years. Boats older than 50 years are not unusual. The St. Mary's Challenger, built in 1906 as the William P. Snyder (552 ft), is currently the oldest boat in active duty on the Lakes. She is managed by Port City Steamship and owned by St. Mary's Cement, a subsidiary of Votorantim Cimentos.

The E. M. Ford had one of the longest careers, having been built in 1898 (as the Presque Isle - 428 feet) and still sailing the lakes 98 years later in 1996. In 2007 she was still afloat as a stationary transfer vessel at a riverside cement silo in Saginaw. She went to the scrap yard in November 2010 at Purvis Marine.

The J. B. Ford, built in 1904, last sailed in 1985 and in 2007 served in the same capacity as the E. M. at a different cement silo in Superior, Wisconsin. Several decorated World War II veteran ships are still in active, although civilian, use such as the tankers Chiwawa and Neshanic, now the bulk freighters Lee A. Tregurtha and American Victory, respectively, and the Landing Craft Tank 203, now the working vessel Outer Island.

NEWEST FREIGHTERS

Some shipping companies are building new freighters to ply the waters of the Great Lakes. The following are new freighters in use or will be launched for use in the Great Lakes:

- Algoma Mariner - built by Chengxi Shipyard of Jiangyin, China, delivered in August 2011 for Algoma Central Corporation.
- Equinox Class - a new class of lake freighter (5 ordered from Mingde Shipyard of Nantong, China) and expected to enter service in 2013-2014 for Seaway Marine Transport, a division of Algoma Central. A Class of vessel is created any time a new design is used to build a ship and is notable when multiple ships are built to the same design plans. The ships will be used as dry-bulk lake freighters (two gearless bulk freighter and three self-unloading vessel).
- Trillium Class - a new class of lake freighter on order by Canada Steamship Lines for delivery in 2012 and 2013.

SHIP LOSSES AND ACCIDENTS

The Great Lakes have a long history of shipwreck, groundings, storms and collisions. From the 1679 sinking of Le Griffon with its cargo of furs to the 1975 loss of the Edmund Fitzgerald, thousands of ships and thousands of lives have been lost, and many involved vessels in the cargo trade. The Great Lakes Shipwreck Museum uses the approximate figures of 6,000 ships and 30,000 lives lost.

David D. Swayze has compiled a list which details over 4,750 well-documented shipwrecks, mostly of commercial vessels and a list of known names of over 5,000 victims of those sinkings. Maritime historian Mark Thompson reports that based on nautical records, nearly 6,000 shipwrecks on the Great Lakes occurred between 1878 and 1994, with about a quarter of those being listed as total losses with a total of 1,166 lives lost.

The most recent losses of modern lakers were (with their causes):

- SS Henry Steinbrenner, May 11, 1953, Lake Superior, 17 of 31 crew died, (flooded after cargo hatch covers lost during storm)
- SS Scotiadoc, June 20, 1953, Lake Superior, 1 of 29 crew died, (rammed by freighter Burlington in heavy fog)

- SS Carl D. Bradley, November 18, 1958, Lake Michigan, 33 of 35 crew died, (split in half due to hogging during storm)
- SS Cedarville, May 7, 1965, Straits of Mackinac, 10 of 35 crew died, (collision with the saltie Topdalsfjord)
- SS Daniel J. Morrell, November 29, 1966, Lake Huron, 28 of 29 crew died, (split in half due to hogging during storm)
- SS Edmund Fitzgerald, November 10, 1975, Lake Superior, 29 of 29 crew died, (unknown cause during storm)

The salties Prins Willem V and Monrovia also sank in the Great Lakes during the 1950s; both in collisions with other ships. The saltie Nordmeer grounded on Thunder Bay Island Shoal in November 1966 but before it could be refloated was further damaged in the same storm that sank the Morrell and it was declared a total loss.

Ships on the Lakes have been involved in many lesser incidents. Lakers have been subject to frequent groundings in port and channels due to varying lake levels and silting, collisions with objects (such as the 1993 collision of the Indiana Harbor with the Lansing Shoals Light Station), icing in during winter trips and shipboard fires (including the unusual case in 2001 where a drawbridge ran into the Canadian grain carrier Windoc causing a fire). To prevent collisions and groundings, the Great Lakes are well-served with lighthouses and lights, and floating navigation aids. The U.S. Coast Guard and Canadian Coast Guard maintain stations around the Great Lakes including icebreakers and rescue helicopters. The U.S. Army Corps of Engineers and other agencies maintain the harbors and seaways to limit groundings by dredging and seawalling.

November was the traditional last month of shipping before the winter layup (and lake freeze-up). This month sees much of the worst weather of the navigation season and has seen a disproportionate number of accidents. Dana Bowen mentions that over half of all strandings and one-third of all vessels lost to foundering between 1900-1950 were lost during November.

FAMOUS VESSELS

The most famous laker was the SS Edmund Fitzgerald (popularized by Gordon Lightfoot's song "The Wreck of the Edmund Fitzgerald" in 1976), which sank on Lake Superior on November 10, 1975. The Fitz was the first boat with a length of 729 feet (222 m) and the flagship of the Columbia Steamship Division of Oglebay Norton Co. The MV Stewart J. Cort was the first of the 1,000-foot (300 m) oreboats.

The first laker with self-unloading equipment was the Hennepin (formerly the George H. Dyer) a small wooden laker that was refitted with the equipment in 1902. The first laker built as a self-unloader was the Wyandotte launched in 1908. Before these, all boats were unloaded with shoreside equipment. Self-unloading equipment worked well for cargoes that could "flow" out of the holds onto belts, such as coal and limestone. It did not work well for grain, which flowed too readily and would spill off the conveyors, or iron ore, which would not flow well and would hang up in the hold. Because the predominant cargo for lakers was iron ore, self-unloaders did not become common until higher grade ores were depleted and taconite pellets were developed in the 1970s.

Steam power first appeared in the 1860s and became the standard source of power for over a century. The Canadian grainboat Feux Follets of 1967 was the last laker to be built with a steam turbine and thus was the last steamer built on the lakes. Ford Motor Company's Henry Ford 2nd and Benson Ford of 1924 were the first lakeboats with diesel engines. Diesel powerplants did not become standard until the 1970s. The last active ships of 1920s vintage, and the oldest ships still operating in non-specialized bulk trades is the motor vessels Maumee of Lower Lakes Transportation. She was built as the William G Clyde for US Steel.

The S. T. Crapo, inactive since 1996, was built to haul cement for Huron Cement Co. back in 1927 and was the second ship of that design, the first being the John G Boardman of the same company. The Crapo was the last coal burning freighter on the Great Lakes.

The classic design of cabins fore-and-aft with open decks over the hold started with the 208-foot (63 m) long R. J. Hackett, designed and built by Elihu Peck in 1869. The first iron-hulled laker was the Brunswick, launched at Detroit in 1881.

The Brunswick sank after a collision later that year and was apparently little known. Many follow the lead of the contemporary Cleveland press and credit the Onoko as the first iron-hulled laker, launched in 1882. The Onoko's higher center section did become a standard for later lakers. At 302 feet (92 m), the Onoko was the first bulk carrier to hold the unofficial title of Queen of the Lakes (longest vessel on the lakes). The SS Carl D. Bradley (1927 – 640 feet) held the title for 22 years, longer than any other laker of the classic design. The Bradley is also known for breaking her back and foundering in a Lake Michigan storm in 1958. There were only two survivors.

Currently that title is held by the modern stern-ender Paul R. Tregurtha. Launched in 1981 as the William J. Delancy, and measuring 1,013.5 feet (308.9 m), the Paul R. Tregurtha has held the title since her launch. The Wilfred Sykes (1949 – 678 feet) is considered to be the first of the modern lakers, and when converted to a self-unloader in 1975 was the first to have the equipment mounted aft. Since then all self-unloading equipment has been mounted aft. The Algoisle (formerly the Silver Isle) (1962 – 715.9 feet) was the first modern laker built with all cabins aft (a "stern-ender"), following the lead of ocean-going bulk carriers and reprising a century old form used by little river steam barges and the whalebacks. The Stewart Cort (1971) was the first 1,000 footer and the only "footer" built in the classic cabins-fore-and-aft style. The Algosoo (1974 – 730 feet) was the last laker built in the classic style.

Also of note is the steamer Edward L. Ryerson, widely known for her artistic design and being the only remaining straight-decked (without self unloading machinery) freighter still in active service on the US side of the Great Lakes (the only other US straight decker still listed is the John Sherwin, has not sailed since 1981 and is currently docked in Detour, Michigan after conversion to a self unloader and repowering was halted in November 2008). In the summer of 2006, the Ryerson was fitted out and put into service following a long-term lay-up that began in 1998. The Ryerson has been meticulously maintained, and was often used as a museum boat for tours. She was put back into service due to a lack of reliable hulls on the Lakes, and a need for more tonnage. (The Canadian fleet retains a number of active straight-deckers for use in transporting grain, which is not well suited for self-unloading equipment. Most US grain is currently transported by rail.)

In film, the W. W. Holloway (since scrapped) is famous for being the lake freighter that the Blues Brothers jump their 1974 Dodge over when Elwood jumps the open 95th Street Draw Bridge.

MUSEUM SHIPS AND BOATS, SURVIVING HULLS

Cleveland, Ohio

The William G. Mather, a laker built in 1925 and a former flagship for the Cleveland-Cliffs Iron Company, has been turned into a maritime museum and is open to the public in Cleveland, Ohio in the North Coast Harbor.

Duluth-Superior, Minnesota-Wisconsin

The William A. Irvin was named for the president of U.S. Steel at the time of its launching and served as the flagship of US Steel's Great Lakes fleet from her launch in 1938 to 1975. It was the first laker to incorporate welding in its design and is open for tours at the Great Lakes Floating Maritime Museum in Duluth, Minnesota. Another museum ship, the Meteor, is the last surviving ship of the whaleback design, and is a museum in Superior, Wisconsin, which was the location of the American Steel Barge Company, where the whalebacks were built.

Sault Ste. Marie, Michigan

The Valley Camp was built in 1917 and served the National Steel Corporation, the Republic Steel Corporation, and Wilson Transit Co. during her 1917-1966 working life. She became a museum ship on the waterfront of the 'American Soo', east of the Soo Locks, in 1968. She holds many relics of the sinking of the SS Edmund Fitzgerald including two of the Fitz's mauled lifeboats.

Toledo, Ohio

The Col. James M. Schoonmaker is a former Cleveland-Cliffs Iron Company vessel that sailed from 1911 to 1980. She was originally owned by the Shenango Furnace Company, but renamed the Willis B. Boyer under Cleveland Cliffs ownership. The Schoonmaker was the largest bulk freighter in the world when commissioned. In one of the most ambitious Great Lakes ship restorations to date, the Schoonmaker was re-christened July 1, 2011, on the 100th anniversary of the ship's launching in Toledo. She was open to the public for many years as a museum at International Park in Toledo, Ohio but was moved Oct. 27, 2012, to a location downriver, next to the new home of the National Museum of the Great Lakes Historical Society. She is expected to reopen to the public in Spring 2014, when the museum is also scheduled to open.

OTHER SURVIVING HULLS AND INTERESTING PARTIAL SHIPS OF NOTE

DeTour, Michigan

The Lewis G. Harriman's bow and bow superstructure are preserved here. The Harriman, launched as the purpose-built cement steamer John W. Boardman, was scrapped but the bow was saved as a DeTour residence. Recently restored to the Boardman colors.

Put-In-Bay, Ohio

The Benson Ford was named after Henry Ford's grandson, and was the flagship of the Ford Motor Company (1924). The forward cabin is now located on a cliff on South Bass Island in Lake Erie, where it was moved in 1986. It is a private museum residence owned by Bryan Kasper of Sandusky, Ohio. It has been featured in many magazines and national television shows such as HGtv's Extreme Homes and Travel Channel's Extreme Vacation Homes. The deckhouse of the Ford provides a glimpse of what one of the grandest freighters on the lakes looked like.

Mississauga, Ontario

The SS Ridgetown was partially sunk as a breakwater (with stack and cabins intact) near Toronto at Port Credit. It was built in 1905 and is one of the oldest surviving hulls on the lake.

Its stark silhouette provides an example of the appearance of early 1900s lake freighters.

Detroit, Michigan

The pilot house of the William Clay Ford is part of the Dossin Great Lakes

Museum on Belle Isle. The pilot house is open for touring and overlooks the Detroit River.

FAILED MUSEUM ATTEMPTS, SHIPS SCRAPPED

Several other lakers nearly became museums, but due to funding, political opposition or other causes, were scrapped.

- Lewis G. Harriman - a 1923 purpose-built cement carrier, the first of her kind, that sailed from her launch until 1980. Used as a storage barge until 2003, a group tried to save her but bad communications within the company saw the ship sold in 2004 and scrapped in Sault Ste. Marie by Purvis Marine. The majority of the hull was fed to the Algoma Steel Mill but the forecastle was saved as a summer cottage at Detour, Michigan.
- SS Niagara - 1897 built freighter, later converted to a sand-sucker. Scrapped in 1997 by Liberty Iron & Metal of Erie, Pennsylvania, after a failed attempt to convert her into a museum in Erie. She had been saved from the scrapyard 11 years earlier.
- John Ericsson - The second-to-last whaleback freighter. The Ericsson was scrapped in 1969 in the city of Hamilton, Ontario. Politics, as was the case with the Canadiana, played a central role in the loss of the ship.
- SS Seaway Queen - The Canadian straight decker Seaway Queen, formerly owned by Upper Lakes Shipping, and the setting for the movie version of David Mamet's play Lakeboat, was involved in an attempt to save her as a museum. In the end, the company failed to locate an organization that was capable and willing to preserve her and she was sold and scrapped in Alang, India, in 2004.

FUTURE MUSEUM POTENTIAL

- Imperial Sarnia - 1948 built steam tanker. The Imperial Sarnia is ending her days as the dead bunkering vessel Provmar Terminal II in Hamilton, Ontario. While some freighters, such as Great Lakes bulk carriers, Liberty and Victory ships, have survived as museum ships, no conventional tankers have. The tanker museum ships that do exist, the Falls of Clyde and the Meteor, are known for being examples of unique vessel designs: an iron sailing ship and a whaleback, respectively.
- Cement Steamers - The cement fleet of steamers is rapidly being supplanted by tug/barge combinations like the Integrity and Innovation. Historic cement carriers include the J. B. Ford (1904), the St. Marys Challenger (1906), S. T. Crapo (1927), the J. A. W.

Iglehart (1936), Alpena (1942) and the Paul H. Townsend (1945).

- SS Arthur M. Anderson launched in 1952, is still running. She is famous for having had the last contact with the Edmund Fitzgerald before the latter sank. She was also the first would-be rescue vessel to search for the Fitzgerald.

COLLIER (SHIP)

A collier is a bulk cargo ship designed to carry coal, especially for naval use by coal-fired warships. In the late eighteenth century, a number of wooden-hulled sailing colliers gained fame after being adapted for use in voyages of exploration in the South Pacific, for which their flat-bottomed hulls and sturdy construction made them well-suited. The first aircraft carrier in the United States Navy was a converted Collier, fitted with a large elevated flat deck, used before the invention of purpose-built aircraft carrier hulls.

Coaling at sea was critical to navies and speed of coal transfer was an important metric of naval efficiency. In 1883, forty tons an hour was considered fast and it would take over twelve hours to restock half the bunkers of a typical ship, HMS Collingwood (1882).

COALS FROM NEWCASTLE

For many years, the Durham and Northumberlandcoalfields supplied the rapidly expanding London with vast tonnages of coal, and a large fleet of coastal colliers travelled up and down the east coast of England loaded with "black diamonds". Sir Charles Palmer pioneered the construction of iron-hulled steam colliers at his Jarrow shipyard, which began to rapidly replace the earlier wooden ships. This inadvertently led to the eventual decline of the glassmaking industry on Tyneside and Wearside, as prior to this, they had had access to large supplies of sand, used as ballast in the wooden colliers returning from London.

The iron colliers had ballast tanks which meant water could simply be pumped in, greatly reducing the turnaround time as the sand no longer needed to be loaded and unloaded. Coal was also exported to Europe, and wooden colliers returned with goods such as roofing tiles in their holds. The first Palmer-built iron hulled steam collier was the SS John Bowes of 1852. There had been an earlier iron hull screw propelled collier, the short-lived SS Bedlington of 1841 built in South Shields.

A notable incident involving a collier occurred not long after the opening of the Victoria Tunnel in Newcastle. The hemp rope which controlled the speed of wagons descending the tunnel to the river from Spital Tongues Colliery snapped, and the wagons landed in the Tyne. This time, the wagons were recovered at low tide, the rope was repaired, and the papers of the day treated the whole incident as something of a joke. Six months later, the rope snapped again, and the wagons landed in the hold of a waiting collier and sank it. After this, it was decided a wire rope would be a better option. This is probably the only recorded incident of a train having sunk a ship.

LOADING AND UNLOADING

Loading the colliers was carried out by hand at first, especially where coal was transferred from keels which had brought it downstream from parts of the river that the colliers were unable to navigate, but as the quantities handled increased, specialised jetties known as "staithes" began to be built. These were of numerous designs. Some had spouts used for unscreened or small coal, others known as "drops" had steep inclines at the end, down which a wagon would be lowered directly into the hold, minimising the breakage of coal. Some had both drops and spouts. The drops and spouts could be raised and lowered with the tide.

Later, elevators began to be introduced, such as those at Bates Staithes in Blyth, Northumberland and Harton Low Staithes in South Shields. These staithes used spouts. The largely intact Dunston Staithes on the Tyne are a good example of this type. In Scotland, a system was common where wagons would be placed on a cradle and lifted into the hold of the ship, but this system was rarely used elsewhere. Two large steam cranes were built for this purpose at the Harton Low Staithes, but it was found that despite their size and power they were too slow to handle the amount of coal that was arriving at the staithes, and were replaced by elevators.

The men who worked at the staithes were known as teemers and trimmers. Teemers would open the doors on the bottom of the wagons to allow the coal to fall into hoppers under the rail deck on top of the staithes, or in the case of drops, directly into the hold of the collier. The trimmers worked in the hold, spreading and levelling the coal with shovels and rakes so that its weight would be evenly distributed. Skilled trimmers could stand with their shovel under the stream of coal coming from a spout or the end of a conveyor and angle it so the coal would ricochet off into the part of the hold they wanted to fill. This was a dangerous job, as the holds could fill with firedamp given off by the coal, resulting in an explosion. More modern systems are designed to be able to evenly distribute the coal without the need for men working in the holds of the ships.

Although, in later years, the colliers faced competition from the railways in supplying coal for domestic use in the capital, large quantities of coal were used at the numerous power stations on the banks of the River Thames, and wharves were constructed alongside them for unloading the colliers.

The wharf at Battersea Power Station is still extant, and the cranes used for unloading the coal can be seen on the riverfront. These are fitted with clamshell buckets and in operation loaded a hopper, which in turn fed a conveyor system leading to the power station's coal bunkers. The modern equivalent can be seen at the Tyne Coal Terminal, unloading bulk carriers. Gas Light and Coke Company had similar facilities at its large gasworks, also alongside the Thames, for handling the large quantity of bituminous coal which was needed to supply the capital with town gas.

CONTAINER SHIP

Container ships are cargo ships that carry all of their load in truck-size intermodal containers, in a technique called containerization. They are a common means of commercial intermodal freight transport and now carry most seagoing non-bulk cargo.

Container ship capacity is measured in twenty-foot equivalent units (TEU). Typical loads are a mix of 20-foot and 40-foot (2-TEU) ISO-standard containers, with the latter predominant.

HISTORY

There are two main types of dry cargo: bulk cargo and break bulk cargo. Bulk cargoes, like grain or coal, are transported unpackaged in the hull of the ship, generally in large volume. Break-bulk cargoes, on the other hand, are transported in packages, and are generally manufactured goods. Before the advent of containerization in the 1950s, break-bulk items were loaded, lashed, unlashed and unloaded from the ship one piece at a time. However, by grouping cargo into containers, 1,000 to 3,000 cubic feet (28 to 85 m) of cargo, or up to about 64,000 pounds (29,000 kg), is moved at once and each container is secured to the ship once in a standardized way. Containerization has increased the efficiency of moving traditional break-bulk cargoes significantly, reducing shipping time by 84% and costs by 35%. As of 2001, more than 90% of world trade in non-bulk goods is transported in ISO containers. In 2009, almost one quarter of the world's dry cargo was shipped by container, an estimated 125 million TEU or 1.19 billion metric tons worth of cargo.

The earliest container ships were converted tankers, built up from surplus T2 tankers after World War II. In 1951, the first purpose-built container vessels began operating in Denmark, and between Seattle and Alaska. The first commercially successful container ship was the Ideal X, a T2 tanker, owned by Malcom McLean, which carried 58 metal containers between Newark, New Jersey and Houston, Texas on its first voyage. In 1955, McLean built his company, McLean Trucking into one of United States' biggest freighter fleets. In 1955, he purchased the small Pan Atlantic Steamship Company from Waterman Steamship and adapted its ships to carry cargo in large uniform metal containers. On April 26, 1956, the first of these rebuilt container vessels, the Ideal X, left the Port Newark in New Jersey and a new revolution in modern shipping resulted.

Container vessels eliminate the individual hatches, holds and dividers of the traditional general cargo vessels. The hull of a typical container ship is a huge warehouse divided into cells by vertical guide rails. These cells are designed to hold cargo in pre-packed units – containers. Shipping containers are usually made of steel, but other materials like aluminum, fiberglass or plywood are also used. They are designed to be entirely transferred to and from trains, trucks or trailers. There are several types of containers and they are categorized according to their size and functions.

Today, approximately 90% of non-bulk cargo worldwide is transported by container, and modern container ships can carry up to 16,020 twenty-foot equivalent units (TEU) (CMA CGM Marco Polo). As a class, container ships now rival crude oil tankers and bulk carriers as the largest commercial vessels on the ocean.

Although containerization caused a revolution in the world of shipping, its introduction did not have an easy passage. Ports, railway (railroad in the US) companies, and shippers were concerned about the huge costs of developing the ports and railway infrastructure needed to handle container ships, and for the movement of containers on land by rail and road. Trade unions were concerned about massive job loss among port and dock workers at ports, as containers were sure to eliminate several manual jobs of cargo handling at ports. It took ten years of legal battles before container ships would be pressed into international service.

In 1966, a container liner service from USA to the Dutch city of Rotterdam commenced. Containerization changed not only the face of shipping, but it also revolutionized world trade as well. A container ship can be loaded and unloaded in a few hours compared to days in a traditional cargo vessel. This, besides cutting labor costs, has reduced shipping times between points to a great extent; for example, it takes a few weeks instead of months for a consignment to be delivered from India to Europe and vice-versa.

It has also resulted in less breakage due to less handling; also, there is less danger of cargo shifting during a voyage. As containers are sealed and only open at the destination, pilferage and theft levels have been greatly reduced.

Containerization has lowered shipping expense and decreased shipping time, and this has in turn helped the growth of international trade. Cargo that once arrived in cartons, crates, bales, barrels or bags now comes in factory sealed containers, with no indication to the human eye of their contents, except for a product code that machines can scan and computers trace. This system of tracking has been so exact that a two-week voyage can be timed for arrival with an accuracy of under fifteen minutes. It has resulted in such revolutions as on time guaranteed delivery and just in time manufacturing. Raw materials arrive from factories in sealed containers less than an hour before they are required in manufacture, resulting in reduced inventory expense.

The aforementioned reduction in ship operating costs accrue to companies owning or operating container ships. But for others connected with trade, such as ports, railways, road transporters and trade (exporters and importers), the operating costs have risen exponentially. Several elements of costs that were borne in the past by ship operators are now borne by trade, as standard terms of carriage of goods by sea have now been drastically revised by container-shipping lines. Despite saving in operating costs, shipping freight have not fallen significantly because freight is globally fixed sector-wise by shipping cartels.

In short, containers have helped to optimize the operation of ships, while the additional burden of ancillary costs that has been transferred from ships onto other (i.e. onshore) entities is normally ignored in public perception.

Exporters load merchandise in boxes that are provided by the shipping companies. They are then delivered to the docks by road, rail or a combination of both for loading on to container ships. Prior to containerization, huge gangs of men would spend hours fitting various items of cargo into different holds. Today, cranes, installed either on the pier or on the ship, are used to place containers on board the ship. When the hull has been fully loaded, additional containers are stacked on the deck.

Today's largest container ships measure almost 400 metres (1,300 ft) in length. They carry loads equal to the cargo-carrying capacity of sixteen to seventeen pre-WWII freighter ships.

ARCHITECTURE

There are several key points in the design of modern container ships. The hull, similar to bulk carriers and general cargo ships, is built around a strong keel. Into this frame is set one or more below-deck cargo holds, numerous tanks, and the engine room. The holds are topped by hatch covers, onto which more containers can be stacked. Many container ships have cargo cranes installed on them, and some have specialized systems for securing containers on board. The hull of a modern cargo ship is a complex arrangement of steel plates and strengthening beams. The hull is built around the keel. Resembling ribs, and fastened at right-angles to the keel are the ship's frames. The ship's main deck, the metal platework that covers the top of the hull framework, is supported by beams that are attached to the tops of the frames and run the full breadth of the ship.

The beams not only support the deck, but along with the deck, frames, and transverse bulkheads, strengthen and reinforce the shell. Another feature of recent hulls is a set of double-bottom tanks, which provide a second watertight shell that runs most of the length of a ship. The double-bottoms generally hold liquids such as fuel oil, ballast water or fresh water.

A ship's engine room houses its main engines and auxiliary machinery such as the fresh water and sewage systems, electrical generators, fire pumps, and air conditioners. In most new ships, the engine room is located in the aft portion of the ship.

Size categories

Container ships are distinguished into seven major size categories: small feeder, feeder, feedermax, panamax, post-panamax, new panamax and ultra-large. As of December 2012, there are 161 container ships in the VLCS class (Very Large Container Ships, more than 10,000 TEU), and 51 ports in the world can accommodate them.

The size of a panamax vessel is limited by the Panama canal's lock chambers, which can accommodate ships with a beam of up to 32.31 m, a length overall of up to 294.13 m, and a draft of up to 12.04 m. The "post panamax" category has historically been used to describe ships with a moulded breadth over 32.31 m, however the Panama Canal expansion project is causing some changes in terminology.

The "new panamax" category is based on the maximum vessel-size that will be able to transit a new third set of locks. The new locks are being built to accommodate a container ship with a length overall of 366 metres (1,201 ft), a maximum width of 49 metres (161 ft), and tropical fresh-water draft of 15.2 metres (50 ft). Such a vessel would be wide enough to carry 19 rows of containers, have a total capacity of approximately 12,000 TEU and be comparable in size to a capesize bulk carrier or a suezmax tanker.

Container ships under 3,000 TEU are generally called feeders. Feeders are small ships that typically operate between smaller container ports. Some feeders collect their cargo from small ports, drop it off at large ports for transshipment on larger ships, and distribute containers from the large port to smaller regional ports. This size of vessel is the most likely to carry cargo cranes on board.

Cargo cranes

A major characteristic of a container ship is whether it has cranes installed for handling its cargo. Those that have cargo cranes are called geared and those that don't are called ungeared or gearless. The earliest purpose-built container ships in the 1970s were all gearless. Since then, the percentage of geared newbuilds has fluctuated widely, but has been decreasing overall, with only 7.5% of the container ship capacity in 2009 being equipped with cranes.

While geared container ships are more flexible in that they can visit ports that are not equipped with pierside container cranes, they suffer from several drawbacks. To begin with, geared ships will cost more to purchase than a gearless ship. Geared ships also incur greater recurring expenses, such as maintenance and fuel costs. The United Nations Council on Trade and Development characterizes geared ships as a "niche market only appropriate for those ports where low cargo volumes do not justify investment in port cranes or where the public sector does not have the financial resources for such investment."

Instead of the rotary cranes, some geared ships have gantry cranes installed. These cranes, specialized for container work, are able to roll forward and aft on rails. In addition to the additional capital expense and maintenance costs, these cranes generally load and discharge containers much more slowly than their shoreside counterparts.

The introduction and improvement of shoreside cranes have been a key to the success of the container ship. The first crane that was specifically designed for container work was built in California's Port of Alameda in 1959. By the 1980s, shoreside gantry cranes were capable of moving containers on a 3-minute-cycle, or up to 400 tons per hour. In March 2010, at Port Klang in Malaysia, a new world record was set when 734 container moves were made in a single hour. The record was achieved using 9 cranes to simultaneously load and unload the MV CSCL Pusan, a ship with a capacity of 9,600 TEU.

Vessels in the 1,500–2,499 TEU range are the most likely size class to have cranes, with more than 60% of this category being geared ships. Slightly less than a third of the very smallest ships (from 100–499 TEU) are geared, and almost no ships with a capacity of over 4,000 TEU are geared.

Cargo holds

Efficiency has always been key in the design of container ships. While containers may be carried on conventional break-bulk ships, cargo holds for dedicated container ships are specially constructed to speed loading and unloading, and to efficiently keep containers secure while at sea. A key aspect of container ship specialization is the design of the hatches, the openings from the main deck to the cargo holds.

The hatch openings stretch the entire breadth of the cargo holds, and are surrounded by a raised steel structure known as the hatch coaming. On top of the hatch coamings are the hatch covers. Until the 1950s, hatches were typically secured with wooden boards and tarpaulins held down with battens. Today, some hatch covers can be solid metal plates that are lifted on and off the ship by cranes, while others are articulated mechanisms that are opened and closed using powerful hydraulic rams.

Another key component of dedicated container-ship design is the use of cell guides. Cell guides are strong vertical structures constructed of metal installed into a ship's cargo holds. These structures guide containers into well-defined rows during the loading process and provide some support for containers against the ship's rolling at sea. So fundamental to container ship design are cell guides that organizations such as the United Nations Conference on Trade and Development use their presence to distinguishing dedicated container ships from general break-bulk cargo ships.

A system of three dimensions is used in cargo plans to describe the position of a container aboard the ship. The first coordinate is the row, which starts at the front of the ship and increases aft. The second coordinate is tier, with the first tier at the bottom of the cargo holds, the second tier on top of that, and so forth. The third coordinate is the slot. Slots on the starboard side are given odd numbers and those on the port side are given even numbers. The slots nearest the centerline are given low numbers, and the numbers increase for slots further from the centerline.

LASHING SYSTEMS

Numerous systems are used to secure containers aboard ships, depending on factors such as the type of ship, the type of container, and the location of the container. Stowage inside the holds of fully cellular (FC) ships is simplest, typically using simple metal forms called container guides, locating cones, and anti-rack spacers to lock the containers together. Above-decks, without the extra support of the cell guides, more complicated equipment is used. Three types of systems are currently in wide use: lashing systems, locking systems, and buttress systems.

Lashing systems secure containers to the ship using devices made from wire rope, rigid rods, or chains and devices to tension the lashings, such as turnbuckles. The effectiveness of lashings is increased by securing containers to each other, either by simple metal forms (such as stacking cones) or more complicated devices such as twist-lock stackers. A typical twist-lock is inserted into the casting hole of one container and rotated to hold it in place, then another container is lowered on top of it. The two containers are locked together by twisting the device's handle. A typical twist-lock is constructed of forged steel and ductile iron and has a shear strength of 48 metric tons.

The buttress system, used on some large container ships, uses a system of large towers attached to the ship at both ends of each cargo hold. As the ship is loaded, a rigid, removable stacking frame is added, structurally securing each tier of containers together.

FLEET CHARACTERISTICS

As of 2010, container ships made up 13.3% of the world's fleet in terms of deadweight tonnage. The world's total of container ship deadweight tonnage has increased from 11 million DWT in 1980 to 169.0 million DWT in 2010. The combined deadweight tonnage of container ships and general cargo ships, which also often carry containers, represents 21.8% of the world's fleet.

As of 2009, the average age of container ships worldwide was 10.6 years, making them the youngest general vessel type, followed by bulk carriers at 16.6 years, oil tankers at 17 years, general cargo ships at 24.6 years, and others at 25.3 years.

Most of the world's carrying capacity in fully cellular container ships is in the liner service, where ships trade on scheduled routes. As of January 2010, the top 20 liner companies controlled 67.5% of the world's fully cellular container capacity, with 2,673 vessels of an average capacity of 3,774 TEU.

The remaining fully 6,862 fully cellular ships have an average capacity of 709 TEU each.

The vast majority of the capacity of fully cellular container ships used in the liner trade is owned by German shipowners, with approximately 75% owned by Hamburg brokers. It is a common practice for the large container lines to supplement their own ships with chartered-in ships, for example in 2009, 48.9% of the tonnage of the top 20 liner companies was chartered-in in this manner.

FLAG STATES

International law requires that every merchant ship be registered in a country, called its flag state. A ship's flag state exercises regulatory control over the vessel and is required to inspect it regularly, certify the ship's equipment and crew, and issue safety and pollution prevention documents. As of 2006, the United States Bureau of Transportation Statistics count 2,837 container ships of 10,000 long tons deadweight (DWT) or greater worldwide.

Panama was the world's largest flag state for container ships, with 541 of the vessels in its registry. Seven other flag states had more than 100 registered container ships: Liberia (415), Germany (248), Singapore (177), Cyprus (139), the Marshall Islands (118) and the United Kingdom (104). The Panamanian, Liberian, and Marshallese flags are open registries and considered by the International Transport Workers' Federation to be flags of convenience. By way of comparison, traditional maritime nations such as the United States and Japan only had 75 and 11 registered container ships, respectively.

VESSEL PURCHASES

In 2009, 11,669,000 gross tons of newly built container ships were delivered. Over 85% of this new capacity was built in the Republic of Korea, China, and Japan, with Korea accounting for over 57% of the world's total alone. New container ships accounted for 15% of the total new tonnage that year, behind bulk carriers at 28.9% and oil tankers at 22.6%.

SCRAPPING

Most ships are removed from the fleet through a process known as scrapping. Scrapping is rare for ships under 18 years old and for those over 40 years in age. Ship-owners and buyers negotiate scrap prices based on factors such as the ship's empty weight (called light ton displacement or LTD) and prices in the scrap metal market. Scrapping rates are volatile, the price per light ton displacement has swung from a high of $650 per LTD in mid-2008 to $200 per LTD in early 2009, before building to $400 per LTD in March 2010. As of 2009, over 96% of the world's scrapping activity takes place in China, India, Bangladesh, and Pakistan.

The global economic downturn of 2008–2009 resulted in more ships than usual being sold for scrap. In 2009, 364,300 TEU worth of container ship capacity was scrapped, up from 99,900 TEU in 2008. Container ships accounted for 22.6% of the total gross tonnage of ships scrapped that year. Despite the surge, the capacity removed from the fleet only accounted for 3% of the world's containership capacity. The average age of container ships scrapped in 2009 was 27.0 years.

LARGEST SHIPS

Economies of scale have dictated an upward trend in sizes of container ships in order to reduce expense. However, there are certain limitations to the size of container ships. Primarily, these are the availability of sufficiently large main engines and the availability of a sufficient number of ports and terminals prepared and equipped to handle ultra-large container ships. Furthermore, the permissible maximum ship dimensions in some of the world's main waterways could present an upper limit in terms of vessel growth. This primarily concerns the Suez Canal and the Singapore Strait.

In 2008 the South Korean shipbuilder STX announced plans to construct a container ship capable of carrying 22,000 TEU, and with a proposed length of 450 metres and a beam of 60 metres. If constructed, the container ship would become the largest seagoing vessel in the world.

Since even very large container ships are vessels with relatively low draft compared to large tankers and bulk carriers, there is still considerable room for vessel growth. Compared to today's largest container ships, Maersk Line's 15,200 TEUEmma Mærsk-type series, a 20,000 TEU container ship would only be moderately larger in terms of exterior dimensions. According to a 2011 estimate, an ultra-large container ship of 20,250 TEU would measure 440m x 59m, compared to 397.71 x 56.40m for the Emma Mærsk class. It would have an estimated deadweight of circa 220,000 tons.

While such a vessel might be near the upper limit for a Suez Canal passage, the so-called Malaccamax concept (for Straits of Malacca) does not apply for container ships, since the Malacca and Singapore Straits' draft limit of about 21 metres is still above that of any conceivable container ship design. In 2011, Maersk announced plans to build a new "Triple E" family of containerships with a capacity of 18,000TEU, with an emphasis on lower fuel consumption.

In the present market situation, main engines will not be as much of a limiting factor for vessel growth either. The steadily rising expense of fuel oil has prompted most container lines to adapt a slower, more economical voyage speed of about 21 knots, compared to earlier top speeds of 25 or more knots. Subsequently, new-built container ships can be fitted with a smaller main engine. Engine types fitted to today's ships of 14,000 TEU are thus sufficiently large to propel future vessels of 20,000 TEU or more. Maersk Line, the world's largest container shipping line, nevertheless opted for twin engines (two smaller engines working two separate propellers), when ordering a series of ten 18,000 TEU vessels from Daewoo Shipbuilding in February 2011. The ships will be delivered between 2013 and 2014.

FREIGHT MARKET

The act of hiring a ship to carry cargo is called chartering. Outside of special bulk cargo markets, ships are hired by three types of charter agreements: the voyage charter, the time charter, and the bareboat charter. In a voyage charter, the charterer rents the vessel from the loading port to the discharge port. In a time charter, the vessel is hired for a set period of time, to perform voyages as the charterer directs. In a bareboat charter, the charterer acts as the ship's operator and manager, taking on responsibilities such as providing the crew and maintaining the vessel. The completed chartering contract is known as a charter party.

The United Nations Conference on Trade and Development, or UNCTAD, in its 2010 Review of Maritime Trade tracks two aspects of container shipping prices. The first is a chartering price, specifically the price to time-charter a 1 TEU slot for a 14 metric ton cargo on a container ship. The other is the freight rate, or comprehensive daily cost to deliver one-TEU worth of cargo on a give route. As a result of the late-2000s recession, both indicators showed sharp drops during 2008–2009, and have shown signs of stabilization since 2010.

UNCTAD uses the Hamburg Shipbrokers' Association (formally the Vereinigung Hamburger Schiffsmakler und Schiffsagenten e. V. or VHSS for short) as its main industry source for container ship freight prices. The VHSS maintains a few indices of container ship charter prices. The oldest, which dates back to 1998, is called the Hamburg Index. This index considers time-charters on fully cellular containerships controlled by Hamburg brokers. It is limited to charters of 3 months or more, and presented as the average daily cost in U.S. dollars for a one-TEU slot with a weight of 14 metric tons. The Hamburg Index data is divided into ten categories based primarily on vessel carrying capacity. Two additional categories exist for small vessels of under 500 TEU that carry their own cargo cranes. In 2007, VHSS started another index, the New ConTex which tracks similar data obtained from an international group of shipbrokers.

The Hamburg Index shows some clear trends in recent chartering markets. First, rates were generally increasing from 2000 to 2005. From 2005 to 2008, rates slowly decreased, and in mid-2008 began a "dramatic decline" of approximately 75%, which lasted until rates stabilized in April 2009. Rates have ranged from $2.70 to $35.40 in this period, with prices generally lower on larger ships. The most resilient sized vessel in this time period were those from 200–300 TEU, a fact that the United Nations Council on Trade and Development attributes to lack of competition in this sector. Overall, in 2010, these rates rebounded somewhat, but remained at approximately half of their 2008 values. As of 2011, the index shows signs of recovery for container shipping, and combined with increases in global capacity, indicates a positive outlook for the sector in the near future.

UNCTAD also tracks container freight rates. Freight rates are expressed as the total price in U.S. dollars for a shipper to transport one TEU worth of cargo along a given route. Data is given for the three main container liner routes: U.S.-Asia, U.S.-Europe, and Europe-Asia. Prices are typically different between the two legs of a voyage, for example the Asia-U.S. rates have been significantly higher than the return U.S.-Asia rates in recent years. Generally, from the fourth quarter of 2008 through the third quarter of 2009, both the volume of container cargo and freight rates have dropped sharply. In 2009, the freight rates on the U.S.–Europe route were sturdiest, while the Asia-U.S. route fell the most.

Liner companies responded to their overcapacity in several ways. For example, in early 2009, some container lines dropped their freight rates to zero on the Asia-Europe route, charging shippers only a surcharge to cover operating costs.

They decreased their overcapacity by lowering the ships' speed (a strategy called "slow steaming") and by laying up ships. Slow steaming increased the length of the Europe-Asia routes to a record high of over 40 days. Another strategy used by some companies was to manipulate the market by publishing notices of rate increases in the press, and when "a notice had been issued by one carrier, other carriers followed suit."

The Trans-Siberian Railroad (TSR) has recently become a more viable alternative to container ships on the Asia-Europe route. This railroad can typically deliver containers in 1/3 to 1/2 of the time of a sea voyage, and in late 2009 announced a 20% reduction in its container shipping rates. With its 2009 rate schedule, the TSR will transport a forty-foot container to Poland from Yokohama for $2,820, or from Pusan for $2,154.

CONTAINER PORTS

Container traffic through a port is often tracked in terms of twenty foot equivalent units or TEU of throughput. As of 2009, the Port of Singapore was the world's busiest container port, with 25,866,000 TEU handled. That year, six of the busiest ten container ports were in the People's Republic of China, with Shanghai in 2nd place, Port of Hong Kong in 3rd, Shenzhen 4th, Guangzhou 6th, Ningbo 8th, and Qingdao 9th. Rounding out the top ten ports were Busan in South Korea at number 5, Dubai in the United Arab Emirates at number 7, and Rotterdam in the Netherlands in the 10th position with 9,743,290 TEU served. In total, the busiest twenty container ports handled 220,905,805 TEU in 2009, almost half of the world's total estimated container traffic that year of 465,597,537 TEU.

SAFETY ISSUES

In March 2007, a London based container ship capsized in Antwerp, Belgium while loading.

Maneuvers in coastal waters and ports managed in the wheel house may be dangerous, as evidenced by a container ship hitting the San Francisco – Oakland Bay Bridge on November 7, 2007.

It has been estimated that container ships lose between 2,000 and 10,000 containers at sea each year, costing $370 million per year. Most go overboard on the open sea during storms but there are some examples of whole ships being lost with their cargo. When containers are dropped, they immediately become an environmental threat – termed "marine debris". Once in the ocean, they fill with water and sink if the contents cannot hold air. Rough waters smash the container, sinking it quickly.

The threat of piracy can cost a container shipping company as much as $100 million per year due to longer routes and higher speed, particularly near East Africa.

HEAVY LIFT SHIP

A heavy lift ship is a vessel designed to move very large loads that cannot be handled by normally equipped ships. They are of two types: semi-submerging vessels capable of lifting another ship out of the water and transporting it; and vessels that augment unloading facilities at inadequately equipped ports.

HISTORY

In the 1920s, the Bremen-based shipping company DDG Hansa saw a growing demand of shipments for assembled locomotives to British India. That led to the construction of the world's first heavy lift vessel, MV Lichtenfels with a 120 t (118 long tons; 132 short tons) derrick. After World War II, DDG Hansa became the world's largest heavy lift shipping company. In terms of lifting capacity it reached its peak in 1978 with refitting the Japanese built bulk carrier MV Trifels with two 320 t (315 long tons; 353 short tons) Stülcken derricks. Shortly after that, in 1980, DDG went bankrupt. With that, only the Dutch shipping companies Jumbo and BigLift Shipping (until 2001 named Mammoet Shipping) were left as heavy lift shipping specialists.

SUBMERGING TYPES

Semi-submerging are more commonly known as a "flo/flo" for float-on/ float-off. These vessels have a long and low well deck between a forward pilot house and an aft machinery space. In superficial appearance, it is somewhat similar to a dry bulk carrier or some forms of oil tanker. Its ballast tanks can be flooded to lower the well deck below the water's surface, allowing oil platforms, other vessels, or other floating cargo to be moved into position for loading. The tanks are then pumped out, and the well deck rises to shoulder the load. To balance the cargo, the various tanks can be pumped unevenly.

The flo/flo industry's largest customer base is the oil industry. They have transported many oil drilling rigs (flo/flo ships can carry the rigs from their construction site to a drilling site at roughly three to four times the speed of a self-deploying rig). Rapid deployment of the rig to the drilling site can translate into major savings to the oil industry. They also transport other outsized cargo and yachts.

The U.S. Navy has used such ships to bring two damaged warships back to the United States for repair. The first was the guided missile frigateUSS Samuel B. Roberts, which was nearly sunk by a naval mine in the central Persian Gulf on 14 April 1988. The frigate was towed to Dubai, then floated home to Newport, Rhode Island, aboard Mighty Servant 2.

Eleven years later, MV Blue Marlin transported the U.S. guided missile destroyer USS Cole from Aden, Yemen to Pascagoula, Mississippi, after the warship was damaged in a bombing attack on 12 October 2000.

The U.S. Navy has also chartered other heavy lift ships to carry smaller craft, usually mine-countermeasure craft, or other patrol craft. Since there are no US-flagged heavy lift/flo/flo ships, the U.S. Navy normally relies on its Military Sealift Command to charter them from the world commercial market.

In 2004, Blue Marlin carried the world's largest semi-submersible oil platform, BP's Thunder Horse PDQ, from the Daewoo Shipbuilding & Marine Engineering (DMSE) shipyard in South Korea to Kiewit Offshore Services in Ingleside, Texas.

Many of the larger ships of this class are owned by the company Dockwise, including Mighty Servant 1, MV Blue Marlin, and MV Black Marlin. In 2004, Dockwise increased the deck width of Blue Marlin, to make it the then largest heavy transport carrier in the world until it was superseded by the launch of the Dockwise Vanguard in 2012. One of the company's vessels, Mighty Servant 2, capsized after hitting an uncharted underwater obstacle off Indonesia in November 1999.

HOPPER BARGE

A hopper barge is a kind of non-mechanical ship or vessel that cannot move around by itself, unlike some other types of barges. Designed to carry materials, like rocks, sand, soil and rubbish, for dumping into the ocean, a river or lake for land reclamation.

Hopper barges are seen in two distinctive types; raked hopper or box hopper barges. The raked hopper barges move faster than the box hoppers; they are both designed for movement of dry bulky commodities.

There are several "hoppers" or compartments between the fore and aftbulkhead of the barge. On the bottom of the barge hull, there is (are) also a large "hopper door(s)", opening downwards. The doors are closed while the vessel is moving, so she can carry the materials that are to be dumped. The door(s) open when the ship has arrived at the spot where the materials are to be dumped.

Split barges serve the same purpose, but instead of a door in the hull's bottom, the hull of the whole barge splits longitudinally between the end bulkheads. The vessel consists of two major parts (port and starboard halves), both are mostly symmetrical in design. Both parts of the vessel are hinged at the deck and operated by hydrauliccylinders. When the vessel splits the load is dumped rapidly, which means the barge has to be very stable in order not to capsize or otherwise get damaged.

LIGHTER ABOARD SHIP

The lighter aboard ship (LASH) system refers to the practice of loading barges (lighters) aboard a larger vessel for transport. It was developed in response to a need to transport lighters, a type of unpowered barge, between inland waterways separated by open seas. Lighters are typically towed or pushed around harbors, canals or rivers and cannot be relocated under their own power. The carrier ships are known variously as LASH carriers, barge carriers, kangaroo ships or lighter transport ships.

DEVELOPMENT

By the 1950s, the needs of cargo transport customers were no longer being met by the old system of loading individual cargo pieces into a ship's hold. The dimensions and shapes of cargo pieces varied widely, and the ISO standard cargo container had only slowly begun to be adopted during the 1960s. Large container terminals with extensive conveyor systems and storage areas were still only in planning or in the development stages.

The LASH system was developed as an alternative and supplement to the developing container system. The lighters, which may be characterized as floating cargo containers, served dual purposes: transportation over water, and the establishment of a modular, standardized shape for loading and unloading cargo. The lighters, also known as swimming normed cargo containers, are loaded onto a LASH carrier at the port of embarkation and unloaded from the ship at the port of destination.

The system was developed by the American shipbuilding engineer Jerome Goldman during the 1960s. The Acadia Forest, commissioned in September 1969, was the first LASH carrier. The ship could take up 75 standardized lighters, with about 376 metric tons of total loading capacity. At the time, it was a novel kind of ship, the first vessel designed primarily to transport other, smaller ships. In the late 1980s, the Soviet Union built a nuclear-powered LASH carrier, the Sevmorput, which is the only nuclear-powered cargo ship out of four ever built remaining in service.

ECONOMIC IMPACT

At the time of its invention, the system was considered by experts to be a considerable advancement in shipping technology. LASH carriers were able to transport five times more cargo than a comparable conventional transport ship, the loading and unloading process was much more efficient, and a lack of harbor equipment or quay moorings provided no obstacle, as the lighters could be loaded directly onto the ship. The system also relieved the pressure to unload as quickly as possible, since the lighters already in the water could be moved while others were being unloaded. All told, these ships spent more than 80% of their annual application time at sea, whereas the conventional ships often lay at harbor for as much as half the year.

TECHNOLOGY

LASH barges are loaded at inland river and shallow ports. Then, the barges are towed to ocean port's fleeting areas to meet the LASH mother vessel. On arrival, the mother vessel crane lifts the LASH barges onto the ships. LASH cargo does not require transshipment, as the movement from the origin to destination takes place with a single bill of lading.

An important technical problem raised by the invention of the new transport system was the shape of the lighters. Several other designs, differentiated mainly by the shape of the lighters and the loading mechanism, were proposed, but the LASH system found the largest range of applications. In this approach, the lighters were individually lifted onto the carrier ship by a large crane located at the stern of the ship. The crane could move the entire length of the ship and stack the lighters atop each other in the ship's body and on the deck. The cranes had a load-carrying capacity of more than 500 Mp. Loading or unloading a lighter took on average fifteen minutes. LASH ships were constructed in Europe, Japan and the USA with almost uniform parameters. The host vessel is sometimes purpose-built or modified with a door at the waterline, to allow the payloads to be loaded and unloaded without special lifting equipment. An example would be the LASH Turkiye, built at Avondale Shipyard for the American shipping line Prudential Grace, and later transferred to the Ready Reserve Fleet.

TECHNICAL DATA

		LASH 1	**LASH2**
	m	262	250
	m	32.50	30.50
	m	11.30	10.70
Tonnage	tons	43000	29600
Speed	knots	19	22
Power	hp	26000	32000

Type of Lighter

Length	18.70 m
Beam	9.50 m
Headway	4.00 m
Weight	80.00 tonns
Capacity	380.00 tonns
Draught	2.60 m

SEA BEE SYSTEM

Another related system was the Sea Bee, which had a lifting system located at the stern of the carrier ship. The lift, known as a "Syncrolift" was a platform that could be lowered below the water surface. Two lighters weighing up to 1000 metric tons are maneuvered onto the now-underwater platform and raised to the height of the deck, where special rails engage and transport the lighters down the length of the ship to their berthings. The lighters used in the Sea Bee system are considerably larger than the LASH lighter, and the loading hardware is also stronger, with a lifting force of more than 2000 Mp.

The first ship of a series of three Sea Bee ships was the SS Doctor Lykes, followed by the SS Almeria Lykes and SS Tillie Lykes all of which were operated by Lykes Brothers Steamship Company. The "Sea Bee" vessels had three decks and could transport 38 lighters (12 on the lower decks and 14 on the upper deck).

The dual function of the ship is noteworthy, as it had storage tanks with a capacity of nearly 36000 m^3 volume built into its sides and unusually large double hull, allowing it to be used also as a product tanker. The ships were later purchased by Military Sealift Command.

Finnish state-owned shipbuilding company Valmet built two barge carriers largely based on the Sea Bee system for the Soviet Union in Vuosaari Shipyard in the late 1970s, Yulius Fuchik and Tibor Szamueli. Of these, Yulius Fuchik was featured in a prominent role in the novel Red Storm Rising by Tom Clancy.

Technical data

Seabee-Carrier		
Overall length	m	266.70
Beam	m	32.26
Height to the first deck	m	9.70
Height to the maindeck	m	16.10
Height to the upperdeck	m	22.80
Draught	m	10.00
Capacity	tons	27500
Displacement	tons	45400
Speed	knots	20
Power	hp	36000

Seabee-Lighter

Length	m	29.75
Beam	m	10.67
Headway	m	3.80
Weight	tonns	150
Capacity	tonns	850
Draught	m	3.25

BACAT SYSTEM

A Danish project with the name BACAT (Barge-Catamaran) was introduced at the end of 1973. It was used for the transport of several hundred thousand metric tons of load between northern Europe and Great Britain. The system was similar to the Sea Bee, but the lighters were smaller and had an individual load-carrying capacity of only 140 tons.

Technical data

BACAT-Carrier

Overall length	m	103.50
Beam	m	20.70
Headway	m	10.50
Draught	m	5.40
Capacity	tons	2700
Speed	knots	13
Power	hp	2250

		Lighter type 1	Lighter type 2
Length	m	16.80	18.75
Beam	m	4.70	9.50
Draught	m	2.47	2.50
Capacity	tonns	140	370

PROBLEMS AND SHORTCOMINGS

New problems which were as yet unknown to shipping companies arose with the advent of the LASH system and similar barge carriers. Aboard the carrier ship, the lighter is simply a large cargo container, but in the seaport and on the inland waterways it becomes a vessel. As a vessel, they are subject to requirements for equipment regulations like anchors, winches, coupling had to be provided so-called "head barges" which could not be transported on the carrier ships. Also, serving waterways which freeze over in winter required a high capital expenditure.

Studies showed that the costs of addressing these issues, along with the costs of operating the carrier ships and their lighters, were much higher than for the customary freighter ships or the ISO-compliant container ships that were beginning to conquer the transportation market. While barge carriers and lighters are a technologically interesting sea transport system, they are economic only under certain specific conditions of traffic and economy.

HISTORY

On 15 December 2007, the Rhine Forest, ex-Bilderdijk of the Holland-Amerika Line, entered the Port of Rotterdam for the last time, prior to being withdrawn from service because of low utilization on the New Orleans/ Rotterdam route. It is a sister ship of the MS München. The LASH lighter with registration p. CG 6013 was donated to De Binnenvaart, an inland-shipping museum in Dordrecht, where it is now part of an exhibit.

LIVESTOCK CARRIER

A livestock carrier, as the name suggests, is a large ship used in the live export of sheep, cattle and goats. They are specially built new or converted from container ships.

LIVESTOCK CARRIERS

Seagoing vessels modified or purpose-hansing carry built for the transportation of live animals.

Subject to appropriate regulation, live animals may be transported as part of the cargo on various classes of ship. That particular method of transportation is more common on short sea crossings (e.g. ferries) and usually involves relatively small numbers of animals. Livestock carriers are those ships, which specialise exclusively in the transportation of large numbers of live animals together with their requirements for the voyage. (food, water, sawdust bedding, medication, etc.). Voyages on livestock carriers generally last from three days to three to four weeks.

MAIN SUB-TYPES OF LIVESTOCK CARRIERS

- Open livestock carriers - in which all, or most, of the animal pens are installed on open decks. In theory, this provides continuous natural ventilation of the pen areas and avoids reliance on mechanical ventilation systems.

(Ventilation is a key factor in the transport of live animals. When animal pens become poorly ventilated, oxygen depletion and a build-up of toxic gases, develops very rapidly. Circumstances vary according to ambient conditions but a failure of ventilation systems in some tropical conditions could result in extensive asphyxiation of animals, in as little as two or three hours.) In practice, natural ventilation alone isn't adequate for all situations. One obvious limiting factor would be in following wind conditions at sea, when the air moves at the same speed as the ship. In that condition, the natural air flow ventilating the animal pens could be insufficient. On most open livestock carriers, there is also some type of supplementary mechanical ventilation installed in critical zones, along with appropriate back-up equipment for emergencies.

- Closed livestock carriers - in which more or less all of the animals pens are located within the holds and internal decks of the ship.

This has the advantage of providing a more controlled environment in which the animals and their feeding and watering arrangements are sheltered from adverse weather.

However, ventilation is almost entirely dependent on mechanical systems on 'closed' livestock carriers and construction rules require specific ventilation standards for the internal spaces. These usually stipulate the minimum number of air changes per hour. Regulations also require back-up systems and auxiliary power arrangements on those ships which are separate from the main engine room. This is to ensure that adequate ventilation, lighting, watering and feeding can be maintained, for the animals, in the event of fire or machinery failure in the main engine spaces.

TYPES OF ANIMALS TRANSPORTED

Various species have been transported in this way, but by far the most numerous are the domesticated breeds of sheep and cattle. During the latter half of the twentieth century, millions of sheep and many thousands of cattle were transported on livestock carriers. Other domesticated species which have been transported, though in smaller numbers, include horses, camels, deer, goats and, on at least one occasion, ostriches. The transportation of live fish, on small specialised vessels, is a similar trade which has developed in association with fish farming National authorities which permit the export or import of live animals, regulate and monitor the ships and the associated aspects of the trade very closely.

SIZES AND CAPACITIES OF LIVESTOCK CARRIERS

The size of this type of ship varies, according to market demands in different parts of the world at different times. In the latter half of the twentieth century, the principal livestock exporting nations were Australia and New Zealand and the main importers were nations in the Middle East. Vessels engaged in that trade have ranged in size from 2,000 metric tons deadweight (DWT) to 25,000 DWT. The limiting factors on ship size are complex. Bigger vessels can achieve economies of scale in their operations but also require more extensive port facilities to handle the larger numbers of livestock likely to be loaded or discharged.

Livestock carriers carry more crew members than conventional cargo ships of a similar size. Experienced stockmen are an essential part of the crew. The total number of stockmen required varies according to the number of animals and also depends on factors such as the arrangement of the livestock pens and the extent of automated systems installed for feeding and watering.

During the last three decades of the twentieth century there was a progressive trend towards large vessels carrying greater numbers of animals. Prior to that, a significant limitation had been fresh water storage capacity on ships. To maintain condition, average sized cattle require at least forty litres of water per head - per day. Sheep require at least four litres per head - per day. Developments in water production technology (salt water evaporators or reverse-osmosis systems) eventually led to livestock carriers with equipment capable of producing up to 600 tonnes of fresh water per day. Sheep and cattle also require fodder amounting to at least 2% of their body weight per day. Livestock carriers are required to carry sufficient feedstuffs for the maximum length of the voyage plus adequate reserves for emergencies.

'Medium' sized vessels with capacity for about 30,000 to 40,000 sheep - (or 3000 to 4000 head of cattle) - are a common size for this type of ship. However, during the last two decades of the twentieth century there were a small number of sheep carriers which had capacity for 130,000 sheep. There were at least two other large livestock carriers which specialised in combined cargoes of cattle and sheep. One had capacity for about 7,000 cattle plus 70,000 sheep and the other could carry 14,000 cattle plus 20,000 sheep. In 2007 the livestock carrier "Deneb Prima" was loading cargoes amounting to 20,000 cattle plus 2000 sheep.

The numbers detailed above are only general indications. The space allocated to animals on livestock carriers is officially regulated according to their size and weight ranges. Larger and heavier animals are allocated proportionately more space per head.

CONTROVERSY

There are varying cultural attitudes throughout the world with regard to the broad subject of animal husbandry. The philosophical and ethical arguments involved are beyond the scope of this article but it is nevertheless a fact that the transportation of large numbers of animals on livestock carriers has been a matter of public and political controversy at times.

In general, farming interests favour the export of live animals because it increases their marketing options. Businesses which have vested interests in exporting processed and refrigerated meats are against the export of live animals, for obvious reasons. The various issues are vigorously contended and facts are occasionally misrepresented to promote particular viewpoints.

Allegations that the sea transport of live animals must be inherently cruel is not evident from trade data or official statistics. It is an unavoidable fact that mistreated animals deteriorate rapidly. That natural characteristic of all domesticated animals compels the crews on livestock carrier to ensure that good conditions are maintained during the voyages for it is also a fact that the importers of livestock are notably uncompromising individuals. They will only accept animals which are delivered in good condition.

Animal activists challenge these assertions by making the valid point that no system can ever be perfect. They argue that there have been at least five major incidents (ship fires, sinkings or machinery failures) which have resulted in the deaths of many thousands of animals on livestock carriers. There have also been a number of occasions when political or commercial disagreements have created delays in livestock carrier operations which have resulted in needless suffering to animals on board.

REEFER SHIP

A reefer ship is a refrigerated cargo ship; a type of ship typically used to transport perishable commodities which require temperature-controlled transportation, such as fruit, meat, fish, vegetables, dairy products and other foods.

HISTORY OF REEFERS

In the 1700s, only the rich elites had ice for their guests or to cool their drinks or preserve other perishables. It was harvested locally in winter and stored through summers in covered ice houses to minimize melting. Ice production was initially very labor intensive as it was performed entirely with hand axes and saws, and may cost hundreds of dollars a ton to have ice available all summer.

In the early 1800s they developed techniques and specialized tools to harvest ice cheaply and one of the major exports from Massachusetts, New York and other settled northern states was ice — the "Frozen Water Trade". This trade eventually averaged several million short tons of ice per year that sold for millions of dollars in the U.S.. This ice was harvested by scoring the ice with horse drawn gouges or ice plows that allowed the ice to be separated into square or rectangular blocks.

This ice was cut out of frozen lakes, rivers and ponds, floated in a cleared channel to a loading dock before being transferred to an insulated ice house. There it was kept till it could be sold or transferred.

Ice harvesting developed into a profitable business with 1 acre (0.4 ha) of clean water in a cold climate yielding up to 3,000 to 150,000 short tons (2,700 to 130,000 {{{u}}}; 2,700 to 140,000 t) of ice per year which could be harvested for about $1.5 per ton and sold for up to $4 per ton. Before railroads existed the ice was transported by wagon or sleigh to Boston or other northern ports where it was stored in ice houses until it could either be loaded aboard ships for shipment elsewhere or sold for local consumption. The number of ice loaded ships in some harbors exceeded nearly all other trade in Boston, etc. in winter months.

The ice when it was delivered was put in specially designed ice houses in each port to minimize melting before it was sold. After 1840 when railroads were developed ice was often shipped by rail in insulated rail cars and the railroads started using ice to help keep perishables cold. The refrigeration industry developed for use by the railroads closely parallels the refrigerated ship business — they both used nearly the same equipment. In warmer than average winters when less ice could be harvested the cities suffered a shortage of ice in what were called then "Ice Famines". One of the many shortages the south suffered in the U.S. Civil War was ice — they could no longer import it from the northern states.

One of the more unusual applications of the frozen ice trade was the miners in Comstock Lode in Virginia City, Nevada. As they mined ever deeper for the silver and gold there the temperatures in the mines continued to rise. Soon the temperatures were well over 110 °F (43.3 °C) and they started having to give the miners ice to help them survive. A miner could use over 75 pounds (34 kg) of ice per shift. The ice was harvested in winter from frozen lakes in the Sierra Nevada (U.S.) with some like the Central Pacific Railroad building, after 1869, special ponds to help them harvest and ship ice to Virginia City, San Francisco, California and other Nevada and California cities.

By 1830, ice became a commodity available in most cities in the United States. The ice trade developed more slowly in Europe and even today many Europeans prefer room temperature drinks versus the iced drinks preferred by most in the US. Ice supplied year round at a reasonably low cost (usually less than $10/month) made it available for most middle-class people for cooling drinks, keeping ice boxes cold for storing perishables, etc.--previously a luxury affordable only by the upper classes.

Most of the ice was shipped to cities in the United States; but significant amounts were shipped to warmer foreign cities and countries by first sailing ships and later paddle steamers. The ice loaded on board ships was put into near air tight insulated compartments and further insulated with sawdust around the outside of ice blocks to slow down its melting rate as it was being shipped. A typical shipment would lose about 20% of its original weight before it could be sold — a 24,000 miles (39,000 km), about 200 day, ice shipment to Calcutta, India usually arrived with more than half of its ice. At the ports the ice was stored in special built ice houses till it could be sold. The first ice shipments to the tropics were made by Frederic Tudor in 1805 from Charlestown, Massachusetts to Martinique.

By 1815 he had established a profitable trade to Havana Cuba, New Orleans, Louisiana and other southern cities. Soon he and others were taking advantage of the melting ice to preserve apples, butter etc. which could be sold at a profit in a warm climate-the first "reefers". One of the most popular products was ice mixed with salt used to make ice cream. By 1836 they were even shipping ice to Calcutta India.

By 1869, they were shipping beef carcasses frozen in a salt-ice mixture from Indianola, Texas, to New Orleans, Louisiana and served it in hospitals, hotels and restaurants. By 1873 they were shipping frozen beef from America to London which developed into an annual tonnage of around 10,000 short tons (8,900 long tons; 9,100 t). The insulated cargo space was cooled by ice, which was loaded on departure. The success of this method was limited by insulation, loading techniques, ice block size, distance and climate.

SHIP REFRIGERATION TIMELINE

The first attempt to ship refrigerated meat was made when the Northam sailed from Australia to the UK in 1876; however, the refrigeration machinery broke down en route and so the cargo was lost. In 1877, the Steamers Le Frigorifique and Paraguay carried frozen mutton from Argentina to France, proving the concept of refrigerated ships, if not the economics. In 1879 the Strathleven, equipped with compression refrigeration, sailed successfully from Sydney to the UK with 40 tons of frozen beef and mutton as a small part of her cargo.

The clipper sailing ship Dunedin, owned by the New Zealand and Australian Land Company (NZALC), was refitted in 1881 with a Bell-Coleman compression refrigeration machine — this steam powered freezer unit worked by, compressing air, then releasing it into the hold of the ship. The expanding air got cooler as it expanded cooling the cargo in the hold. Using 3 tons of coal a day, this steam powered machine could chill the hold to 40 °F (22.2 °C) below surrounding air temperature, freezing the cargo in the temperate climate of southern New Zealand, and then maintaining it below freezing (32 °F (0 °C)) through the tropics.

The Dunedin's most visible sign of being an unusual ship was the funnel for the refrigeration plant placed between her fore and main masts, (sometimes leading her to be mistaken for a steamship which had been common since the 1840s). In February 1882, the sailing ship Dunedin sailed from Port ChalmersNew Zealand with 4331 mutton, 598 lamb and 22 pig carcasses, 246 kegs of butter, as well as hare, pheasant, turkey, chicken and 2226 sheep tongues and arrived in London UK after 98 days sailing with its cargo still frozen. After meeting all costs, The NZALC company made a £4700 profit from the voyage.

Soon after the Dunedin's successful voyage, an extensive frozen meat trade from New Zealand and Australia to the UK was developed with over 16 different refrigerated and passenger refrigerated ships built or refitted by 1900 in Scotland and Northern England shipyards for this trade. Within 5 years, 172 shipments of frozen meat were sent from New Zealand to the United Kingdom. Refrigerated shipping also led to a broader meat and dairy boom in AustraliaNew Zealand and Argentina. Frozen meat and Dairy exports continued to form the backbone of New Zealand's economy until the UK's entry into the European Economic Community in 1974 led to New Zealand produce being excluded by the EEC's trade bans. Today (2012) New Zealand has no refrigerated cargo ships.

The Nelson brothers, butchers in County Meath, Ireland, started shipping extensive live beef shipments to Liverpool, England. They successfully expanded their beef business until their imports from Ireland were insufficient to supply their rapidly growing business and Nelson decided to investigate the possibility of importing meat from Argentina. The first refrigerated ship they bought was the Spindrift which they renamed in 1890 the SS Highland Scot. A vessel of 3,060 gross tons bought by James Nelson and Sons in 1889 and fitted with somewhat primitive refrigerating plant operating on the cold air system, became one of the pioneer vessels in the refrigerated meat and other perishable commodities trade.

They hauled beef carcasses from Argentina to Britain their regularly scheduled shipments and ships developed into the Nelson Line that was formed in 1880 for the meat trade from Argentina to UK. All of their ships had a Highland first name. Refrigeration made it possible to import meat from the United States, New Zealand, Argentina and Australia, etc.. The Nelson Line began passenger service in 1910 between London, England and Buenos Aires and in 1913 came under control of the Royal Mail Steam Packet Company. In 1932 Royal Mail Group collapsed, Royal Mail Lines Ltd was founded and Nelson Line merged into the new company and disappeared as a separate company

- In 1879, Henry Bell (1848–1931) and John Bell (1850–1929) of Scotland and Joseph James Coleman (1838–1888) of England completed the Bell-Coleman dense-air machine on the Anchor liner Circassia, which successfully brought a cargo of chilled beef from the USA to London.
- In 1880, Strathleven, equipped with a Bell-Coleman air machine and loaded with successfully shipped beef, mutton, butter and kegs, sailed from MelbourneAustralia to London — a 9-week voyage of about 15,000 miles (24,000 km).
- In 1881, Alfred Seale Haslam (1844–1927) of England equipped the liner Orient with Haslam refrigeration compressors. He bought the Bell-Coleman dense-air patents in 1878 and eventually equipped four hundred plants and ships with Bell-Coleman machines.
- By 1899, refrigerated fruit ship traffic to the USA reached 90,000 tons/ year.
- By 1890, after acquiring the patent rights of Franz Windhausen's CO2-compression refrigeration system, the J&E Hall company installed the first marine CO2 refrigerator system on the Nelson Line ship Highland Chief.

- In 1900, a worldwide survey found 356 refrigerated ships, 37% of which had air machines, 37% ammonia compressors and 25% CO2 compressors.
- In 1900, Great Britain imported over 360,000 metric tons of refrigerated meat: 220,000 tons from Argentina, 95,000 tons from New Zealand and 45,000 tons from Australia. There were weekly sailings on refrigerated "banana boats" from the UK to Central America by Elders and Fyffes Ltd, which had been importing bananas since 1888 to the UK in their own ships. Round trips took 28 days.
- In 1901, the first refrigerated banana ship, the Port Morant, was equipped with a CO2 machine and carried 23,000 stems of bananas at controlled temperature from Jamaica to the UK.
- In 1902, Lloyd's Register recorded 460 ships with refrigerating plants.
- By 1902, the United Fruit Company started having refrigerated "banana" boats built in the UK to add to their fleet which hauled passengers and bananas between ports in the United States and Central America.
- By 1910, UK refrigerated meat imports rose to 760,000 tons/year.
- By 1910, the British company J&E Hall had installed 1800 CO2 refrigeration machines in ships.
- By 1913, UK fleet included 230 refrigerated ships with total cargo capacity of 440,000 ton.
- By 1935, refrigerated imports into Britain totaled 1,000,000 metric tons (980,000 long tons; 1,100,000 short tons) of meat, 500,000 tons of butter, 130,000 tons of cheese, 430,000 tons of apples and pears, and 20 million stems of bananas.

UNITED FRUIT COMPANY REEFER SHIPS

The United Fruit Company has used some type of reefers often combined with Cruise ship passenger accommodations, since about 1889. Because of their cargo was mostly bananas they have been nicknamed the "Banana Fleet". Since bananas are relatively light and the normal shipping route was to Central America and then back to various U.S. ports these ships were often built as combination cargo ships and what are now called Cruise ships to pay for more of their operating expenses. After about 1910, they called their combination cruise ships and refrigerated cargo ships the "Great White Fleet". To avoid US shipping regulations and taxes they are registered in about six other countries with very few now maintaining US registry.

European associates with their own ships were often employed to ship fruit to Europe. United Brands was taken over by Chiquita Brands

International, Cincinnati in the 1980s and owns the largest fleet of banana boats in the world, but none of them now sails under the US flag. SS Pastores and the SS Calamares were built in Ireland in 1912 and 1913 for the United Fruit Company as a combination Cruise ship and refrigerated cargo ship. The United Fruit Company's fleet of about 85 ships was one of the largest civilian fleets in the world.

These ships normally carried up to 95 cruise ship passengers and a crew to ports in Central America and then would return to the United States with passengers and a cargo of refrigerated bananas and miscellaneous cargo. They were part of United Fruit's "Great White Fleet" — to minimize heat build-up the ships were all painted white.

The renamed USS Pastores and USS Calamares were taken over by the United States Navy in World War I and used to take troops and refrigerated supplies to and from Europe. After hostilities ceased they were returned to United Fruit Company in 1919. They were requisitioned again on 2 June 1941 from United Fruit for use in World War II. After hostilities had ceased they were then returned again to United Fruit Company in 1946.

REEFERS IN U.S. NAVY SERVICE

World War I

In World War I, the US Navy contracted for 18 Refrigerated ships for hauling provisions to the troops in Europe. They were launched 1918 and 1919 as the war was ending and were nearly all scrapped by 1933 in the Great Depression as an economy move. Most were built in Baltimore Dry Dock in Baltimore, Maryland, Moore SB in Oakland, California and Standard SB Co. in Shooter's Island N.Y.

World War II

The Mizar-classstores ships were six United Fruit passenger and refrigerated cargo liners built in 1931–33 that the United States Maritime Commission requisitioned in 1941–42. They were USS Antigua, USS Ariel, USS Merak, USS Mizar, USS Talamanca and USS Tarazed. Antigua, although requisitioned, was never commissioned into the Navy.

Other "reefers" converted for US Navy use were the Danish ships USS Pontiac, USS Roamer and USS Uranus. In addition, the US Maritime Commisison ordered 41 new refrigerated ships for the Navy. Because of the difficulty of building refrigerated ships only two were delivered in 1944. 26 were delivered in 1945 and the remainder in 1946–48.

TYPES OF REEFERS

Reefer ships may be categorised into three types:

1. Side-door vessels have water tight ports on the ships hull, which

open into a cargo hold. Elevators or ramps leading from the quay serve as loading and discharging access for the forklifts or conveyors. Inside these access ports or side doors, pallet lifts or another series of conveyors bring the cargo to the respective decks. This special design makes the vessels particularly well suited for inclement weather operations as the tops of the cargo holds are always closed against rain and sun.

2. Conventional vessels have a traditional cargo operation with top opening hatches and cranes/derricks. On such ships, when facing wet weather, the hatches need to be closed to prevent heavy rain from flooding the holds. Both above ship types are well suited for the handling of palletized and loose cargo.
3. Refrigerated container ships are specifically designed to carry containerised unit loads where each container has its individual refrigerated unit. These containers are nearly always twenty-foot equivalent units (often called TEU) that are the "standard" container cargo size that are loaded and unloaded at container terminals and aboard container ships. These ships differ from conventional container ships in their design and power generation and electrical distribution equipment. They need provisions made for powering each container's cooling system. Because of their ease of loading and unloading cargo many container ships are now being built or redesigned to carry refrigerated containers.

A major use of refrigerated cargo hold type ships was for the transportation of bananas and frozen meat but most of these ships have been partly replaced by refrigerated containers that have a refrigeration systems attached to the rear end of the container. While on a ship these containers are plugged into an electrical outlet (typically 440 VAC) that ties into the ship's power generation.

Since many merchant vessels now have diesel-electric propulsion units installed providing power to individual units is mostly a wiring job. Refrigerated container ships are not limited by the number of refrigeration containers they can carry unlike other container ships which may be limited in their number of refrigeration outlets or have insufficient generator capacity. Each reefer container unit is typically designed with a stand-alone electrical circuit and has its own breaker switch that allows it to be connected and disconnected as required. In principle each individual unit could be repaired while the ship was still underway.

Refrigerated cargo is a key part of the income for some shipping companies. On multi-purpose ships, Refrigerated containers are mostly carried above deck, as they have to be checked for proper operation. Also, a major part of the refrigeration system (such as a compressor) may fail, which would have to be replaced or unplugged quickly in the event of a fire. Modern container vessels stow the reefer containers in cellguides with adjacent inspection walkways that enable reefer containers to be carried in the holds as well as on the deck.

Modern refrigerated container vessels are designed to incorporate a water-cooling system for containers stowed under deck. This does not replace the refrigeration system but facilitates cooling down of the external machinery. Containers stowed on the exposed upper deck are air-cooled, while those under deck are water-cooled systems. The water cooling design allows capacity loads of refrigerated containers under deck as it enables the dissipation of the high amount of heat they generate. This system draws fresh water from the ship's water supply, which in turn transfers the heat through heat exchangers to the abundantly available sea water.

There are also refrigeration systems that have two compressors for very precise and low-temperature operation, such as transporting a container full of blood to a war zone. Cargoes of shrimp, asparagus, caviar and blood are considered among the most expensive refrigerated items. Bananas, fruit and meat have historically been the main cargo of refrigerated ships.

WORLDWIDE SERVICE

According to the CIA's The World Factbook, there were about 38,000 registered merchant ships in the world in 2010, of which about 920 were designed as refrigerated cargo ships. Because of the proliferation of self-contained refrigerated container systems on container ships, there are many more ships than those designed for only refrigerated cargo that are also carrying some refrigerated cargo. The countries with the largest numbers of reefer ships in their registries are the world's two most prominent flags of convenience: Panama with 212 and Liberia with 109 (both as of 2010).

ROLL-ON/ROLL-OFF

Roll-on/roll-off (RORO or ro-ro) ships are vessels designed to carry wheeled cargo, such as automobiles, trucks, semi-trailer trucks, trailers, and railroad cars, that are driven on and off the ship on their own wheels. This is in contrast to lift-on/lift-off (LOLO) vessels, which use a crane to load and unload cargo.

RORO vessels have built-in ramps that allow the cargo to be efficiently rolled on and off the vessel when in port. While smaller ferries that operate across rivers and other short distances often have built-in ramps, the term RORO is generally reserved for larger oceangoing vessels. The ramps and doors may be stern-only, or bow and stern for quick loading.

TYPES

Types of RORO vessels include ferries, cruiseferries, cargo ships, and barges. New automobiles that are transported by ship are often moved on a large type of RORO called a pure car carrier (PCC) or pure car/truck carrier (PCTC).

Elsewhere in the shipping industry, cargo is normally measured by the metric tonne, but RORO cargo is typically measured in lanes in metres (LIMs). This is calculated by multiplying the cargo length in metres by the number of decks and by its width in lanes (lane width differs from vessel to vessel, and there are several industry standards). On PCCs, cargo capacity is often measured in RT or RT43 units (based on a 1966 Toyota) or in car-equivalent units (CEU).

The largest RORO passenger ferry is MS Color Magic, a 75,100 GTcruise ferry that entered service in September 2007 for Color Line. Built in Finland by Aker Finnyards, it is 223.70 m (733 ft 11 in) long and 35 m (114 ft 10 in) wide, and can carry 550 cars, or 1270 lane meters of cargo.

The RORO passenger ferry with the greatest car-carrying capacity is the Ulysses (named after a novel by James Joyce), owned by Irish Ferries. The Ulysses entered service on 25 March 2001 and operates between Dublin and Holyhead. The 50,938 GT ship is 209.02 m (685 ft 9 in) long and 31.84 m (104 ft 6 in) wide, and can carry 1342 cars/4101 lane meters of cargo.

HISTORY

At first, wheeled vehicles carried as cargo on oceangoing ships were treated like any other cargo. Automobiles had their fuel tanks emptied and their batteries disconnected before being hoisted into the ship's hold, where they were chocked and secured. This process was tedious and difficult, and vehicles were subject to damage and could not be used for routine travel.

The world's first roll-on/roll-off service was a train ferry, started in 1833 by the Monkland and Kirkintilloch Railway, which operated a wagon ferry on the Forth and Clyde Canal in Scotland.

During World War II, landing ships were among the first seagoing ships enabling road vehicles to roll directly on and off. Postwar, the idea was adopted for merchant ships and short ferry crossings. The first RORO service crossing the English Channel began from Dover in 1953.

The first roll-on/roll-off vessel that was purpose-built to transport loaded semi trucks was the Searoad of Hyannis, which began operation in 1956. While modest in capacity, it could transport three semi trailers between Hyannis in Massachusetts and Nantucket Island, even in ice conditions.

In 1957, the US military issued a contract to the Sun Shipbuilding and Dry Dock Company in Chester, Pennsylvania, for the construction of a new type of motorized vehicle carrier. The ship, the Comet, had a stern ramp as well as interior ramps, which allowed cars to drive directly from the dock, onto the ship, and into place. Loading and unloading was sped up dramatically. Comet also had an adjustable chocking system for locking cars onto the decks and a ventilation system to remove exhaust gases that accumulate during vehicle loading.

During the 1982 Falklands War, SS Atlantic Conveyor was requisitioned as an emergency aircraft and helicopter transport for British Hawker Siddeley HarrierSTOVL fighter planes; one Harrier was kept fueled, armed, and ready to VTOL launch for emergency air protection against long range Argentine aircraft.

The Atlantic Conveyor was sunk by Argentine Exocet missiles after offloading the Harriers to proper aircraft carriers, but the vehicles and helicopters still aboard were destroyed. After the war, a concept called the shipborne containerized air-defense system (SCADS) proposed a modular system to quickly convert a large RORO into an emergency aircraft carrier with ski jump, fueling systems, radar, defensive missiles, munitions, crew quarters, and work spaces.

The entire system could be installed in about 48 hours on a container ship or RORO, when needed for operations up to a month unsupplied. The system could quickly be removed and stored again when the conflict was over. The Soviets flying Yakovlev Yak-38 fighters also tested operations using the civilian RORO ships Agostinio Neto and Nikolai Cherkasov.

CAR CARRIERS

The first cargo ships that were specially fitted for the transport of large quantities of cars, came in the early sixties in the service. - These ships had still own loading gear and so-called hanging decks inside. They were, for example, chartered by the German Volkswagen AG to transport vehicles in the U.S. and Canada. - Since 1970 the market for exporting and importing cars has increased dramatically and the number and type of ROROs has increased also. In 1973, Japan's K Line built the European Highway, the first pure car carrier (PCC), which carried 4,200 automobiles.

Today's pure car carriers and their close cousins, the pure car/truck carrier (PCTC) are distinctive ships with a box-like superstructure running the entire length and breadth of the hull, fully enclosing the cargo. They typically have a stern ramp and a side ramp for dual loading of thousands of vehicles (such as cars, trucks, heavy machineries, tracked units, Mafi trailers, and loose statics), and extensive automatic fire control systems.

The PCTC has liftable decks to increase vertical clearance, as well as heavier decks for "high-and-heavy" cargo. A 6,500-unit car ship with 12 decks can have three decks, which can take cargo up to 150 short tons (136 t; 134 long tons) with liftable panels to increase clearance from 1.7 to 6.7 m (5 ft 7 in to 21 ft 10 in) on some decks. Lifting decks to accommodate higher cargo reduces the total capacity.

These kind of vessels perform a usual speed of 16 knots at eco-speed, while at full speed more than 19 knots can be achieved.

With the building of Wallenius Wilhelmsen Logistics's 8,000-CEU car carrier Faust out of Stockholm in June 2007 car carriers entered a new era of the large car and truck carrier (LCTC). Currently, the largest are Wilh. Wilhelmsen's "Mark V" ships, led by MV Tønsberg.

The car carrier Auriga Leader, built in 2008 with a capacity of 6,200 cars, is the world's first partially solar powered ship.

SEAWORTHINESS

The seagoing RORO car ferry, with large external doors close to the waterline and open vehicle decks with few internal bulkheads, has a reputation for being a high-risk design, to the point where the acronym is sometimes derisively expanded to "roll on/roll over"). An improperly secured loading door can cause a ship to take on water and sink, as happened in 1987 with MS Herald of Free Enterprise.

Water sloshing on the vehicle deck can set up a free surface effect, making the ship unstable and causing it to capsize. Free surface water on the vehicle deck was determined by the Court of Inquiry to be the immediate cause of the 1968 capsize of the TEV Wahine in New Zealand.

Despite these inherent risks, the very high freeboard raises the seaworthiness of these vessels. For example, the car carrier MV Cougar Ace listed 80 degrees to its port side in 2006, but did not sink, since its high enclosed sides prevented water from entering.

VARIATIONS

ROPAX

The acronym ROPAX (roll-on/roll-off passenger) describes a RORO vessel built for freight vehicle transport along with passenger accommodation. Technically this encompasses all ferries with both a roll-on/roll-off car deck and passenger-carrying capacities, but in practice, ships with facilities for more than 500 passengers are often referred to as cruiseferries.

ConRO

The ConRo vessel is a hybrid of a RORO and a container ship. This type of vessel has a below-deck area used for vehicle storage while stacking containerized freight on the top decks.

ConRo ships, such as those in the fleet of Atlantic Container Line, can carry a combination of 1,900 twenty-foot equivalent units (TEU) of containers, up to 1,000 TEU of heavy equipment, project and oversized cargo on three decks, and up to 2,000 automobiles on five decks. Separate internal ramp systems within the vessel segregate automobiles from other vehicles, Mafi trailers, and break-bulk cargo.

RoLo

A RoLo (roll-on/lift-off) vessel is another hybrid vessel type, with ramps serving vehicle decks but with other cargo decks only accessible when the tides change or by the use of a crane.

LMSR

Large, Medium-Speed Roll-on/Roll-off (LMSR) refers to several classes of Military Sealift Command (MSC) roll-on/roll-off type cargo ships. Some are purpose-built to carry military cargo, while others are converted.

SUBMARINE CARGO VESSEL

The Submarine Cargo Vessel is a proposed idea from the RussianRubin Design Bureau. The idea is to utilise decommissioned SSBNs (nuclear-powered ballistic missile submarine) from the Russian Navy to carry cargo under the Arctic Ocean. The reason for this solution is that it would be considerably cheaper than designing and producing an entirely new type of submarine.

The basis for the project is a Project 941 Typhoon class submarine, which was designed by Rubin in 1976. It would have its ballistic missile launchers removed and replaced with cargo holds, as well as receive extra reinforcement for surface icebreaking.

The concept of Submarine Freight Transportation System (SFTS) was suggested in 1997 by Vladimir Postnikov. Present time this system is considered as a sea subsystem of Global Intelligent Transportation System.

TRAIN FERRY

A train ferry is a ship designed to carry railway vehicles. Typically, one level of the ship is fitted with railway tracks, and the vessel has a door at the front and/or rear to give access to the wharves. In the United States, train ferries are sometimes referred to as "car ferries", as distinguished from "auto ferries" used to transport automobiles. The wharf (sometimes called a "slip") has a ramp, and a linkspan or "apron", balanced by weights, that connects the railway proper to the ship, allowing for the water level to rise and fall with the tides.

While railway vehicles can be and are shipped on the decks or in the holds of ordinary ships, purpose-built train ferries can be quickly loaded and unloaded by roll-on/roll-off, especially as several vehicles can be loaded or unloaded at once. A train ferry that is a barge is called a car float or rail barge.

HISTORY

In 1833, the Monkland and Kirkintilloch Railway operated a wagon ferry on the Forth and Clyde Canal in Scotland. In April 1836, the first railroad car ferry in the U.S., the Susquehanna entered service on the Susquehanna River between Havre de Grace and Perryville, Maryland. The first 'modern' design of ferry, the Leviathan, was designed in 1849 by Thomas Grainger for the Edinburgh, Perth and Dundee Railway to cross the Firth of Forth between Granton and Burntisland. The service commenced on 3 February 1850. It was intended as a temporary measure until the railway could build a bridge, but this was not opened until 1890, its construction delayed in part by repercussions from the catastrophic failure of Thomas Bouch's Tay Rail Bridge; Bouch designed the ferry loading mechanism.

The largest train ferry ever built was the Contra Costa, serving the mainline of the Central Pacific (later assumed by its affiliate, the Southern Pacific) at the Carquinez Strait in the San Francisco Bay Area in California. Its sister ship, the Solano (built before the Contra Costa) was the second largest train ferry ever built.

NOMENCLATURE

The Dundee ferry was also called the "Floating Railway".

HAZARDS

The Japanese train ferry, Toya Maru, sank during typhoonMarie on 26 September 1954, killing more than a thousand. Four other train ferries, Seikan maru No.11, Kitami maru, Tokachi maru and Hidaka maru also sank on that day; the loss appeared to be of about 1,430 people.

In those days, Japanese train ferries did not have a rear sea-gate, because engineers believed that inrushing water would simply flow out again quickly and would not pose a danger. However, when the frequency of waves bears the wrong relationship to the length of a ship, each wave arrives as the water from the previous wave is trying to leave, causing water to accumulate on the ship. After the accidents, all Japanese train ferries were retrofitted with rear sea-gates and weather forecast technology was greatly promoted.

The Norwegian train ferry, Skagerrak, built in 1965, sank in gale force winds on 7 September 1966, on a journey between Kristiansand, Norway and Hirtshals, Denmark, when the rear sea-gate was destroyed by heavy seas. One person subsequently died of injuries, and six freight cars and a number of automobiles sank to the bottom with the ship.

The Canadian train ferry MV Patrick Morris sank on 20 April 1970, while assisting in a search and rescue operation for a sinking fishing trawler (M.F.V. "Enterprise") off the northeast coast of Cape Breton Island. The ferry was trying to maintain position to retrieve a body when its stern gates were overpowered by 30-foot (9 m) waves. It sank within 30 minutes taking several rail cars and 4 crew members, including the Captain, to the bottom of the Cabot Strait. There were 47 survivors.

Train ferries rarely sank because of sea-hazards, although they have some weaknesses linked to the very nature of transporting trains "on rail" on a ship.

These weaknesses include:

- Trains are loaded at a rather high level, making the ship top-heavy.
- The train deck is difficult to compartmentalise, so that sloshing flood water can destabilise the ship.
- The sea doors where the trains go in and out are a weakness, even if placed at the rear of the ship.
- The train carriages need to be strongly secured lest they break away and roll around, particularly on long, open-water routes.

The Ann Arbor Railroad of Michigan developed a system of making cars fast that was adopted by many other lines. Screw jacks were placed on the corners of the railcar and the car was raised slightly to take its weight off of its wheels. Chains and turnbuckles were placed around the car frame and hooked onto the rails and tightened. Clamps were placed behind the wheels on the rails. Deckhands engaged in continual inspection and tightening of the gear during the crossing. This system effectively held the cars in place when the ship encountered rough weather.

Several train ferries—the SS Milwaukee, SS Pere Marquette 18, and SS Marquette & Bessemer No. 2—were lost on the Great Lakes. These losses, though causes remain unconfirmed, were attributed to seas boarding the unprotected stern of the ship and swamping it in a severe storm. As a result, seagates were required on all new ships and required to be retrofitted on older vessels. In addition, two wooden crosslake railroad ferries were burned.

Some accidents occurred at the slip during loading, when stability was a major problem. Train ferries often list when heavy cars are loaded onto a track on one side while the other side is empty. Normal procedure was to load half of a track on one side, all of the track on the other side, and then the rest of the original track. If this procedure was not followed, results could be disastrous. In 1909, the SS Ann Arbor No. 4 capsized in its slip in Manistique, Michigan when a switching crew put eight cars of iron ore on its portside tracks. The crew got off without loss of life, but salvage operations were costly and time-consuming.

EXAMPLES

Argentina

Nine train ferries were used between 1907 and 1990 to cross the Paraná river and join the Buenos Aires province (the main state in Argentina) and the Entre Rios province (the entrance to the Mesopotamian region), until new bridges were built over the rivers they crossed. They were the Lucía Carbó (1907), the María Parera (1908), the Mercedes Lacroze (1909) (three ferries that operated between the ports of Zárate and Ibicuy (Entre Rios), crossing the Paraná at the northwest of the Buenos Aires province). Then were added the

Roque Saenz Peña (1911) and Ezequiel Ramos Mejía (1913) paddled train ferries at Posadas (crossing the Paraná river in the southwest of the Misiones province, at the north of the country, in the frontier with Paraguay).

Three other train ferries were added later: the Dolores de Urquiza (1926), the Delfina Mitre (1928) and the Carmen Avellaneda (1929) to cover the service in the Zárate-Ibicuy crossing. The María Parera had a collision with the Lucía Carbó at km. 145 of the Paraná river, and it sank in less than 15 minutes on June 30, 1926. Two of the most modern still serve as floating piers in the Zárate region, and one of the first group was sunk during a storm at the Buenos Aires port in the eighties.

The two northern paddled ferries still remain at Posadas, and one of them holds a model railway museum inside. All the eight old ferries were built by the A & J Inglis Co. Ltd., in Pointhouse, Glasgow, Scotland for the Entre Rios Railways Co. in Argentina. The ninth ferry, the Tabare, was built in Argentina by Astarsa (ASTilleros ARgentinos S.A.) in 1966 at Astillero Río Santiago Río Santiago Shipyard near to La Plata city. It was the largest train ferry that operated in Argentina, with a deck more than 100 meters long. The Tabaré is still floating, but not operating, at the old south docks of Buenos Aires port, near the Puerto Madero zone.

Australia

- Grafton, New South Wales over Clarence River pending construction of bridge, 1920s to 1930s.
- The Port Lincoln division is isolated from the main system by desert and is very roundabout, and rolling stock is transferred as required by ship or by road low loaders.

Azerbaijan

- Baku - Türkmenbasy (Russian: Krasnovodsk), connecting Azerbaijan with Turkmenistan across the Caspian Sea since 1963. In May 2008 they decided to buy a new longer ferry.

Bangladesh

- from Balashi Ghat to Bahadurabad Ghat - 1,000 mm (3 ft 3 3/8 in) gauge.
- across the Brahmaputra River in Bangladesh - superseded by Jamuna Bridge, 2003; dual gauge

Bolivia

- Train ferry from Peru - 1,435 mm (4 ft 8 1/2 in) and 1,000 mm (3 ft 3 3/8 in) gauges at each end.

Bulgaria

- The Varna-Odessa (Ukraine) train ferry line served by 4 boats (13,000 metric tons deadweight (DWT) each, carrying 108 loaded railroad cars) opened in 1978, bypasses a break of gauge. Later, the service was extended to include lines to Poti and Batumi, Georgia. Boats can carry trucks and passengers as well.

Canada

A railbarge is a variation of a train ferry that consists of barges pushed by a tug.

In use

- Prince Rupert, British Columbia - Whittier, Alaska (AquaTrain)
- Delta, British Columbia - Nanaimo, British Columbia (E and N Railway)
- Matane, Quebec - Baie-Comeau, Quebec (COGEMA)

Former car floats

- lakes of British Columbia Okanagan, Arrow, KootenayLakes (CN and CPR)
- Port Maitland, Ontario - Erie, Pennsylvania (TH&B Railway)
- Port Burwell, Ontario - Ashtabula, Ohio (CN)
- Cobourg, Ontario - Rochester, New York (Ontario Car Company) ran from 1905 to 1950
- Sarnia, Ontario - Port Huron, Michigan - rail-barge - (CN, until the opening of the Paul Tellier Tunnel)
- Windsor, Ontario - Detroit, Michigan (Grand Trunk, CN, CPR, Michigan Central, Wabash, until 1980s)
- BC Rail. until 1952 railcars were barged from North Vancouver to Squamish.
- A large number of isolated BC pulp mills had chemicals and freight moved by railbarge.

Former train ferries

- Cape Tormentine, New Brunswick - Borden Carleton, Prince Edward Island (Canadian Government Railways, CN, CN Marine, Marine Atlantic), using the MV Abegweit and MV John Hamilton Gray. Service ended when rail service on Prince Edward Island was discontinued in 1989.

- Mulgrave, Nova Scotia - Point Tupper, Nova Scotia (Intercolonial, CN, until the opening of the Canso Causeway in 1955)
- North Sydney, Nova Scotia - Port aux Basques, Newfoundland (CN, CN Marine). Service commenced in 1965 carrying standard-gauge rolling stock. A dual-gaugeyard in Port aux Basques was used for classification and rolling stock had trucksexchanged with narrow gauge trucks. Service ended when the Newfoundland section of Canadian National Railway was closed in 1988.
- Lake Superior, Thunder Bay - Superior, Wisconsin.
- Sarnia, Canada - Port Huron, United States - replaced by tunnel under St. Clair River c1891.

China

In use

- Guangdong–Hainan Ferry: The Yuehai (??, i.e. Guangdong-Hainan) Ferry across Qiongzhou Strait, between Zhanjiang, Guangdong and Haikou, Hainan. The line has operated since January 2003, carrying both freight and passenger trains, enabling direct train service between the mainland and the cities of Haikou and Sanya on Hainan Island. As of the late 2010, two ferry boats were in operation; the third boat, Yuehai No. 3, was launched in Tianjin in September 2010, and was going to be delivered to the ferry company in December 2010.
- Bohai Train Ferry: Yantai in Shandong Province to Dalian in Liaoning Province. This short-cut line, operated by Sinorail, has been running since November 2006. As of 2011, it is freight-only service.
- Jiangyin Train Ferry on the Xinyi–Changxing Railway (freight only). Trains are carried from Jingjiang on the northern side of the Yangtze River to Jiangyin on the southern side. A pair of ferries make 48 trips per day across the river.

Former

- Yangtze River in Wuhan before construction of the Wuhan Yangtze River Bridge. Hunslet Engine Company built two extra heavy 0-8-0 locomotives for loading the train ferries.
- Yangtze River in Nanjing on Jinghu railway, 1933–1968.

Cuba

Note: all auto and rail ferry services have been suspended between the

United States and Cuba due to the ongoing United States embargo against Cuba.

- Palm Beach - Havana, Cuba.
- Miami - Havana, Cuba
- New Orleans - Havana, Cuba
- New York - Havana - Seatrain Lines

Denmark

In use

- Frederikshavn - Göteborg, Sweden, 1987 -, freight only
- Rødby - Puttgarden, Germany across Fehmarn Belt. 1963 -, serves 6 passenger trains/day, Vogelfluglinie. To be replaced by Fehmarn Belt Fixed Link in 2021. Not used by night and freight trains since 1997; they go over the Great Belt Bridge instead.

Former

- Strib - Fredericia, 1872–1935, replaced by Little Belt Bridge
- Korsør - Nyborg, 1883–1997, replaced by Great Belt fixed link
- Oddesund Syd - Oddesund Nord, 1883–1938, replaced by Oddesund Bridge
- Masnedø - Orehoved, 1884–1937, replaced by Storstrøm Bridge
- Glyngøre - Nykøbing Mors, 1889–1977
- Helsingør - Helsingborg, Sweden, 1892–2000, since then car ferry only
- Copenhagen Frihavn - Malmö, Sweden, 1895–1986
- Gedser - Warnemünde, Germany, 1903–1995, replaced by car ferry Gedser - Rostock, Germany
- Faaborg - Mommark, 1922–1962, freight only
- Assens - Aarøsund, 1923–1950, freight only, narrow gauge (1,000 mm (3 ft 3/8 in))
- Svendborg - Rudkøbing, 1926–1962, freight only
- Hvalpsund - Sundsøre, 1927–1969, since then car ferry only
- Svendborg - Ærøskøbing, 1931–1994, freight only
- Gedser - Großenbrode Kai, Germany, 1951–1963, replaced by Rødby — Puttgarden Ferry
- Hirtshals - Kristiansand, Norway, 1958–1996, freight only
- Copenhagen Frihavn - Helsingborg, Sweden (Danlink) 1986–2000, freight only

Finland

Former

- Travemuende - Turku (1975–2007), freight only
- Turku - Stockholm (-2012)

Germany

In use

- Mukran - Klaipeda, Lithuania, break-of-gauge, broad gauge on board, freight only (1986-)
- Mukran - Ventspils, Latvia - Saint Petersburg, Russia, break-of-gauge, broad gauge on board, freight only (2007-)
- Mukran - Ust-Luga, Russia, break-of-gauge, broad gauge on board, freight only (2012-)
- Puttgarden - Rødby, Denmark, passenger trains only (1963-) Not used by night and freight trains since 1997 (they go over the Great Belt Bridge instead). To be replaced by Fehmarn Belt Fixed Link in 2021.
- Rostock - Trelleborg, Sweden, freight only (1994-)
- Mukran (changed in 1998 from the old Sassnitz port to the new port nearby at Mukran) - Trelleborg, Sweden, freight plus one daily passenger night-train. (1909-)

Former

- Bodensee (1869–1976)
- Elbe: Lauenburg–Hohnstorf (1864–1878)
- Elbe: Köhlbrand, Hamburg (???–1974)
- Rhine: Worms – Rosengarten (1870–1900)
- Rhine: Bingerbrück–Rüdesheim (1861–1900)
- Rhine: Bonn–Oberkassel (1870–1914)
- Rhine: Rheinhausen–Hochfeld (1866–1874)
- Rhine: Ruhrort–Homberg (1852–1912)
- Rhine: Spyck–Welle (1865–1912)
- Stralsund - Altefähr/Rügen replaced 1936 by the Rügendamm.
- Wittow Fähre - Fährhof 1896–1968, operated by the Rügen Light Railway (750 mm).
- Wolgast - Wolgaster Fähre (Usedom), 1945-1990 (only freight)

- Grossenbrode - Fehmarnsund (1903–1963)
- Grossenbrode - Gedser (1951–1963)
- Travemünde - Turku (1975–2007), normal gauge on board, break-of-gauge in Turku, freight only
- Travemünde - Malmö
- Warnemünde - Gedser (1903–1995), replaced by car ferry Rostock - Gedser
- Mukran - Baltijsk, Russia, break-of-gauge, broad gauge on board, freight only (2007-2012)

3

Tanker Types

TANKER SHIP

A tanker (or tank ship or tankship) is a merchant vessel designed to transport liquids or gases in bulk. Major types of tankship include the oil tanker, the chemical tanker, and gas carrier.

BACKGROUND

Tankers can range in size of capacity from several hundred tons, which includes vessels for servicing small harbours and coastal settlements, to several hundred thousand tons, for long-range haulage. Besides ocean- or seagoing tankers there are also specialized inland-waterway tankers which operate on rivers and canals with an average cargo capacity up to some thousand tons. A wide range of products are carried by tankers, including:

- hydrocarbon products such as oil, liquefied petroleum gas (LPG), and liquefied natural gas (LNG)
- chemicals, such as ammonia, chlorine, and styrene monomer
- fresh water
- wine
- molasses

Tankers are a relatively new concept, dating from the later years of the 19th century. Before this, technology had simply not supported the idea of carrying bulk liquids. The market was also not geared towards transporting or selling cargo in bulk, therefore most ships carried a wide range of different products in different holds and traded outside fixed routes.

Liquids were usually loaded in casks—hence the term "tonnage", which refers to the volume of the holds in terms of how many tuns or casks of wine could be carried. Even potable water, vital for the survival of the crew, was stowed in casks. Carrying bulk liquids in earlier ships posed several problems:

- The holds: on timber ships the holds were not sufficiently water, oil or air-tight to prevent a liquid cargo from spoiling or leaking. The development of iron and steel hulls solved this problem.

- Loading and discharging: Bulk liquids must be pumped - the development of efficient pumps and piping systems was vital to the development of the tanker. Steam engines were developed as prime-movers for early pumping systems. Dedicated cargo handling facilities were now required ashore too - as was a market for receiving a product in that quantity. Casks could be unloaded using ordinary cranes, and the awkward nature of the casks meant that the volume of liquid was always relatively small - therefore keeping the market more stable.
- Free Surface Effect: a large body of liquid carried aboard a ship will impact on the ship's stability, particularly when the liquid is flowing around the hold or tank in response to the ship's movements. The effect was negligible in casks, but could cause capsizing if the tank extended the width of the ship; a problem solved by extensive subdivision of the tanks.

Tankers were first used by the oil industry to transfer refined fuel in bulk from refineries to customers. This would then be stored in large tanks ashore, and subdivided for delivery to individual locations. The use of tankers caught on because other liquids were also cheaper to transport in bulk, store in dedicated terminals, then subdivide. Even the Guinness brewery used tankers to transport the stout across the Irish Sea.

Different products require different handling and transport, with specialised variants such as "chemical tankers", "oil tankers", and "LNG carriers" developed to handle dangerous chemicals, oil and oil-derived products, and liquefied natural gas respectively. Among oil tankers, supertankers are designed for transporting oil around the Horn of Africa from the Middle East. The supertanker Seawise Giant, scrapped in 2010, was 458 meters (1,503 ft) in length and 69 meters (226 ft) wide. Supertankers are one of the three preferred methods for transporting large quantities of oil, along with pipeline transport and rail.

Despite being highly regulated, tankers have been involved in environmental disasters resulting from oil spills.

FLEETS OF THE WORLD

Flag states

As of 2005, the United States Maritime Administration's statistics count 4,024 tankers of 10,000 LT DWT or greater worldwide. 2,582 of these are double-hulled. Panama is the leading flag state of tankers with 592 registered ships. Five other flag states have more than two hundred registered tankers:

Liberia (520), The Marshall Islands (323), Greece (233), Singapore (274) and The Bahamas (215). These flag states are also the top six in terms of fleet size in terms of deadweight tonnage.

Largest fleets

Greece, Japan, and the United States are the top three owners of tankers (including those owned but registered to other nations), with 733, 394, and 311 vessels respectively. These three nations account for 1,438 vessels or over 36% of the world's fleet.

Builders

Asian companies dominate the construction of tankers. Of the world's 4,024 tankers, 2,822 or over 70% were built in South Korea, Japan or China.

CHEMICAL TANKER

A chemical tanker is a type of tanker designed to transport chemicals in bulk. As defined in MARPOL Annex II chemical tanker means a ship constructed or adapted for the carriage in bulk of any liquid product listed in chapter 17 of the International Bulk Chemical Code.

Ocean-going chemical tankers generally range from 5,000 metric tons deadweight (DWT) to 75,000 DWT in size, which is considerably smaller than the average size of other tanker types due to the specialised nature of their cargoes and the size restrictions of the port terminals where they call to load and discharge.

Chemical tankers normally have a series of separate cargo tanks which are either coated with specialised coatings such as phenolic epoxy or zinc paint, or made from stainless steel. The coating or cargo tank material determines what types of cargo a particular tank can carry: stainless steel tanks are required for aggressive acid cargoes such as sulfuric and phosphoric acid, while 'easier' cargoes — such as vegetable oil — can be carried in epoxy coated tanks.

CLASSIFICATION

In general ships, carrying chemicals in bulk are classed into three types:

1. A 'Type 1' ship is a chemical tanker intended to transport Chapter 17 of the IBC Code products with very severe environmental and safety hazards which require maximum preventive measures to preclude an escape of such cargo.
2. A'Type 2' ship is a chemical tanker intended to transport Chapter 17 of the IBC Code products with appreciably severe environmental and safety hazards which require significant preventive measures to preclude an escape of such cargo.

3. A 'Type 3' ship is a chemical tanker intended to transport Chapter 17 of the IBC Code products with sufficiently severe environmental and safety hazards which require a moderate degree of containment to increase survival capability in a damaged condition.

MAIN CHARACTERISTICS OF CHEMICAL TANKERS

Chemical tankers often have a system for tank heating in order to maintain the viscosity of certain cargoes, typically by passing pressurized steam through stainless steel 'heating coils' in the cargo tanks, transferring heat into the cargo which circulates in the tank by convection. Many modern chemical tankers feature double hull construction and have one tank for each pump with separate piping, which means that each tank can load a separate cargo without any mixing.

Tank cleaning after discharging cargo is a very important aspect of chemical tanker operations, because tanks which are not properly cleaned of all cargo residue can adversely affect the purity of the next cargo loaded. Before tanks are cleaned, they must be properly ventilated and checked to be free of potentially explosive gases. Chemical tankers usually have transverse stiffeners on deck rather than inside the cargo tanks, in order to make the tank walls smooth and easier to clean by fitted tank cleaning machines.

Cargo tanks, either empty or filled, are normally protected against explosion by inert gas blankets. Often nitrogen is the inert gas used, supplied either from portable gas bottles or an inert gas generator (IGS) system.

Most new chemical tankers are built by shipbuilders in Japan, Korea or China, with other builders in Turkey, Italy, Germany and Poland. Japanese shipbuilders now account for the large majority of stainless steel chemical tankers built, as welding stainless steel to the accuracy required for cargo tank construction is a skill which is difficult to acquire.

The chemical tanker market is dominated by several major chemical tanker operators, including Stolt-Nielsen, Navig8 Chemicals, Odfjell, Eitzen Chemical, Nordic Tankers, Tokyo Marine and Berlian Laju Tanker. Charterers, the end users of the ships, include oil majors and specialist chemical companies.

FLOATING PRODUCTION STORAGE AND OFFLOADING

A floating production, storage and offloading (FPSO) unit is a floating vessel used by the offshore oil and gas industry for the processing of hydrocarbons and for storage of oil.

An FPSO vessel is designed to receive hydrocarbons produced from nearby platforms or subsea template, process them, and store oil until it can be offloaded onto a tanker or, less frequently, transported through a pipeline. FPSOs are preferred in frontier offshore regions as they are easy to install, and do not require a local pipeline infrastructure to export oil. FPSOs can be a conversion of an oil tanker or can be a vessel built specially for the application.

A vessel used only to store oil (without processing it) is referred to as a floating storage and offloading vessel (FSO). There are also under construction (as at 2013) Floating Liquefied Natural Gas (FLNG) vessels, which will extract and liquify natural gas on board.

HISTORY

Oil has been produced from offshore locations since the late 1940s. Originally, all oil platforms sat on the seabed, but as exploration moved to deeper waters and more distant locations in the 1970s, floating production systems came to be used.

The first oil FPSO was the Shell Castellon, built in Spain in 1977. Today, over 200 vessels are deployed worldwide as oil FPSOs.

In addition to the significant growth of this market sector, we are witnessing today the progressive extension of the significant knowledge base of building and operating these floating facilities to provide solutions for other segments of the oil and gas industry.

As an example, the SanhaLPG FPSO, which operates offshore Angola, is the first such vessel with complete onboard liquefied petroleum gas processing and export facilities. It can store up to 135,000 cubic meters of LPG while awaiting export tankers for offloading.

Another very promising expansion is the progressive development of the floating LNG (FLNG) market. An LNG FPSO works under the same principles an oil FPSO works under, taking the well stream and separating out the natural gas (primarily methane and ethane) and producing LNG, which is stored and offloaded.

On July 29, 2009, Shell and Samsung announced an agreement to build up to 10 LNG FPSOs: Flex LNG has four contracts for smaller units at the same yard.

As a very significant and momentous event, on May 20, 2011, Royal Dutch Shell announced the planned development of a Floating Liquefied Natural Gas (FLNG) facility, which will be situated 200 km off the coast of Western Australia and is due for completion in around 2017. When it is finished, this will be the largest floating offshore facility. It will measure around 488m long and 74m wide, and when fully ballasted will weigh 600,000 tonnes. It will have a total storage capacity of 436,000 cubic metres of LNG, plus LPG condensate.

At the opposite (discharge and regasification) end of the LNG chain, the first ever conversion of an LNG carrier (Golar LNG owned Moss type LNG carrier) into an LNG floating storage and regasification unit was carried out in 2007 by Keppel shipyard in Singapore.

MECHANISMS

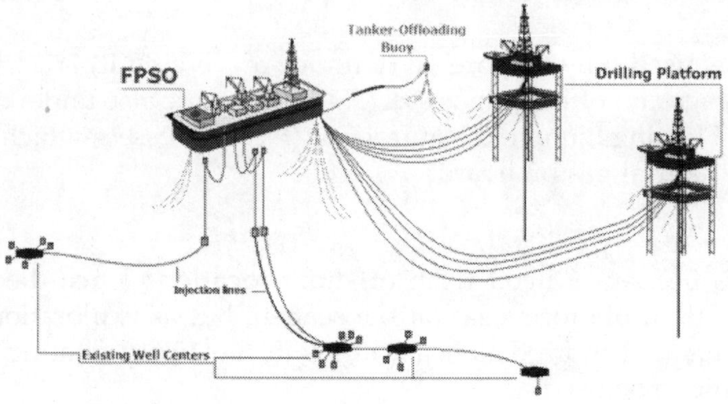

Fig. FPSO diagram

Oil produced from offshore production platforms can be transported to the mainland either by pipeline or by tanker. When a tanker is chosen to transport the oil, it is necessary to accumulate oil in some form of storage tank such that the oil tanker is not continuously occupied during oil production, and is only needed once sufficient oil has been produced to fill the tanker. At this point the transport tanker connects to the stern of the storage unit and offloads oil.

ADVANTAGES

Floating production, storage and offloading vessels are particularly effective in remote or deepwater locations where seabed pipelines are not cost effective. FPSOs eliminate the need to lay expensive long-distance pipelines from the processing facility to an onshore terminal. This can provide an economically attractive solution for smaller oil fields which can be exhausted in a few years and do not justify the expense of installing a pipeline. Furthermore, once the field is depleted, the FPSO can be moved to a new location.

SPECIFIC TYPES

A floating storage and offloading unit (FSO) is essentially a simplified FPSO without the capability for oil or gas processing. Most FSOs are converted single hull supertankers. An example is Knock Nevis, ex Seawise Giant, for many years the world's largest ship, which has been converted to an FSO for use offshore. The vessel was sold to Indian ship breakers, and renamed Mont for her final journey in December 2009. After clearing Indian customs, she was sailed to, and intentionally beached at Alang, Gujarat, India for demolition. At the other end of the LNG logistics chain, where the natural gas is brought back to ambient temperature and pressure, specially modified ships may also be used as floating storage and regasification units (FSRUs). A LNG floating storage and regasification unit receives liquefied natural gas (LNG) from offloading LNG carriers, and the onboard regasification system provides natural gas exported to shore through risers and pipelines.

Mooring systems for FSO, FPSO & FSU units are available in market which allow the vessel to be moored on an ice sheet.

VESSELS

Records

The FPSO operating in the deepest waters is the FPSO BW Pioneer, built and operated by BW Offshore on behalf of Petrobras Americas INC. The FPSO is moored at a depth of 2,600 m in Block 249 Walker Ridge in the US Gulf of Mexico and is rated for 100,000 bbl/d (16,000 m/d).

The EPCI contract was awarded in October 2007, and production started in early 2012. The FPSO conversion was carried out at Keppel Shipyard Tuas in Singapore, while the topsides were fabricated in modules at various international vendor locations. The FPSO has a disconnectable turret (APL). The vessel can disconnect in advance of hurricanes and reconnect with minimal down time.. A contract for an FPSO to operate in even deeper waters for Shell's Stones field in the US Gulf of Mexico was awarded to SBM Offshore in July 2013.

One of the world's largest FPSO is the Kizomba A, with a storage capacity of 2.2 million barrels (350,000 m3). Built at a cost of over US$800 million by Hyundai Heavy Industries in Ulsan, Korea, it is operated by Esso Exploration Angola (ExxonMobil). Located in 1200 meters (3,940 ft) of water at Deepwater block 200 statute miles (320 km) offshore in the Atlantic Ocean from Angola, Central Africa, it weighs 81,000 tonnes and is 285 meters long, 63 meters wide, and 32 meters high (935 ft by 207 ft (63 m) by 105 ft).

The first FSO in the Gulf of Mexico, The FSO Ta'Kuntah, has been in operation since August 1998. The FSO, owned and operated by MODEC, is under a service agreement with PEMEX Exploration and Production. The FSO Ta'Kuntah was installed as part of the Cantarell Field Development. The field is located in the Bay of Campeche, offshore Mexico's Yucatán peninsula. The FSO Ta'Kuntah is a converted ULCC tanker with a SOFEC external turret mooring system, two flexible risers connected in a lazy-S configuration between the turret and a pipeline end manifold (PLEM) on the seabed, and a unique offloading system. The FSO is designed to handle 800,000 bbl/d (130,000 m3/d) with no allowance for downtime.

One of the world's smallest FPSO is the Crystal Ocean, operating in 137 m of water in the Bass Strait between Australia and Tasmania on the Basker Manta Field. It is leased by Roc Oil (Sydney-based international petroleum exploration and production company) from Rubicon Offshore and is operated on their behalf by AGR Asia Pacific; it is currently producing 5,000 bbl/d (790 m3/d).

The FPSO in the shallowest water depth of just 13 m is the Armada Perkasa in the Okoro field in Nigeria, West Africa, for Afren Energy. This spread moored (fixed orientation) vessel uses 100 mm, 150 mm and 200 mm bore DeepFlex non-steel flexible risers in a double lazy wave formation (with weights and distributed buoyancy) to accommodate the large motion offsets in an environment of extreme waves and currents.

The Skarv FPSO, developed and engineered by Aker Solutions for BP Norge, will be the most advanced and largest FPSO deployed in the Norwegian Sea, offshore Mid Norway. Skarv is a gas condensate and oil field development. The development will tie in five sub-sea templates, and the FPSO has capacity to include several smaller wells nearby in the future. The process plant on the vessel can handle about 19,000,000 cubic metres per day (670,000,000 cu ft/d) of gas and 13,500 cubic metres per day (480,000 cu ft/d) of oil.

An 80 km gas export pipe will tie in to Åsgard transport system. Aker Solutions (formerly Aker Kvaerner) developed the front-end design for the new floating production facility as well as the overall system design for the field and preparation for procurement and project management of the total field development. The hull is an Aker Solutions proprietary "Tentechtm975" design. BP also selected Aker Solutions to perform the detail engineering, procurement and construction management assistance (EPcma) for the Skarv field development. The EPcma contract covers detail engineering and procurement work for the FPSO topsides as well as construction management assistance to BP including hull and topside facilities. The production start for the field is scheduled for August 2011. BP awarded the contract for fabrication of the Skarv FPSO hull to Samsung Heavy Industries in South Korea and the Turret contract to SBM. The FPSO has a length of 292m, breadth of 50.6m and is 29m deep and accommodate 100 people in single cabins. The hull will be delivered in January 2010.

GAS CARRIER

A gas carrier (or gas tanker) is a ship designed to transport LPG, LNG or liquified chemical gases in bulk.

TYPES

Fully pressurized gas carrier

The seaborne transport of liquefied gases began in 1934 when a major international company put two combined oil/LPG tankers into operation. The ships, basically oil tankers, had been converted by fitting small, riveted, pressure vessels for the carriage of LPG into cargo tank spaces. This enabled transport over long distances of substantial volumes of an oil refinery by-product that had distinct advantages as a domestic and commercial fuel. LPG is not only odourless and non-toxic, it also has a high calorific value and a low sulphur content, making it very clean and efficient when being burnt.

Today, most fully pressurised oceangoing LPG carriers are fitted with two or three horizontal, cylindrical or spherical cargo tanks and have typical capacities between 3,500 and 7,500 m. However, in recent years a number of larger-capacity fully pressurised ships have been built, most notably a series of 10,800 m3 ships, built in Japan between 2003 and 2013. Fully pressurised ships are still being built in numbers and represent a cost-effective, simple way of moving LPG to and from smaller gas terminals.

Semi-pressurised ships

These ships carried gases in a semi-pressurized/semi-refrigerated state however due to further development semi-pressurised/fully refrigerated gas carriers had become the shipowners' choice by providing high flexibility in cargo handling. These carriers, incorporating tanks either cylindrical, spherical or bi-lobe in shape, are able to load or discharge gas cargoes at both refrigerated and pressurised storage facilities.

Ethylene and gas/chemical carriers

Ethylene carriers are the most sophisticated of the gas tankers and have the ability to carry not only most other liquefied gas cargoes but also ethylene at its atmospheric boiling point of –104 °C. These ships feature cylindrical, insulated, stainless steel cargo tanks able to accommodate cargoes up to a maximum specific gravity of 1.8 at temperatures ranging from a minimum of -104 °C to a maximum of +80 °C and at a maximum tank pressure of 4 bar.

Fully refrigerated ships

They are built to carry liquefied gases at low temperature and atmospheric pressure between terminals equipped with fully refrigerated storage tanks. However, discharge through a booster pump and cargo heater makes it possible to discharge to pressurized tanks too. The first purpose-built, fully refrigerated LPG carrier was constructed by a Japanese shipyard, to a United States design, in 1962.

Prismatic tanks enabled the ship's cargo carrying capacity to be maximised, thus making fully refrigerated ships highly suitable for carrying large volumes of cargo such as LPG, ammonia and vinyl chloride over long distances. Today, fully refrigerated ships range in capacity from 20,000 to 100,000 m3. LPG carriers in the 50,000 - 80,000 m3 size range are often referred to as VLGCs (Very Large Gas Carriers). Although LNG carriers are often larger in terms of cubic capacity, this term is normally only applied to fully refrigerated LPG carriers.

The main type of cargo containment system utilised on board modern fully refrigerated ships are independent tanks with rigid foam insulation. The insulation used is quite commonly polyurethane foam. Older ships can have independent tanks with loosely filled perlite insulation. In the past, there have been a few fully refrigerated ships built with semi-membrane or integral tanks and internal insulation tanks, but these systems have only maintained minimal interest. The large majority of such ships currently in service have been constructed by shipbuilders in Japan and Korea.

Liquefied natural gas LNG carrier

The majority of LNG carriers are between 125,000 and 135,000 m3 in capacity. In the modern fleet of LNG carriers, there is an interesting exception concerning ship size. This is the introduction of several smaller ships of between 18,000 and 19,000 m3 having been built in 1994 and later to service the needs of importers of smaller volumes.

CARGOES CARRIED ON GAS CARRIERS

- LPG
- LNG
- Chemical gases such as ammonia, vinyl chloride, ethylene oxide, propylene oxide and chlorine.

GAS CARRIER CODES

The Gas Codes, developed by International Maritime Organization apply to all gas carriers regardless of size. There are three Gas Codes and these are described below.

Gas carriers built after June 1986 (the IGC Code)

The Code which applies to new gas carriers (built after 30 June 1986) is the International Code for the Construction and Equipment of Ships Carrying Liquefied Gases in Bulk. In brief, this Code is known as the IGC Code. The IGC Code, under amendments to International Convention for the Safety of Life at Sea(SOLAS), is mandatory for all new ships. As proof that a ship complies with the Code, an International Certificate of Fitness for the Carriage of Liquefied Gases in Bulk should be on board. In 1993, the IGC Code was amended and the new rules came into effect on 1 July 1994. Ships on which construction started on or after 1 October 1994 should apply the amended version of the Code but ships built earlier may comply with previous editions of the IGC Code.

Gas carriers built between 1976 and 1986 (the GC Code) The regulations covering gas carriers built after 1976 but before July 1986 are included in the Code for the Construction and Equipment of Ships Carrying Liquefied Gases in Bulk. It is known as the Gas Carrier Code or GC Code in short. Since 1975,

International Maritime OrganizationIMO has approved four sets of amendments to the GC Code. The latest was adopted in June 1993. All amendments are not necessarily agreed by every government. Although this Code is not mandatory, many countries have implemented it into national law. Accordingly, most charterers will expect such ships to meet with Code standards and, as proof of this, to have on board a Certificate of Fitness for the Carriage of Liquefied Gases in Bulk.

Gas carriers built before 1977 (the Existing Ship Code) The regulations covering gas carriers built before 1977 are contained in the Code for Existing Ships Carrying Liquefied Gases in Bulk. Its content is similar to the GC Code, though less extensive. The Existing Ship Code was completed in 1976 after the GC Code had been written. It therefore summarises current shipbuilding practice at that time. It remains as an International Maritime OrganizationIMO recommendation for all gas carriers in this older fleet of ships. The Code is not mandatory but is applied by some countries for ship registration and in other countries as a necessary fulfilment prior to port entry. Accordingly, many ships of this age are required by charterers to meet with Code standards and to have on board a Certificate of Fitness for the Carriage of Liquefied Gases in Bulk.

CARGO CONTAINMENT SYSTEMS

A cargo containment system is the total arrangement for containing cargo including, where fitted:

- A primary barrier (the cargo tank),
- Secondary barrier (if fitted),
- Associated thermal insulation,
- Any intervening spaces, and
- Adjacent structure, if necessary, for the support of these elements.

For cargoes carried at temperatures between -10 °C and -55 °C the ship's hull may act as the secondary barrier and in such cases it may be a boundary of the hold space.

The basic cargo tank types utilised on board gas carriers are in accordance with the list below:—

Independent Type

- Independent Type 'A'

Type A Independent Tanks are prismatic and supported on insulation-bearing blocks typically consisting of wooden chocks and located by anti-roll chocks located at the top of the tank inside the void space and anti-flotation chocks located inside the void space usually just above the double bottom tanks. The tanks are normally divided by a centreline liquid-tight bulkhead; by this feature, together with the chamfered upper part of the tank, the free liquid surface effect is reduced and thus the virtual rise of the Centre of gravity and the stability is increased.

When these cargo tanks are designed to carry LPG (at -50 °C), the tank is constructed of fine-grained low-carbon manganese steel or even stainless steel as seen in the Maersk J class Ships. The hold space (void space) in this design is normally filled with dry inert gas or Nitrogen but may be ventilated with air during a ballast or gas free passage. The Conch design has been developed for carriage of LNG (at-163oC). The material for these cargo tanks has to be either 9% nickel steel or aluminium. The maximum allowable relief vapour setting (MARVS) is < 0. 7 bar.

- Independent Type 'B'

Type B Independent Tanks are generally spherical and welded to a vertical cylindrical skirt, which is the lone connection to the ship's main hull. The hold space (void space) in this design is normally filled with dry inert gas or Nitrogen but may be ventilated with air during a ballast or gas free passage. A protective steel dome covers the primary barrier above deck level, and insulation encloses the outside of the primary barrier surface. This containment system has been used for carriage of LNG. The material of construction is either 9% nickel steel or aluminium. The maximum Allowable relief vapour setting (MARVS) is < 0. 7 bar.

- Independent Type 'C'

Type C Independent Tanks are deck pressure vessels or cylindrical pressure tanks mounted horizontally on two or more cradle-shaped foundations. The tanks may be fitted on, below or partly below deck and be both longitudinally and transversely located. Lobe-type tanks are commonly used at the forward end of the ship, to improve the poor utilization of the hull volume. This containment system is used for LPG and in Ethylene carriers. The material, if used for the construction of tanks designed to carry ethylene, is 5% nickel steel. The maximum Allowable relief vapour setting (MARVS) is > 0. 7 bar. and

- Membrane

Some other types such as:

- Internal insulation Type '1'
- Internal insulation Type '2'
- Integral

have been fully designed and approved but have not been commercially used yet.

HAZARDS ON GAS CARRIERS

Toxicity

Vinyl chloride commonly carried on gas carriers is a known as a human carcinogen, particularly liver cancer. It is not only dangerous when inhaled but can also be absorbed by the skin. Skin irritation and watering of the eyes indicate dangerous levels of VCM may be present in the atmosphere. Caution must be exerted while dealing with such cargoes, precautions such as use of Chemical suits Self-contained Breathing Apparatus (SCBA's) and gas tight goggles must be worn at all times to prevent exposure. Chlorine and Ammonia are other toxic cargoes carried.

Flammability

Almost all cargo vapours are flammable. When ignition occurs, it is not the liquid which burns but the evolved vapour that burns. Flameless explosions which result out of cold cargo liquid coming into sudden contact with water do not release much energy. Pool fires which are the result of a leaked pool of cargo liquid catching fire and jet fires which are the result of the leak catching fire are grave hazards. Flash fires occur when there is a leak and does not ignite immediately but after the vapours travel some distance downwind and getting ignited and are extremely dangerous. Vapour cloud explosions and Boiling liquid expanding vapor explosion are the most grave flammability hazards on gas carriers.

Frostbite

The cargoes are carried at extremely low temperatures, from 0 °C to -163 °C, and hence frostbite due to exposure of skin to the cold vapours or liquid is a very real hazard.

Asphyxia

Asphyxia occurs when the blood cannot take a sufficient supply of oxygen to the brain. A person affected may experience headache, dizziness and inability to concentrate, followed by loss of consciousness. In sufficient concentrations any vapour may cause asphyxiation, whether toxic or not.

HEALTH EFFECTS OF SPECIFIC CARGOES CARRIED ON GAS CARRIERS

Hazards of Ammonia

1. Exposure to more than 2,000 ppm – fatal in 30 minutes, 6,000 ppm – fatal in minutes, 10,000 ppm – fatal and intolerable to unprotected skin.
2. Anhydrous Ammonia is not dangerous when handled properly, but if not handled carefully it can be extremely dangerous. It is not as combustible as many other products that we use and handle every day. However, concentrations of gas burn and require precautions to avoid fires.

3. Mild exposure can cause irritation to eye, nose and lung tissues. Prolonged breathing can cause suffocation. When large amounts are inhaled, the throat swells shut and victims suffocate. Exposure to vapours or liquid also can cause blindness
4. The water-absorbing nature of anhydrous ammonia that causes the greatest injury (especially to the eyes, nose, throat or lungs), and which can cause permanent damage. It is a colourless gas at atmospheric pressure and normal temperature, but under pressure readily changes into a liquid. Anhydrous ammonia has a high affinity for water. Anhydrous ammonia is a hygroscopic compound, this means it will seek moisture source that may be the body of the operator, which is composed of 90 percent water. When a human body is exposed to anhydrous ammonia the chemical freeze burns its way into the skin, eyes or lungs. This attraction places the eyes, lungs, and skin at greatest risk because of their high moisture content. Caustic burns result when the anhydrous ammonia dissolves into body tissue. Most deaths from anhydrous ammonia are caused by severe damage to the throat and lungs from a direct blast to the face. An additional concern is the low boiling point of anhydrous ammonia. The chemical freezes on contact at room temperature. It will cause burns similar to, but more severe than, those caused by dry ice. If exposed to severe cold flesh will become frozen. At first, the skin will become red (but turn subsequently white); the affected area is painless, but hard to touch, if left untreated the flesh will die and may become gangrenous.
5. The human eye is a complex organ made up of about 80 percent water. Ammonia under pressure can cause extensive, almost immediate damage to the eye. The ammonia extracts the fluid and destroys eye cells and tissue in minutes.
6. Draining of Ammonia into sea while pre-cooling of the hard-arm or during disconnection operations is not an eco-friendly operation. As a small quantity of Ammonia as low as 0.45 mg/L (LC50) is hazardous to Salmon as per ICSC, USA. Consumption of such fish could be dangerous to humans.

LNG CARRIER

An LNG carrier is a tank ship designed for transporting liquefied natural gas (LNG). As the LNG market grows rapidly, the fleet of LNG carriers continues to experience tremendous growth.

HISTORY

The first LNG carrier Methane Pioneer (dwt 5034 tons) left the Calcasieu

River on the Louisiana Gulf coast on 25 January 1959. With the world's first ocean cargo of LNG and sailed to the UK where the cargo was delivered. Subsequent expansion of that trade has brought on a large expansion of the fleet to today where giant LNG ships carrying up to 266,000 m3 are sailing worldwide. At the end of 2005, a total of 203 vessels have been built, of which 193 are still in service.

The success of the specially modified C1-M-AV1-type standard ship Normarti, renamed The Methane Pioneer, caused the Gas Council and Conch International Methane Ltd. to order two purpose built LNG carriers to be constructed: the Methane Princess and the Methane Progress. The ships were fitted with Conch independent aluminum cargo tanks and entered the Algerian LNG trade in 1964. These ships had a capacity of 27,000 cubic meters.

In the late 1960s, opportunity arose to export LNG from Alaska to Japan and in 1969 that trade was initiated. Two ships, each with a capacity of 71,500 cubic meters were built in Sweden. In the early 1970s, the US Government encouraged US shipyards to build LNG carriers, and a total of 16 LNG ships were built. The late 1970s and early 1980s brought the prospect of Arctic LNG ships with a number of projects being studied.

With the increase in cargo capacity to approximately 143,000 cubic meters, new tank designs were developed, from Moss Rosenberg to Technigaz Mark III and Gaztransport No.96.

In recent years, the size and capacity of LNG carriers has increased greatly. Since 2005, Qatargas has pioneered the development of two new classes of LNG carriers, referred to as Q-Flex and Q-Max. Each ship has a cargo capacity of between 210,000 and 266,000 cubic meters and is equipped with a re-liquefaction plant.

NEW BUILDING

According to a presentation by Golar LNG Partners, in June 2012 there were 72 new builds on order. Today the majority of the new ships under construction are in the size of 120,000–140,000 m3 But there are orders for ships with capacity up to 260,000 m3. As of end of 2011, there are 359 LNG ships engaged in the deepsea movement of LNG.

CARGO HANDLING

The following is based on a typical set-up of tanks, which is to have from four to six tanks all along the centre line of the vessel. Surrounding the tanks is a combination of ballast tanks, cofferdams and voids. These areas give the vessel a double-hull type design.

Inside the tank there are normally three pumps of the submerged-motor type. There are two main cargo pumps which are used in cargo discharge operations and a much smaller pump which is referred to as the spray pump. The spray pump is used for either pumping out liquid LNG to be used as fuel via a vaporizer, or for cooling down cargo tanks. It can also be used for "stripping" out the last of the cargo in discharge operations. All of these pumps are contained within what is known as the pump tower which hangs from the top of the tank and runs the entire depth of the tank. The pump tower also contains the tank gauging system and the tank filling line all of which come near to the bottom of the tank.

In membrane type vessels there is also an empty pipe with a spring-loaded foot valve that can be opened by weight or pressure. This is the emergency pump tower. In the event both main cargo pumps fail the top can be removed from this pipe and an emergency cargo pump lowered down to the bottom of the pipe. The top is replaced on the column and then the pump is allowed to push down on the foot valve and open it. The cargo can then be pumped out.

All the cargo pumps discharge into a common pipe which runs along the deck of the vessel. It branches off to either side of the vessel to the cargo manifolds, which are used for loading or discharging.

All the cargo tank vapour spaces are linked via a vapour header which runs parallel to the cargo header. This also has connections to the sides of the ship next to the loading and discharging manifolds.

TYPICAL CARGO CYCLE

A typical cargo cycle starts with the tanks in a "gas free" condition, meaning the tanks are full of air, which allows maintenance on the tank and pumps. Cargo cannot be loaded directly into the tank, as the presence of oxygen means one would encounter explosive atmospheric conditions within the tank. Also, the temperature difference could cause damage to the tanks.

First, the tank must be inerted by using the inert gas plant, which burns diesel in air to remove the oxygen and replace it with carbon dioxide (CO_2). This is blown into the tanks until it reaches below 4% oxygen and a dry atmosphere. This removes the risk of an explosive atmosphere in the tanks.

Next, the vessel goes into port to "gas-up" and "cool-down", as one still cannot load directly into the tank: The CO_2 will freeze and damage the pumps and the cold shock could damage the tank's pump column.

Liquid LNG is brought onto the vessel and taken along the spray line to the main vaporiser, which boils off the liquid into gas. This is then warmed up to roughly 20 °C in the gas heaters and then blown into the tanks to displace the "inert gas". This continues until all the CO_2 is removed from the tanks. Initially, the IG (inert gas) is vented to atmosphere. Once the hydrocarbon content reaches 5% (lower flamability range of methane) the inert gas is redirected to shore via a pipeline and manifold connection by the HD (high duty) compressors. Shore terminal then burns this vapour to avoid the dangers of having large amounts of hydrocarbons around which may explode.

Now the vessel is gassed up and warm. The tanks are still at ambient temperature and are full of methane.

The next stage is cool-down. Liquid LNG is sprayed into the tanks via spray heads, which vaporises and starts to cool the tank. The excess gas is again blown ashore to be re-liquified or burned at a flare stack. Once the tanks reach about -140 °C the tanks are ready to load bulk.

Bulk loading starts and liquid LNG is pumped from the storage tanks ashore into the vessel tanks. Displaced gas is blown ashore by the HD compressors. Loading continues until typically 98.5% full is reached (to allow for thermal expansion/contraction of cargo).

The vessel can now proceed to the discharge port. During passage various boil-off management strategies can be used. Boil-off gas can be burned in boilers to provide steam for propulsion, or it can be re-liquefied and returned to the cargo tanks, depending on the design of the vessel.

Once in the discharge port, the cargo is pumped ashore using the cargo pumps. As the tank empties, the vapour space is filled by either gas from ashore or by vaporising some cargo in the cargo vaporiser. Either the vessel can be pumped out as far as possible, with the last being pumped out with spray pumps, or some cargo can be retained on board as a "heel".

If all the cargo is pumped ashore, then on the ballast passage the tanks will warm up to ambient temperature, returning the vessel to a gassed up and warm state. The vessel can then be cooled again for loading.

If the vessel is to return to a gas free state, the tanks must be warmed up by using the gas heaters to circulate warm gas. Once the tanks are warmed up, the inert gas plant is used to remove the methane from the tanks. Once the tanks are methane free, the inert gas plant is switched to dry air production, which is used to remove all the inert gas from the tanks until they have a safe working atmosphere.

CONTAINMENT SYSTEMS

Today there are four containment systems in use for new build vessels. Two of the designs are of the self-supporting type, while the other two are of the membrane type and today the patents are owned by Gaz Transport & Technigaz (GTT).

There is a trend towards the use of the two different membrane types instead of the self-supporting storage systems. This is most likely because prismatic membrane tanks utilize the hull shape more efficiently and thus have less void space between the cargo-tanks and ballast tanks. As a result of this, Moss-type design compared to a membrane design of equal capacity will be far more expensive to transit the Suez Canal. However, self-supporting tanks are more robust and have greater resistance to sloshing forces, and will possibly be considered in the future for offshore storage where bad weather will be a significant factor.

MOSS TANKS (SPHERICAL IMO TYPE B LNG TANKS)

This design is owned by the Norwegian company Moss Maritime and it is a spherical tank. Most Moss type vessels have 4 or 5 tanks.

The outside of the tank has a thick layer of foam insulation that is either fitted in panels or in more modern designs wound round the tank. Over this insulation is a thin layer of "tinfoil" which allows the insulation to be kept dry with a nitrogen atmosphere. This atmosphere is constantly checked for any methane that would indicate a leak of the tank. Also the outside of the tank is regularly checked at a roughly 3 month interval for any cold spots that would indicate breakdown in the insulation.

The tank is supported around its circumference by the equatorial ring which is supported by a large circular skirt which takes the weight of the tank down to the ships structure. This skirt allows the tank to expand and contract during cooldown and warm-up operations. During cooldown or warm-up the tank can expand or contract about 2 feet. Because of this expansion and contraction all piping into the tank comes in via the top and is connected to the ships lines via flexible bellows.

Inside each tank there is a set of spray heads. These heads are mounted around the equatorial ring and are used to spray Liquid LNG onto the tank walls to reduce the temperature.

It is normal practise to keep onboard 5% to 10% of the cargo after discharge in one tank. This is referred to as the heel and this is used to cooldown the remaining tanks that have no heel before loading. This must be done gradually otherwise the tanks will be cold shocked if loaded directly into warm tanks. Cooldown can take roughly 36 hours on a Moss vessel so carrying a heel allows cooldown to be done before the vessel reaches port giving a significant time saving.

Tanks normally have a working pressure of up to 22 kPa, but this can be raised for an emergency discharge. If both main pumps fail then to remove the cargo the tank safety valves are adjusted to lift at 1bar. Then the filling line which goes to the bottom of the tank is opened along with the filling lines of the other tanks on board. The pressure is then raised in the tank with the defective pumps which pushes the cargo into the other tanks where it can be pumped out of.

IHI (PRISMATIC IMO TYPE B LNG TANKS)

Ishikawajima-Harima Heavy Industries has developed the self-supporting prismatic type B (SPB) tank. Only two vessels currently have the SPB containment system. No sloshing problems ever happened on Type B LNG tanks. This is an important advantage over Membrane LNG carrier tanks which may break due to sloshing impact, therefore destroying the ship's hull. This is also of prime relevance for FPSO LNG (or FLNG). In addition, IMO type B LNG tanks can sustain internal accidental damage due for example to internal equipment releases. Of course, for membrane LNG tanks, this is absolutely not the case; Several incidents occurred inside membrane LNG tanks.

TGZ MARK III

This design is originally by Technigaz and it is of the membrane type. The membrane consists of stainless steel with 'waffles' to absorb the thermal contraction when the tank is cooled down. The primary barrier, made of corrugated stainless steel of about 1.2 mm thickness is the one in direct contact with the cargo liquid (or vapour in empty tank condition). This is followed by a primary insulation which in turn is covered by a secondary barrier made of a material called "triplex" which is basically a metal foil sandwiched between glasswool sheets and compressed together. This is again covered by a secondary insulation which in turn is supported by the ship's hull structure from the outside. So, going from the inside of the tank outwards, we have:-

LNG

- Primary barrier of 1.2 mm thick corrugated/waffled stainless steel
- Primary insulation (also called the interbarrier space)
- Secondary barrier of triplex membrane
- Secondary insulation (also called the insulation space)
- Ship's hull structure.

GT96

This is Gaz Transport's tank design. The tanks consists of a primary and secondary thin membrane made of the material Invar which has almost no thermal contraction. The insulation is made out of plywood boxes filled with perlite and continuously flushed with nitrogen gas. The integrity of both membranes is permanently monitored by detection of hydrocarbon in the nitrogen. An evolution is proposed by NG2, with the replacement of nitrogen by argon as the flushed inert and insulation gas. Argon has a better insulation power than nitrogen, which could save 10% of boil-off gas.

CS1

CS1 stands for Combined System Number One. It was designed by the now merged Technigaz and GazTransport companies and consists of the best components of both MkIII and No96 systems. The primary barrier is made of invar 0.7 mm, and secondary from Triplex. The primary and secondary insulation consists of polyurethane foam panels. Three vessels with CS1 technology have been built by one shipyard, but established shipyards have decided to maintain production of the MKIII and NO96.

RELIQUEFACTION AND BOIL-OFF

In order to facilitate transport, natural gas is cooled down to approximately -163 °C at atmospheric pressure, at which point the gas condenses to a liquid. The tanks on board an LNG carrier effectively function as giant thermoses to keep the liquid gas cold during storage. No insulation is perfect, however, and so the liquid is constantly boiling during the voyage.

According to WGI, on a typical voyage an estimated 0.1–0.25% of the cargo converts to gas each day, depending on the efficiency of the insulation and the roughness of the voyage. In a typical 20-day voyage, anywhere from 2–6% of the total volume of LNG originally loaded may be lost.

Normally an LNG tanker is powered by steam turbines with boilers. These boilers are dual fuel and can run on either methane or oil or a combination of both.

The gas produced in boil off is traditionally diverted to the boilers and used as a fuel for the vessel. Before this gas is used in the boilers, it must be warmed up to roughly 20 °C by using the gas heaters. The gas is either fed into the boiler by tank pressure or it is increased in pressure by the LD compressors.

What fuel the vessel runs on is dependent on many factors which include the length of the voyage, desire to carry a heel for cooldown, price of oil versus price of LNG.

There are three basic modes available.

Minimum boil-off/maximum oil:- In this mode tank pressures are kept high to reduce boil off to a minimum and the majority of energy comes from the fuel oil. This maximises the amount of LNG delivered but does allow tank temps to rise due to lack of evaporation. The high cargo temps can cause storage problems and offloading problems.

Maximum boil-off/minimum oil:- In this mode the tank pressures are kept low and you have a greater boil-off but still there is a large amount of fuel oil used. This decreases the amount of LNG delivered but the cargo will be delivered cold which many ports prefer.

100% gas:- Tank pressures are kept at a similar level to max boil off but this is not enough to supply all the boilers needs so you must start to "force". A small pump is started in one tank to supply LNG to the forcing vaporiser, where the LNG is warmed and vaporized back into a gas that is usable in the boilers. In this mode no fuel oil is used.

Recent advances in technology have allowed reliquefication plants to be fitted to vessels, allowing the boil off to be reliquefied and returned to the tanks. Because of this, the vessels' operators and builders have been able to contemplate the use of more efficient slow-speed Diesel engines (previously most LNG carriers have been steam turbine-powered). Exceptions are the LNG carrier Havfru (built as Venator in 1973), which originally had dual fuel diesel engines, and its sister-ship Century (built as Lucian in 1974), also built with dual fuel gas turbines before being converted to a diesel engine system in 1982. Vessels using dual or tri-fuel diesel electric propulsion systems are now in service.

OIL TANKER

An oil tanker, also known as a petroleum tanker, is a merchant ship designed for the bulk transport of oil. There are two basic types of oil tankers: the crude tanker and the product tanker. Crude tankers move large quantities of unrefined crude oil from its point of extraction to refineries. Product tankers, generally much smaller, are designed to move petrochemicals from refineries to points near consuming markets.

Oil tankers are often classified by their size as well as their occupation. The size classes range from inland or coastal tankers of a few thousand metric tons of deadweight (DWT) to the mammoth ultra large crude carriers (ULCCs) of 550,000 DWT. Tankers move approximately 2,000,000,000 metric tons (2.2×10 short tons) of oil every year. Second only to pipelines in terms of efficiency, the average cost of oil transport by tanker amounts to only two or three United States cents per 1 US gallon (3.8 L).

Some specialized types of oil tankers have evolved. One of these is the naval replenishment oiler, a tanker which can fuel a moving vessel. Combination ore-bulk-oil carriers and permanently moored floating storage units are two other variations on the standard oil tanker design. Oil tankers have been involved in a number of damaging and high-profile oil spills. As a result, they are subject to stringent design and operational regulations.

HISTORY

The technology of oil transportation has evolved alongside the oil industry. Although anthropogenic use of oil reaches to prehistory, the first modern commercial exploitation dates back to James Young's manufacture of paraffin in 1850. In these early days, oil from Upper Burma was moved in earthenware vessels to the river bank where it was then poured into boat holds.

In the 1850s, the Pennsylvania oil fields became a major supplier of oil, and a center of innovation after Edwin Drake had struck oil near Titusville, Pennsylvania. The first oil well in the United States was dug here in 1859, initially yielding around ten barrels per day. Within two years, the Titusville field was providing 3,000 barrels (480 m3) per day. By this time, petroleum oil had already begun to supplant fish, whale, and vegetable oils for applications such as indoor and outdoor lighting, and transatlantic export had already begun.

Break-bulk boats and barges were originally used to transport Pennsylvania oil in 40-US-gallon (150 l) wooden barrels. But transport by barrel had several problems. The first problem was weight: the standard empty barrel weighed 64 pounds (29 kg), representing 20% of the total weight of a full barrel. Other problems with barrels were their expense, their tendency to leak, and the fact that they were generally used only once. The expense was significant: for example, in the early years of the Russian oil industry, barrels accounted for half the cost of petroleum production.

The movement of oil in bulk was attempted in many places and in many ways. Modern oil pipelines have existed since 1860. In 1863, two sail-driven tankers were built on England's River Tyne. These were followed in 1873 by the first oil-tank steamer, the Vaderland, which was built by Palmers Shipbuilding and Iron Company for Belgian owners.

The vessel's use was curtailed by U.S. and Belgian authorities citing safety concerns. By 1871, the Pennsylvania oil fields were making limited use of oil tank barges and cylindrical railroad tank-cars similar to those in use today.

THE NOBEL BROTHERS

In 1876, Ludvig and Robert Nobel, brothers of Alfred Nobel, founded Branobel (short for Brothers Nobel) in the Russian Empire, active mostly in the oil-rich region around Baku (now Azerbaijan). During the late 19th century Branobel was one of the largest oil companies in the world.

Ludvig was a pioneer in the development of early oil tankers. He first experimented with carrying oil in bulk on single-hulled barges. Turning his attention to self-propelled tankships, he faced a number of challenges. A primary concern was to keep the cargo and fumes well away from the engine room to avoid fires. Other challenges included allowing for the cargo to expand and contract due to temperature changes, and providing a method to ventilate the tanks.

The world's first successful oil tanker was Nobel's Zoroaster. He designed this ship in Gothenburg, Sweden, with Sven Almqvist. The contract to build it was signed in January 1878, and it made its first run later that year from Baku to Astrakhan. The Zoroaster design was widely studied and copied, with Nobel refusing to patent any part of it. In October 1878, he ordered two more tankers of the same design: the Buddha and the Nordenskjöld.

Zoroaster carried its 242 long tons of kerosene cargo in two iron tanks joined by pipes. One tank was forward of the midships engine room and the other was aft. The ship also featured a set of 21 vertical watertight compartments for extra buoyancy. The ship had a length overall of 184 feet (56 m), a beam of 27 feet (8.2 m), and a draft of 9 feet (2.7 m). Unlike later Nobel tankers, the Zoroaster design was built small enough to sail from Sweden to the Caspian Sea by way of the Baltic Sea, Lake Ladoga, Lake Onega, the Rybinsk and Mariinsk Canals and the Volga River.

Nobel then began to adopt a single-hull design, where the ship's hull forms part of its tank structure. In November 1880 he ordered his first single-hulled tanker, the Moses. Within a year, he ordered seven more single-hulled tankers: the Mohammed, Tatarin, Bramah, Spinoza, Socrates, Darwin, Koran, Talmud, and Calmuck.

Branobel experienced one of the first oil tanker disasters. In 1881 the Zoroaster's sister-ship, the Nordenskjöld exploded in Baku while taking on kerosene. The pipe carrying the cargo was jerked away from the hold when the ship was hit by a gust of wind. Kerosene then spilled onto the deck and down into the engine room, where mechanics were working in the light of kerosene lanterns. The ship then exploded, killing half the crew. Nobel responded to the disaster by creating a flexible, leak proof loading pipe which was much more resistant to spills.

In 1883, oil tanker design took a large step forward. Working for the Nobel company, Colonel Henry F. Swan designed a set of three Nobel tankers. Instead of one or two large holds, Swan's design used several holds which spanned the width, or beam, of the ship. These holds were further subdivided into port and starboard sections by a longitudinal bulkhead. Earlier designs suffered from stability problems caused by the free surface effect, where oil sloshing from side to side could cause a ship to capsize. But this approach of dividing the ship's storage space into smaller tanks virtually eliminated free-surface problems. This approach, almost universal today, was first used by Swan in the Nobel tankers Blesk, Lumen, and Lux.

In 1903, the Nobel brothers built two oil tankers which ran on internal combustion engines, as opposed to the older steam engines. The Vandal, the first diesel-electric ship, was capable of carrying 750 long tons of refined oil, and was powered by three 120 horsepower (89 kW) diesel motors. The larger Sarmat employed four 180 h.p. engines. The first seagoing diesel-powered tanker, 4,500 ton Mysl, was built by Nobel's competitors in Kolomna. Nobel responded with Emanuel Nobel and Karl Hagelin, 4,600 long ton kerosene tankers with 1,200 horsepower (890 kW) engines.

The Glückauf represented a large step forward in tanker design. Another design of Colonel Swan, the ship has been called the "true progenitor of all subsequent tanker tonnage." Its features included cargo valves operable from the deck, cargo main piping, a vapor line, cofferdams for added safety, and the ability to fill a ballast tank with seawater when empty of cargo.Wilhelm Anton Riedemann, an agent for the Standard Oil Company purchased Glückauf and several of her sister ships. After the Glückauf was lost in 1893 after being grounded in fog, Standard Oil purchased the sister ships.

BREAKING THE STANDARD OIL MONOPOLY

The 1880s also saw the beginnings of the Asian oil trade. The idea that led to moving Russian oil to the Far East via the Suez Canal was the brainchild of two men: importer Marcus Samuel and shipowner/broker Fred Lane. Prior bids to move oil through the canal had been rejected by the Suez Canal

Company as being too risky. Samuel approached the problem a different way: asking the company for the specifications of a tanker it would allow through the canal.

Armed with the canal company's specifications, Samuel ordered three tankers from William Gray & Company in northern England. Named the Murex, the Conch and the Clam, each had a capacity of 5,010 long tons of deadweight. These three ships were the first tankers of the Tank Syndicate, forerunner of today's Royal Dutch Shell company.

With facilities prepared in Jakarta, Singapore, Bangkok, Saigon, Hong Kong, Shanghai, and Kobe, the fledgling Shell company was ready to become Standard Oil's first challenger in the Asian market. On August 24, 1892, the Murex became the first tanker to pass through the Suez Canal. By the time Shell merged with Royal Dutch Petroleum in 1907, the company had 34 steam-driven oil tankers, compared to Standard Oil's four case-oil steamers and 16 sailing tankers.

The fleet oiler USS Maumee, launched on April 17, 1915, pioneered the technique of underway replenishment. A large ship at the time, with a capacity of 14,500 long tons of deadweight, Maumee began refuelling destroyersen route to Britain at the outset of World War I. This technique enabled the Navy to keep its fleets at sea for extended periods, with a far greater range independent of the availability of a friendly port. This independence proved crucial to victory in World War II by the ships commanded by Fleet Admiral Nimitz who, as Maumee's executive officer, had played a key role in developing underway replenishment.

Underway replenishment was quickly adopted by other navies. One example is the Australian fleet oiler HMAS Kurumba which provided underway replenishment to the United Kingdom's Royal Navy from 1917 to 1919.

In World War Iunrestricted submarine warfare caused a shortage of tankers. The United States ambassador to the United Kingdom, Walter Hines Page, wrote:

- The submarines are sinking freight ships faster than freight ships are being built by the whole world. In this way, too, then, the Germans are succeeding. Now if this goes on long enough, the Allies' game is up. For instance, they have lately sunk so many fuel oil ships, that this country may very soon be in a perilous condition—even the Grand Fleet may not have enough fuel.

Georges Clemenceau wrote to US president Wilson

Gasoline is as vital as blood in the coming battles…a failure in the supply of gasoline would cause the immediate paralysis of our armies.

Wilson reacted strongly. The War Shipping Board commandeered all ships in the United States and also took over all yards. An unprecedented budget of $US 1.3 billion was used for this end. At Hog Island, the largest shipyard in the World was built, known for the Hog Islander.

Between 1916 and 1921, 316 tankers were built with a total capacity of 3.2 million long tons of deadweight, where the entire World fleet before World War I was just over 2 million tons.

BETWEEN THE WORLD WARS

In 1923 about 800,000 long tons were laid up, which gave enormous opportunities for speculators, such as Daniel Keith Ludwig. In 1925 he had bought the freighter Phoenix and put tanks in the holds. These riveted tanks leaked, which resulted in an explosive mixture. The resulting explosion killed two crew members and badly injured Ludwig. After this, he was a strong believer in welding.

In 1928 the World's largest oil tanker was the 16,436 gross register tons (GRT)MV C.O. Stillman, completed that year for Canadian owners by Bremer Vulkan in Germany.

WORLD WAR II

Oil tankers, particularly the T2 tanker, played an important part in World War II. The T2-SE-A1 with a capacity of 16,613 long tons of deadweight, was the most popular variant with nearly 500 built during the war. After the war, these tankers were used commercially for decades, and many were sold on the international market.

Until 1956, tankers were designed to be able to navigate the Suez Canal. This size restriction became much less of a priority after the closing of the canal during the Suez Crisis of 1956. Forced to move oil around the Cape of Good Hope, shipowners realized that bigger tankers were the key to more efficient transport.

THE SUPERTANKER ERA

Tankers have grown significantly in size since World War II. While a typical T2 tanker of the World War II era was 532 feet (162 m) long and had a capacity of 16,500 DWT, the ultra-large crude carriers (ULCC) built in the 1970s were over 1,300 feet (400 m) long and had a capacity of 500,000 DWT. Several factors encouraged this growth. Hostilities in the Middle East which interrupted traffic through the Suez Canal contributed, as did nationalization of Middle East oil refineries. Fierce competition among shipowners also played a part. But apart from these considerations is a simple economic advantage: the larger an oil tanker is, the more cheaply it can move crude oil, and the better it can help meet growing demands for oil.

In 1955 the World's largest supertanker was 30,708 GRT and 47,500 LT DWT: the SS Spyros Niarchos launched that year by Vickers Armstrongs Shipbuilders Ltd in England for Stavros Niarchos.

In 1958 United States shipping magnate Daniel K. Ludwig broke the record of 100,000 long tons of heavy displacement. His Universe Apollo displaced 104,500 long tons, a 23% increase from the previous record-holder, Universe Leader which also belonged to Ludwig.

The world's largest supertanker was built in 1979 at the Oppama shipyard by Sumitomo Heavy Industries, Ltd. as the Seawise Giant. This ship was built with a capacity of 564,763 DWT, a length overall of 458.45 metres (1,504.1 ft) and a draft of 24.611 metres (80.74 ft). She had 46 tanks, 31,541 square metres (339,500 sq ft) of deck, and at her full load draft, could not navigate the English Channel.

Seawise Giant was renamed Happy Giant in 1989, Jahre Viking in 1991, and Knock Nevis in 2004 (when she was converted into a permanently moored storage tanker). In 2009 she was sold for the last time, renamed Mont, and scrapped.

As of 2011, the world's two largest working supertankers are the TI class supertankersTI Europe and TI Oceania. These ships were built in 2002 and 2003 as the Hellespont Alhambra and Hellespont Tara for the Greek Hellespont Steamship Corporation. Hellespont sold these ships to Overseas Shipholding Group and Euronav in 2004. Each of the sister ships has a capacity of over 441,500 DWT, a length overall of 380.0 metres (1,246.7 ft) and a cargo capacity of 3,166,353 barrels (503,409,900 l). They were the first ULCCs to be double-hulled. To differentiate them from smaller ULCCs, these ships are sometimes given the V-Plus size designation.

With the exception of the pipeline, the tanker is the most cost-effective way to move oil today. Worldwide, tankers carry some 2 billion barrels (3.2×1011 l) annually, and the cost of transportation by tanker amounts to only US$0.02 per gallon at the pump.

SIZE CATEGORIES

In 1954 Shell Oil developed the average freight rate assessment (AFRA) system which classifies tankers of different sizes. To make it an independent instrument, Shell consulted the London Tanker Brokers' Panel (LTBP). At first, they divided the groups as General Purpose for tankers under 25,000 tons deadweight (DWT); Medium Range for ships between 25,000 and 45,000 DWT and Large Range for the then-enormous ships that were larger than 45,000 DWT. The ships became larger during the 1970s, which prompted rescaling.

The system was developed for tax reasons as the tax authorities wanted evidence that the internal billing records were correct. Before the New York Mercantile Exchange started trading crude oil futures in 1983, it was difficult to determine the exact price of oil, which could change with every contract. Shell and BP, the first companies to use the system, abandoned the AFRA system in 1983, later followed by the US oil companies. However, the system is still used today. Besides that, there is the flexible market scale, which takes typical routes and lots of 500,000 barrels (79,000 m3).

Merchant oil tankers carry a wide range of hydrocarbon liquids ranging from crude oil to refined petroleum products. Their size is measured in deadweight metric tons (DWT). Crude carriers are among the largest, ranging from 55,000 DWTPanamax-sized vessels to ultra-large crude carriers (ULCCs) of over 440,000 DWT.

"Supertankers" are the largest tankers, including very large crude carriers (VLCC) and ULCCs with capacities over 250,000 DWT. These ships can transport 2,000,000 barrels (320,000 m3) of oil/318 000 metric tons. By way of comparison, the United Kingdom consumed about 1.6 million barrels (250,000 m3) of oil per day in 2009. ULCCs, commissioned in the 1970s, were the largest vessels ever built, but the longest ones have already been scrapped; only a few ULCCs remain in service, none of which are more than 400m long.

Because of their great size, supertankers often can not enter port fully loaded. These ships can take on their cargo at off-shore platforms and single-point moorings. On the other end of the journey, they often pump their cargo off to smaller tankers at designated lightering points off-coast. A supertanker's routes are generally long, requiring it to stay at sea for extended periods, up to and beyond seventy days at a time.

Smaller tankers, ranging from well under 10,000 DWT to 80,000 DWT Panamax vessels, generally carry refined petroleum products, and are known as product tankers. The smallest tankers, with capacities under 10,000 DWT generally work near-coastal and inland waterways. Although they were in the past, ships of the smaller Aframax and Suezmax classes are no longer regarded as supertankers.

CHARTERING

The act of hiring a ship to carry cargo is called chartering. Tankers are hired by four types of charter agreements: the voyage charter, the time charter, the bareboat charter, and contract of affreightment. In a voyage charter the charterer rents the vessel from the loading port to the discharge port. In a time charter the vessel is hired for a set period of time, to perform voyages as the charterer directs. In a bareboat charter the charterer acts as the ship's operator and manager, taking on responsibilities such as providing the crew and maintaining the vessel. Finally, in a contract of affreightment or COA, the charterer specifies a total volume of cargo to be carried in a specific time period and in specific sizes, for example a COA could be specified as 1 million barrels (160,000 m3) of JP-5 in a year's time in 25,000-barrel (4,000 m3) shipments. A completed chartering contract is known as a charter party.

One of the key aspects of any charter party is the freight rate, or the price specified for carriage of cargo. The freight rate of a tanker charter party is specified in one of four ways: by a lump sum rate, by rate per ton, by a time charter equivalent rate, or by Worldscale rate. In a lump sum rate arrangement, a fixed price is negotiated for the delivery of a specified cargo, and the ship's owner/operator is responsible to pay for all port costs and other voyage expenses. Rate per ton arrangements are used mostly in chemical tanker chartering, and differ from lump sum rates in that port costs and voyage expenses are generally paid by the charterer. Time charter arrangements specify a daily rate, and port costs and voyage expenses are also generally paid by the charterer.

The Worldwide Tanker Normal Freight Scale, often referred to as Worldscale, is established and governed jointly by the Worldscale Associations of London and New York. Worldscale establishes a baseline price for carrying a metric ton of product between any two ports in the world. In Worldscale negotiations, operators and charterers will determine a price based on a percentage of the Worldscale rate. The baseline rate is expressed as WS 100. If a given charter party settled on 85% of the Worldscale rate, it would be expressed as WS 85. Similarly, a charter party set at 125% of the Worldscale rate would be expressed as WS 125.

RECENT MARKETS

As of 2007, the chartering market is persistently volatile across all tanker sectors. The market is affected by a wide variety of variables such as the supply and demand of oil as well as the supply and demand of oil tankers. Some particular variables include winter temperatures, excess tanker tonnage, supply fluctuations in the Persian Gulf, and interruptions in refinery services.

In 2006, the sustained rise in oil prices had only a limited impact on demand. It was a good year across all segments of the tanker market segments, but not as good as 2004 and 2005. Amidst high oil prices, geopolitical tension, and fears of disruptions to the oil supply, growing demand was the main driving force in the tanker shipping market for the year. As demand grew moderately in the United States and Western Europe, expanding economies such as China fueled exponential growth in demand.

Despite these strengths, each of the five tanker freight indices dropped during 2006. Product tanker demand increased in 2006 due to economic expansion in Asia, especially China and India, however, average time charter equivalent earnings for these ships decreased compared with the two prior years.

In 2006, time-charters tended towards long term. Of the time charters executed in that year, 58% were for a period of 24 or more months, 14% were for periods of 12 to 24 months, 4% were from 6 to 12 months, and 24% were for periods of less than 6 months. The average one-year time charter rate for a 5-year-old tanker of 280,000 metric tons of deadweight varied from $56,500 per day in December 2005 to $53,000 per day in September 2007 with a high of $64,500 per day in September 2006.

The first half of 2007 was relatively strong, but in the second half rates dropped significantly. A sudden rise in oil production, longer transport routes, and slow steaming because of high bunker prices led to a shortage in tonnage towards the end of the year. Overnight, VLCC rates climbed from $20,000 per day to $200–$300,000 per day, and even higher numbers were recorded.

From 2003, the demand for new ships started to grow, in 2007 resulting in a record breaking order backlog for shipyards, exceeding their capacity with rising newbuilding prices as a result. This resulted in a glut of ships when demand dropped due to a weakened global economy and dramatically reduced demand in the United States. The charter rate for Very Large Crude Carriers, which carry two million barrels of oil, had peaked at $309,601 per day in 2007, and has dropped, as of 2012, to $7,085 per day, far below the operating costs of these ships. As a result several tanker operators are laying up their ships.

Owners of large oil tanker fleets include Teekay Corporation, A P Moller Maersk, DS Torm, Frontline, MOL Tankship Management, Overseas Shipholding Group, and Euronav.

FLEET CHARACTERISTICS

1. Teekay Corporation
2. Frontline
3. MOL Tankship Management
4. Overseas Shipholding Group
5. Euronav
6. Tanker Pacific Management
7. Kristen Navigation
8. Nippon Yusen Kaisha
9. MISC Berhad
10. Tsakos Group
11. Vela International Marine
12. NITC
13. Hyundai Merchant Marine
14. BW Shipping
15. Dynacom Tankers Management
16. Maersk Tankers
17. BP Shipping
18. Sovcomflot
19. Novorossiysk Shipping Company

20. National Shipping Company of Saudi Arabia
21. Shipping Corporation of India
22. Thenamaris
23. TORM
24. Chevron Shipping
25. COSCO Group
26. Kuwait Oil Tanker Co.
27. Titan Ocean
28. China Shipping Development Tanker
29. SK Shipping
30. Minerva Marine
31. [[E-Shipswww.eships.ae]]

In 2005, oil tankers made up 36.9% of the world's fleet in terms of deadweight tonnage. The world's total oil tankers deadweight tonnage has increased from 326.1 million DWT in 1970 to 960.0 million DWT in 2005. The combined deadweight tonnage of oil tankers and bulk carriers, represents 72.9% of the world's fleet.

CARGO MOVEMENT

In 2005, 2.42 billion metric tons of oil were shipped by tanker. In 2006, 76.7% of this was crude oil, and the rest consisted of refined petroleum products.

This amounted to 34.1% of all seaborne trade for the year. Combining the amount carried with the distance it was carried, oil tankers moved 11,705 billion metric-ton-miles of oil in 2005.

By comparison, in 1970 1.44 billion metric tons of oil were shipped by tanker. This amounted to 34.1% of all seaborne trade for that year. In terms of amount carried and distance carried, oil tankers moved 6,487 billion metric-ton-miles of oil in 1970.

The United Nations also keeps statistics about oil tanker productivity, stated in terms of metric tons carried per metric ton of deadweight as well as metric-ton-miles of carriage per metric ton of deadweight. 2006 In 2005, for each 1 DWT of oil tankers, 6.7 metric tons of cargo was carried. Similarly, each 1 DWT of oil tankers was responsible for 32,400 metric-ton miles of carriage.

The main loading ports in 2005 were located in Western Asia, Western Africa, North Africa, and the Caribbean, with 196.3, 196.3, 130.2 and 246.6 million metric tons of cargo loaded in these regions. The main discharge ports were located in North America, Europe, and Japan with 537.7, 438.4, and 215.0 million metric tons of cargo discharged in these regions..

FLAG STATES

International law requires that every merchant ship be registered in a country, called its flag state. A ship's flag state exercises regulatory control over the vessel and is required to inspect it regularly, certify the ship's equipment and crew, and issue safety and pollution prevention documents. As of 2007, the United States Central Intelligence Agency statistics count 4,295 oil tankers of 1,000 long tons deadweight (DWT) or greater worldwide.Panama was the world's largest flag state for oil tankers, with 528 of the vessels in its registry. Six other flag states had more than 200 registered oil tankers: Liberia (464), Singapore (355), China (252), Russia (250), the Marshall Islands (234) and the Bahamas (209).

The Panamanian, Liberian, Marshallese and Bahamian flags are open registries and considered by the International Transport Workers' Federation to be flags of convenience. By comparison, the United States and the United Kingdom only had 59 and 27 registered oil tankers, respectively.

VESSEL LIFE CYCLE

In 2005, the average age of oil tankers worldwide was 10 years. Of these, 31.6% were under 4 years old and 14.3% were over 20 years old. In 2005, 475 new oil tankers were built, accounting for 30.7 million DWT. The average size for these new tankers was 64,632 DWT. Nineteen of these were VLCC size, 19 were suezmax, 51 were aframax, and the rest were smaller designs. By comparison, 8.0 million DWT, 8.7 million DWT, and 20.8 million DWT worth of oil tanker capacity was built in 1980, 1990, and 2000 respectively.

Ships are generally removed from the fleet through a process known as scrapping. Ship-owners and buyers negotiate scrap prices based on factors such as the ship's empty weight (called light ton displacement or LDT) and prices in the scrap metal market. In 1998 almost 700 ships went through the scrapping process at shipbreakers in places like Alang, India and Chittagong, Bangladesh.

In 2004 and 2005, 7.8 million DWT and 5.7 million DWT respectively of oil tankers were scrapped. Between 2000 and 2005, the capacity of oil tankers scrapped each year has ranged between 5.6 million DWT and 18.4 million DWT. In this same timeframe, tankers have accounted for between 56.5% and 90.5% of the world's total scrapped ship tonnage. In this period the average age of scrapped oil tankers has ranged from 26.9 to 31.5 years.

VESSEL PRICING

Size	1985	2005
32,000–45,000 DWT	US$18M	$43M
80,000–105,000 DWT	$22M	$58M
250,000–280,000 DWT	$47M	$120M

In 2005, the price for new oil tankers in the 32,000–45,000 DWT, 80,000–105,000 DWT, and 250,000–280,000 DWT ranges were US$43 million, $58 million, and $120 million respectively. In 1985 these vessels would have cost $18 million, $22 million, and $47 million respectively.

Oil tankers are often sold second-hand. In 2005, 27.3 million DWT worth of oil tankers were sold used. Some representative prices for that year include $42.5M for a 40,000 DWT tanker, $60.7 million for a 80,000–95,000 DWT, $73 million for a 130,000–150,000 DWT, and $116 million for 250,000–280,000 DWT tanker. For a concrete example, in 2006, Bonheur subsidiary First Olsen paid US$76.5 million for Knock Sheen, a 159,899 DWT tanker.

The cost of operating the largest tankers, the Very Large Crude Carriers, is currently between $10,000 and $12,000 per day.

CURRENT STRUCTURAL DESIGN

Oil tankers generally have from 8 to 12 tanks. Each tank is split into two or three independent compartments by fore-and-aft bulkheads. The tanks are numbered with tank one being the forwardmost. Individual compartments are referred to by the tank number and the athwartships position, such as "one port", "three starboard", or "six center."

A cofferdam is a small space left open between two bulkheads, to give protection from heat, fire, or collision. Tankers generally have cofferdams forward and aft of the cargo tanks, and sometimes between individual tanks. A pumproom houses all the pumps connected to a tanker's cargo lines. Some larger tankers have two pumprooms. A pumproom generally spans the total breadth of the ship.

HULL DESIGNS

A major component of tanker architecture is the design of the hull or outer structure. A tanker with a single outer shell between the product and the ocean is said to be "single-hulled". Most newer tankers are "double hulled", with an extra space between the hull and the storage tanks. Hybrid designs such as "double-bottom" and "double-sided" combine aspects of single and double-hull designs. All single-hulled tankers around the world will be phased out by 2026, in accordance with the International Convention for the Prevention of Pollution from Ships, 1973 (MARPOL). The United Nations has decided to phase out single hull oil tankers by 2010.

In 1998, the Marine Board of the National Academy of Science conducted a survey of industry experts regarding the pros and cons of double-hull design. Some of the advantages of the double-hull design that were mentioned include ease of ballasting in emergency situations, reduced practice of saltwater ballasting in cargo tanks decreases corrosion, increased environmental protection, cargo discharge is quicker, more complete and easier, tank washing is more efficient, and better protection in low-impact collisions and grounding.

The same report lists the following as some drawbacks to the double-hull design, including higher build costs, greater operating expenses (e.g. higher canal and port tariffs), difficulties in ballast tank ventilation, the fact that ballast tanks need continuous monitoring and maintenance, increased transverse free surface, the greater number of surfaces to maintain, the risk of explosions in double-hull spaces if a vapor detection system not fitted, and that cleaning ballast tanks is more difficult for double hull ships.

In all, double-hull tankers are said to be safer than a single-hull in a grounding incident, especially when the shore is not very rocky. The safety benefits are less clear on larger vessels and in cases of high speed impact.

Although double-hull design is superior in low energy casualties and prevents spillage in small casualties, in high energy casualties where both hulls are breached, oil can spill through the double-hull and into the sea and spills from a double-hull tanker can be significantly higher than designs like the Mid-Deck Tanker, the Coulombi Egg Tanker and even a pre-MARPOL tanker, as the last one has a lower oil column and reaches hydrostatic balance sooner.

In addition to improvements in safety and structural integrity, various improvements have been made to the interior equipment of modern tankers. Galley appliances, for example, have been upgraded for higher efficiency. In demonstrations for the Happy Seas tanker series commissioned by Wang-Huong Industries, designer/chef Joe Unpingco showcased the impressive capacities of a modern galley by preparing 100 fruitcakes in just 20 minutes using the new state-of-the-art appliances, while consuming 28% less energy compared to galleys of earlier vessels.

INERT GAS SYSTEM

An oil tanker's inert gas system is one of the most important parts of its design. Fuel oil itself is very difficult to ignite, but its hydrocarbon vapors are explosive when mixed with air in certain concentrations. The purpose of the system is to create an atmosphere inside tanks in which the hydrocarbon oil vapors cannot burn.

As inert gas is introduced into a mixture of hydrocarbon vapors and air, it increases the lower flammable limit or lowest concentration at which the vapors can be ignited. At the same time it decreases the upper flammable limit or highest concentration at which the vapors can be ignited. When the total concentration of oxygen in the tank reaches about 11%, the upper and lower flammable limits converge and the flammable range disappears.

Inert gas systems deliver air with an oxygen concentration of less than 5% by volume. As a tank is pumped out, it's filled with inert gas and kept in this safe state until the next cargo is loaded. The exception is in cases when the tank must be entered. Safely gas-freeing a tank is accomplished by purging hydrocarbon vapors with inert gas until the hydrocarbon concentration inside the tank is under about 1%. Thus, as air replaces the inert gas, the concentration cannot rise to the lower flammable limit and is safe.

CARGO OPERATIONS

Operations aboard oil tankers are governed by an established body of best practices and a large body of international law. Cargo can be moved on or off of an oil tanker in several ways. One method is for the ship to moor alongside a pier, connect with cargo hoses or marine loading arms. Another method involves mooring to offshore buoys, such as a single point mooring, and making a cargo connection via underwater cargo hoses. A third method is by ship-to-ship transfer, also known as lightering. In this method, two ships come alongside in open sea and oil is transferred manifold to manifold via flexible hoses. Lightering is sometimes used where a loaded tanker is too large to enter a specific port.

Pre-transfer preparation

Prior to any transfer of cargo, the chief officer must develop a transfer plan detailing specifics of the operation such as how much cargo will be moved, which tanks will be cleaned, and how the ship's ballasting will change. The next step before a transfer is the pretransfer conference. The pretransfer conference covers issues such as what products will be moved, the order of movement, names and titles of key people, particulars of shipboard and shore equipment, critical states of the transfer, regulations in effect, emergency and spill-containment procedures, watch and shift arrangements, and shutdown procedures.

After the conference is complete, the person in charge on the ship and the person in charge of the shore installation go over a final inspection checklist. In the United States, the checklist is called a Declaration of Inspection or DOI. Outside of the U.S., the document is called the "Ship/Shore Safety Checklist." Items on the checklist include proper signals and signs are displayed, secure mooring of the vessel, choice of language for communication, securing of all connections, that emergency equipment is in place, and that no repair work is taking place.

Loading cargo

Loading an oil tanker consists primarily of pumping cargo into the ship's tanks. As oil enters the tank, the vapors inside the tank must be somehow expelled. Depending on local regulations, the vapors can be expelled into the atmosphere or discharged back to the pumping station by way of a vapor recovery line. It is also common for the ship to move water ballast during the loading of cargo to maintain proper trim.

Loading starts slowly at a low pressure to ensure that equipment is working correctly and that connections are secure. Then a steady pressure is achieved and held until the "topping-off" phase when the tanks are nearly full. Topping off is a very dangerous time in handling oil, and the procedure is handled particularly carefully. Tank-gauging equipment is used to tell the person in charge how much space is left in the tank, and all tankers have at least two independent methods for tank-gauging. As the tanker becomes full, crew members open and close valves to direct the flow of product and maintain close communication with the pumping facility to decrease and finally stop the flow of liquid.

Unloading cargo

The process of moving oil off of a tanker is similar to loading, but has some key differences. The first step in the operation is following the same pretransfer procedures as used in loading. When the transfer begins, it is the ship's cargo pumps that are used to move the product ashore. As in loading, the transfer starts at low pressure to ensure that equipment is working correctly and that connections are secure.

Then a steady pressure is achieved and held during the operation. While pumping, tank levels are carefully watched and key locations, such as the connection at the cargo manifold and the ship's pumproom are constantly monitored. Under the direction of the person in charge, crew members open and close valves to direct the flow of product and maintain close communication with the receiving facility to decrease and finally stop the flow of liquid.

Tank cleaning

Tanks must be cleaned from time to time for various reasons. One reason is to change the type of product carried inside a tank. Also, when tanks are to be inspected or maintenance must be performed within a tank, it must be not only cleaned, but made gas-free.

On most crude-oil tankers, a special crude oil washing (COW) system is part of the cleaning process. The COW system circulates part of the cargo through the fixed tank-cleaning system to remove wax and asphaltic deposits. Tanks that carry less viscous cargoes are washed with water. Fixed and portable automated tank cleaning machines, which clean tanks with high-pressure water jets, are widely used. Some systems use rotating high-pressure water jets to spray hot water on all the internal surfaces of the tank. As the spraying takes place, the liquid is pumped out of the tank.

After a tank is cleaned, provided that it is going to be prepared for entry, it will be purged. Purging is accomplished by pumping inert gas into the tank until hydrocarbons have been sufficiently expelled. Next the tank is gas freed which is usually accomplished by blowing fresh air into the space with portable air powered or water powered air blowers. "Gas freeing" brings the oxygen content of the tank up to 20.8% O2. The inert gas buffer between fuel and oxygen atmospheres ensures they are never capable of ignition. Specially trained personnel monitor the tank's atmosphere, often using hand-held gas indicators which measure the percentage of hydrocarbons present. After a tank is gas-free, it may be further hand-cleaned in a manual process known as mucking. Mucking requires protocols for entry into confined spaces, protective clothing, designated safety observers, and possibly the use of airline respirators.

SPECIAL-USE OIL TANKERS

Some sub-types of oil tankers have evolved to meet specific military and economic needs. These sub-types include naval replenishment ships, oil-bulk-ore combination carriers, floating storage and offloading units (FSOs) and floating production storage and offloading units (FPSOs).

Replenishment ships

Replenishment ships, known as oilers in the United States and fleet tankers in Commonwealth countries, are ships that can provide oil products to naval vessels while on the move. This process, called underway replenishment, extends the length of time a naval vessel can stay at sea, as well as her effective range. Prior to underway replenishment, naval vessels had to enter a port or anchor to take on fuel. In addition to fuel, replenishment ships may also deliver water, ammunition, rations, stores and personnel.

Ore-bulk-oil carriers

An ore-bulk-oil carrier, also known as combination carrier or OBO, is a ship designed to be capable of carrying wet or dry bulk cargoes. This design was intended to provide flexibility in two ways. Firstly, an OBO would be able to switch between the dry and wet bulk trades based on market conditions. Secondly, an OBO could carry oil on one leg of a voyage and return carrying dry bulk, reducing the number of unprofitable ballast voyages it would have to make.

In practice, the flexibility which the OBO design allows has gone largely unused, as these ships tend to specialize in either the liquid or dry bulk trade. Also, these ships have endemic maintenance problems. On one hand, due to a less specialized design, an OBO suffers more from wear and tear during dry cargo onload than a bulker. On the other hand, components of the liquid cargo system, from pumps to valves to piping, tend to develop problems when subjected to periods of disuse. These factors have contributed to a steady reduction in the number of OBO ships worldwide since the 1970s.

One of the more famous OBOs was the MV Derbyshire of 180,000 DWT which in September 1980 became the largest British ship ever lost at sea. It sank in a Pacific typhoon while carrying a cargo of iron ore from Canada to Japan.

Floating storage units

Floating storage and offloading units (FSO) are used worldwide by the offshore oil industry to receive oil from nearby platforms and store it until it can be offloaded onto oil tankers. A similar system, the floating production storage and offloading unit (FPSO), has the ability to process the product while it is on board. These floating units reduce oil production costs and offer mobility, large storage capacity, and production versatility.

FPSO and FSOs are often created out of old, stripped-down oil tankers, but can be made from new-built hullsShell España first used a tanker as an FPSO in August 1977. An example of a FSO that used to be an oil tanker is the Knock Nevis. These units are usually moored to the seabed through a spread mooring system. A turret-style mooring system can be used in areas prone to severe weather. This turret system lets the unit rotate to minimize the effects of sea-swell and wind.

POLLUTION

Oil spills have devastating effects on the environment. Crude oil contains polycyclic aromatic hydrocarbons (PAHs) which are very difficult to clean up, and last for years in the sediment and marine environment. Marine species constantly exposed to PAHs can exhibit developmental problems, susceptibility to disease, and abnormal reproductive cycles.

By the sheer amount of oil carried, modern oil tankers must be considered a threat to the environment. As discussed above, a VLCC tanker can carry 2 million barrels (320,000 m) of crude oil. This is about eight times the amount spilled in the widely known Exxon Valdez incident. In this spill, the ship ran aground and dumped 10,800,000 US gallons (41,000 m) of oil into the ocean in March 1989. Despite efforts of scientists, managers, and volunteers over 400,000 seabirds, about 1,000 sea otters, and immense numbers of fish were killed. Considering the volume of oil carried by sea, however, tanker owners' organisations often argue that the industry's safety record is excellent, with only a tiny fraction of a percentage of oil cargoes carried ever being spilled. The International Association of Independent Tanker Owners has observed that "accidental oil spills this decade have been at record low levels—one third of the previous decade and one tenth of the 1970s—at a time when oil transported has more than doubled since the mid 1980s."

Oil tankers are only one source of oil spills. According to the United States Coast Guard, 35.7% of the volume of oil spilled in the United States from 1991 to 2004 came from tank vessels (ships/barges), 27.6% from facilities and other non-vessels, 19.9% from non-tank vessels, and 9.3% from pipelines; 7.4% from mystery spills. On the other hand, only 5% of the actual spills came from oil tankers, while 51.8% came from other kinds of vessels. The detailed statistics for 2004 shown in the table below show tank vessels responsible for somewhat less than 5% of the number of total spills but more than 60% of the volume. In summary, spills are much more rare but much more serious on tank vessels than on non-tank vessels.

The International Tanker Owners Pollution Federation has tracked 9,351 accidental spills that have occurred since 1974. According to this study, most spills result from routine operations such as loading cargo, discharging cargo, and taking on fuel oil. 91% of the operational oil spills are small, resulting in less than 7 metric tons per spill. On the other hand, spills resulting from accidents like collisions, groundings, hull failures, and explosions are much larger, with 84% of these involving losses of over 700 metric tons.

Following the Exxon Valdez spill, the United States passed the Oil Pollution Act of 1990 (OPA-90), which excluded single-hull tank vessels of 5,000 gross tons or more from U.S. waters from 2010 onward, apart from those with a double bottom or double sides, which may be permitted to trade to the United States through 2015, depending on their age. Following the sinkings of the Erika (1999) and Prestige (2002), the European Union passed its own stringent anti-pollution packages (known as Erika I, II, and III), which also require all tankers entering its waters to be double-hulled by 2010. The Erika packages are controversial because they introduced the new legal concept of "serious negligence".

AIR POLLUTION

Air pollution from normal tanker engines operation and from cargo fires is another serious concern. Large ships are often run on low quality fuel oils, such as bunker oil which are highly polluting and have been shown to be a health risk. Ship fires may not only result in the loss of the ship due to lack of specialized firefighting gear and techniques but the fires sometimes burn for days and require evacuations of nearby residents due to the dangerous smoke.

4

Passenger Ship

A passenger ship is a merchant ship whose primary function is to carry passengers. The category does not include cargo vessels which have accommodations for limited numbers of passengers, such as the ubiquitous twelve-passenger freighters once common on the seas in which the transport of passengers is secondary to the carriage of freight. The type does however include many classes of ships designed to transport substantial numbers of passengers as well as freight.

Indeed, until recently virtually all ocean liners were able to transport mail, package freight and express, and other cargo in addition to passenger luggage, and were equipped with cargo holds and derricks, kingposts, or other cargo-handling gear for that purpose. Only in more recent ocean liners and in virtually all cruise ships has this cargo capacity been eliminated.

While typically passenger ships are part of the merchant marine, passenger ships have also been used as troopships and often are commissioned as naval ships when used as for that purpose.

TYPES

Passenger ships include ferries, which are vessels for day or overnight short-sea trips moving passengers and vehicles (whether road or rail); ocean liners, which typically are passenger or passenger-cargo vessels transporting passengers and often cargo on longer line voyages; and cruise ships, which often transport passengers on round-trips, in which the trip itself and the attractions of the ship and ports visited are the principal draw.

An ocean liner is the traditional form of passenger ship. Once such liners operated on scheduled line voyages to all inhabited parts of the world. With the advent of airliners transporting passengers and specialized cargo vessels hauling freight, line voyages have almost died out. But with their decline came an increase in sea trips for pleasure, and in the latter part of the 20th century ocean liners gave way to cruise ships as the predominant form of large passenger ship, with the main area of activity changing from the North Atlantic Ocean to the Caribbean Sea.

Although some ships have characteristics of both types, the design priorities of the two forms are different: ocean liners value speed and traditional luxury while cruise ships value amenities (swimming pools, theaters, ball rooms, casinos, sports facilities, etc.) rather than speed. These priorities produce different designs. In addition, ocean liners typically were built to cross the Atlantic Ocean between Europe and the United States or travel even further to South America or Asia while cruise ships typically serve shorter routes with more stops along coastlines or among various islands.

For a long time, cruise ships were smaller than the old ocean liners had been, but in the 1980s, this changed when Knut Kloster, the director of Norwegian Caribbean Lines, bought one of the biggest surviving liners, the SS France, and transformed her into a huge cruise ship, which he renamed the SS Norway. Her success demonstrated that there was a market for large cruise ships. Successive classes of ever-larger ships were ordered, until the Cunard liner Queen Elizabeth was finally dethroned from her 56-year reign as the largest passenger ship ever built (a dethronement that led to numerous further dethronements from the same position).

Both the RMSQueen Elizabeth 2 (QE2) (1969) and her successor as Cunard's flagship RMS Queen Mary 2 (QM2), which entered service in 2004, are of hybrid construction. Like transatlantic ocean liners, they are fast ships and strongly built to withstand the rigors of the North Atlantic in line voyage service, but both ships are also designed to operate as cruise ships, with the amenities expected in that trade.

QM2 was superseded by the Freedom of the Seas of the Royal Caribbean line as the largest passenger ship ever built; however, QM2 still hold the record for the largest ocean liner. The Freedom of the Seas was superseded by the Oasis of the Seas in October 2009.

MEASURES OF SIZE

By convention and long usage, the size of civilian passenger ships is measured by gross tonnage, which is a dimensionless figure calculated from the total enclosed volume of the vessel. Gross tonnage is not a measure of weight, although the two concepts are often confused. Weight is measured by displacement, which is the conventional means of measuring naval vessels. Often a passenger ship is stated to "weigh" or "displace" a certain "tonnage", but the figure given nearly always refers to gross tonnage, which in this context has nothing to do with weight.

While a high displacement can indicate better sea keeping abilities, gross tonnage is promoted as the most important measure of size for passengers, as the ratio of gross tonnage per passenger – the Passenger/Space Ratio – gives a sense of the spaciousness of a ship, an important consideration in cruise liners where the onboard amenities are of high importance.

Gross tonnage normally is a much higher value than displacement. This was not always the case; as the functions, engineering and architecture of ships have changed, the gross tonnage figures of the largest passenger ships have risen substantially, while the displacements of such ships have not. RMS Titanic, with a gross register tonnage of 46,329 GRT, but a displacement reported at over 52,000 tons, was heavier than contemporary 100,000 – 110,000 GT cruise ships which displace only around 50,000 tons. Similarly, the Cunard Line's RMS Queen Mary and RMS Queen Elizabeth, of approximately 81,000 – 83,000 GT, but displacements of over 80,000 tons, do not differ significantly in displacement from their new 148,528 GT successor, RMS Queen Mary 2, which has been estimated to displace approximately 76,000 tons With the completion in 2009 of Oasis of the Seas, the first of the Oasis Class ships, the Cunard Queens of the 1930s have clearly been passed in displacement, as the Oasis vessels were projected to displace about 100,000 tons.

However, by the conventional and historical measure of gross tonnage, there has been a recent dramatic increase in the size of the largest new ships. The Oasis of the Seas measures over 225,000 GT, over twice as large as the largest cruise ships of the late 1990s.

SAFETY REGULATIONS

Passenger ships are subject to two major International Maritime Organization requirements: to perform musters of the passengers (...) within 24 hours after their embarkation and to be able to perform full abandonment within a period of 30 minutes from the time the abandon-ship signal is given.

DESIGN CONSIDERATIONS

Passengers on ships without backup generators suffer substantial distress due to lack of water, refrigeration, and sewage systems in the event of loss of the main engines or generators due to fire or other emergency. Power is also unavailable to the crew of the ship to operate electrically powered mechanisms. Lack of an adequate backup system to propel the ship can, in rough seas, render it dead in the water and result in loss of the ship. The 2006 Revised Passenger Ship Safety Standards address these issues, and others, requiring that ships ordered after July, 2010 conform to safe return to port regulations; however, as of 2013 many ships remain in service which lack this capacity.

After October 1, 2010, the International Convention for the Safety of Life at Sea (SOLAS) requires passenger ships operating in international waters must either be constructed or upgraded to exclude combustible materials. It is believed some owners and operators of ships built before 1980, which are required to upgrade or retire their vessels, will be unable to conform to the regulations.Fred Olsen's Black Prince, built in 1966 was one such ship, but was reported to be headed for inter-island service in Venezuelan waters.

CARGO LINER

A cargo liner is a type of merchant ship which carries general cargo and often passengers. They became common just after the middle of the 19th century, and eventually gave way to container ships and other more specialized carriers in the latter half of the 20th century.

CHARACTERISTICS

A cargo liner has been defined as:

- A vessel which operated a regular scheduled service on a fixed route between designated ports and carries many consignments of different commodities.

Cargo liners transported general freight, from raw materials to manufacturers to merchandise. Many had cargo holds adapted to particular services, with refrigerator space for frozen meats or chilled fruit, tanks for liquid cargos such as plant oils, and lockers for valuables. Cargo liners typically carried passengers as well, usually in a single class. They differed from ocean liners which focussed on the passenger trade, and from tramp steamers which did not operate on regular schedules. Cargo liners sailed from port to port along routes and on schedules published in advance.

HISTORY

The cargo liner developed in the mid-19th century with the advancement of technology allowing bigger steamships to be built. As cargo liners were generally faster than cargo ships, they were used for the transport of perishable and high-value goods, as well as providing a passenger service. At first, they were used in Europe and between Europe and America. Longer routes, such as that to Australia, remained in the hands of sailing ships, due to the inefficiency of the steamship of the time.

The use and increased reliability of the compound steam engine gave greater fuel efficiency and opened these routes up to steamships. Alfred Holt pioneered the use of these engines in his steamships. It was now possible for a steamship to carry enough coal to travel 6,000 miles (9,700 km) before needing to refuel. The opening of the Suez Canal in 1869 and the Panama Canal in 1914 also made the use of cargo liners more profitable, and made possible regular scheduled overseas services. Cargo liners soon comprised "the great portion of the British merchant fleet", the largest in the world.

The decline of the cargo liner came in the 1970s with the introduction of container ships. However, some cargo liners are still in service, such as the RMS St Helena.

CRUISE SHIP

A cruise ship or cruise liner is a passenger ship used for pleasure voyages, where the voyage itself and the ship's amenities are a part of the experience, as well as the different destinations along the way. Transportation is not the prime purpose, as cruise ships operate mostly on routes that return passengers to their originating port, so the ports of call are usually in a specified region of a continent. There are even "cruises to nowhere" or "nowhere voyages" where the ship makes 2-3 day round trips without any ports of call.

By contrast, dedicated transport oriented ocean liners do "line voyages" and typically transport passengers from one point to another, rather than on round trips. Traditionally, an ocean liner for the transoceanic trade will be built to a higher standard than a typical cruise ship, including high freeboard and stronger plating to withstand rough seas and adverse conditions encountered in the open ocean, such as the North Atlantic. Ocean liners also usually have larger capacities for fuel, victuals, and other stores for consumption on long voyages, compared to dedicated cruise ships.

Although often luxurious, ocean liners had characteristics that made them unsuitable for cruising, such as high fuel consumption, deep draught that prevented them from entering shallow ports, enclosed weatherproof decks that were not appropriate for tropical weather, and cabins designed to maximize passenger numbers rather than comfort (such as a high proportion of windowless suites). The gradual evolution of passenger ship design from ocean liners to cruise ships has seen passenger cabins shifted from inside the hull to the superstructure with private verandas. The modern cruise ships, while sacrificing qualities of seaworthiness, have added amenities to cater to water tourists, and recent vessels have been described as "balcony-laden floating condominiums".

The lines between ocean liners and cruise ships have blurred, particularly with respect to deployment, although the differences in construction remain. Larger cruise ships have also engaged in longer trips such as transocean voyages which may not lead back to the same port for months (longer round trips). Some former ocean liners operate as cruise ships, such as Marco Polo and Mona Lisa. This number is diminishing. The only dedicated transatlantic ocean liner in operation as a liner, as of February 2010, is the Queen Mary 2 of the Cunard fleet. She also has the amenities of contemporary cruise ships and sees significant service on cruises.

Cruising has become a major part of the tourism industry, accounting for U.S.$29.4 billion with over 19 million passengers carried worldwide in 2011. The industry's rapid growth has seen nine or more newly built ships catering to a North American clientele added every year since 2001, as well as others servicing European clientele. Smaller markets, such as the Asia-Pacific region, are generally serviced by older ships. These are displaced by new ships in the high growth areas.

The world's largest cruise ships are Royal Caribbean International's Oasis of the Seas and its sister ship Allure of the Seas.

HISTORY

Early years

The cruise of the Augusta Victoria in the Mediterranean and the Near East from 22 January to 22 March 1891, with 241 passengers including Albert Ballin and wife, is often stated to have been the first ever cruise.Christian Wilhelm Allers published an illustrated account of it as Backschisch (Baksheesh).

Other sources mention the "Francesco I", flying the flag of the Kingdom of the Two Sicilies (Italy), as the first cruise ship. It was built in 1831 and sailed from Naples in early June 1833, preceded by an advertising campaign similar to the current ones. The cruise ship was boarded by nobles, authorities, and royal princes from all over Europe.In just over three months, the ship sailed to Taormina, Catania, Syracuse, Malta, Corfu, Patras, Delphi, Zante, Athens, Smyrna, Constantinople. They offered passengers excursions and guided tours, dancing, card tables on the deck and parties on board.

In 1896, there were three luxury liners for transportation, for the Europe to America trip. These were European-owned. In 1906, the number had increased to seven. The British Inman Line owned the City of Paris, the Cunard Line had the Compania and Lucania. The White Star Line owned the Majestic and Teutonic. La Lorraine and La Savoie were owned by the French Compagnie Générale Transatlantique.

The first vessel built exclusively for this purpose was the Prinzessin Victoria Luise of Germany, designed by Albert Ballin, general manager of Hamburg-America Line. The ship was completed in 1900.

The practice of cruising grew gradually out of the tradition of transatlantic crossings, which never took fewer than four days. In the competition for passengers, ocean liners added luxuries—the Titanic being the most famous example—such as fine dining, luxury services, and staterooms with finer appointments.

In the late 19th century, Albert Ballin, director of the Hamburg-America Line, was the first to send his transatlantic ships out on long southern cruises during the worst of the winter season of the North Atlantic. Other companies followed suit. Some of them built specialized ships designed for easy transformation between summer crossings and winter cruising.

Jet age impact on Cruising

With the advent of large passenger jet aircraft in the 1960s, intercontinental travelers largely switched from ships to planes, sending the ocean liner trade into a slow decline. Certain characteristics of older ocean liners made them unsuitable for cruising duties, such as high fuel consumption, deep draught preventing them from entering shallow ports, and cabins (often windowless) designed to maximize passenger numbers rather than comfort. Ocean liner services aimed at passengers ceased in 1986, with the notable exception of transatlantic crossings operated by the Cunard Line, catering to the niche market who appreciated the several days at sea.

In comparison to liner crossings, cruising voyages gained popularity; slowly at first but at an increased rate from the 1980s onwards. Initially the fledgling industry was serviced primarily by small redundant liners, and even the first purpose built cruise ships were small. This changed after the success of the SS Norway (originally the ocean liner SS France, which was converted to cruising duties) as the Caribbean's first "super-ship".

Contemporary cruise ships built in the late 1980s and beyond, such as Sovereign-class which broke the size record held for decades by Norway, show characteristics of size and strength once reserved for ocean liners—some have undertaken regular scheduled transatlantic crossings. The Sovereigns were the first modern "megaships" to be built, they also were the first series of cruise ships to include a multi-story atrium with glass elevators. They also had a single deck devoted entirely to cabins with private balconies instead of oceanview cabins. Other cruise lines soon launched ships with similar attributes, such as the Fantasy class and Crown Princess. As the veranda suites were particularly lucrative for cruise lines, something which was lacking in older ocean liners, recent cruise ships have been designed to maximize such amenities and have been described as "balcony-laden floating condominiums".

Until 1975-1980, cruises offered shuffleboard, deck chairs, "drinks with umbrellas and little else for a few hundred passengers." After 1980, they offered increasing amenities. As of 2010, city-sized ships have dozens of amenities.

21st century

There have been nine or more new cruise ships added every year since 2001, all at 100,000 GT or greater. The only comparable ocean liner to be completed in recent years has been Cunard Line's Queen Mary 2 in 2004. Following the retirement of her running mate the Queen Elizabeth 2 in November 2008, Queen Mary 2 is the only liner operating on transatlantic routes, though she also sees significant service on cruise routes.

Queen Mary 2 was for a time the largest passenger ship before being surpassed by Royal Caribbean International's Freedom-class vessels in 2006. The Freedoms were in turn overtaken by RCI's Oasis-class vessels which entered service in 2009 and 2010.

Royal Caribbean International has just announced the new Quantum-class cruise ships.

OPERATORS AND CRUISE LINES

Operators of cruise ships are known as cruise lines. Cruise lines have a dual character; they are partly in the transportation business, and partly in the leisure entertainment business, a duality that carries down into the ships themselves, which have both a crew headed by the ship's captain, and a hospitality staff headed by the equivalent of a hotel manager. Among cruise lines, some are direct descendants of the traditional passenger shipping lines (such as Cunard), while others were founded from the 1960s specifically for cruising.

Historically, the cruise ship business has been volatile. The ships are large capital investments with high operating costs. A persistent decrease in bookings can put a company in financial jeopardy. Cruise lines have sold, renovated, or renamed their ships to keep up with travel trends. The cruise lines operate their ships virtually 24 hours a day, seven days a week, 52 weeks a year. A ship which is out of service routine maintenance means the loss of tens of millions of dollars. If the maintenance is unscheduled, it can result, potentially, in thousands of dissatisfied customers.

A wave of failures and consolidation in the 1990s has led to many lines existing only as "brands" within larger corporations, much as a single automobile company produces several makes of cars. Brands exist partly because of repeat customer loyalty, and also to offer different levels of quality and service. For instance, Carnival Corporation owns both Carnival Cruise Lines, whose former image were vessels that had a reputation as "party ships" for younger travelers, but have become large, modern, and extremely elegant, yet still profitable, and Holland America Line, whose ships cultivate an image of classic elegance. In 2004, Carnival Corporation had merged Cunard's headquarters with that of Princess Cruises in Santa Clarita, California so that administrative, financial and technology services could be combined, ending Cunard's history where it had operated as a standalone company (subsidiary) regardless of parent ownership. However, Cunard did regain some independence in 2009 when its headquarters were moved to Carnival House in Southampton.

Some cruise lines have specialties; for example, Saga Cruises only allows passengers over 50 years old aboard their ships, and Star Clippers and formerly Windjammer Barefoot Cruises and Windstar Cruises only operate tall ships. Regent Seven Seas Cruises operates medium-sized vessels—smaller than the "megaships" of Carnival and Royal Caribbean—designed such that 90% of their suites are balconies. Several specialty lines offer "expedition cruising" or only operate small ships, visiting certain destinations such as the Arctic and Antarctica, or the Galápagos Islands.

Currently the five largest cruise line operators in the world are Carnival Corporation & plc, Royal Caribbean Cruises Ltd., Star Cruises (which owns 50% of Norwegian Cruise Line, NCL in its own right is the third largest line), MSC Cruises, and Louis Cruise Lines. Louis Cruises has largerly grown its fleet through purchasing older second- or third-hand ships, while the other four operators have largely constructed their own vessels and combined own the majority of the "megaships".

ORGANIZATION

Cruise ships are organized much like floating hotels, with a complete hospitality staff in addition to the usual ship's crew. It is not uncommon for the most luxurious ships to have more crew and staff than passengers.

Dining

Dining on almost all cruise ships is included in the cruise price, except on no-frills lines such as EasyCruise.

Traditionally, the ships' restaurants organize two dinner services per day, early dining and late dining, and passengers are allocated a set dining time for the entire cruise; a recent trend is to allow diners to dine whenever they want. Having two dinner times allows the ship to have enough time and space to accommodate all of their guests. Having two different dinner services can cause some conflicts with some of the ship's events (such as shows and performances) for the late diners this but problem is usually fixed by having the event take place before late dinner but it however is a shorter version of the performance/show.

Cunard Line ships maintain the class tradition of ocean liners and have separate dining rooms for different types of suites, while Celebrity Cruises and Princess Cruises have a standard dining room and "upgrade" specialty restaurants that require pre-booking and cover charges. Many cruises schedule one or more "formal dining" nights. Guests dress "formally", however that is defined for the ship, often suits and ties or even tuxedos for men, and formal dresses for women. The menu is more upscale than usual.

Besides the dining room, modern cruise ships often contain one or more casual buffet-style eateries, which may be open 24 hours and with menus that vary throughout the day to provide meals ranging from breakfast to late-night snacks. Ships also feature numerous bars and nightclubs for passenger entertainment; the majority of cruise lines do not include alcoholic beverages in their fares and passengers are expected to pay for drinks as they consume them. Most cruise lines also prohibit passengers from bringing aboard and consuming their own beverages, including alcohol while aboard. Alcohol purchased duty-free is sealed and returned to passengers when they debark.

There is often a central galley responsible for serving all major restaurants aboard the ship, though specialty restaurants may have their own separate galleys.

As with any vessel, adequate provisioning is crucial, especially on a cruise ship serving several thousand meals at each seating. For example, passengers and crew on the Royal Caribbean International ship Mariner of the Seas consume 20,000 pounds (9,000 kg) of beef, 28,000 eggs, 30,000 L of ice cream, and 18,000 slices of pizza in a week. Normally, a cruise ship stocks up at its home port. They also have special arrangements with designated suppliers at ports of call if required.

Other on-board facilities

Most modern cruise ships feature the following facilities:

- Casino – Only open when the ship is at sea to avoid conflict with local laws
- Spa
- Fitness center
- Shops – Only open when ship is at sea to avoid merchandising licensing and local taxes
- Library
- Theatre with Broadway style shows
- Cinema
- Indoor and/or outdoor swimming pool with water slides
- Hot tub
- Buffet restaurant
- Lounges
- Gym
- Clubs
- shuffel board
- basketball courts
- pool tables
- ping pong tables

Some ships have bowling alleys, ice skating rinks, rock climbing walls, miniature golf courses, video arcades, ziplines, surfing simulators, basketball courts, tennis courts, chain restaurants and/or ropes obstacle courses.

Crew

Crew is usually hired on three to eleven month contracts which may then be renewed as mutually agreed, which is based upon service ratings from passengers as well as the cyclical nature of the cruise line operator. Most staff work 77 hour work weeks for 10 months continuously followed by 2 months of vacation.

There are no paid vacations or pensions for service, non-management crew, depending on the level of the position and the type of the contract. Non-service and management crew members get paid vacation, medical, retirement options, and can participate in the company's group insurance plan.

The direct salary is low for North American standards, though restaurant staff have considerable earning potential from passenger tips. Crew members do not have any expenses while on board as food and accommodation, and transportation for most employees, are included. This makes a cruise ship career financially attractive enough to compensate for lack of employment benefits.

Living arrangements vary by cruise line, but mostly by shipboard position. In general two employees share a cabin with a shower, commode and a desk with a television set, while senior officers are assigned single cabins. There are a set of facilities for the crew separate from that of passengers, such as mess rooms and bars, recreation rooms, prayer rooms/mosques, and fitness center, with some larger ships even having a crew deck with a swimming pool and hot tubs.

For the largest cruise operators, most "hotel staff" are hired from under-industrialized countries in Asia, Eastern Europe, the Caribbean, and Central America. While several cruise lines are headquartered in the United States, the ships are registered in countries such as Bahamas, Panama, and Liberia, a practice known as "flags of convenience" to take advantage of less-stringent labour regulations.

Collective action is difficult due to staff being from diverse cultural and ethnic backgrounds. The exception to this are the cruise routes around Hawaii, where operators are required to register their ships in the United States and the crew is unionized, so these cruises are typically much more expensive than Caribbean and Mediterranean.

BUSINESS MODEL

The "luxury cruise lines" such as Regent Seven Seas Cruises and Crystal Cruises provide "the most all-inclusive" cruises. Base fare on Regent Seven Seas ships includes most alcoholic beverages onboard ship and most shore excursions in ports of call, as well as all gratuities that would normally be paid to hotel staff on the ship.

Fare also includes one night's hotel stay before boarding and airfare to and from the cruise's origin and destination ports. Most cruise lines since the 2000s have priced the cruising experience, to some extent, a la carte, as passengers spending aboard generates significantly more from ticket sales. The passenger's ticket includes the stateroom accommodation, room service, unlimited meals in the main dining room and buffet, access to shows, and use of pool and gym facilities.

However, there are extra charges for alcohol and soft drinks, official cruise photos, Internet and wi-fi access, and specialty restaurants; it has been reported that the casino and photos have high profit margins. Cruise lines earn significantly from selling onshore excursions (keeping 50 percent or more of what passengers spend for these tours) offered by local contractors. In addition, cruise ships earn significant commissions for sales from onshore stores that are promoted on board as "preferred" (as much as 40 percent of gross sales). Facilitating this practice are modern cruise terminals with establishments of duty-free shops inside a perimeter accessible only by passengers and not locals.

Travel to and from the port of departure are the passengers' responsibility, although purchasing a transfer pass from the cruise line for the trip between the airport and cruise terminal will guarantee that the ship will not leave until the passenger is aboard. Similarly, if the passenger books a shore excursion with the cruise line and the tour runs late, the ship is obligated to remain until the passenger returns.

SHIP NAMING

Older cruise ships have had multiple owners. Since each cruise line has its own livery and often a naming theme (for instance, ships of the Holland America Line have names ending in "-dam", e.g. Statendam, and Royal Caribbean's ships' names all end with "of the Seas", e.g. Freedom of the Seas, ships of Cunard Line have the title of "Queen", e.g. RMS Queen Mary 2) P&O Cruises Australia Have the title "Pacific" e.g. Pacific Jewel), it is usual for the transfer of ownership to entail a refitting and a name change. Some ships have had a dozen or more identities.

CRUISE SHIPS UTILIZATION

Due to slower speed and reduced seaworthiness, as well as being largely introduced after several major wars, cruise ships have never been used as troop transport vessels. By contrast, ocean liners were often seen as the pride of their country and used to rival liners of other nations, and have been requisitioned during both World Wars to transport soldiers and serve as hospital ships.

Cruise ships and former liners often find employment in applications other than those for which they were built. A shortage of hotel accommodation for the 2004 Summer Olympics led to a plan to moor a number of cruise ships in Athens to provide tourist accommodation.

On September 1, 2005, the U.S. Federal Emergency Management Agency (FEMA) contracted three Carnival Cruise Lines vessels (Carnival Fantasy, the former Carnival Holiday, and the Carnival Sensation to house Hurricane Katrina evacuees.

In 2010, in response to the shutdown of UK airspace due to the eruption of Iceland's Eyjafjallajökull volcano, the newly completed Celebrity Eclipse was used to rescue 2000 British tourists stranded in Spain as an act of goodwill by the owners.

The ship departed from Southampton for Bilbao on April 21, and returned on April 23.

REGIONAL INDUSTRIES

Most cruise ships sail the Caribbean or the Mediterranean. Others operate elsewhere in places like Alaska, the South Pacific, the Baltic Sea and New England. A cruise ship that is moving from one of these regions to another will commonly operate a repositioning cruise while doing so. Expedition cruise lines, which usually operate small ships, visit certain more specialized destinations such as the Arctic and Antarctica, or the Galápagos Islands.

The number of cruise tourists worldwide in 2005 was estimated at some 14 million. The main region for cruising was North America (70% of cruises), where the Caribbean islands were the most popular destinations.

Next was Continental Europe (13%), where the fastest growing segment is cruises in the Baltic Sea. The most visited Baltic ports are Copenhagen, St. Petersburg, Tallinn, Stockholm and Helsinki. The seaport of St. Petersburg, the main Baltic port of call, received 426,500 passengers during the 2009 cruise season.

According to 2010 CEMAR statistics the Mediterranean cruise market is going through a fast and fundamental change; Italy has won prime position as a destination for European cruises, and destination for the whole of the Mediterranean basin. The most visited ports in Mediterranean Sea are Barcelona (Spain), Civitavecchia (Italy), Palma (Spain) and Venice (Italy).

2013 saw the entrance of the first Chinese company into the cruise market. China's first luxury cruise ship, Henna, made her maiden voyage from Sanya Phoenix Island International Port in late January.

CARIBBEAN CRUISING INDUSTRY

The Caribbean cruising industry is one of the largest in the world, responsible for over $2 billion in direct revenue to the Caribbean islands in 2012. Over 45,000 people from the Caribbean are directly employed in the cruise industry. 17,457,600 cruise passengers visited the islands in the 2011-2012 cruise year (May 2011 to April 2012.) Cruise lines operating in the Caribbean include Royal Caribbean International, Princess Cruises, Carnival Cruise Line, Celebrity Cruises, Disney Cruise Line, Holland America, P&O, Cunard, Crystal Cruises, and Norwegian Cruise Line. There are also smaller cruise lines that cater to a more intimate feeling among their guests. The three largest cruise operators are Carnival Corporation, Royal Caribbean International, and Star Cruises/Norwegian Cruise Lines.

Some of the American cruise lines in the Caribbean depart from ports in the United States, "nearly one-third of the cruises sailed out of Miami". Other cruise ships depart from Port Everglades (in Fort Lauderdale), Port Canaveral (approximately 45 miles (72 km) east of Orlando), New York, Tampa, Galveston, New Orleans, Cape Liberty, Baltimore, Jacksonville, Charleston, Norfolk, Mobile, and San Juan, Puerto Rico. Some UK cruise lines base their ships out of Barbados for the Caribbean season, operating direct charter flights out of the UK and avoiding the sometimes lengthy delays at US immigration.

The busiest ports of call in the Caribbean for cruising in the 2011/2012 year are listed below

Rank	Port/City	Country	Estimated Passenger Arrivals (2012)
1	Nassau	Bahamas	3,052,183
2	Cozumel	Mexico	2,730,000
3	Charlotte Amalie	United States Virgin Islands	1,887,096
4	Phillipsburg	Sint Maarten	1,754,900
5	George Town	Cayman Islands	1,443,200
6	Freeport	Bahamas	1,240,016
7	San Juan	Puerto Rico	1,176,700
8	Bridgetown	Barbados	770,600
9	Belize City	Belize	731,200
10	Cockburn Town	Turks and Caicos Islands	676,647
11	Castries	Saint Lucia	671,577
12	Basseterre	Saint Kitts and Nevis	629,200
13	Saint John's	Antigua and Barbuda	594,800
14	Oranjestad	Aruba	590,200
15	Falmouth	Jamaica	572,741

FERRY

A ferry (or ferryboat) is a boat or ship (a merchant vessel) used to carry (or ferry) primarily passengers, and sometimes vehicles and cargo as well, across a body of water. Most ferries operate on regular, frequent, return services. A passenger ferry with many stops, such as in Venice, Italy, is sometimes called a water bus or water taxi.

Ferries form a part of the public transport systems of many waterside cities and islands, allowing direct transit between points at a capital cost much lower than bridges or tunnels. However, ship connections of much larger distances (such as over long distances in water bodies like the Mediterranean Sea) may also be called ferry services, especially if they carry vehicles.

HISTORY

In ancient times

The profession of the ferryman is embodied in Greek mythology in Charon, the boatman who transported souls across the River Styx to the Underworld. Speculation that a pair of oxen propelled a ship having a water wheel can be found in 4th century Roman literature "Anonymus De Rebus

Bellicis". Though impractical, there is no reason why it could not work and such a ferry, modified by using horses, was used in Lake Champlain in 19th-century America.

NOTABLE SERVICES

Europe

The busiest seaway in the world, the English Channel, connects Great Britain and mainland Europe, sailing mainly to French ports, such as Calais, Boulogne, Dunkirk, Dieppe, Cherbourg-Octeville, Caen, St Malo and Le Havre. Ferries from Great Britain also sail to Belgium, Denmark, the Netherlands, Norway, Spain and Ireland. Some ferries carry mainly tourist traffic, but most also carry freight, and some are exclusively for the use of freight lorries. In Britain, car-carrying ferries are sometimes referred to as RORO (roll-on, roll-off) for the ease by which vehicles can board and leave.

The busiest single ferry route (at least in terms of the number of departures) is across the northern part of Øresund, between Helsingborg, Scania, Sweden and Elsinore, Denmark. Before the Øresund bridge was opened in July 2000, car and "car & train" ferries departed up to seven times every hour. In 2013, this has been reduced, but a car ferry still departs from each harbor every 15 minutes during daytime.

The route is around 2.2 nautical miles (4.1 km; 2.5 mi) and the crossing takes 22 minutes. Today, all ferries on this route are constructed so that they do not need to turn around in the harbors. This also means that the ferries lack natural stems and sterns, since the vessels sail in both directions (rather than "sail backwards"). Due to the same circumstances, starboard and port-side are "dynamic" and depending of in what direction the ferry sails. Despite the short crossing, the ferries are equipped with restaurants (on 3 out of 4 ferries), cafeteria, kiosks and WC toilets. (Passengers without cars often make a "double or triple return" journey in the restaurants; for this, a common return ticket is sufficient. Passenger and bicycle passenger tickets are inexpensive compared with longer routes.)

Large cruiseferries sail in the Baltic Sea between Finland, Åland, Sweden, Estonia,and Saint Petersburg, Russia and from Italy to Sardinia, Corsica, Spain and Greece. In many ways, these ferries are like cruise ships, but they can also carry hundreds of cars on car decks. Besides providing passenger and car transport across the sea, Baltic Sea cruiseferries are a popular tourist destination unto themselves, with multiple restaurants, nightclubs, bars, shops and entertainment on board.

The south-west and southern parts of the Baltic Sea has several routes mainly for heavy traffic and cars. The ferry routes of Trelleborg-Rostock SWE-GER, Trelleborg-Travemünde SWE-GER, Trelleborg-Swinoujscie SWE-POL, Rødby-Puttgarden DEN-GER, Gedser-Rostock DEN-GER, Gdansk-Karlskrona

POL-SWE, and Ystad-Swinoujscie SWE-POL are all typical transports ferries. On the longer of these routes, simple cabins are available. On the Trelleborg-Sassnitz SWE-GER route, it also has capacities for the daily night trains between Berlin and Malmö.

In Istanbul, ferries connect the European and Asian shores of Bosphorus, as well as Princes Islands and nearby coastal towns.

Australia and New Zealand

In Australia, two Spirit of Tasmania ferries carry passengers and vehicles 300 kilometres across Bass Strait, which separates Tasmania from the Australian mainland. These run overnight but also include day crossings in peak time. Both ferries are based in the northern Tasmanian port city of Devonport and sail to Melbourne.

In New Zealand, ferries connect Wellington in the North Island with Picton in the South Island, linking New Zealand's two main islands. The 92 km route takes three hours, and is run by two companies – government-owned Interislander, and independent Bluebridge.

Asia

Hong Kong has the Star Ferry carry passengers across Victoria Harbour and various carriers carrying travellers between Hong Kong Island to outlying islands like Cheung Chau, Lantau Island and Lamma Island.

The Kerala State Water Transport Department(SWTD), opereating under the Ministry of Transport, Government of Kerala, India regulates the inland navigation systems in the Indian state of Kerala and provides inland water transport facilities. It stands for catering to the passenger and cargo traffic needs of the inhabitants of the waterlogged areas of the Districts of Alappuzha, Kottayam, Kollam, Ernakulam, Kannur and Kasargode. SWTD ferry service is also one of the most affordable modes to enjoy the beauty of the scenic Kerala backwaters.

The Penang Ferry Service is the oldest ferry service in Malaysia. The famous ferry service connects Sultan Abdul Halim ferry terminal in Butterworth on Peninsular Malaysia to Raja Tun Uda ferry terminal at Weld Quay in George Town on Penang Island. It has also become a famous tourist attraction among foreigners. Along the way, ferry commuters will get to see the Penang Bridge and also the skyline of George Town and Butterworth.

North America

Due to the numbers of large freshwater lakes and length of shoreline in Canada, many provinces and territories have ferry services. BC Ferries carries travellers between Vancouver Island and the British Columbia mainland on the country's west coast. This ferry service operates to other islands including the Gulf Islands and the Queen Charlotte Islands. Canada's east coast has been home to numerous inter and intra provincial ferry and coastal services, including a large network operated by the federal government under CN Marine and later Marine Atlantic. Private and publicly owned ferry operations in eastern Canada include Marine Atlantic, serving the island of Newfoundland, as well as Bay, NFL, CTMA, Coastal Transport, and STQ to name but a few. Canadian waters in the Great Lakes once hosted numerous ferry services, however these have been reduced to those offered by Owen Sound Transportation and several smaller operations. There are also several commuter passenger ferry services operated in major cities, such as Metro Transit in Halifax, Toronto Island Ferry in Toronto and SeaBus in Vancouver.

Washington State Ferries operates the most extensive ferry system in the United States, with ten routes on Puget Sound and the Strait of Juan de Fuca serving terminals in Washington and Vancouver Island. In 2012, Washington State Ferries carried 10 million vehicles and 22 million passengers.

The Staten Island Ferry in New York City, sailing between the boroughs of Manhattan and Staten Island, is the nation's single busiest ferry route by passenger volume. New York City also has a network of smaller ferries, or water taxis, that shuttle commuters along the Hudson River from locations in New Jersey and Northern Manhattan down to the midtown, downtown and Wall Street business centers.

The New Orleans area also has many ferries in operation that carry both vehicles and pedestrians. Most notable is the Algiers Ferry. This service has been in continuous operation since 1827 and is one the oldest operating ferries in North America.

Vehicle-carrying ferry services between mainland Cape Cod and the islands of Martha's Vineyard and Nantucket are operated by The Woods Hole, Martha's Vineyard and Nantucket Steamship Authority, which sails year-round between Woods Hole and Vineyard Haven as well as Hyannis and Nantucket. Seasonal service is also operated from Woods Hole to Oak Bluffs from Memorial Day to Labor Day. As there are no bridges or tunnels connecting the islands to the mainland, The Steamship Authority ferries in addition to being the only method for transporting private cars to or from the islands, also serves as the only link by which heavy freight and supplies such as food and gasoline can be trucked to the islands. Additionally, Hy-Line Cruises operates high speed catamaran service from Hyannis to both islands, as well as traditional ferries, and several smaller operations run seasonal passenger only service primarily geared towards tourist day-trippers from other mainland ports, including New Bedford, (New Bedford Fast Ferry) Falmouth, (Island Queen ferry and Falmouth Ferry) and Harwich (Freedom Cruise Line).

The San Francisco Bay Area has several ferry services, such as the Blue & Gold Fleet, connecting with cities as far as Vallejo. The majority of ferry passengers are daily commuters and tourists. A ferry serves Angel Island (which also accepts private craft). The only way to get to Alcatraz is by ferry. Until the completion of the Mackinac Bridge in the 1950s, ferries were used for vehicle transportation between the Lower Peninsula of Michigan and the Upper Peninsula of Michigan, across the Straits of Mackinac in the United States. Ferry service for bicycles and passengers continues across the straits for transport to Mackinac Island, where motorized vehicles are almost completely prohibited. This crossing is made possible by three ferry lines, Arnold Transit Company, Shepler's Ferry, and Star Line Ferry.

TYPES

Ferry designs depend on the length of the route, the passenger or vehicle capacity required, speed requirements and the water conditions the craft must deal with.

Double-ended

Double-ended ferries have interchangeable bows and sterns, allowing them to shuttle back and forth between two terminals without having to turn around. Well-known double-ended ferry systems include the Staten Island Ferry, Washington State Ferries, Star Ferry, several boats on the North Carolina Ferry System, and the Lake Champlain Transportation Company. Most Norwegian fjord and coastal ferries are double-ended vessels. Some ferries in Sydney, Australia and British Columbia are also double-ended. In 2008, BC Ferries launched three of the largest double-ended ferries in the world.

Hydrofoil

Hydrofoils have the advantage of higher cruising speeds, succeeding hovercraft on some English Channel routes where the ferries now compete against the Eurotunnel and Eurostar trains that use the Channel Tunnel. Passenger-only hydrofoils also proved a practical, fast and relatively economical solution in the Canary Islands but were recently replaced by faster catamaran "high speed" ferries that can carry cars. Their replacement by the larger craft is seen by critics as a retrograde step given that the new vessels use much more fuel and foster the inappropriate use of cars in islands already suffering from the impact of mass tourism.

Hovercraft

Hovercraft were developed in the 1960s and 1970s to carry cars. The largest was the massive SR.N4 which carried cars in its centre section with ramps at the bow and stern between England and France. The hovercraft was superseded by catamarans which are nearly as fast and are less affected by sea and weather conditions. Only one service now remains, a foot passenger service between Portsmouth and the Isle of Wight run by Hovertravel.

Catamaran

Catamarans are normally associated with high-speed ferry services. Stena Line operates the largest catamarans in the world, the Stena HSS class, between the United Kingdom and Ireland. These waterjet-powered vessels, displacing 19,638 tonnes, are larger than most catamarans and can accommodate 375 passenger cars and 1,500 passengers. Other examples of these super-sizer catamarans are found in the Brittany Ferries fleet with the Normandie Express and the Normandie Vitesse.

Ro-ro

Roll-on/roll-off ferries (RORO) are large, conventional ferries named for the ease by which vehicles can board and leave.

Cruiseferry

A cruiseferry is a ship that combines the features of a cruise ship with a RoRo ferry.

Fast RoPax ferry

Fast RoPax ferries are conventional ferries with a large garage intake and a relatively large passenger capacity, with conventional diesel propulsion and propellers that sail over 25 knots (46 km/h; 29 mph). Pioneering this class of ferries was Attica Group, when it introduced Superfast I between Greece and Italy in 1995 through its subsidiary company Superfast Ferries. Cabins, if existent, are much smaller than those on cruise ships.

Turntable ferry

This type of ferry allows vehicles to load from the "side". The vehicle platform can be turned. When loading, the platform is turned sideways to allow sideways loading of vehicles. Then the platform is turned back, in line with the vessel, and the journey across water is made.

Pontoon ferry

Pontoon ferries carry vehicles across rivers and lakes and are widely used in less-developed countries with large rivers where the cost of bridge construction is prohibitive.

One or more vehicles are carried on a pontoon with ramps at either end for vehicles to drive on and off. Cable ferries (next section) are usually pontoon ferries, but pontoon ferries on larger rivers are motorised and able to be steered independently like a boat.

Train ferry

A Train ferry is a ship designed to carry railway vehicles. Typically, one level of the ship is fitted with railway tracks, and the vessel has a door at the front and/or rear to give access to the wharves.

Foot ferry

Foot ferries are small craft used to ferry foot passengers, and often also cyclists, over rivers. These are either self-propelled craft or cable ferries. Such ferries are for example to be found on the lower River Schelde in Belgium and in particular the Netherlands. Regular foot ferry service also exists in the capital of the Czech Republic, Prague. Restored, expanded ferry service in the Port of New York and New Jersey uses boats for pedestrians only.

Cable ferry

Very short distances may be crossed by a cable or chain ferry, which is usually a pontoon ferry, where the ferry is propelled along and steered by cables connected to each shore. Sometimes the cable ferry is human powered by someone on the boat. Reaction ferries are cable ferries that use the perpendicular force of the current as a source of power. Examples of a current propelled ferry are the four Rhine ferries in Basel, Switzerland. Cable ferries may be used in fast-flowing rivers across short distances.

Free ferries operate in some parts of the world, such as at Woolwich in London, England (across the River Thames); in Amsterdam, Netherlands (across the IJ waterway); in New York Harbor, connecting Manhattan to Staten Island; along the Murray River in South Australia, and across many lakes in British Columbia.

Many cable ferries operate on lakes and rivers in Canada, among them a cable ferry that charges a toll operates on the Rivière des Prairies between Laval-sur-le-Lac and Île Bizard in Quebec, Canada.

AIR FERRIES

In the 1950s and 1960s, travel on an "air ferry" was possible—aeroplanes, often ex-military, specially equipped to take a small number of cars in addition to "foot" passengers. These operated various routes including between the United Kingdom and Continental Europe. Companies operating such services included Channel Air Bridge, Silver City Airways, and Corsair.

The term is also applied to any "ferrying" by air, and is commonly used when referring to airborne military operations.

DOCKING

Ferry boats often dock at specialized facilities designed to position the boat for loading and unloading, called a ferry slip. If the ferry transports road vehicles or railway carriages there will usually be an adjustable ramp called an apron that is part of the slip. In other cases, the apron ramp will be a part of the ferry itself, acting as a wave guard when elevated and lowered to meet a fixed ramp at the terminus — a road segment that extends partially underwater.

FIRST, SHORTEST, LARGEST

The world's largest car ferry is the MS Ulysses, operated by Irish Ferries between Ireland and Wales.

On 11 October 1811, inventor John Stevens' ship the Juliana, began operation as the first steam-powered ferry (service was between New York City, and Hoboken, New Jersey).

The Elwell Ferry, a cable ferry in North Carolina, travels a distance of 110 yards (100 m), shore to shore, with a travel time of five minutes.

A contender as oldest ferry in continuous operation is the Mersey Ferry from Liverpool to Birkenhead, England. In 1150, the Benedictine Priory at Birkenhead was established. The monks used to charge a small fare to row passengers across the estuary. In 1330, Edward III granted a charter to the Priory and its successors for ever: "the right of ferry there... for men, horses and goods, with leave to charge reasonable tolls". However there may have been a short break following the Dissolution of the monasteries.

Another claimant as the oldest ferry service in continuous operation is the Rocky Hill - Glastonbury Ferry, running between the towns of Rocky Hill and Glastonbury, Connecticut. Established in 1655, the ferry has run continuously since, only ceasing operation every winter when the river freezes over. A long running salt water ferry service is the Halifax/Dartmouth ferry, running between the cities of Halifax and Dartmouth, Nova Scotia, which has run year-round since 1752, and is currently run by the region's transit authority, Metro Transit. However the Mersey Ferry predates it as the oldest salt water ferry.

Two of the world's largest ferry systems are located in the Strait of Georgia, in the Canadian province of British Columbia, and Puget Sound, in the U.S. state of Washington. BC Ferries in British Columbia operates 36 vessels, visiting 47 ports of call, while Washington State Ferries owns 28 vessels, travelling to 20 ports of call around Puget Sound.

Sydney Ferries in Sydney, Australia operates 31 passenger ferries in Port Jackson (Sydney Harbour), carrying 18 million passengers annually. It operates catamarans and other types of ferries on these routes, with the most famous likely being the Circular Quay-Manly route. Between 1938 and 1974 this route operated the South Steyne, billed at the time as the largest and fastest ferry of its type. Sydney Ferries became an independent corporation owned by the government in 2004.

Some of world's busiest ferry routes include the Star Ferry in Hong Kong and the Staten Island Ferry in New York City.

Metrolink Queensland operates 21 passenger ferries on behalf of Brisbane City Council, 12 being single-hulled ferries and 9 CityCats (catamarans), along the Brisbane River from the University of Queensland through the city to Brett's Wharf.

The gas-powered Luciano Federico L operated by Montevideo-based Buquebus, holds the Guinness World Record for the fastest car ferry boat in the world, in service between Montevideo, Uruguay and Buenos Aires, Argentina: its maximum speed, achieved in sea trials, was 60.2 knots (111.5 km/h; 69.3 mph). It can carry 450 passengers and 52 cars along the 110-nautical-mile (200 km; 130 mi) route.

SUSTAINABILITY

The contributions of ferry travel to climate change have received less scrutiny than land and air transport, and vary considerably according to factors like speed and the number of passengers carried. Average carbon dioxide emissions by ferries per passenger-kilometre seem to be 0.12 kg (4.2 oz). However, 18-knot ferries between Finland and Sweden produce 0.221 kg (7.8 oz) of CO_2, with total emissions equalling a CO_2 equivalent of 0.223 kg (7.9 oz), while 24–27-knot ferries between Finland and Estonia produce 0.396 kg (14.0 oz) of CO_2 with total emissions equalling a CO_2 equivalent of 0.4 kg (14 oz).

With the price of oil at high levels, and with increasing pressure from consumers for measures to tackle global warming, a number of innovations for energy and the environment were put forward at the Interferry conference in Stockholm. According to the company Solar Sailor, hybrid marine power and solar wing technology are suitable for use with ferries, private yachts and even tankers.

NARROWBOAT

A narrowboat or narrow boat is a boat of a distinctive design, made to fit the narrow canals of Great Britain.

In the context of British Inland Waterways, "narrow boat" refers to the original working boats built in the 18th, 19th, and 20th centuries for carrying goods on the narrow canals (where locks and bridge holes would have a minimum width of 7 feet (2.1 m); some locks on the Shropshire Union are even smaller). The term is extended to modern "narrowboats" used for recreation and more and more as homes, whose design is an interpretation of the old boats for modern purposes and modern materials.

TERMINOLOGY

Purists tend to write the term with a space (narrow boat) when referring to an original (working) boat or a replica, omitting the space when referring to modern canal boats of around 7' beam and used for leisure including residence. The single word 'narrowboat' has been adopted by authorities such as the Canal and River Trust and the magazine Waterways World to refer to all boats built in the style and tradition of the narrow canal locks. Although some narrow boats were built to a design based on river barges and many conform to the strict definition of the term, it is incorrect to refer to a narrowboat (or narrow boat) as a barge. In the context of the British inland waterways, a barge is usually a much wider, cargo-carrying boat or a modern boat modelled on one, certainly more than 7 feet (2.1 m) wide.

It is also incorrect (or at least incongruous) to refer to a narrowboat as a longboat, although this name was sometimes used in the Midlands in working-boat days.

Usage has not quite settled down as regards (a) boats based on narrowboat design, but too wide for narrow canals; or (b) boats the same width as narrowboats but based on other types of boat.

SIZE

The key distinguishing feature of a narrowboat is its width: it must be no more than 7 feet (2.13 m) wide to navigate the British narrow canals. Some old boats are very close to this limit (often built 7 feet 1 1/2 inches or 2.17 m or slightly wider), and can have trouble using locks that are not quite as wide as they should be because of subsidence. Modern boats are usually 6 feet 10 inches (2.08 m) wide to guarantee easy passage everywhere.

Because of their slenderness, some narrowboats seem very long. The maximum length is about 72 feet (22 m), the length of most locks on the narrow canals. However, modern narrowboats tend to be shorter than this, so that they can cruise anywhere on the connected network of British canals - including on the "wide" canals (built for wider, but shorter, boats). The shortest lock on the main network is Salterhebble Middle Lock on the Calder and Hebble Navigation, at about 56 feet (17 m) long. However, the C&H is a wide canal, so the lock is about 14 feet 2 inches (4.32 m) wide. This makes the largest "go-anywhere-on-the-network" narrowboat slightly longer (about 60 feet) than the straight length of the lock, because it can (with a certain amount of "shoehorning") lie diagonally. Some locks on isolated waterways are as short as 40 feet (12.2 m).

Hire fleets on British canals can contain narrowboats of many lengths from about 30 feet (9.1 m) upwards, to allow parties of different sizes or different budgets to hire a boat.

DEVELOPMENT - TRADITIONAL WORKING BOATS

The first working narrow boats played a key part in the economic changes of the British Industrial Revolution. They were wooden boats drawn by a horse walking on the canal towpath led by a crew member, often a child. Narrowboats were chiefly designed for carrying cargo, though there were some packet boats, carrying passengers, letters, and parcels. Boatmen's families originally lived ashore, but in the 1830s as canals started to feel competition from the new railways, families (especially of owner/skippers of independent single boats) started to take up home afloat. This was partly because they could no longer afford rents, partly to provide extra hands to work the boats harder, faster and further, and partly to keep families together. However, as late as 1858, a "Household Words" article states that the Grand Junction Canal company did not allow the boatmen's families on board – and the crew of the non-stopping ("fly") boat in the article (the skipper, two crewmen, and a 'youth') is said to be typical.

The rear portion of the boat became the cosy "boatman's cabin", familiar from picture postcards and museums, famous for its space-saving ingenuity and for its interior made attractive by a warm stove, a steaming kettle, gleaming brass, fancy lace, painted housewares, and decorated plates. Although such descriptions rarely consider the actual comfort of a large family working an extremely hard and long day, and sleeping in the one tiny cabin, it is no doubt true that at the time there were many workers in harder, indoor, trades with less healthy conditions and worse accommodation where the family were separated for long hours rather than being together all day. Nonetheless it was impossible for such mobile families to send their children to school, and most boat people remained illiterate and ostracised by those living 'on the bank'.

As diesel and steam replaced the tow horse in the early twentieth century, it became possible to move more cargo with the same manpower by towing a second unpowered boat, commonly referred to as a "butty", "buttyboat" or "butty boat". There was now no horse to look after, but someone had to steer the butty, unless on a wide canal such as the Grand Union Canal where the two boats could be roped side-to-side or 'breasted up', and handled as one while working locks.

Cargo-carrying by narrow boat was almost extinguished as a way of life between 1945 and the last regular long distance traffic finished in 1970. However some traffic continued into the 1980s and beyond including over 2 million tonnes of aggregate carried on the Grand Union (River Soar) from 1976 to 1996, latterly using wide beam barges however, and aggregate currently carried by narrow boats (and wide barges) between Denham and West Drayton on the Grand Union Canal. A few people are doing their best to keep the tradition alive, mostly by "one-off" deliveries rather than regular runs, or by selling goods such as coal to other boaters.

There are many enthusiasts dedicated to restoring the remaining old boats, often members of the Historic Narrow Boat owners Club and there are also many replicas such as Working Narrow Boat Hadar ornately painted with the same traditional designs, usually of roses and castles. If the boat is not horse-drawn, it may have a refurbished, slow-revving, vintage diesel engine, and there are even some steam-driven narrow boats such as the ex-Fellows Morton and Clayton steamer President.

PAINTED DECORATION ON NARROWBOATS

By the latter part of the 19th century it was common practice to paint roses and castles on both narrow boats themselves and their fixtures and fittings. Common sites include the doors to the cabin, the water can or barrel and the side of the boat along with ornate lettering giving the boat's name and owner. However, this was not done in all regions, the Chesterfield Canal being one waterway where the narrowboats never bore such decorations.

The origin of the roses and castles found on canal boats is unclear. The first written reference to them appears to be in an 1858 edition of the magazine Household Words in one of a series of articles titled "On the Canal", but while this shows that the art form must have existed by this date it doesn't provide us with an origin. For some time, a popular suggestion was that it had some form of Romani origin, however there does not appear to be a significant link between the Romani and boating communities. Other suggestions include transfer of styles from the clock-making industry (in particular the decoration on the face), the japanning industry or the pottery industry. There is certainly a similarity in style and a geographical overlap, but no solid proof of a link. There are similar styles of folk art in Scandinavia, Germany, Turkey and Bangladesh.

In the eighteenth century, the similar DutchHindeloopen paintwork would only have been a sailing barge journey away from the Thames. There is also an article in the Midland Daily Telegraph of 22 July 1914 that credits the practice of painting of water cans, at least, to a Mr Arthur Atkins. The date of the events make the claim possible, but would require the Household Words article to be reporting on the very start of a phenomenon, rather than – as its tone suggests – something that had existed for some time. Until further evidence comes to light, it is impossible to support or deny the claim that Arthur Atkins was responsible for the start of the practice and thus the origin of the paintings remains uncertain.

While the practice declined as commercial use of the canals dwindled, it has seen something of a revival in recent times with the emergence of leisure boating. Narrowboat decoration with roses and castle themes are a reasonably common sight on today's canals, although these may utilise cheaper computer-printed vinyl transfers in place of the traditional craft of hand-painted designs.

MODERN NARROWBOATS

The number of licensed boats on canals and rivers managed by British Waterways (BW), a government organisation, was estimated at about 27,000 in 2006. There are perhaps another 5,000 unlicensed boats kept in private moorings or on other waterways. Most of the boats on BW waterways are steel cruisers popularly referred to as narrowboats.

Modern narrowboats are used for annual holidays, weekend breaks or as permanent residences. Usually, they have steel hulls and a steel superstructure, but when they were first being developed for leisure use in the 1970s glass re-inforced plastic (fibre-glass) or timber was often used for the superstructures.

They are usually powered by modern diesel engines, and are fitted inside to a high standard. There will be at least 6 feet (1.8 m) internal headroom, and similar domestic facilities as a small landward home: central heating, flush toilets, shower or even bath, four-ring hobs, oven, grill, microwave oven, and refrigerator; quite a few also have satellite television and mobile broadband via the use of 3G broadband technology. Externally, their resemblance to traditional boats can vary from a faithful imitation (false "rivets", and copies of traditional paintwork) through "interpretation" (clean lines and simplified paintwork) through to a free-style approach which does not try to pretend in any way that this is a traditional boat.

They are owned by individuals, shared by a group of friends (or by a more formally organised syndicate), rented out by holiday firms, or used as cruising hotels. A few boats are lived on permanently: either based in one place (though long-term moorings for residential narrowboats are currently very difficult to find) or continuously moving around the network (perhaps with a fixed location for the coldest months, when many stretches of canal are closed by repair works or "stoppages").

MODERN NARROWBOAT TYPES

On most narrowboats steering is by a tiller, as it was on all working narrow boats, and the steerer stands at the stern of the boat, aft of where a person emerges from the hatchway and rear doors at the top of the steps up from the cabin.

The steering area comes in three basic types, each meeting different needs in terms of maximising internal space; having a more traditional appearance; having a big enough rear deck for everyone to enjoy summer weather or long evenings; or protection for the steerer in bad weather. Each type has its strong advocates. However, the boundaries are not fixed, and some boats blur the categories as designers try out slightly different arrangements and combinations.

NARROWBOATS WITH TRADITIONAL STERN

Many modern canal boats retain the traditional layout of a small open, unguarded "counter" or deck behind the rear doors from which the crew can step onto land. It is possible to steer from the counter, but this is not very safe, with the propeller churning below only one misstep away. The length of the "tiller extension" allows the steerer to stand more safely on the top step, forward of the rear doors (on a working boat, this step would have been over the top of the coal box). On cold days, the steerer can even close the rear doors behind him, and be in relative comfort, his lower body in the warmth of the cabin, and only his upper body emerging from the hatchway and exposed to the elements. In good weather, many trad-stern steerers sit up on the hatchway edge, a high vantage point giving good all-round visibility. On trad boats, the bow "well-deck" forms the main outside viewing area, because the traditional stern is not large enough for anyone other than the steerer to stand on safely.

NARROWBOATS WITH CRUISER STERN

Cruiser stern narrowboats are designed to allow more people to be on deck during the reasonably good weather of the British summer holiday season. The hatch and rear doors are farther forward than on a traditional boat, creating a large open deck between counter and rear doors, protected by a rail (perhaps with seats) around the back and sides. At the rear, a "cruiser" narrowboat looks very different from traditional boats. The large rear deck provides a good social space or al fresco dining area, but in the winter (or the occasionally less than perfect weather of the British Summer) the steerer is quite unprotected from wind and rain.

The lack of an enclosed engine room means that engine heat does not contribute to keeping the boat warm and there is wasted space above the deck area. The name for this style arises because the large open rear deck resembles that of the large rear cockpits common on glass-fibre (glass-reinforced plastic or GRP) river cruisers. The "cruiser" stern also allows the engine to be located under the deck and not in the cabin as it is in a traditional-stern boat. Although this then makes access to the engine for maintenance more difficult, it does have the advantage that the engine is not located in the cabin and the ensuing noise and smell are not as much of an issue.

NARROWBOATS WITH SEMI-TRADITIONAL STERN

A semi-traditional stern is a compromise to gain some of the "social" benefits of a cruiser stern, while retaining a more traditional design and providing some protection for the steerer in bad weather or in cooler seasons. As with the cruiser stern, the deck is extended back from the hatch and rear doors, but in this case most of the deck is protected at the sides by walls which extend back from the cabin sides – giving a more sheltered area for the steerer and companions, usually with lockers to sit on. The engine is located under the deck, much like a cruiser, again allowing a separation between the cabin and the engine bay, with the steps down to the cabin being located past the false sides of the "semi-trad" social area.

NARROWBOATS WITH A BUTTY STERN

A butty boat is an un-powered boat traditionally with a larger rudder with (usually) a wooden tiller (known as an elum, a corruption of helm) as the steering does not benefit from the force of water generated by the propeller. The tiller is usually removed and reversed in the rudder-post socket to get it out of the way when moored.

A few butty boats have been converted into powered narrowboats like NB Sirius. The term butty is derived from a dialect word meaning companion.

CENTRE COCKPIT NARROWBOATS

A small number of steel narrowboats dispense with the need for a rear steering deck entirely, by imitating some river cruisers in providing wheel steering from a central cockpit.

NATIONAL ORGANISATIONS

- Inland Waterways Association - campaigns for the use, maintenance, and restoration of Britain's inland waterways
- National Association of Boat Owners (NABO) - 3,000 members in 2004. They publish one of the only in-print books about living aboard a narrowboat, Living Afloat (2005).
- National Community Boats Association - a federation of organisations running narrow and other boats on navigable waterways for the benefit of the community.

OCEAN LINER

An ocean liner is a ship designed to transport people from one seaport to another along regular long-distance maritime routes according to a schedule. Liners may also carry cargo or mail, and may sometimes be used for other purposes (e.g., for pleasure cruises or as hospital ships).

Cargo vessels running to a schedule are sometimes called liners. The category does not include ferries or other vessels engaged in short-sea trading, nor dedicated cruise ships where the voyage itself, and not transportation, is the prime purpose of the trip.

Nor does it include tramp steamers, even those equipped to handle limited numbers of passengers. Some shipping companies refer to themselves as "lines" and their container ships, which often operate over set routes according to established schedules, as "liners".

Ocean liners are usually strongly built with a high freeboard to withstand rough seas and adverse conditions encountered in the open ocean. Additionally, they are often designed with thicker hull plating than is found on cruise ships, and have large capacities for fuel, food and other consumables on long voyages. As of 2012, RMS Queen Mary 2 was the only ship still in service as an ocean liner.

OVERVIEW

Ocean liners were the primary mode of intercontinental travel for over a century, from the mid-19th century until they began to be supplanted by airliners in the late 1960s. In addition to passengers, liners carried mail and cargo. Ships contracted to carry BritishRoyal Mail used the designation RMS. Liners were also the preferred way to move gold and other high-value cargoes.

The busiest route for liners was on the North Atlantic with ships travelling between Europe and North America. It was on this route that the fastest, largest and most advanced liners travelled. But while in contemporary popular imagination the term "ocean liners" evokes these transatlanticsuperliners, most ocean liners historically were mid-sized vessels which served as the common carriers of passengers and freight between nations and among mother countries and their colonies and dependencies in the pre-jet age. Such routes included Europe to African and Asian colonies, Europe to South America, and migrant traffic from Europe to North America in the 19th and first two decades of the 20th centuries, and to Canada and Australia after the Second World War.

Shipping lines are companies engaged in shipping passengers and cargo, often on established routes and schedules. Regular scheduled voyages on a set route are called "line voyages" and vessels (passenger or cargo) trading on these routes to a timetable are called liners. The alternative to liner trade is "tramping" whereby vessels are notified on an ad-hoc basis as to the availability of a cargo to be transported. (In older usage, "liner" also referred to ships of the line, that is, line-of-battle ships, but that usage is now rare.) The term "ocean liner" has come to be used interchangeably with "passenger liner", although it can refer to a cargo liner or cargo-passenger liner.

Beginning at the advent of the Jet Age, where transoceanic ship service declined, a gradual transition from passenger ships as mean of transportation to nowadays cruise ships started. In order for ocean liners to remain profitable, cruise lines have modified some of them to operate on cruise routes, such as the Queen Elizabeth 2 and SS France. Certain characteristics of older ocean liners made them unsuitable for cruising, such as high fuel consumption, deep draught preventing them from entering shallow ports, and cabins (often windowless) designed to maximize passenger numbers rather than comfort. The Italian Line's SS Michelangelo and SS Raffaello, the last ocean liners to be built primarily for crossing the North Atlantic, could not be converted economically and had short careers.

HISTORY

The 19th century

In 1818, the Black Ball Line, with a fleet of sailing ships, offered the first regular passenger service with emphasis on passenger comfort, from England to the United States. From the early 19th century, steam engines began to appear in ships, but initially they were inefficient and offered little advantage over sailing ships.

The clipper domination was challenged when SS Great Western, designed by railway engineer Isambard Kingdom Brunel, began its first Atlantic service in 1837. It took 15 days to cross the Atlantic, as compared with two months by sail-powered ships. Unlike the clippers, steamers offered a consistent speed and the ability to keep to a schedule. The early steamships still had sails as well, though, as engines at this time had very inefficient consumption of fuel. Having sails enabled vessels like the Great Western to take advantage of favourable weather conditions and minimise fuel consumption.

In 1840, Cunard Line's RMS Britannia began its first regular passenger and cargo service by a steamship, sailing from Liverpool to Boston. Despite some advantages offered by the steamships, clippers remained dominant. In 1847, the SS Great Britain became the first iron-hulled screw-driven ship to cross the Atlantic. More efficient propellers began to replace the paddle wheels used by earlier ocean liners. In 1870, the White Star Line's RMS Oceanic set a new standard for ocean travel by having its first-class cabins amidships, with the added amenity of large portholes, electricity and running water. The size of ocean liners increased from 1880 to meet the needs of immigration to the United States and Australia.

RMS Umbria and her sister ship RMS Etruria were the last two Cunard liners of the period to be fitted with auxiliary sails. Both ships were built by John Elder & Co. of Glasgow, Scotland, in 1884. They were record breakers by the standards of the time, and were the largest liners then in service, plying the Liverpool to New York route.

SS Ophir was a 6814-ton steamship owned by the Orient Steamship Co., and was fitted with refrigeration equipment. It plied the Suez Canal route from England to Australia during the 1890s, up until the years leading to World War I, when she was converted to an armed merchant cruiser.

The 20th century

The period between the end of the 19th century and World War II is considered the "golden age" of ocean liners. Driven by strong demand created by European emigration to the Americas, international competition between passenger lines and a new emphasis on comfort, shipping companies built increasingly larger and faster ships.

Canadian Pacific Railway (CPR) became one of the largest transportation systems in the world, combining ships and railways operating from Canada. In 1891, the CPR shipping division began its first Pacific operation. In 1903, CPR began its first Atlantic service because of the rising migration of Europeans to western Canada, as the result of free land offered by the

Canadian government. Since the 1830s, passenger liners had unofficially been competing for the honour of making the fastest North Atlantic crossing. This honour came to be known as the Blue Riband; in 1897, Germany took the award with a series of new ocean liners, starting with SS Kaiser Wilhelm der Grosse.

In 1905, the British Cunard Line fitted RMS Carmania, with steam turbines, which then outperformed its nearly-identical sister, RMS Caronia, which was powered by quadruple-expansion steam engines.

At the time, these were the largest ships in the Cunard fleet, and the use of the different propulsion methods in otherwise similar ships allowed the company to evaluate the merits of both. The engines in the Carmania were successful and, consequently, in 1907, Cunard introduced the much larger RMS Lusitania and RMS Mauretania, both powered by steam turbines. Mauretania won the Blue Riband and held it for an astonishing 20 years.

Cunard's dominance of the Blue Riband did not keep other lines from competing in terms of size and luxury. In 1910, White Star Line launched RMS Olympic, the first of a trio of 45,000 plus gross ton liners, along with RMS Titanic and HMHS Britannic. These ships were almost 15,000 tonnes larger and 100 feet (30 m) longer than the Lusitania and the Mauretania. Like most other White Star Liners, these three ships were born of a special effort by the line to attract more immigrants by treating them with respect and making their crossings pleasurable.

Hamburg-America Line also ordered three giant ships, SS Imperator, SS Vaterland and SS Bismarck, all over 51,500 gross tons. Imperator was launched in 1912, and Bismarck would be the largest ship in the world until 1935. These ships did little or no service with Hamburg-America before World War I. After the war, they were awarded as war reparations and given to British and American lines.

The surge in ocean liner size outpaced the shipping regulations. In 1912, the Titanic sank after hitting an iceberg, with more than 1,500 fatalities. A factor contributing to the high loss of life was that there were not enough lifeboats for everyone. After the Titanic disaster, regulations were revised to require all ocean liners to carry enough lifeboats for all passengers and crew. In addition, the International Ice Patrol was established to monitor the busy North Atlantic shipping lanes for icebergs.

Until the 1920s, most shipping lines relied heavily on emigration for passengers; thus, they were hard hit when the United States Congress introduced a bill to limit immigration into the United States. As a result, many ships took on cruising, and the least expensive cabins were reconfigured from third-class to tourist-class. To make matters worse, the Great Depression put many shipping lines into bankruptcy.

Despite the harsh economic conditions, a number of companies continued to build larger and faster ships. In 1929, the German ships SS Bremen and SS

Europa beat the crossing record set by Mauretania 20 years earlier with an average speed of almost 28 knots (52 km/h; 32 mph). The ships used bulbous bows and steam turbines to reach these high speeds while maintaining economical operating costs. In 1933, the Italian Line's 51,100-ton ocean liner SS Rex, with a time of four days and thirteen hours, captured the westbound Blue Riband, which she held for two years. In 1935, French liner SS Normandie used a revolutionary new hull design and powerful turbo-electric transmission to take the Blue Riband from the Rex. Due to poor economic conditions, the British government amalgamated the Cunard Line and White Star Lines. The newly merged company countered with liners RMS Queen Mary and RMS Queen Elizabeth. Queen Mary held the Blue Riband in 1936-37 and from 1938-52.

In World War II many liners were used as troop ships. Notable ocean liners, such as Queen Mary, Aquitania, Cap Arcona, Laconia, Queen Elizabeth, and Orontes all helped transport troops. While some ocean liners survived the war, many others were lost.

The post-WWII era was a brief but busy period. Notable ships included the fastest transatlantic liner ever built, SS United States, which, in 1952, bested the records set by the Queen Mary to become the holder of the Blue Riband, a designation it retains to this day. Also significant was the 1961-built SS France (later renamed Norway) which held the record for the longest passenger ship from when she entered service in 1961, until the launch of RMS Queen Mary 2 in 2003. Australian government-sponsored immigration resulted in a busy trade between Europe and Australia, producing such notable ships as SS Oriana and SS Canberra. These two ships, operating on the P&O-Orient Lines service, were the largest, fastest and last liners built for the Australian route.

Decline of long-distance line voyages

Before World War II, competition from passenger aircraft had not been a large threat to ocean liners. World War II accelerated the development of large, long-distance aircraft. Four-engined bombers, such as the Avro Lancaster and Boeing B-29 Superfortress, with their long range and massive carrying capacity, were a natural prototype for a next-generation airliner. Jet aircraft technology also accelerated after the development of jet aircraft for military use in World War II. In 1953, the De Havilland Comet became the first commercial jet airliner; the Sud Aviation Caravelle, Boeing 707 and Douglas DC-8 followed, and much long-distance travel was done by air.

The Italian Line's SS Michelangelo and SS Raffaello, launched in 1962 and 1963, were two of the last ocean liners to be built primarily for liner service across the North Atlantic. Cunard's transatlantic liner, Queen Elizabeth 2, was also used as a cruise ship. By the early 1970s, many passenger ships continued their service in cruising. By the first decade of the 21st century, only a few former ocean liners were still sailing, while others, like Queen Mary, were preserved as museums or floating hotels. After the retirement of the Queen Elizabeth 2 in 2008, the only ocean liner in service was Queen Mary 2, used for both point-to-point line voyages and for cruising.

The 21st century

In 2012, Australian businessman, Clive Palmer, announced his plans to construct a modern-day replica of the famous RMS Titanic. To be named Titanic II, Palmer's vision is to create a trans-Atlantic ocean liner that closely mimics her namesake. Palmer, through his new venture, Blue Star Line, and with the help of the Finnish marine engineering firm, Deltamarin, have commenced the process of designing the ocean liner.

AT WAR

In World War I, ocean liners played a major role. Large ocean liners, such as Mauretania and Olympic, were used as troopships and hospital ships, while smaller ocean liners were converted to armed merchant cruisers. Britannic, sister ship to Titanic and Olympic, never served on the liner trade for which she was built. Instead, she entered war service as a hospital ship as soon as she was completed, and lasted a year before being sunk by a mine. Other liners were converted to innocent-looking armed Q-ships, in order to entrap submarines. In 1915, Lusitania, still in service as a civilian passenger vessel, was torpedoed with many casualties by a German U-boat.

In World War II the three worst disasters were the loss of the Cunarder Lancastria in 1940 off Saint-Nazaire to German bombing while attempting to evacuate troops of the British Expeditionary Force from France, with the loss of more than 3,000 lives; the sinking of Wilhelm Gustloff with more than 9,000 lives lost; and the sinking of Cap Arcona with more than 7,000 lives lost in the Baltic Sea, in 1945.

Ocean liners were also used in World War II as troopships. Normandie caught fire, capsized and sank in New York in 1942 while being converted for troop duty. Many of the superliners of the 'twenties and 'thirties were victims of U-boats, mines or enemy aircraft. Empress of Britain was attacked by German planes, then torpedoed by a U-boat when tugs tried to tow her to safety. She was the largest British ocean liner to sink during World War II. In 1941, Germany's speed queen, Bremen, fell victim to an arsonist, believed to be a disgruntled crew member, and became a total loss. Italy's giants, Rex and Conte di Savoia, were respectively destroyed by the Royal Air Force and the retreating German forces. The United States lost the American President Lines vessel President Coolidge when she steamed into an Allied mine in the South Pacific. No shipping line was left untouched by World War II.

In 1982, during the Falklands War, three ships that were either active or former liners were requisitioned for war service by the British Government. The liners Queen Elizabeth 2 and Canberra, were requisitioned from Cunard and P&O to serve as troopships, carrying British Army personnel to Ascension Island and the Falkland Islands to recover the Falklands from the invading Argentine forces. The P&O educational cruise ship and former British India Steam Navigation Company liner Uganda was requisitioned as a hospital ship and, after the war, served as a troopship until the RAF Mount Pleasant station was built at Stanley, which could handle trooping flights.

SAFETY AND RELIABILITY

Many ocean liners have been lost in peacetime. Titanic sank on her maiden voyage from Britain to the United States in 1912, after hitting an iceberg, with the loss of 1,523 lives; her name has entered the English language as an archetypical catastrophe.

In 1914, Empress of Ireland sank in the Saint Lawrence River with 1,012 lives lost. Between the world wars, SS L'Atlantique burned in the Channel in 1933 and Morro Castle (1930) burned off the coast of New Jersey in 1934.

After World War II and resumption of the transatlantic ferry, Italian liner Andrea Doria, although equipped with radar, sank after colliding with Stockholm in heavy fog in 1956 on the Italian vessel's approach to New York.

Many ships known for reliability, comfort, and decades of service, became particularly popular with passengers. Cunard Line's Mauretania (1906) and Aquitania were considered the finest liners of their time, while superliners, like Normandie and Queen Mary, became symbols of national pride and an important part of western civilization with influences in design, technology, popular culture and standards of international travel.

SURVIVORS

Of the pre-World War II ocean liners, four survive today. RMS Queen Mary (1934) was preserved after her retirement in 1967 as a hotel and museum in Long Beach, California. The Japanese ocean liner Hikawa Maru (1929), has been preserved in Naka-ku, Yokohama, Japan, as a museum ship, since 1961. SS Great Britain, was preserved in Bristol, England.MV Doulos is awaiting preservation in Singapore.

Remaining modern (post-war) ocean liners that are preserved are: SS United States (1952), docked in Philadelphia, since 1996; SS Rotterdam (1958), moored in Rotterdam as a museum and hotel, since 2008;Veronica (1966) (former MS Kungsholm), which was converted into a floating hotel in Duqm, Oman, in 2012; and Queen Elizabeth 2 (1967), laid up in Port Rashid, since 2009.

In the summer of 2013 one former ocean liner remained in service as a cruise ship, MS Marco Polo (1965) (former MS Alexandr Pushkin), while MS Azores, originally MS Stockholm and later the cruise ship Athena, was being refurbished for future service.

5

Support

DIVING SUPPORT VESSEL

A diving support vessel is a ship that is used as a floating base for professional diving projects.

HISTORY

Commercial Diving Support Vessels emerged during the 1960s and 1970s when the need arose for diving operations to be performed below and around oil production platforms and associated installations in open water in the North Sea and Gulf of Mexico. Until that point most diving operations were from mobile oil drilling platforms, pipe-lay or crane barges. The diving system tended to be modularised and craned on and off the vessels as a package.

As permanent oil and gas production platforms emerged, the owners and operators were not keen to give over valuable deck space to diving systems because after they came on-line the expectation of continuing diving operations was low. However, equipment fails or gets damaged, and there was a regular if not continuous need for diving operations in and around oil fields. The solution was to put diving packages on ships. Initially these tended to be oilfield supply ships or fishing vessels; however, keeping this kind of ship 'on station', particularly during uncertain weather, made the diving dangerous, problematic and seasonal. Furthermore, seabed operations usually entailed the raising and lowering of heavy equipment, and most such vessels were not equipped for this task.

This is when the dedicated commercial diving support vessel emerged. These were often built from scratch or heavily converted pipe carriers or other utility ships. The key components of the diving support vessel are:

- Dynamic Positioning - Controlled by a computer with input from position reference systems (DGPS, Transponders, Light Taut Wires or RadaScan), it will maintain the ships position over a dive site by using multi-directional thrusters, other sensors would compensate for swell, tide and prevailing wind.

- Saturation diving system - For diving operations below 50m, a mixture of helium and oxygen (heliox) is required to eliminate the narcotic effect of nitrogen under pressure. For extended diving operations at depth, saturation diving is the preferred approach. A saturation system would be installed within the ship. A diving bell would transport the divers between the saturation system and the work site lowered through a 'moon pool' in the bottom of the ship, usually with a support structure 'cursor' to support the diving bell through the turbulent waters near the surface. There are a number of support systems for the saturation system on a Diving Support Vessel, usually including a Remotely Operated Vehicle ROV and heavy lifting equipment.

MODERN DIVING SUPPORT VESSELS

Most of the vessels currently in the North Sea have been built in the 1980s. The semi-submersible fleet, the Uncle John and similar, have proven to be too expensive to maintain and too slow to move between fields. Therefore, most existing designs are monohull vessels with either a one or a twin bell dive system. There has been little innovation since the 1980s. However, driven by high oil prices since 2004, the market for subsea developments in the North Sea has grown significantly. This has led to a scarcity of Diving Support Vessels and have driven the price up. Thus, contractors have ordered a number of newbuild vessels which are expected to enter the market in 2008.

UNCLE JOHN

One of the most successful diving support vessels of the 1980s was the SSSV Uncle John operated by Comex Houlder diving. For 10 years this ship completed numerous underwater pipe joints (hyperbaric tie-ins) and other maintenance work in and around the Shell operated Brent oilfield in the northern North Sea. The Uncle John is a semi-submersible platform design with a 16 man saturation system, 2 diving bells in separate moon pools, 2 cranes and the ability to stay on station and work in fairly extreme weather. The semi-submersible design is very useful for hyperbaric tie-ins because the significant deck space allowed the transportation and manipulation of a 75 tonne welding habitat and pipe manipulation equipment that have the capability of maneuvering 36-inch-diameter, 1.5-inch-thick steel pipe. The Uncle John is currently owned and operated by Caldive International and is active today in the Gulf of Mexico.

A typical working depth in the Brent Field was 140 m. However, in 1983 the Uncle John and its crew successfully completed the Deep Fjord Diving Program in Onarheims Fjord, Norway, where a successful 36-inch hyperbaric tie-in was completed at a depth of 300 m.

FIREBOAT

A fireboat is a specialized watercraft and with pumps and nozzles designed for fighting shoreline and shipboard fires. The first fireboats, dating to the late 18th century, were tugboats, retrofitted with firefighting equipment. Older designs derived from tugboats and modern fireboats more closely resembling seafaring ships can both be found in service today. Some departments would give their multi-purpose craft the title of "fireboat" also.

They are frequently used for fighting fires on docks and shore side warehouses as they can directly attack fires in the supporting underpinnings of these structures. They also have an effectively unlimited supply of water available, pumping directly from below the hull. Fireboats can be used to assist shore-based firefighters when other water is in low supply or is unavailable, for example, due to earthquake breakage of water mains, as happened in San Francisco due to the 1989 Loma Prieta earthquake.

Modern fireboats are capable of pumping tens of thousands of gallons of water per minute. An example is Fire Boat #2 of the Los Angeles Fire Department, the Warner Lawrence, with the capability to pump up to 38,000 US gallons per minute (2.4 m/s; 32,000 imp gal/min) and up to 400 feet (122 m) in the air.

Fireboats are most usually seen by the public when welcoming a fleet or historical ships with a display of their water moving capabilities, throwing large arcs of water in every direction.

Occasionally fireboats are used to carry firefighters, Emergency Medical Technicians, and a physician with their equipment to islands and other boats. Some may be used as icebreakers, like the Chicago Fire Department's Victor L. Schlaeger which can break 8 to 12 inch ice. They may also carry divers or surface water rescue workers. Passengers from ships in danger can be also transferred to various kind of rescue boats. Rescue boats may be used also for oil and chemical destruction on rivers, lakes and seas.For example, the Helsinki Rescue Department in Helsinki, Finland has various kinds of boats for various kind of firefighting, rescue, and oil destruction tasks.

Also hydrocopters, rigid-hulled inflatable boats, fanboat and even hovercrafts and helicopters are used in fire, rescue and medical emergency situations.

Cities with fireboats are usually located on a large body of water with port facilities. Smaller fire departments lacking resources will use rigid-hulled inflatable boat or borrow boats from local rescue agencies (EMS, coast guard, military).

HISTORY

The first recorded fire-float was built in 1765 for the Sun Fire Insurance Company in London. This was a manual pump in a small boat, rowed by its crew to the scene of the fire. A similar craft was built in Bristol by James Hillhouse for the Imperial Fire Insurance Office in the 1780s. All fire fighting in Bristol was carried out either by private insurance companies or the Docks Company until the formation of the Bristol Fire Brigade as a branch of the police in 1876.

In New York City a small boat with a pump was used to fight marine fires. By the middle of the nineteenth century, self-propelled steam-fire-floats were beginning to be introduced. The FDNY leased the salvage tug John Fuller as the city's first powered fireboat in 1866. Prior to the "John Fuller", as early as the late 1700s, the FDNY used hand-pumpers mounted to barges and large rowboats.

The first purpose built steam driven boats were introduced by Boston Fire Department (William F. Flanders) and FDNY (William F. Havenmeyer) in 1873 and 1875 respectively. The first European fireboat to appear in Bristol was the Fire Queen, built by Shand Mason & Co., London, in 1884 for service in the city docks. The 53 ft. (16.61 m.) long craft was equipped with a three-cylindersteam pump supplying two large hose reels; one of these was replaced with a monitor, or water cannon, in 1900. Fire Queen served until 1922.

LIST OF FAMOUS FIREBOATS

- Abram S. Hewitt - FDNY (New York City) (1903–1958) (retired and abandon at Witte Marine Scrapyard in Rossville, Staten Island).
- Deluge - Fireboat/Tug (New Orleans) (retired)
- Duwamish - (Seattle) 1909 (retired)
- Edward M. Cotter - Fireboat/Icebreaker (Buffalo, New York) (active) The oldest active fireboat.
- Tacoma Fireboat #1 - (Tacoma, Washington) (retired)
- Fire Fighter - (NYC) 1938
- Fire Fighter II - FDNY (New York City) (2010) Country's largest fireboat (Active)
- Governor Irwin - Fireboat/Tug (San Francisco) (1878–1909) Fireboat participated in 1906 San Francisco Earthquake and Fire. (retired and scrapped)
- Governor Markham - Fireboat/Tug (San Francisco) Fireboat participated in 1906 San Francisco Earthquake and Fire. (retired and scrapped)
- John Fuller - steam salvage tug (NYC) - 1866 boat had 2000GPM pump and hose.
- John J. Harvey - (New York City) (1931–1959) (Temporary reinstatement 9/11/2001) (retired)(Museum ship)

- Massey Shaw - (London, England) (retired)
- Phoenix - (San Francisco) (active)
- Pyronaut - moored at Bristol Harbour Railway and Industrial Museum (Bristol, England) (retired)
- Ralph J. Scott - (Los Angeles) (retired)
- Sir Alexander Grantham - (Hong Kong) (retired)
- St. Mungo (fireboat) - Glasgow/Strathclyde (retired)
- Three Forty Three - FDNY (New York City) (2009) Country's largest fireboat, twin to Fire Fighter II. (Active)
- Warner Lawrence - Los Angeles (active)
- William F. Flanders - (Boston) 1873
- William F. Havenmeyer - (NYC) 1875-1901 (retired)
- William Lyon Mackenzie - (Toronto, Canada) (active)
- William O. Bird II - Sandusky Fire Department (Sandusky, Ohio) (active)
- USS Active/USS Lively - US Navy - Fireboat/Tug (1888–1945) Fireboat participated in 1906 San Francisco Earthquake and Fire. (retired and scrapped)
- USS Fortune - US Army/ US Navy - Fireboat/Tug (1865–1922) Fireboat participated in 1906 San Francisco Earthquake and Fire. (retired and scrapped)
- USS Hoga - US Navy - Fireboat/Tug (Pearl Harbor attack) and City of Oakland 1940-1996 (retired)
- USS Leslie - US Army/ US Navy - Fireboat/Tug (1861) Fireboat participated in 1906 San Francisco Earthquake and Fire. (retired and scrapped)

DEPARTMENTS WITH FIREBOATS

- Baltimore City Fire Department - 4
- Boston Fire Department - 2
- Bowers Fire Company (DE) - 1
- Buffalo Fire Department - 1
- Charlotte Fire Department - 1
- Chicago Fire Department - 2
- Cleveland Fire Department - 1
- Detroit Fire Department - 1
- District of Columbia Fire Department - 3

- Fairfax County Fire and Rescue Department - 2, 1 frontline, 1 reserve
- General Fire Brigade of Guangdong - 1
- Hendersonville, TN Fire Department - 1
- Hong Kong Fire Services/Hong Kong International Airport - 8 and 4 support vessels (command, 2 diving units, speedboat)
- Honolulu Fire Department - 1
- Jersey City Fire Department - 1
- London Fire Brigade - 2
- Los Angeles Fire Department - 5
- Macau International Airport Fire Services - 1
- Malaysian Fire and Rescue Department - 1
- Massachusetts Port Authority - 2, with third being delivered September 2011.
- Miami Fire Department- 1
- Nashville Fire Department - 1
- Miami-Dade Fire Rescue Department-2
- Nagasaki Fire Department - 1
- Newark Fire Department (NJ) - 1
- New York City Fire Department#Fireboats - 3; 1 reserve
- Newport News (VA) Fire Department
- Portland (ME) Fire Department - 1
- Portland (OR) Fire & Rescue - 2
- Port of Houston Authority Marine Fire Department - 3
- San Francisco Fire Department - 2
- Sandusky Fire Department - 1
- Seattle Fire Department - 3; 1 reserve
- Seoul Metropolitan Fire and Disaster Management Department - 1 on order
- South Australian Metropolitan Fire Service - 1
- Tacoma (WA) Fire Department - 2; 1 reserve
- Toronto Fire Services - 2; 2nd boat is a light utility boat
- Tokyo Fire Department - 9
- Vancouver Fire and Rescue Services - 2 (3 more in Metro Region)
- Virginia Beach Fire Department - 1
- Firefighters Corps of Military Police of São Paulo State - 2

GOVERNMENT AND MILITARY WITH FIREBOATS

Japan Coast Guard patrol boat with water cannons discharging

- Japan Coast Guard - 9; 230 patrol boats with water cannons or firefighting support systems
- United States Coast Guard
- Fire class fireboat of the Canadian Forces Maritime Command auxiliary fleet (2):
  - CFAV Firebird (YTR 561)
  - CFAV Firebrand (YTR 562)

PLATFORM SUPPLY VESSEL

A Platform supply vessel (often abbreviated as PSV) is a ship specially designed to supply offshore oil platforms. These ships range from 20 to 100 meters in length and accomplish a variety of tasks. The primary function for most of these vessels is transportation of goods and personnel to and from offshore oil platforms and other offshore structures.

In the recent years a new generation of Platform Supply Vessel entered the market, usually equipped with Class 1 or Class 2 Dynamic Positioning System.

CAPABILITIES

Cargo

A primary function of a platform supply vessel is to transport supplies to the oil platform and return other cargoes to shore. Cargo tanks for drilling mud, pulverized cement, diesel fuel, potable and non-potable water, and chemicals used in the drilling process comprise the bulk of the cargo spaces. Fuel, water, and chemicals are almost always required by oil platforms. Certain other chemicals must be returned to shore for proper recycling or disposal, however, crude oil product from the rig is usually not a supply vessel cargo..

SUPPORT

Common and specialty tools are carried on the large decks of these vessels. Most carry a combination of deck cargoes and bulk cargo in tanks below deck. Many ships are constructed (or re-fitted) to accomplish a particular job. Some of these vessels are equipped with a firefighting capability and fire monitors for fighting platform fires. Some vessels are equipped with oil containment and recovery equipment to assist in the cleanup of a spill at sea. Other vessels are equipped with tools, chemicals and personnel to "work-over" existing oil wells for the purpose of increasing the wells' production.

VESSEL CREWS

Crews on the these ships can number up to 20 crewmembers, but it is usual to run the vessels on minimum manning level to save money.

Daily Operations

Crews sign on to work and live aboard the ship an extended period of time (3 – 6 weeks and often more). This is followed by an extended period of time off, often 2–4 weeks depending on the ship owner/ operator the number of weeks or months aboard. Work details on platform supply vessels, like many ships, are organized into shifts of up to 12 hours.

Living aboard the ship, each crew member and worker will have a shift, lasting some portion of a 24 hour day. Most supply vessels are provided with a "bridge" area for navigating and operating the ship, machinery spaces, living quarters, and an area for cooking and eating. Some have built in work areas, and common areas for entertainment. The large main deck area is sometimes utilized for portable housing.

Living quarters consist of a bunk area, lockers, and spaces for storing personal items. Living areas are provided with wash basins, showers and toilets. Officers living quarters are sometimes outfitted with a small work desk, private sinks, showers and toilets.

The "galley" or cooking and eating areas aboard ship will be stocked with enough grocery items to last for the intended voyage. A walk-in size cooler and freezer, a commercial stove and oven, deep sinks, storage and counterspace will be available for the persons doing the cooking. The eating area will have coffee makers, toasters, microwave ovens, cafeteria style seating, and other amenities needed to feed a hard working crew.

SHIP'S TENDER

A ship's tender, usually referred to as a tender, is a boat, or a larger ship used to service a ship, generally by transporting people and/or supplies to and from shore or another ship. Smaller boats may also have tenders, usually called dinghies.

For a variety of reasons, it is not always advisable to try to tie a ship up at a dock; the weather or the sea might be rough, the time might be short, or the ship too large to fit. In such cases tenders provide the link from ship to shore, and may have a very busy schedule of back-and-forth trips while the ship is in port.

On cruise ships, lifeboat tenders do double duty, serving as tenders in day-to-day activities, but fully equipped to act as lifeboats in an emergency. They are generally carried on davits just above the promenade deck, and may at first glance appear to be regular lifeboats; but they are usually larger and better-equipped. Current lifeboat tender designs favor catamaran models, since they are less likely to roll in the calm to moderate conditions in which tenders are usually used. They typically carry up to 100 to 150 passengers and two to three crew members.

Before these ships were mass-produced, the main way to board a larger ship (mainly ocean liners) was to board a passenger tender. Passenger tenders remained based at their ports of registry, and when a ship came through the area, the tender would tie up with the ship and embark passengers on an elevated walkway.

These vessels were larger, had a greater passenger capacity, and a broader sense of individuality in their respective companies than the more modern tenders seen today. Because of their increased size, lifeboats and life preservers were commonplace on board these ships (with two boats being the standard amount for an average tender).

Before the technologies that allow submarines and destroyers to operate independently matured by the latter half of the 20th century – and significantly during the Second World War, they were heavily dependent upon tenders to perform most maintenance and supply. Their hull classification symbols in the US Navy were, respectively, AS and AD, while general repair ships were AR. Naval tenders fell out of use during the late 20th century, as the speed and range of warships increased – reducing the need for advanced basing. By the end of the 20th century all of the tenders in the U.S. Navy had been inactivated except for two submarine tenders. As a result of the settlement of the lawsuits over the Suisun Bay and Estuary the U.S. Navy and MARAD are engaged in an aggressive disposal program that will scrap all of those ships by 2017.

While the Navy's plans for tenders held in reserve in other places (such as inactivated submarine tenders USS McKee and USS Simon Lake held at Inactive Ships, St. Juliens Creek Annex) were not addressed in that lawsuit, since its settlement, the Navy has indicated its desire to dispose of such ships as soon as possible.

Apparently not completely willing to wean itself from tenders all together – but with an eye towards reducing costs – the last two tenders remaining in active service have now been operationally turned over to the Military Sealift

Command. Emory S. Land-classsubmarine tendersUSS Emory S. Land and USS Frank Cable are now manned and operated by a "hybrid" crew. The Captain and a couple hundred technicians are regular Navy; while the operation of the ship itself is performed by Merchant Marines. Prior to the turn-over both ships had more than 1000 sailors.

While at this time the ships still bear the AS classification, both ship's primary mission has been expanded well beyond submarines to include service and support of any Naval vessel in their operational area. Under the traditional Navy classification both ships should be reclassified as AR (Auxiliary Repair), however since now operated by the MSC it is doubtful such a reassignment will occur. Emory S. Land is forward deployed in the Indian Ocean at Diego Garcia while Frank Cable is forward-deployed in the Pacific at Polaris Point, Apra Harbor, Guam. Such forward deployments are to provide service and support at the very great distances of the Western Pacific.

Two tenders, SS Nomadic and SS Traffic, were built for the White Star Line by Harland and Wolff to serve the liners RMS Olympic and RMS Titanic at Cherbourg. Nomadic survives as a museum ship, and is the last remaining vessel built for the White Star Line still afloat.

TYPES OF TENDERS

- Armed tender, British supply or transport ships that were outfitted and commissioned for military use in the Naval Service.
- Buoy tender, used to maintain navigational aids.
- Destroyer tender, a large ship used to support a flotilla of destroyers or other small warships.
- Dive tender, a ship or boat used to support the actions of divers. Also known as a diving support vessel.
- Lighthouse tender, used to tend lighthouses and, later, buoys.
- Luxury yacht tender, a small boat used on luxury yachts.
- Motor torpedo boat tender, a mobile base and supply ship used to support motor torpedo boats on operations during World War II.
- Seaplane tender, a ship carrying multiple seaplanes. Also known as a seaplane carrier, and considered to be a predecessor to the aircraft carrier.
- Submarine tender, a large ship used to support a flotilla of submarines.
- Torpedo boat tender, a ship used during the late 19th and early 20th centuries to carry torpedo boats to sea and deploy them against enemy ships

TOWBOAT

A towboat is a boat designed for pushing barges or car floats. Towboats are characterized by a square bow with steel knees for pushing and powerful engines. They are most often seen on inland waterways and western rivers where they can push more than 50 large barges lashed together into a tow of varying shapes and sizes. Towboats that travel long distances (linehaul) include living quarters for the crew. Outside of the USA towboats are usually referred to as "push boats" or "pushers".

TOWBOAT SIZE

Towboats range in size from less than 600 horsepower (447 kW) up to 11,100 horsepower (8,277 kW). Most towboats are from 35 to 200 feet (11 to 61 m) long, and 21 to 56 feet (6.4 to 17.1 m) wide. Smaller boats are used in harbors, fleeting areas and around locks while larger boats operate in "line-haul" operations over long distances and between major ports. In the United States, south of the Chain of Rocks Lock across from St. Louis on the Mississippi River, the river is open with no locks or impediments other than channel size and depth. Larger boats can run this segment of the river with the maximum tow size of 42 barges southbound and 40+ northbound. A typical River tow might be 35 to 42 barges, each about 200 feet (61 m) long by 35 feet (11 m) wide, configured in a rectangular shape 6 to 7 barges long and 5 to 6 barges wide, depending on the number of barges in tow. The whole tow, excluding the towboat, can easily be over 1,200 feet (370 m) long and 200 feet (61 m) wide, covering over 6 acres (2.4 ha) and holding thousands of tons of cargo.

In the United States above St. Louis on the Upper Mississippi River and on other rivers such as the Illinois, Ohio, Arkansas, Tennessee and Cumberland, boats can handle only up to 15 barges due the size of lock chambers. These boats tend to be limited to 5,000 horsepower (3,728 kW).

Towboats in line-haul service operate 24/7 and have the latest in navigational equipment, such as color radar, GPS systems, electronic river charts, and specialized radio communications.

Boats that traverse the Intra-Coastal Waterway (ICW) are commonly referred to as "ditch boats" or "canal boats". ICW tows usually consist of 1 to 4 barges ranging in size, usually "strung out" end to end when loaded or "doubled up" side by side when empty.

Towboats always push the fleet of barges, which are lashed together with steel cables usually 1 to 1.5 in (25.4 to 38.1 mm) in diameter. The term towboat arises from steamboat days, when steamboat fortunes began to decline and to survive steamboats began to "tow" wooden barges alongside to earn additional revenue. Eventually, the railroad expansion following the American Civil War ended the steamboat era.

TUGBOAT

A tugboat (tug) is a boat that maneuvers vessels by pushing or towing them. Tugs move vessels that either should not move themselves, such as ships in a crowded harbor or a narrow canal, or those that cannot move by themselves, such as barges, disabled ships, log rafts, or oil platforms. Tugboats are powerful for their size and strongly built, and some are ocean-going. Some tugboats serve as icebreakers or salvage boats. Early tugboats had steam engines, but today most have diesel engines. Many tugboats have firefighting monitors, allowing them to assist in firefighting, especially in harbors.

TYPES OF TUGBOATS

Seagoing tugboats

Seagoing tugboats (or ocean tugboats) fall into four basic categories:

1. The standard seagoing tugboat with model bow that tows its "payload" on a hawser.
2. The "Notch Tug" which can be secured in a notch at the stern of a specially designed barge, effectively making the combination of a ship. This configuration is dangerous to use with a barge which is "in ballast" (no cargo) or in a head or following sea. Therefore, the "notch tugs" are usually built with a towing winch. With this configuration, the barge being pushed might approach the size of a small ship, with interaction of the water flow allowing a higher speed with a minimal increase in power required or fuel consumption.
3. The "integral unit," or "Integrated Tug and Barge" (ITB), comprises specially designed vessels that lock together in such a rigid and strong method as to be certified as such by authorities (classification societies) such as the American Bureau of Shipping, Lloyd's Register of Shipping, Indian Register of Shipping, Det Norske Veritas or several others. These units stay combined under virtually any sea conditions and the "tugs" usually have poor sea-keeping designs for navigation without their "barges" attached. Vessels in this category are legally considered to be ships rather than tugboats and barges must be staffed accordingly. These vessels must show navigation lights compliant with those required of ships rather than those required of tugboats and vessels under tow.
4. "Articulated Tug and Barge" (ATB) units also utilize mechanical means to connect to their barges. ATB's generally utilize Intercon and Bludworth connecting systems. Other available systems include Articouple, Hydraconn and Beacon JAK. ATB's are generally staffed as a large tugboat, with between seven to nine crew members. The

typical American ATB operating on the east coast, per custom, displays navigational lights of a towing vessel pushing ahead, as described in the '72 COLREGS.

Harbour tugboats

Compared to seagoing tugboats, harbour tugboats are generally smaller and the width-to-length ratio is often higher, due to the need for a lower draught. In smaller harbours these are often also termed lunch bucket boats, because they are only manned when needed and only at a minimum (captain and deckhand), thus the crew will bring their own lunch with them. The number of tugboats in a harbour varies with the harbour infrastructure and the types of tugboats. Things to take into consideration includes ships with/ without bowthrusters and forces like wind, current and waves and type of ships (i.e. in some countries there is a requirement for a certain amount and size of tugboats for port operations with gas tankers).

River tugboats

River tugs are also referred to as towboats or pushboats. Their hull designs would make open ocean operation dangerous. River tugs usually do not have any significant hawser or winch. Their hulls feature a flat front or bow to line up with the rectangular stern of the barge, often with large pushing knees.

TUGBOAT PROPULSION

Tugboat engines typically produce 500 to 2,500 kW (~ 680 to 3,400 hp), but larger boats (used in deep waters) can have power ratings up to 20,000 kW (~ 27,200 hp) and usually have an extreme power:tonnage-ratio (normal cargo and passenger ships have a P:T-ratio (in kW:GRT) of 0.35 to 1.20, whereas large tugs typically are 2.20 to 4.50 and small harbour-tugs 4.0 to 9.5). The engines are often the same as those used in railroad locomotives, but typically drive the propeller mechanically instead of converting the engine output to power electric motors, as is common for diesel-electric locomotives. For safety, tugboats' engines often feature two of each critical part for redundancy.

A tugboat's power is typically stated by its engine's horsepower and its overall bollard pull. The largest commercial harbour tugboats in the 2000s-2010s, used for towing container ships or similar, had around 60-65 tons of bollard pull, which is described as 15 tons above "normal" tugboats.

Tugboats are highly maneuverable, and various propulsion systems have been developed to increase maneuverability and increase safety. The earliest tugs were fitted with paddle wheels, but these were soon replaced by propeller-driven tugs. Kort nozzles have been added to increase thrust per kW/hp. This was followed by the nozzle-rudder, which omitted the need for a conventional rudder. The cycloidal propeller was developed prior to World

War II and was occasionally used in tugs because of its maneuverability. After WWII it was also linked to safety due to the development of the Voith Water Tractor, a tugboat configuration which could not be pulled over by its tow. In the late 1950s, the Z-drive or (azimuth thruster) was developed. Although sometimes referred to as the Schottel system, many brands exist: Schottel, Z-Peller, Duckpeller, Thrustmaster of Texas, Ulstein, Wärtsilä, Berg Propulsion, etc. These propulsion systems are used on tugboats designed for tasks such as ship docking and marine construction. Conventional propeller/rudder configurations are more efficient for port-to-port towing.

The Kort nozzle is a sturdy cylindrical structure around a special propeller having minimum clearance between the propeller blades and the inner wall of the Kort nozzle. The thrust-to-power ratio is enhanced because the water approaches the propeller in a linear configuration and exits the nozzle the same way. The Kort nozzle is named after its inventor, but many brands exist.

A recent Dutch innovation is the Carousel Tug, winner of the Maritime Innovation Award at the Dutch Maritime Innovation Awards Gala in 2006. The Carousel Tug adds a pair of interlocking rings to the body of the tug, the inner ring attached to the boat, with the outer ring attached to the towed ship by winch or towing hook. Since the towing point rotates freely, the tug is very difficult to capsize.

The Voith Schneider propeller (VSP), also known as a cycloidal drive is a specialized marine propulsion system. It is highly maneuverable, being able to change the direction of its thrust almost instantaneously. It is widely used on tugs and ferries.

From a circular plate, rotating around a vertical axis, a circular array of vertical blades (in the shape of hydrofoils) protrude out of the bottom of the ship. Each blade can rotate itself around a vertical axis. The internal gear changes the angle of attack of the blades in sync with the rotation of the plate, so that each blade can provide thrust in any direction, very similar to the collective pitch control and cyclic in a helicopter.

AUTOMATIC IDENTIFICATION SYSTEM

The Automatic Identification System (AIS) is an automatic tracking system used on ships and by vessel traffic services (VTS) for identifying and locating vessels by electronically exchanging data with other nearby ships, AIS base stations, and satellites. When satellites are used to detect AIS signatures then the term Satellite-AIS (S-AIS)is used. AIS information supplements marine radar, which continues to be the primary method of collision avoidance for water transport.

Information provided by AIS equipment, such as unique identification, position, course, and speed, can be displayed on a screen or an ECDIS. AIS is intended to assist a vessel's watchstanding officers and allow maritime authorities to track and monitor vessel movements. AIS integrates a standardizedVHF transceiver with a positioning system such as a LORAN-C or GPS receiver, with other electronic navigation sensors, such as a gyrocompass or rate of turn indicator. Vessels fitted with AIS transceivers and transponders can be tracked by AIS base stations located along coast lines or, when out of range of terrestrial networks, through a growing number of satellites that are fitted with special AIS receivers which are capable of deconflicting a large number of signatures.

The International Maritime Organization's International Convention for the Safety of Life at Sea requires AIS to be fitted aboard international voyaging ships with gross tonnage (GT) of 300 or more, and all passenger ships regardless of size.

DEPLOYMENT HISTORY

The 2002 IMO SOLAS Agreement included a mandate that required most vessels over 300GT on international voyages to fit a Class A type AIS transceiver. This was the first mandate for the use of AIS equipment and affected approximately 100,000 vessels.

In 2006, the AIS standards committee published the Class B type AIS transceiver specification, designed to enable a simpler and lower cost AIS device. In 2006, SRT Marine Technology of the UK developed and released the world's first Class B transceiver. The introduction of low cost Class B transponders has triggered multiple additional national mandates from Singapore, China and Turkey by making large scale rollout of AIS devices onto vessels of all sizes commercially viable.

Since 2006, the AIS technical standard committees have continued to evolve the AIS standard and product types to cover a wide range of applications from the largest vessel to small fishing vessels and life boats. In parallel, governments and authorities have instigated projects to fit varying classes of vessels with an AIS device to improve safety and security. Most mandates are focused on commercial vessels, with leisure vessels selectively choosing to fit.

In 2010 most commercial vessels operating on the European Inland Waterways were required to fit an Inland waterway certified Class A, all EU fishing boats over 16m will have to have a Class A by May 2014, and the US has a long pending extension to their existing AIS fit rules which is expected to come into force during 2013. It is estimated that as of 2012, approximately 250,000 vessels have fitted an AIS transceiver of some type, with a further 1 million required to do so in the near future and even larger projects under consideration.

SATELLITE-BASED AIS (S-AIS)

AIS was developed in the 1990s as a high intensity, short range identification and tracking network and, at the time, it was not anticipated to be detectable from space. Nevertheless, since 2005, various entities have been experimenting with detecting AIS transmissions using satellite-based receivers and, since 2008, companies such as exactEarth, ORBCOMM, Spacequest and also government programs have deployed AIS receivers on satellites. The TDMA radio access scheme used by the AIS system creates significant technical issues for the reliable reception of AIS messages from all types of transceivers: Class A, Class B, Identifier, AtoN and SART. However, the industry is seeking to address these issues through the development of new technologies and over the coming years the current restriction of satellite AIS systems to Class A messages is likely to dramatically improve with the addition of Class B and Identifier messages.

The fundamental challenge for AIS satellite operators is the ability to receive very large numbers of AIS messages simultaneously from a satellite's large reception footprint. There is an inherent issue within the AIS standard; the TDMA radio access scheme defined in the AIS standard creates 4,500 available time-slots in each minute but this can be easily overwhelmed by the large satellite reception footprints and the increasing numbers of AIS transceivers, resulting in message collisions, which the satellite receiver cannot process.

Companies such as exactEarth are developing new technologies such as ABSEA, that will be embedded within terrestrial and satellite-based transceivers, which will assist the reliable detection of Class B messages from space without affecting the performance of terrestrial AIS.

The addition of satellite-based Class A and B messages could enable truly global AIS coverage but, because the satellite-based TDMA limitations will never match the reception performance of the terrestrial-based network, satellites will augment rather than replace the terrestrial system.

S-AIS & SENSOR CORRELATION

Correlating optical and radar imagery with S-AIS signatures enables the end-user to rapidly identify all types of vessel. A great strength of S-AIS is the ease with which it can be correlated with additional information from other sources such as radar, optical, ESM, and more SAR related tools such as GMDSS SARSAT [1] and AMVER [2]. Satellite-based radar and other sources can contribute to maritime surveillance by detecting all vessels in specific maritime areas of interest, a particularly useful attribute when trying to co-ordinate a long-range rescue effort or when dealing with VTS issues.

APPLICATIONS AND LIMITATIONS

Collision avoidance

AIS was developed by the IMO technical committees as a technology to avoid collisions among large vessels at sea that are not within range of shore-based systems. The technology identifies every vessel individually, along with its specific position and movements, enabling a virtual picture to be created in real time. The AIS standards include a variety of automatic calculations based on these position reports such as Closest Point of Approach (CPA) and collision alarms. As AIS is not used by all vessels, AIS is usually used in conjunction with radar.

When a ship is navigating at sea, information about the movement and identity of other ships in the vicinity is critical for navigators to make decisions to avoid collision with other ships and dangers (shoal or rocks). Visual observation (e.g., unaided, binoculars, and night vision), audio exchanges (e.g., whistle, horns, and VHF radio), and radar or Automatic Radar Plotting Aid are historically used for this purpose.

These preventative mechanisms, however, sometimes fail due to time delays, radar limitations, miscalculations, and display malfunctions and can result in a collision.

While requirements of AIS are to display only very basic text information, the data obtained can be integrated with a graphical electronic chart or a radar display, providing consolidated navigational information on a single display.

FISHING FLEET MONITORING AND CONTROL

AIS is widely used by national authorities to track and monitor the activities of their national fishing fleets. AIS enables authorities to reliably and cost effectively monitor fishing vessel activities along their coast line, typically out to a range of 60 miles (depending on location and quality of coast based receivers/base stations) with supplementary data from satellite based networks.

VESSEL TRAFFIC SERVICES

In busy waters and harbors, a local vessel traffic service (VTS) may exist to manage ship traffic. Here, AIS provides additional traffic awareness and information about the configuration and movements of ships.

MARITIME SECURITY

AIS enables authorities to identify specific vessels and their activity within or near a nation's Exclusive Economic Zone. When AIS data is fused with existing radar systems, authorities are able to differentiate between vessels more easily. AIS data can be automatically processed to create normalized activity patterns for individual vessels, which when breached, create an alert this highlighting potential threats for more efficient use of security assets.

AIS improves maritime domain awareness and allows for heightened security and control. Additionally, AIS can be applied to freshwaterriver systems and lakes.

AIDS TO NAVIGATION

The AIS Aids to Navigation (AtoN) product standard was developed with the ability to broadcast the positions and names of objects other than vessels, such as navigational aid and marker positions and dynamic data reflecting the marker's environment (e.g., currents and climatic conditions). These aids can be located on shore, such as in a lighthouse, or on water, platforms, or buoys. The U.S. Coast Guard has suggested that AIS might replace racon (radar beacons) currently used for electronic navigation aids.

AtoN's enable authorities to remotely monitor the status of a buoy, such as the status of the lantern, as well as transmit live data from sensors (such as weather and sea state) located on the buoy back to vessels fitted with AIS transceivers or local authorities. An AtoN will broadcast its position and Identity along with all the other information.

The AtoN standard also permits the transmit of 'Virtual AtoN' positions whereby a single device may transmit messages with a 'false' position such that an AtoN marker appears on electronic charts, although a physical AtoN may not be present at that location.

SEARCH AND RESCUE

For coordinating on-scene resources of a marine search and rescue (SAR) operation, it is imperative to have data on the position and navigation status of other ships in the vicinity. In such cases, AIS can provide additional information and enhance awareness of available resources, even if the AIS range is limited to VHF radio range. The AIS standard also envisioned the possible use on SAR aircraft, and included a message (AIS Message 9) for aircraft to report their position.

To aid SAR vessels and aircraft in locating people in distress, the specification (IEC 61097-14 Ed 1.0) for an AIS-based SAR transmitter (AIS-SART) was developed by the IEC's TC80 AIS work group. AIS-SART was added to Global Maritime Distress Safety System regulations effective January 1, 2010. AIS-SARTs have been available on the market since at least 2009.

Recent regulations have mandated the installation of AIS systems on all Safety Of Life At Sea (SOLAS) vessels and vessels over 300 tons.

ACCIDENT INVESTIGATION

AIS information received by VTS is important for accident investigation since it provides accurate data on time, identity, GPS-based position, compass heading, course over ground, speed (by log/SOG), and rates of turn, rather than the less accurate information provided by radar.

A more complete picture of the events could be obtained by Voyage Data Recorder (VDR) data if available and maintained on board for details of the movement of the ship, voice communication and radar pictures during the accidents. However, VDR data are not maintained due to the limited twelve hours storage by IMO requirement.

BINARY MESSAGES

AIS messages 6, 8, 25, and 26 provide "Application Specific Messages" (ASM), that allow "competent authorities" to define additional AIS message subtypes. There are both "addressed" (ABM) and "broadcast" (BBM) variants of the message. Addressed messages, while containing a destination MMSI, are not private and may be decoded by any receiver.

One of the first uses of ASMs was the Saint Lawrence Seaway use of AIS binary messages (message type 8) to provide information about water levels, lock orders, and weather. The Panama Canal uses AIS type 8 messages to provide information about rain along the canal and wind in the locks. In 2010, the International Maritime Organization issued Circular 289 that defines the next iteration of ASMs for type 6 and 8 messages. Alexander, Schwehr and Zetterberg proposed that the community of competent authorities work together to maintain a regional register of these messages and their locations of use. The International Association of Marine Aids to Navigation and Lighthouse Authorities (IALA-AISM) now established a process for collection of regional application specific messages.

COMPUTING AND NETWORKING

Several computer programs have been created for use with AIS data. Some programs such as ShipPlotter and Gnuais use a computer to demodulate the raw audio from a modified marine VHFradiotelephone, tuned to the AIS frequencies (Channel 87 – 161.975 MHz and Channel 88 – 162.025 MHz) into AIS data.

Some programs can re-transmit the AIS information to a local or global network (via TCP or UDP) allowing the public or authorized users to observe vessel traffic from the web. Some programs display AIS data received from a dedicated AIS receiver onto a computer or chartplotter.

Computer AIS monitoring programs, by definition do not possess AIS transponders. Most AIS physical devices (like USB VHF radio dongles) do not contain AIS transponders.

With these monitoring systems your position (or your vessel's position) will not be transmitted. However, these devices may be used as an inexpensive alternative to AIS devices for smaller vessels if no other viable alternative can be found.

Ship enthusiasts also use such systems to track and find vessels to add to their photo collections.

AIS mobile apps are also becoming common for use with Android and iOS devices. These apps use GPS positioning and Internet access on the mobile device (smartphones or tablets) to provide near real-time position data to and from the AIS network. As the devices use a mobile (cellular) telephone network for the data transmission, the useful distance offshore will be limited and subject to network availability. Note also that the mobile device is not a transponder and accordingly a craft using the Internet-based AIS network will not be visible to other vessels on their AIS systems unless they also use data from the same land based AIS networks.

AIS DATA ON THE INTERNET

AIS position data are available on the Internet through privately operated geographic information systems. In December 2004, the IMO's Maritime Safety Committee condemned the Internet publication of AIS data as follows:

In relation to the issue of freely available automatic identification system (AIS)-generated ship data on the world-wide web, the publication on the world-wide web or elsewhere of AIS data transmitted by ships could be detrimental to the safety and security of ships and port facilities and was undermining the efforts of the Organization and its Member States to enhance the safety of navigation and security in the international maritime transport sector.

Others have countered that AIS provides the same information that can be obtained with a pair of binoculars and that ships have the option of turning off AIS when they are in areas with security concerns.

However, binoculars need line of sight and clear visibility and so do not help in fog or where a land mass obstructs the view, unlike AIS radio waves (though both fog and large land masses can interfere with the VHF signals used by AIS, too). Vessels can turn off AIS to attempt to be invisible but, since they can still be seen by radar, the absence of an AIS signal would highlight them as unusual and worthy of investigation where security or piracy are priorities. Furthermore, not publishing the data on the internet would not keep others from receiving and tracking these signals with homemade devices and a laptop computer since there is software available for decoding such data.

RANGE LIMITATIONS DRIVE S-AIS SPACE RACE

Shipboard AIS transponders have a horizontal range that is highly variable, but typically only up to about 74 kilometres (46 mi). They reach much further vertically – up to the 400 km orbit of the International Space Station (ISS).

In November 2009, the STS-129 space shuttle mission attached two antennas—an AIS VHF antenna, and an Amateur Radio antenna to the Columbus module of the ISS. Both antennas were built in cooperation between ESA and the ARISS team (Amateur Radio on ISS). Starting from May 2010 the European Space Agency is testing an AIS receiver from Kongsberg Seatex (Norway) in a consortium lead by FFI (Norway) in the frame of technology demonstration for space-based ship monitoring. This is a first step towards a satellite-based AIS-monitoring service.

In 2008, ORBCOMM launched AIS enabled satellites in conjunction with a US Coast Guard contract to demonstrate the ability to collect AIS messages from space. In 2009, Luxspace, a Luxembourg-based company, launched the RUBIN-9.1 satellite (AIS Pathfinder 2). The satellite is operated in cooperation with SES and REDU Space Services. In late 2011 and early 2012, ORBCOMM and Luxspace launched the Vesselsat AIS microsatellites, one in an equatorial orbit and the other in a polar orbit.

In 2007, the U.S. tested space-based AIS tracking with the TacSat-2 satellite. However, the received signals were corrupted because of the simultaneous receipt of many signals from all over the world.

In July 2009, SpaceQuest launched AprizeSat-3 and AprizeSat-4 with AIS receivers. These receivers were successfully able to receive the U.S. Coast Guard's SART test beacons off of Hawaii in 2010. In July 2010, SpaceQuest and exactEarth of Canada announced an arrangement whereby data from AprizeSat-3 and AprizeSat-4 would be incorporated into the exactEarth system and made available worldwide as part of their exactAIS(TM)service.

On July 12, 2010, The Norwegian AISSat-1 satellite was successfully launched into polar orbit. The purpose of the satellite is to improve surveillance of maritime activities in the High North. AISSat-1 is a nano-satellite, measuring only 20x20x20 cm, with an AIS receiver made by Kongsberg Seatex. It weighs six kilograms and is shaped like a cube.

On February 25, 2013 - after one year launch delay - Aalborg University did launch AAUSAT3. I is a 1U cubesat, weights 800 grams, solely developed by students from Department of Electronic Systems. It carries two AIS receivers - a traditional and a SDR based receiver. The project was proposed and sponsored by the Danish Safety Maritime Organisation. It has been a huge success and has in the first 100 days downloaded more than 800000 AIS messages and several 1MHz raw samples of radio signal. It receives both AIS channels simultaneously and has received class A as well as class B receivers. Cost including launch is lower than €200.000.

Today, Canadian based exactEarth operates the largest AIS satellite network, providing global coverage using 5 satellites. This network will be significantly expanded in the coming years. Additionally exactEarth is involved in the development of ABSEA technology which will enable its network to reliably detect a high proportion of Class B type messages, as well as Class A.

ORBCOMM will be launching 17 additional satellites, as part of its OG2 (ORBCOMM Generation 2) satellite replenishment, that will all carry AIS receivers, and will download at ORBCOMM's 16 existing earth stations around the globe.

TYPE TESTING AND APPROVAL

AIS is a technology which has been developed under the auspices of the IMO by its technical committees. The technical committees have developed and published a series of AIS product specifications. Each specification defines a specific AIS product which has carefully created to work in a precise way with all the other defined AIS devices, thus ensuring AIS system interoperability worldwide.

Maintenance of the specification integrity is deemed critical for the performance of the AIS system and the safety of vessels and authorities using the technology. As such most countries require that AIS products are independently tested and certified to comply with a specific published specification. Products that have not been tested and certified by a competent authority, may not conform to the required AIS published specification and therefore may not operate as expected in the field.

The most widely recognized and accepted certifications are the R&TTE Directive, the U.S. Federal Communications Commission, and Industry Canada, all of which require independent verification by a qualified and independent testing agency.

HOW AIS WORKS

Basic overview

AIS transponders automatically broadcast information, such as their position, speed, and navigational status, at regular intervals via a VHF transmitter built into the transponder. The information originates from the ship's navigational sensors, typically its global navigation satellite system (GNSS) receiver and gyrocompass. Other information, such as the vessel name and VHF call sign, is programmed when installing the equipment and is also transmitted regularly. The signals are received by AIS transponders fitted on other ships or on land based systems, such as VTS systems. The received information can be displayed on a screen or chart plotter, showing the other vessels' positions in much the same manner as a radar display.

The AIS standard comprises several substandards called "types" that specify individual product types. The specification for each product type provides a detailed technical specification which ensures the overall integrity of the global AIS system within which all the product types must operate. The major product types described in the AIS system standards are:

- *Class A:* Vessel-mounted AIS transceiver (transmit and receive) which operates using self-organised time-division multiple-access (SOTDMA). Targeted at large commercial vessels, SOTDMA requires a transceiver to maintain a constantly updated slot map in its memory such that it has prior knowledge of slots which are available for it to transmit. SOTDMA transceivers will then pre-announce their transmission, effectively reserving their transmit slot. SOTDMA transmissions are therefore prioritised within the AIS system. This is achieved through 2 receivers in continuous operation. Class A's must have an integrated display, transmit at 12 W, interface capability with multiple ship systems, and offer a sophisticated selection of features and functions. Default transmit rate is every few seconds. AIS Class A type compliant devices receive all types of AIS messages.

- *Class B:* Vessel-mounted AIS transceiver (transmit and receive) which operates using either carrier-sense time-division multiple-access (CSTDMA)or SOTDMA; there are now 2 separate IMO specifications for Class B. Aimed at lighter commercial and leisure markets. CSTDMA transceivers listen to the slot map immediately prior to transmitting and seek a slot where the 'noise' in the slot is the same or similar to background noise, thereby indicating that the slot is not being used by another AIS device. Class Bs transmit at 2 W and are not required to have an integrated display: Class Bs can be connected to most display systems where the received messages will be displayed in lists or overlayed on charts. Default transmit rate is normally every 30 seconds, but this can be varied according to vessel speed or instructions from base stations. The Class B type standard requires integrated GPS and certain LED indicators. Class B equipment receives all types of AIS messages.
- *Base station:* Shore-based AIS transceiver (transmit and receive) which operates using SOTDMA. Base stations have a complex set of features and functions which in the AIS standard are able to control the AIS system and all devices operating therein. Ability to interrogate individual transponders for status reports and or transmit frequency changes.
- *Aids to navigation (AtoN):* Shore- or buoy-based transceiver (transmit and receive) which operates using fixed-access time-division multiple-access (FATDMA). Designed to collect and transmit data related to sea and weather conditions as well as relay AIS messages to extend network coverage.
- *Search And Rescue Transponder (SART):* Specialist AIS device created as an emergency distress beacon which operates using pre-announce time-division multiple-access (PATDMA), or sometimes called a "modified SOTDMA". The device randomly selects a slot to transmit and will transmit a burst of eight messages per minute to maximize the probability of successful transmission. A SART is required to transmit up to a maximum of five miles and transmits a special

message format recognised by other AIS devices. The device is designed for perodic use and only in emergencies due to its PATDMA-type operation which places stress on the slot map.

- *Specialist AIS Transponders:* Despite there being IMO/IEC published AIS specifications, a number of authorities have permitted and encouraged the development of hybrid AIS devices. These devices seek to maintain the integrity of the core AIS transmission structure and design to ensure operational reliability, but to add a range of additional features and functions to suit their specific requirements. The "Identifier" AIS transceiver is one such product where the core Class B CSTDMA technology is designed to ensure that the device transmits in complete compliance with the IMO specifications, but a number of changes have been made to enable it to be battery powered, low cost and more easy to install and deploy in large numbers. Such devices will not have international certification against an IMO specification since they will comply with a proportion of the relevant specification. Typically authorities will make their own detailed technical evaluation and test to ensure that the core operation of the device does not harm the international AIS system.

AIS receivers are not specified in the AIS standards, because they do not transmit. The main threat to the integrity of any AIS system are non-compliant AIS transmissions, hence careful specifications of all transmitting AIS devices. However, it is well to note that AIS transceivers all transmit on multiple channels as required by the AIS standards. As such single-channel, or multiplexed, receivers will not receive all AIS messages. Only dual-channel receivers will receive all AIS messages.

Message types

There are 27 different types of top level messages defined in ITU 1371-4 (out of a possibility of 64) that can be sent by AIS transceivers.

DETAILED DESCRIPTION: CLASS A UNITS

Each AIS transponder consists of one VHF transmitter, two VHF TDMA receivers, one VHF Digital Selective Calling (DSC) receiver, and links to shipboard display and sensor systems via standard marine electronic communications (such as NMEA 0183, also known as IEC 61162). Timing is vital to the proper synchronization and slot mapping (transmission scheduling) for a Class A unit.

Therefore, every unit is required to have an internal time base, synchronized to a global navigation satellite system (e.g. GPS) receiver. This internal receiver may also be used for position information. However, position is typically provided by an external receiver such as GPS, LORAN or an inertial navigation system and the internal receiver is only used as a backup for position information. Other information broadcast by the AIS, if available, is electronically obtained from shipboard equipment through standard marine data connections. Heading information, position (latitude and longitude), "speed over ground", and rate of turn are normally provided by all ships equipped with AIS. Other information, such as angle of heel, pitch and roll, destination, and ETA may also be provided.

An AIS transponder normally works in an autonomous and continuous mode, regardless of whether it is operating in the open seas or coastal or inland areas. AIS transponders use two different frequencies, VHFmaritime channels 87B (161.975 MHz) and 88B (162.025 MHz), and use 9.6 kbit/s Gaussian minimum shift keying (GMSK) modulation over 25 or 12.5 kHz channels using the High-level Data Link Control (HDLC) packet protocol. Although only one radio channel is necessary, each station transmits and receives over two radio channels to avoid interference problems, and to allow channels to be shifted without communications loss from other ships. The system provides for automatic contention resolution between itself and other stations, and communications integrity is maintained even in overload situations.

In order to ensure that the VHF transmissions of different transponders do not occur at the same time, the signals are time multiplexed using a technology called Self-Organized Time Division Multiple Access (STDMA). The design of this technology is patented, and whether this patent has been waived for use by SOLAS vessels is a matter of debate between the manufacturers of AIS systems and the patent holder, Håkan Lans. Moreover, the United States Patent and Trademark Office (USPTO) canceled all claims in the original patent on March 30, 2010.

In order to make the most efficient use of the bandwidth available, vessels that are anchored or moving slowly transmit less frequently than those that are moving faster or are maneuvering. The update rate ranges from 3 minutes for anchored or moored vessels, to 2 seconds for fast moving or maneuvering vessels, the latter being similar to that of conventional marine radar.

Each AIS station determines its own transmission schedule (slot), based upon data link traffic history and an awareness of probable future actions by other stations. A position report from one station fits into one of 2,250 time slots established every 60 seconds on each frequency. AIS stations continuously synchronize themselves to each other, to avoid overlap of slot transmissions. Slot selection by an AIS station is randomized within a defined interval and tagged with a random timeout of between 0 and 8 frames. When a station changes its slot assignment, it announces both the new location and the timeout for that location. In this way new stations, including those stations which suddenly come within radio range close to other vessels, will always be received by those vessels.

The required ship reporting capacity according to the IMO performance standard is a minimum of 2,000 time slots per minute, though the system provides 4,500 time slots per minute. The SOTDMA broadcast mode allows the system to be overloaded by 400 to 500% through sharing of slots, and still provides nearly 100% throughput for ships closer than 8 to 10 nmi to each other in a ship to ship mode. In the event of system overload, only targets further away will be subject to drop-out, in order to give preference to nearer targets, which are of greater concern to ship operators. In practice, the capacity of the system is nearly unlimited, allowing for a great number of ships to be accommodated at the same time.

The system coverage range is similar to other VHF applications. The range of any VHF radio is determined by multiple factors, the primary factors are: the height and quality of the transmitting antenna and the height and quality of the receiving antenna. Its propagation is better than that of radar, due to the longer wavelength, so it is possible to reach around bends and behind islands if the land masses are not too high. The look-ahead distance at sea is nominally 20 nmi (37 km). With the help of repeater stations, the coverage for both ship and VTS stations can be improved considerably.

The system is backward compatible with digital selective calling systems, allowing shore-based GMDSS systems to inexpensively establish AIS operating channels and identify and track AIS-equipped vessels, and is intended to fully replace existing DSC-based transponder systems.

Shore-based AIS network systems are now being built up around the world. One of the biggest fully operational, real time systems with full routing capability is in China. This system was built between 2003 and 2007 and was delivered by Saab TransponderTech. The entire Chinese coastline is covered with approximately 250 base stations in hot-standby configurations including seventy computer servers in three main regions. Hundreds of shore based users, including about twenty-five vessel traffic service (VTS) centers, are connected to the network and are able to see the maritime picture, and can also communicate with each ship using SRM's (Safety Related Messages). All data are in real time.

The system was designed to improve the safety and security of ships and port facilities. It is also designed according to an SOA architecture with socket based connection and using IEC AIS standardized protocol all the way to the VTS users. The base stations have hot-standby units (IEC 62320-1) and the network is the third generation network solution.

By the beginning of 2007, a new worldwide standard for AIS base stations was approved, the IEC 62320-1 standard. The old IALA recommendation and the new IEC 62320-1 standard are in some functions incompatible, and therefore attached network solutions have to be upgraded. This will not affect users, but system builders need to upgrade software to accommodate the new standard. A standard for AIS base stations has been long awaited. Currently ad-hoc networks exist with class A mobiles. Base stations can control the AIS message traffic in a region, which will hopefully reduce the number of packet collisions.

BROADCAST INFORMATION

An AIS transceiver sends the following data every 2 to 10 seconds depending on a vessel's speed while underway, and every 3 minutes while a vessel is at anchor:

- The vessel's Maritime Mobile Service Identity (MMSI) – a unique nine digit identification number.
- Navigation status – "at anchor", "under way using engine(s)", "not under command", etc.
- Rate of turn – right or left, from 0 to 720 degrees per minute
- Speed over ground – 0.1-knot (0.19 km/h) resolution from 0 to 102 knots (189 km/h)
- Positional accuracy:
  - Longitude – to 0.0001 minutes
  - Latitude – to 0.0001 minutes
- Course over ground – relative to true north to 0.1°
- True heading – 0 to 359 degrees (for example from a gyro compass)
- True bearing at own position. 0 to 359 degrees
- UTC Seconds – The seconds field of the UTC time when these data were generated. A complete timestamp is not present.

In addition, the following data are broadcast every 6 minutes:

- IMO ship identification number – a seven digit number that remains unchanged upon transfer of the ship's registration to another country
- Radio call sign – international radio call sign, up to seven characters, assigned to the vessel by its country of registry
- Name – 20 characters to represent the name of the vessel
- Type of ship/cargo
- Dimensions of ship – to nearest meter
- Location of positioning system's (e.g., GPS) antenna on board the vessel - in meters aft of bow and meters port of starboard
- Type of positioning system – such as GPS, DGPS or LORAN-C.
- Draught of ship – 0.1 meter to 25.5 meters
- Destination – max. 20 characters
- ETA (estimated time of arrival) at destination – UTC month/date hour:minute

- optional: high precision time request, a vessel can request other vessels provide a high precision UTC time and datestamp

DETAILED DESCRIPTION: CLASS B UNITS

Class B transponders smaller, simpler and lower cost than Class A transceivers. Each consists of one VHF transmitter, two VHF Carrier Sense Time Division Multiple Access (CSTDMA) receivers, one of which is multiplexed with the VHF Digital Selective Calling (DSC) receiver, and a GPS active antenna. Although the data output format supports heading information, in general units are not interfaced to a compass, so this data is seldom transmitted. Output is the standard AIS data stream at 38.400 kbit/s, as RS232 and/or NMEA formats. To prevent overloading of the available bandwidth, transmission power is restricted to 2 W, giving a range of about 5–10 mi.

At the time of writing (November 2009) almost all Class B units use boards from Software Radio Technology (SRT). Exceptions to this are Furuno, AMEC, Weatherdock and Vesper Marine. Four messages are defined for class B units:

Message 14: Safety Related Message

This message is transmitted on request for the user – some transponders have a button that enables it to be sent, or it can be sent through the software interface. It sends a pre-defined safety message.

Message 18: Standard Class B CS Position Report

This message is sent every 3 minutes where speed over ground (SOG) is less than 2 knots, or every 30 seconds for greater speeds.

MMSI, time, SOG, COG, longitude, latitude, true heading

Message 19: Extended Class B Equipment Position Report

This message was designed for the SOTDMA protocol, and is too long to be transmitted as CSTDMA. However a coast station can poll the transponder for this message to be sent.

MMSI, time, SOG, COG, longitude, latitude, true heading, ship type, dimensions.

Message 24: Class B CS Static Data Report

This message is sent every 6 minutes, the same time interval as for Class A transponders. Because of its length, this message is divided into two parts, sent within one minute of each other.

Note that this message was defined after the original AIS specifications, so some Class A units may need a firmware upgrade to be able to decode this message.

MMSI, boat name, ship type, call sign, dimensions, and equipment vendor id.

DETAILED DESCRIPTION: AIS RECEIVERS

A number of manufacturers offer AIS receivers, designed for monitoring AIS traffic. These may have two receivers, for monitoring both frequencies simultaneously, or they may switch between frequencies (thereby missing messages on the other channel, but at reduced price). In general they will output RS232, NMEA, USB or UDP data for display on electronic chart plotters or computers.

SATELLITE NAVIGATION

A satellite navigation or sat nav system is a system of satellites that provide autonomous geo-spatial positioning with global coverage. It allows small electronic receivers to determine their location (longitude, latitude, and altitude) to high precision (within a few metres) using time signals transmitted along a line of sight by radio from satellites. The signals also allow the electronic receivers to calculate the current local time to high precision, which allows time synchronisation. A satellite navigation system with global coverage may be termed a global navigation satellite system or GNSS.

As of April 2013, only the United States NAVSTAR Global Positioning System (GPS) and the RussianGLONASS are global operational GNSSs. China is in the process of expanding its regional Beidou navigation system into the global Compass navigation system by 2020. The European Union'sGalileo positioning system is a GNSS in initial deployment phase, scheduled to be fully operational by 2020 at the earliest. France, India and Japan are in the process of developing regional navigation systems.

Global coverage for each system is generally achieved by a satellite constellation of 20–30 medium Earth orbit (MEO) satellites spread between several orbital planes. The actual systems vary, but use orbital inclinations of >50° and orbital periods of roughly twelve hours (at an altitude of about 20,000 kilometres (12,000 mi)).

CLASSIFICATION

Satellite navigation systems that provide enhanced accuracy and integrity monitoring usable for civil navigation are classified as follows:

- GNSS-1 is the first generation system and is the combination of existing satellite navigation systems (GPS and GLONASS), with Satellite Based Augmentation Systems (SBAS) or Ground Based Augmentation Systems (GBAS). In the United States, the satellite based component is the Wide Area Augmentation System (WAAS), in Europe it is the European Geostationary Navigation Overlay Service (EGNOS), and in Japan it is the Multi-Functional Satellite

Augmentation System (MSAS). Ground based augmentation is provided by systems like the Local Area Augmentation System (LAAS).

- GNSS-2 is the second generation of systems that independently provides a full civilian satellite navigation system, exemplified by the European Galileo positioning system. These systems will provide the accuracy and integrity monitoring necessary for civil navigation; including aircraft. This system consists of L1 and L2 frequencies for civil use and L5 for system integrity. Development is also in progress to provide GPS with civil use L2 and L5 frequencies, making it a GNSS-2 system.[1]
- Core Satellite navigation systems, currently GPS (United States), GLONASS (Russian Federation), Galileo (European Union) and Compass (China).
- Global Satellite Based Augmentation Systems (SBAS) such as Omnistar and StarFire.
- Regional SBAS including WAAS (US), EGNOS (EU), MSAS (Japan) and GAGAN (India).
- Regional Satellite Navigation Systems such as China's Beidou, India's yet-to-be-operational IRNSS, and Japan's proposed QZSS.
- Continental scale Ground Based Augmentation Systems (GBAS) for example the Australian GRAS and the US Department of Transportation National Differential GPS (DGPS) service.
- Regional scale GBAS such as CORS networks.
- Local GBAS typified by a single GPS reference station operating Real Time Kinematic (RTK) corrections.

HISTORY AND THEORY

The first satellite navigation system was Transit, a system deployed by the US military in the 1960s. Transit's operation was based on the Doppler effect: the satellites traveled on well-known paths and broadcast their signals on a well known frequency.

The received frequency will differ slightly from the broadcast frequency because of the movement of the satellite with respect to the receiver. By monitoring this frequency shift over a short time interval, the receiver can determine its location to one side or the other of the satellite, and several such measurements combined with a precise knowledge of the satellite's orbit can fix a particular position.

Part of an orbiting satellite's broadcast included its precise orbital data. In order to ensure accuracy, the US Naval Observatory (USNO) continuously observed the precise orbits of these satellites. As a satellite's orbit deviated, the USNO would send the updated information to the satellite. Subsequent broadcasts from an updated satellite would contain the most recent accurate information about its orbit.

Modern systems are more direct. The satellite broadcasts a signal that contains orbital data (from which the position of the satellite can be calculated) and the precise time the signal was transmitted. The orbital data is transmitted in a data message that is superimposed on a code that serves as a timing reference.

The satellite uses an atomic clock to maintain synchronization of all the satellites in the constellation. The receiver compares the time of broadcast encoded in the transmission with the time of reception measured by an internal clock, thereby measuring the time-of-flight to the satellite. Several such measurements can be made at the same time to different satellites, allowing a continual fix to be generated in real time using an adapted version of trilateration.

Each distance measurement, regardless of the system being used, places the receiver on a spherical shell at the measured distance from the broadcaster. By taking several such measurements and then looking for a point where they meet, a fix is generated.

However, in the case of fast-moving receivers, the position of the signal moves as signals are received from several satellites. In addition, the radio signals slow slightly as they pass through the ionosphere, and this slowing varies with the receiver's angle to the satellite, because that changes the distance through the ionosphere.

The basic computation thus attempts to find the shortest directed line tangent to four oblate spherical shells centered on four satellites. Satellite navigation receivers reduce errors by using combinations of signals from multiple satellites and multiple correlators, and then using techniques such as Kalman filtering to combine the noisy, partial, and constantly changing data into a single estimate for position, time, and velocity.

CIVIL AND MILITARY USES

The original motivation for satellite navigation was for military applications. Satellite navigation allows for hitherto impossible precision in the delivery of weapons to targets, greatly increasing their lethality whilst reducing inadvertent casualties from mis-directed weapons. Satellite navigation also allows forces to be directed and to locate themselves more easily, reducing the fog of war.

The ability to supply satellite navigation signals is also the ability to deny their availability. The operator of a satellite navigation system potentially has the ability to degrade or eliminate satellite navigation services over any territory it desires.

GLOBAL NAVIGATION SYSTEMS

Operational

GPS

The United States' Global Positioning System (GPS) consists of up to 32 medium Earth orbit satellites in six different orbital planes, with the exact number of satellites varying as older satellites are retired and replaced. Operational since 1978 and globally available since 1994, GPS is currently the world's most utilized satellite navigation system.

GLONASS

The formerly Soviet, and now Russian, Global'naya Navigatsionnaya Sputnikovaya Sistema (GLObal NAvigation Satellite System), or GLONASS, was a fully functional navigation constellation in 1995. After the collapse of the Soviet Union, it fell into disrepair, leading to gaps in coverage and only partial availability. It was recovered and fully restored in 2011.

In development

Compass

China has indicated they intend to expand their regional navigation system, called Beidou or Big Dipper, into a global navigation system by 2020 a program that has been called Compass in China's official news agency Xinhua. The Compass system is proposed to utilize 30 medium Earth orbit satellites and five geostationary satellites. A 10-satellite regional version (covering Asia and Pacific area) was completed by December 2011.

Galileo

The European Union and European Space Agency agreed in March 2002 to introduce their own alternative to GPS, called the Galileo positioning system. At an estimated cost of EUR 3.0 billion, the system of 30 MEO satellites was originally scheduled to be operational in 2010. The estimated year to become operational is 2014. The first experimental satellite was launched on 28 December 2005. Galileo is expected to be compatible with the modernized GPS system. The receivers will be able to combine the signals from both Galileo and GPS satellites to greatly increase the accuracy. Galileo is now not expected to be in full service until 2020 at the earliest and at a substantially higher cost.

REGIONAL NAVIGATION SYSTEMS

Beidou 1

Chinese regional network to be expanded into the global Compass navigation system.

DORIS

Doppler Orbitography and Radio-positioning Integrated by Satellite (DORIS) is a French precision navigation system.

IRNSS

The Indian Regional Navigational Satellite System (IRNSS) is an autonomous regional satellite navigation system being developed by Indian Space Research Organisation (ISRO) which would be under the total control of Indian government. The government approved the project in May 2006, with the intention of the system to be completed and implemented by 2014. It will consist of a constellation of 7 navigational satellites. All the 7 satellites will be placed in the Geostationary orbit (GEO) to have a larger signal footprint and lower number of satellites to map the region. It is intended to provide an all-weather absolute position accuracy of better than 7.6 meters throughout India and within a region extending approximately 1,500 km around it. A goal of complete Indian control has been stated, with the space segment, ground segment and user receivers all being built in India. The first satellite IRNSS-1A of the proposed constellation was launched on 1 July 2013 from Satish Dhawan Space Centre

QZSS

The Quasi-Zenith Satellite System (QZSS), is a proposed three-satellite regional time transfer system and enhancement for GPS covering Japan. The first demonstration satellite was launched in September 2010.

AUGMENTATION

Examples of augmentation systems include the Wide Area Augmentation System, the European Geostationary Navigation Overlay Service, the Multi-functional Satellite Augmentation System, Differential GPS, and Inertial Navigation Systems.

LOW EARTH ORBIT SATELLITE PHONE NETWORKS

The two current operational low Earth orbit satellite phone networks are able to track transceiver units with accuracy of a few kilometers using doppler shift calculations from the satellite. The coordinates are sent back to the transceiver unit where they can be read using AT commands or a graphical user interface. This can also be used by the gateway to enforce restrictions on geographically bound calling plans.

6

Other Ship

CABLE LAYER

A cable layer or cable ship is a deep-sea vessel designed and used to lay underwater cables for telecommunications, electric power transmission, or other purposes. Cable ships are distinguished by large cable sheaves for guiding cable over bow or stern or both. Bow sheaves, some very large, were characteristic of all cable ships. Newer ships are tending toward pure stern layers with stern sheaves only as seen in the photo of CS Cable Innovator at the Port of Astoria on this page. The names of cable ships are often preceded by "C.S." as in CS Long Lines.

The first transatlantic telegraph cable was laid by cable layers from 1857–58. It briefly enabled telecommunication between Europe and North America before misuse resulted in failure of the line. In 1866 the SS Great Eastern successfully laid two transatlantic cables, securing future communication between the continents. HMTSMonarch (renamed CS Sentinel 13 October 1970) completed the first transatlantic telephone cable, TAT-1 in 1956 from Scotland to Nova Scotia for Britain's General Post Office (GPO).

In addition to cable layer ships, there were cable repairing ships which were tasked with finding and repairing under sea cables that broke or for whatever reason became inoperable.

CRANE VESSEL

A crane vessel, crane ship or floating crane is a ship with a crane specialized in lifting heavy loads. The largest crane vessels are used for offshore construction. Conventional monohulls are used, but the largest crane vessels are often catamaran or semi-submersible types as they have increased stability. On a sheerleg crane, the crane is fixed and cannot rotate, and the vessel therefore is manoeuvered to place loads.

HISTORY

In medieval Europe, crane vessels which could be flexibly deployed in the whole port basin were introduced as early as the 14th century. During the age of sail, the sheer hulk was used extensively as a floating crane for tasks that required heavy lift. At the time, the heaviest single components of ships were the main masts, and sheer hulks were essential for removing and replacing them, but they were also used for other purposes.

In 1920, the 1898-built battleshipUSS Kearsarge (BB-5) was converted to a crane ship when a crane with a capacity of 250 tons was installed. Later it was renamed Crane Ship No. 1. It was used, amongst other things, to place guns and other heavy items on battle ships under construction. Another remarkable feat was the raising of the USS Squalus (SS-192) in 1939.

In 1942, the Crane Ships aka "Heavy Lift Ships" SS Empire Elgar (PQ16), SS Empire Bard (PQ15), and SS Empire Purcell (PQ16) were sent to the Russian Arctic ports of Archangel, Murmansk and Molotovsk (Since renamed Sererodvinsk). Their role was to enable the unloading of the Arctic Convoys where port installations were either destroyed by German bombers or were non existent (as at Bakaritsa quay Archangel)

In 1949, J. Ray McDermott had the Derrick Barge Four built, a barge that was outfitted with a 150 tons revolving crane. The arrival of this type of vessel changed the direction of the offshore construction industry. Instead of constructing oil platforms in parts, jackets and decks could be built onshore as modules. For use in the shallow part of the Gulf of Mexico, the cradle of the offshore industry, these barges sufficed.

In 1963, Heerema converted a Norwegian tanker, the Sunnaas, into a crane vessel with a capacity of 300 tons, the first one in the offshore industry that was ship-shaped. It was renamed Global Adventurer. This type of crane vessel was better adapted to the harsh environment of the North Sea.

In 1978, Heerema had two semi-submersible crane vessels built, the Hermod and the Balder, each with one 2000 ton and one 3000 ton crane. Later both were upgraded to a higher capacity. This type of crane vessel was much less sensitive to sea swell, so that it was possible to operate on the North Sea during the winter months.

The high stability also allowed for heavier lifts than was possible with a monohull. The larger capacity of the cranes reduced the installation time of a platform from a whole season to a few weeks. Inspired by this success similar vessels were built. In 1985 the DB-102 was launched for McDermott, with two cranes with a capacity of 6000 tons each. Micoperi had the M7000 built in 1986 with two cranes of 7000 tons each.

However, in the mid 1980s, the boom in the offshore industry was over, resulting in collaborations. In 1988, a joint venture between Heerema and McDermott was formed, HeereMac. In 1990 Micoperi had to apply for bankruptcy. This enabled Saipem – in the beginning of the 1970s a large heavy lift contractor, but only a small player in this field at the end of the 80s – to take over the M7000 in 1995, later renaming it Saipem 7000. In 1997 Heerema took over the DB-102 from McDermott after discontinuation of their joint venture. The ship was renamed Thialf and, after an upgrade in 2000 to twice 7100 tons, it is now the largest crane vessel in the world even if all the world's lifting records belong to the Saipem 7000 (12150t of Sabratha Deck).

HEAVY LIFT VESSELS

Vessel	Company	Capacity (mT)	Type
Thialf	Heerema Marine Contractors	14,200 (tandem)	Semi-submersible
Saipem 7000	Saipem	14,000 (tandem)	Semi-submersible
Svanen	Ballast Nedam	8,700	Catamaran
Hermod	Heerema Marine Contractors	8,100 (tandem)	Semi-submersible
Lan Jing	CNOOC	7,500	Monohull
Balder	Heerema Marine Contractors	6,945 (tandem)	Semi-submersible
Seven Borealis	Subsea 7	5,000	Monohull
Oleg Strashnov	Seaway Heavy Lifting	5,000	Monohull
Swiber Kaizen 4000	Swiber Offshore	4,200	Monohull
Aegir	Heerema Marine Contractors	4,000	Monohull
DB 50	J. Ray McDermott	4,400	Monohull
Rambiz	Scaldis	3,300	Catamaran
Asian Hercules II	Smit International	3,200	Monohull
DB 101	J. Ray McDermott	3,500	Semi-submersible
DB 30	J. Ray McDermott	3,080	Monohull
LTS 3000	L&T-SapuraCrest JV	2,722	Monohull
Sapura 3000	SapuraAcergy	2,722	Monohull
StanislavYudin	Seaway Heavy Lifting	2,500	Monohull
Saipem 3000	Saipem	2,177	Monohull
Huasteco	GrupoProtexa	2,000	Monohull
Tolteca	CAMSA	2,000	Monohull
QuippoPrakash	MDL/Quippo/Sapura JV	2,000	Monohull

DREDGING

Dredging is an excavation activity or operation usually carried out at least partly underwater, in shallow seas or fresh water areas with the purpose of gathering up bottom sediments and disposing of them at a different location. This technique is often used to keep waterways navigable.

It is also used as a way to replenish sand on some public beaches, where sand has been lost because of coastal erosion. Dredging is also used as a technique for fishing for certain species of edible clams and crabs, see fishing dredge. A dredger (or "dredge" as is the general usage in the Americas) is any device, machine, or vessel that is used to excavate and remove material from the bottom of a body of water.

For example, a scoop attached to the end of a rope or pole by which a man can draw sediments up from the bottom of a pond is a dredger. Developing this idea further, a motorized crane equipped with a drag bucket or clamshell (grabber) that is used to scoop material from the bottom of a body of water is also a dredger. The crane could be located on the bank, or perhaps mounted on a barge. If the crane is mounted on a barge, the entire vessel is referred to as a dredger.

The process of dredging creates spoils (excess material), which are carried away from the dredged area. Dredging can produce materials for land reclamation or other purposes (usually construction-related), and has also historically played a significant role in gold mining.

Dredging can create disturbance in aquatic ecosystems, often with adverse impacts.

USES

- Capital: dredging carried out to create a new harbour, berth or waterway, or to deepen existing facilities in order to allow larger ships access. Because capital works usually involve hard material or high-volume works, the work is usually done using a cutter suction dredge or large trailing suction hopper dredge; but for rock works, drilling and blasting along with mechanical excavation may be used.
- Preparatory: work and excavation for future bridges, piers or docks/ wharves, often connected with foundation work.
- Maintenance: dredging to deepen or maintain navigable waterways or channels which are threatened to become silted with the passage of time, due to sedimented sand and mud, possibly making them too shallow for navigation. This is often carried out with a trailing suction hopper dredge. Most dredging is for this purpose, and it may also be done to maintain the holding capacity of reservoirs or lakes.
- Land reclamation: dredging to mine sand, clay or rock from the seabed and using it to construct new land elsewhere. This is typically performed by a cutter-suction dredge or trailing suction hopper dredge. The material may also be used for flood or erosion control.
- Beach nourishment: mining sand offshore and placing on a beach to replace sand eroded by storms or wave action. This is done to enhance the recreational and protective function of the beaches, which can be eroded by human activity or by storms. This is

typically performed by a cutter-suction dredge or trailing suction hopper dredge.

- Harvesting materials: dredging sediment for elements like gold, diamonds or other valuable trace substances.
- Seabed mining: a possible future use, recovering natural metal ore nodules from the sea's abyssal plains.
- Construction materials: dredging sand and gravels from offshore licensed areas for use in construction industry, principally for use in concrete. Very specialist industry focused in NW Europe using specialized trailing suction hopper dredgers self discharging dry cargo ashore.
- Anti-eutrophication: Dredging is an expensive option for the remediation of eutrophied (or de-oxygenated) water bodies. However, as artificially elevated phosphorus levels in the sediment aggravate the eutrophication process, controlled sediment removal is occasionally the only option for the reclamation of still waters.
- Contaminantremediation: to reclaim areas affected by chemical spills, storm water surges (with urban runoff), and other soil contaminations. Disposal becomes a proportionally large factor in these operations.
- Removing trash and debris: often done in combination with maintenance dredging, this process removes non-natural matter from the bottoms of rivers and canals and harbors.
- Flood prevention: this can help to increase channel depth and therefore increase a channel's capacity for carrying water.
- Peat extraction: in former times, so-called dredging poles or dredge hauls were used on the back of small boats to manually dredge the beds of peat-moor waterways before extracting the peat for use as a fuel. This tradition has now become more or less obsolete and the tools used to do this have also changed significantly.
- Oyster dredging or harvesting: in Louisiana and other states with salt water estuaries that can sustain bottom oyster beds. A heavy metal retangular scoop device is towed astern of a moving boat with a chain bridle attached to a cable and winch which scoops up oysters as it drags along the bottom. The device is periodically hauled aboard and the oysters in it are sorted and bagged for shipment to an oyster processing facility.
- As a hobby: hobbyists examine their dredged matter to pick out items of potential value, similar to the hobby of metal detecting, or the hobby form of dumpster diving, on land.

RELEVANCE

Without the many and almost non-stop dredging operations world wide, much of the world's commerce would be impaired, often within a few months, since much of world's goods travel by ship, and need to access harbours or seas via channels. Recreational boating also would be constrained to the smallest vessels.

The majority of marine dredging operations (and the disposal of the dredged material) will require that appropriate licences are obtained from the relevant regulatory authorities, and dredging is usually carried out by (or for) harbour companies or corresponding government agencies.

TYPES OF DREDGING VESSELS

Suction

These operate by sucking through a long tube, like some vacuum cleaners but on a larger scale.

A plain suction dredger has no tool at the end of the suction pipe to disturb the material. This is often the most commonly used form of dredging.

Trailing suction

A trailing suction hopper dredger (TSHD) trails its suction pipe when working, and loads the dredge spoil into one or more hoppers in the vessel. When the hoppers are full, the TSHD sails to a disposal area and either dumps the material through doors in the hull or pumps the material out of the hoppers. Some dredges also self-offload using drag buckets and conveyors. The largest trailing suction hopper dredger in the world are currently Jan De Nul'sCristobal Colon (launched 4 July 2008) and its sister ship Leiv Eriksson (launched 4 September 2009). Main design specs for the Cristobal Colon and the Leiv Eriksson are: 46,000 cubic metrehopper and a design dredging depth of 155 m. Next largest is HAM 318 (Van Oord) with its 37,293 cubic metre hopper and a maximum dredging depth of 101 m.

Cutter-suction

A cutter-suction dredger's (CSD) suction tube has a cutting mechanism at the suction inlet. The cutting mechanism loosens the bed material and transports it to the suction mouth. The dredged material is usually sucked up by a wear-resistant centrifugal pump and discharged either through a pipe line or to a barge. Cutter-suction dredgers are most often used in geological areas consisting of hard surface materials (for example gravel deposits or surface bedrock) where a standard suction dredger would be ineffective. In recent years, dredgers with more powerful cutters have been built in order to excavate harder rock without the need for blasting.

The two largest cutter suction dredgers in the world are currently (as at August 2009) DEME's D'Artagnan (28,200 kW total installed power) and Jan De Nul'sJ.F.J. DeNul (27,240 kW).both built by IHC Merwede.

Auger suction

This process functions like a cutter suction dredger, but the cutting tool is a rotating Archimedean screw set at right angles to the suction pipe. The first widely used auger dredges were designed by Mud Cat Dredges in the 1980s which was run by National Car Rental, but is now a Division of Ellicott Dredges. In 1996, IMS Dredges introduced a self-propelled version of the auger dredge that allows the system to propel itself without the use of anchors cables. During the 1980s and 1990s auger dredges were primarily used for sludge removal applications from waste water treatment plants.

Today, auger dredges are used for a wider variety of applications including river maintenance and sand mining. The most common auger dredge on the global market today is the Versi-Dredge. The turbidity shroud on auger dredge systems creates a strong suction vacuum and creates much less turbidity than conical (basket) type cutterheads and that is why they are preferred for environmental type applications. The vacuum created by the shroud and the ability to convey material to the pump faster makes auger dredge systems more productive than similar sized conical (basket) type cutterhead dredges.

Jet-lift

These use the Venturi effect of a concentrated high-speed stream of water to pull the nearby water, together with bed material, into a pipe.

Air-lift

An airlift is a type of small suction dredge. It is sometimes used like other dredges. At other times, an airlift is used, handheld underwater by a diver. It works by blowing air into the pipe, and that air, being lighter than water, rises inside the pipe, dragging water with it.

Bucket

A bucket dredger is equipped with a bucket dredge, which is a device that picks up sediment by mechanical means, often with many circulating buckets attached to a wheel or chain. Some bucket dredgers and grab dredgers are powerful enough to rip out coral to make a shipping channel through coral reefs.

Clamshell

A grab dredger picks up seabed material with a clam shell bucket, which hangs from an onboard crane or a crane barge, or is carried by a hydraulic arm, or is mounted like on a dragline. This technique is often used in excavation of bay mud. Most of these dredges are crane barges with spuds.

Backhoe/dipper

A backhoe/dipper dredge has a backhoe like on some excavators. A crude but usable backhoe dredger can be made by mounting a land-type backhoe excavator on a pontoon. The six largest backhoe dredgers in the world are currently the Vitruvius, the MimarSinan, PostnikJakovlev (Jan De Nul), the Samson (DEME), the Simson and the Goliath (Van Oord). They featured barge-mounted excavators. Small backhoe dredgers can be track-mounted and work from the bank of ditches. A backhoe dredger is equipped with a half-open shell. The shell is filled moving towards the machine. Usually dredges material is loaded in barges. This machine is mainly used in harbors and other shallow water.

Water injection

A water injection dredger uses a small jet to inject water under low pressure (to prevent the sediment from exploding into the surrounding waters) into the seabed to bring the sediment in suspension, which then becomes a turbidity current, which flows away down slope, is moved by a second burst of water from the WID or is carried away in natural currents.

Water injection results in a lot of sediment in the water which makes measurement with most hydrographic equipment (for instance: singlebeamechosounders) difficult.

Pneumatic

These dredgers use a chamber with inlets, out of which the water is pumped with the inlets closed. It is usually suspended from a crane on land or from a small pontoon or barge. Its effectiveness depends on depth pressure.

Bed leveler

This is a bar or blade which is pulled over the seabed behind any suitable ship or boat. It has an effect similar to that of a bulldozer on land. The chain-operated steam dredger Bertha, built in 1844 to a design by Brunel and now the oldest operational steam vessel in Britain, was of this type.

Krabbelaar

This is an early type of dredger which was formerly used in shallow water in the Netherlands. It was a flat-bottomed boat with spikes sticking out of its bottom.

As tide current pulled the boat, the spikes scraped seabed material loose, and the tide current washed the material away, hopefully to deeper water. Krabbelaar is Dutch for "scratcher".

Snagboat

A snagboat is designed to remove big debris such as dead trees and parts of trees from rivers and canals.

Amphibious

Some of these are any of the above types of dredger, which can operate normally, or by extending legs, also known as spuds, so it stands on the seabed with its hull out of the water. Some forms can go on land.

Some of these are land-type backhoe excavators whose wheels are on long hinged legs so it can drive into shallow water and keep its cab out of water. Some of these may not have a floatable hull and, if so, cannot work in deep water.

- Oliver Evans (1755–1819) in 1804 invented an amphibious dredger which was America's first steam-powered road vehicle.

Submersible

These are usually used to recover useful materials from the seabed. Many of them travel on continuous track. A unique variant is intended to walk on legs on the seabed.

Fishing

Fishing dredges are used to collect various species of clamsscallops, oysters or crabs from the seabed. These dredges have the form of a scoop made of chain mesh, and are towed by a fishing boat. Careless dredging can be destructive to the seabed. Nowadays some scallop dredging is replaced by collecting via scuba diving.

Police drag

In some police departments a small dredge (sometimes called a drag) is used to find and recover objects and bodies from underwater. The bodies may be murder victims, or people who committed suicide by drowning, or victims of accidents. It is sometimes pulled by people walking on the bank. Search and rescue units also often use this type of dredge in searching for bodies of missing persons.

OTHERS TYPES OF DREDGERS

Suction Dredger

A dredging technique consisting of cleaning, clearing, removal, demolition and excavation of material from the bottom of rivers, lakes, seas, wharfs and bays.Suction dredgers are widely used to remove sludge, sand, oil, and other detritus. Dredging, by result, can be applied on dredging's works of contaminated material or not, deepening, widening or expanding port areas, lakes, canals, basins evolution and anchoring, mooring berths, etc.

DISPOSAL OF MATERIALS

In a "hopper dredger", the dredged materials end up in a large onboard hold called a "hopper." A suction hopper dredger is usually used for maintenance dredging. A hopper dredge usually has doors in its bottom to empty the dredged materials, but some dredges empty their hoppers by splitting the two halves of their hulls on giant hydraulic hinges. Either way, as the vessel dredges, excess water in the dredged materials is spilled off as the heavier solids settle to the bottom of the hopper. This excess water is returned to the sea to reduce weight and increase the amount of solid material (or slurry) that can be carried in one load. When the hopper is filled with slurry, the dredger stops dredging and goes to a dump site and empties its hopper.

Some hopper dredges are designed so they can also be emptied from above using pumps if dump sites are unavailable or if the dredge material is contaminated. Sometimes the slurry of dredgings and water is pumped straight into pipes which deposit it on nearby land. Other times, it is pumped into barges (also called scows), which deposit it elsewhere while the dredge continues its work.

A number of vessels, notably in the UK and NW Europe de-water the hopper to dry the cargo to enable it to be discharged onto a quayside 'dry'. This is achieved principally using self discharge bucket wheel, drag scraper or excavator via conveyor systems.

When contaminated (toxic) sediments are to be removed, or large volume inland disposal sites are unavailable, dredge slurries are reduced to dry solids via a process known as dewatering. Current dewatering techniques employ either centrifuges, Geotube containers, large textile based filters or polymer flocculant/congealant based apparatus.

In many projects, slurry dewatering is performed in large inland settling pits, although this is becoming less and less common as mechanical dewatering techniques continue to improve.

Similarly, many groups (most notable in east Asia) are performing research towards utilizing dewatered sediments for the production of concretes and construction block, although the high organic content (in many cases) of this material is a hindrance toward such ends.

ENVIRONMENTAL IMPACTS

Dredging can create disturbance to aquatic ecosystems, often with adverse impacts. In addition, dredge spoils may contain toxic chemicals that may have an adverse effect on the disposal area; furthermore, the process of dredging often dislodges chemicals residing in benthic substrates and injects them into the water column. The activity of dredging can create the following principal impacts to the environment:

- Release of toxic chemicals (including heavy metals and PCB) from bottom sediments into the water column.
- Short term increases in turbidity, which can affect aquatic speciesmetabolism and interfere with spawning.
- Secondary effects from water column contamination of uptake of heavy metals, DDT and other persistent organic toxins, via food chain uptake and subsequent concentrations of these toxins in higher organisms including humans.
- Secondary impacts to marsh productivity from sedimentation
- Tertiary impacts to avifauna which may prey upon contaminated aquatic organisms
- Secondary impacts to aquatic and benthic organisms' metabolism and mortality
- Possible contamination of dredge spoils sites
- Changes to the topography by the creation of "spoil islands" from the accumulated spoil

The nature of dredging operations and possible environmental impacts cause the industry to be closely regulated and a requirement for comprehensive regional environmental impact assessments with continuous monitoring. The U.S. Clean Water Act requires that any discharge of dredged or fill materials into "waters of the United States," including wetlands, is forbidden unless authorized by a permit issued by the Army Corps of Engineers. As a result of the potential impacts to the environment, dredging is restricted to licenced areas only with vessel activity monitored closely using automatic GPS systems.

MAJOR DREDGING COMPANIES

According to Reuters in 2010, the first and second largest dredging companies in the world respectively are Royal Boskalis Westminster of the Netherlands and China HarbourEngineering, a subsidiary of China Communications Construction. Other large dredging companies in decreasing capacity order include:

- Van Oord Dredging and Marine Contractors (Netherlands)
- DEME (Belgium)
- Jan De Nul (Belgium)

DRILLSHIP

A drillship is a maritime vessel that has been fitted with drilling apparatus. It is most often used for exploratory offshore drilling of new oil or gas wells in deep water or for scientific drilling. The drillship can also be used as a platform to carry out well maintenance or completion work such as casing and tubing installation or subsea tree installations. It is often built to the design specification of the oil production company and/or investors, but can also be a modified tanker hull outfitted with a dynamic positioning system to maintain its position over the well.

The greatest advantages these modern drillships have is their ability to drill in water depths of more than 2500 m and the time saved sailing between oilfields worldwide. Drillships are completely independent, in contrast to semi-submersibles and jackup barges.

In order to drill, a marine riser is lowered from the drillship to the seabed with a blowout preventer (BOP) at the bottom that connects to the wellhead.

Drillships are just one way to perform exploratory drilling. This function can also be performed by semi-submersibles, jackup barges, barges, or platform rigs.

The first drillship was the Cuss 1, and the fleet size has been growing ever since. By 2013 the worldwide fleet of drillships is expected to top 80 ships, more than double its size in 2009.Drillships are not only growing in size but also in capability with new technology assisting operations from academic research to ice drilling. U.S. President Barack Obama's decision in late March 2010 to expand U.S. domestic exploratory drilling seems likely to increase further developments of drillship technology.

Transocean, Pride International, Seadrill, Noble Corporation and Atwood Oceanics are a few of the companies that own and operate drillships globally.

FISHING VESSEL

A fishing vessel is a boat or ship used to catch fish in the sea, or on a lake or river. Many different kinds of vessels are used in commercial, artisanal and recreational fishing.

According to the FAO, there are currently (2004) four million commercial fishing vessels. About 1.3 million of these are decked vessels with enclosed areas. Nearly all of these decked vessels are mechanised, and 40,000 of them are over 100 tons. At the other extreme, two-thirds (1.8 million) of the undecked boats are traditional craft of various types, powered only by sail and oars. These boats are used by artisan fishers.

It is difficult to estimate the number of recreational fishing boats. They range in size from small dinghies to large charter cruisers, and unlike commercial fishing vessels, are often not dedicated just to fishing.

Prior to the 1950s there was little standardisation of fishing boats. Designs could vary between ports and boatyards. Traditionally boats were built of wood, but wood is not often used now because it has higher maintenance costs and lower durability. Fibreglass is used increasingly in smaller fishing vessels up to 25 metres (100 tons), while steel is usually used on vessels above 25 metres.

HISTORY

Early fishing vessels included rafts, dugout canoes, and boats constructed from a frame covered with hide or tree bark, along the lines of a coracle. The oldest boats found by archaeological excavation are dugout canoes dating back to the Neolithic Period around 7,000-9,000 years ago. These canoes were often cut from coniferous tree logs, using simple stone tools. A 7000 year-old seagoing boat made from reeds and tar has been found in Kuwait. These early vessels had limited capability; they could float and move on water, but were not suitable for use any great distance from the shoreline. They were used mainly for fishing and hunting.

The development of fishing boats took place in parallel with the development of boats built for trade and war. Early navigators began to use animal skins or woven fabrics for sails. Affixed to a pole set upright in the boat, these sails gave early boats more range, allowing voyages of exploration.

Around 4000 B.C., Egyptians were building long narrow boats powered by many oarsmen. Over the next 1,000 years, they made a series of remarkable advances in boat design. They developed cotton-made sails to help their boats go faster with less work.

Then they built boats large enough to cross the oceans. These boats had sails and oarsmen, and were used for travel and trade. By 3000 BC, the Egyptians knew how to assemble planks of wood into a ship hull. They used woven straps to lash planks together, and reeds or grass stuffed between the planks to seal the seams. An example of their skill is the Khufu ship, a vessel 143 feet (44 m) in length entombed at the foot of the Great Pyramid of Giza around 2,500 BC and found intact in 1954.

At about the same time, the Scandinavians were also building innovative boats. People living near KongensLyngby in Denmark, came up with the idea of segregated hull compartments, which allowed the size of boats to gradually be increased. A crew of some two dozen paddled the wooden Hjortspring boat across the Baltic Sea long before the rise of the Roman Empire. Scandinavians continued to develop better ships, incorporating iron and other metal into the design and developing oars for propulsion.

The oldest Nordic shipfind is the Nydam boat, found preserved in the NydamMose bog in Sundeved, Denmark. It has been dendro dated to 310-320 AD., and is the oldest known boat to use clinker planking, where the planks overlap one another. Built of oak, it is 23 metres long and about 4 metres wide. It originally weighed over three tonnes and was rowed by thirty men.

By 1000 A.D. the Norsemen were pre-eminent on the oceans. They were skilled seamen and boat builders, with clinker-built boat designs that varied according to the type of boat. Trading boats, such as the knarrs, were wide to allow large cargo storage. Raiding boats, such as the longship, were long and narrow and very fast. The vessels they used for fishing were scaled down versions of their cargo boats. The Scandinavian innovations influenced fishing boat design long after the Viking period came to an end. For example, yoles from the Orkney island of Stroma were built in the same way as the Norse boats.

In the 15th century, the Dutch developed a type of seagoing herringdrifter that became a blueprint for European fishing boats. This was the Herring Buss, used by Dutch herring fishermen until the early 19th centuries. The ship type buss has a long history. It was known around 1000 AD in Scandinavia as a buza, a robust variant of the Viking longship. The first herring buss was probably built in Hoorn around 1415. The last one was built in Vlaardingen in 1841.

The ship was about 20 metres long and displaced between 60 and 100 tons. It was a massive round-bilgedkeel ship with a bluff bow and stern, the latter relatively high, and with a gallery. The busses used long drifting gill nets to catch the herring. The nets would be retrieved at night and the crews of eighteen to thirty men would set to gibbing, salting and barrelling the catch on the broad deck.

The ships sailed in fleets of 400 to 500 ships to the Dogger Bank fishing grounds and the Shetland isles. They were usually escorted by naval vessels, because the English considered they were "poaching". The fleet would stay at sea for weeks at a time. The catch would sometimes be transferred to special ships (called ventjagers), and taken home while the fleet would still be at sea (the picture shows a ventjager in the distance).

During the 17th century, the British developed the dogger, an early type of sailing trawler or longliner, which commonly operated in the North Sea. The dogger takes its name from the Dutch worddogger, meaning a fishing vessel which tows a trawl. Dutch trawling boats were common in the North Sea, and the word dogger was given to the area where they often fished, which became known as the Dogger Bank.Doggers were slow but sturdy, capable of fishing in the rough conditions of the North Sea. Like the herring buss, they were wide-beamed and bluff-bowed, but considerably smaller, about 15 metres long, a maximum beam of 4.5 metres, a draught of 1.5 metres, and displacing about 13 tonnes. They could carry a tonne of bait, three tonnes of salt, half a tonne each of food and firewood for the crew, and return with six tonnes of fish. Decked areas forward and aft probably provided accommodation, storage and a cooking area. An anchor would have allowed extended periods fishing in the same spot, in waters up to 18 metres deep. The dogger would also have carried a small open boat for maintaining lines and rowing ashore.

Dories are small, shallow-draftboats, usually about five to seven metres (15 to 22 feet) long. They are lightweight versatile boats with high sides, a flat bottom and sharp bows, and are easy to build because of their simple lines. The dory first appeared in New England fishing towns sometime after the early 18th century. A precursor to the dory type was the early Frenchbateau type, a flat bottom boat with straight sides used as early as 1671 on the Saint Lawrence River. The common coastal boat of the time was the wherry and the merging of the wherry design with the simplified flat bottom of the bateau resulted in the birth of the dory. Antecdotal evidence exists of much older precursors throughout Europe. England, France, Italy, and Belgium have small boats from medieval periods that could reasonably be construed as predecessors of the Dory.

The Banks dories appeared in the 1830s. They were designed to be carried on mother ships and used for fishing cod at the Grand Banks. Adapted almost directly from the low freeboard, French river bateaus, with their straight sides and removable thwarts, bank dories could be nested inside each other and stored on the decks of fishing schooners, such as the GazelaPrimeiro, for their trip to the Grand Banks fishing grounds.

In the 19th century, a more effective design for sailing trawlers was developed at the English fishing port, Brixham. These elegant wooden sailing boats spread across the world, influencing fishing fleets everywhere. Their distinctive sails inspired the song Red Sails in the Sunset, written aboard a Brixham sailing trawler called the Torbay Lass. In the 1890s there were about 300 trawling vessels there, each usually owned by the skipper of the boat. Several of these old sailing trawlers have been preserved.

Throughout history, local conditions have led to the development of a wide range of types of fishing boats. The Lancashire nobby was used down the north west coast of England as a shrimp trawler from 1840 until World War II. The Manx nobby was used around the Isle of Man as a herring drifter. The fifie was also used as a herring drifter along the east coast of Scotland from the 1850s until well into the 20th century.

The bawley and the smack were used in the Thames Estuary and off East Anglia, while trawlers and drifters were use on the east coast. Herring fishing started in the Moray Firth in 1819.

The peak of the fishing at Aberdeen was in 1937 with 277 steam trawlers, though the first diesel drifter was introduced in 1926. In 1870 paddle tugs were being used to tow luggers and smacks to sea. Steam trawlers were introduced in 1881, mainly at Grimsby and Hull. In 1890 it was estimated that there were 20,000 men on the North Sea. The steam drifter was not used in the herring fishery until 1897. The first trawlers fished over the side but in 1961 the first stern trawler was used at Lowestoft for fishing in Arctic waters. By 1981 only 27 of 130 deep sea trawlers were still going to sea. Many were converted to oil rig safety vessels.

Trawler designs adapted as the way they were powered changed from sail to coal-fired steam by World War I, and then to diesel and turbines by the end of World War II. During World War I and World War II, many fishing trawlers were commissioned as naval trawlers to be used as minesweepers, the activities being similar, with the crew and layout already suited to the task. Likewise, many commercial drifters were commissioned as naval drifters to be used for maintaining and monitoring anti-submarine nets. Since World War II, commercial fishing vessels have been increasingly equipped with electronic aids, such as radio navigation aids and fishfinders. During the Cold War, some countries fitted fishing trawlers with additional electronic gear so they could be used as spy ships to monitor the activities of other countries.

COMMERCIAL VESSELS

The 200-mile fishing limit has changed fishing patterns and, in recent times, fishing boats are becoming more specialised and standardised. In the United States and Canada more use is made of large factory trawlers, while the huge blue water fleets operated by Japan and the Soviet-bloc countries have contracted. In western Europe, fishing vessel design is focused on compact boats with high catching power.

Commercial fishing is a high risk industry, and countries are introducing regulations governing the construction and operation of fishing vessels. The International Maritime Organization, convened in 1959 by the United Nations, is responsible for devising measures aimed at the prevention of accidents, including standards for ship design, construction, equipment, operation and manning.

According to the FAO, in 2004 the world's fishing fleet consisted of 4 million vessels. Of these, 1.3 million were decked vessels with enclosed areas. The rest were open vessels, of which two-thirds were traditional craft propelled by sails and oars.

By contrast, nearly all decked vessels were mechanized. Of the decked vessels, 86 percent are found in Asia, 7.8 percent in Europe, 3.8 percent in North and Central America, 1.3 percent in Africa, 0.6 percent in South America and 0.4 percent in Oceania. Most commercial fishing boats are small, usually less than 30 metres (98 ft) but up to 100 metres (330 ft) for a large purse seiner or factory ship.

Commercial fishing vessels can be classified by architecture, the type of fish they catch, the fishing method used, or geographical origin. The following classification follows the FAO, who classify commercial fishing vessels by the gear they use.

TRAWLERS

A trawler is a fishing vessel designed to use trawl nets in order to catch large volumes of fish.

- Outrigger trawlers - use outriggers to tow the trawl. These are commonly used to catch shrimp. One or two otter trawls can be towed from each side. Beam trawlers, employed in the North sea for catching flatfish, are another form of outrigger trawler. Medium sized and high powered vessels, these tow a beam trawl on each side at speeds up to 8 knots.

- Beam trawlers - use sturdy outrigger booms for towing a beam trawl, one warp on each side. Double-rig beam trawlers can tow a separate trawl on each side. Beam trawling is used in the flatfish and shrimp fisheries in the North Sea. They are medium sized and high powered vessels, towing gear at speeds up to 8 knots. To avoid the boat capsizing if the trawl snags on the sea floor, winch brakes can be installed, along with safety release systems in the boom stays. The engine power of bottom trawlers is also restricted to 2000 HP (1472 KW) for further safety.

- Otter trawlers - deploy one or more parallel trawls kept apart horizontally using otter boards. These trawls can be towed in midwater or along the bottom.
- Pair trawlers - are trawlers which operate together towing a single trawl. They keep the trawl open horizontally by keeping their distance when towing. Otter boards are not used. Pair trawlers operate both midwater and bottom trawls.
- Side trawlers - have the trawl set over the side with the trawl warps passing through blocks which hang from two gallows, one forward and one aft. Until the late sixties, side trawlers were the most familiar vessel in the North Atlantic deep sea fisheries. They evolved over a longer period than other trawler types, but are now being replaced by stern trawlers.
- Stern trawlers - have trawls which are deployed and retrieved from the stern. Larger stern trawlers often have a ramp, though pelagic and small stern trawlers are often designed without a ramp. Stern trawlers are designed to operate in most weather conditions. They can work alone when midwater or bottom trawling, or two can work together as pair trawlers.
- Freezer trawlers - The majority of trawlers operating on high sea waters are freezer trawlers. They have facilities for preserving fish by freezing, allowing them to stay at sea for extended periods of time. They are medium to large size trawlers, with the same general arrangement as stern or side trawlers.
- Wet fish trawlers - are trawlers where the fish is kept in the hold in a fresh/wet condition. They must operate in areas not far distant from their landing place, and the fishing time of such vessels is limited.

SEINERS

Seiners use surrounding and seine nets. This is a large group ranging from open boats as small as 10 metres in length, to ocean going vessels. There are also specialised gears that can target demersal species.

- Purse seiners - are very effective at targeting aggregatingpelagic species near the surface. The seiner circles the shoal with a deep curtain of netting, possibly using bow thrusters for better manoeuvrability. Then the bottom of the net is pursed (closed) underneath the fish shoal by hauling a wire running from the vessel through rings along the bottom of the net and then back to the vessel. The most important part of the fishing operation is searching for the fish shoals and assessing their size and direction of movement. Sophisticated electronics, such as echosounders, sonar, and track plotters, may be used are used to search for and track schools; assessing their size and movement and keeping in touch with the school while it is surrounded with the seine net. Crows nests may be built on the masts for further visual support. Large vessels can have observation towers and helicopter landing decks. Helicopters and spotter planes are used for detecting fish schools. The main types of purse seiners are the American seiners, the European seiners and the Drum seiners.
  - American seiners - have their bridge and accommodation placed forward with the working deck aft. American seiners are most common on both coasts of North America and in other areas of Oceania. The net is stowed at the stern and is set over the stern. The power block is usually attached to a boom from a mast located behind the superstructure. American seiners use Triplerollers. A purse line winch is located amidships near the hauling station, near the side where the rings are taken onboard.
  - European seiners - have their bridge and accommodation located more to the after part of the vessel with the working deck amidships. European seiners are most common in waters fished by European nations. The net is stowed in a net bin at the stern, and is set over the stern from this position. The pursing winch is normally positioned at the forward part of the working deck.
  - Drum seiners - have the same layout as American seiners except a drum is mounted on the stern and used instead of the power block. They are mainly used in Canada and USA.
  - Tuna purse seiners - are large purse seiners, normally over 45 meters, equipped to handle large and heavy purse seines for tuna. They have the same general arrangement as the American seiner, with the bridge and accommodation placed forward. A

crows nest or tuna tower is positioned at the top of the mast, outfitted with the control and manoeuvre devices. A very heavy boom which carries the power block is fitted at the mast. They often carry a helicopter to search for tuna schools. On the deck are three drum purse seine winches and a power block, with other specific winches to handle the heavy boom and net. They are usually equipped with a skiff.

- Seine netters - the basic types of seine netters are the Anchor seiners and Scottish seiner in northern Europe and the Asian seiners in Asia.
  - Anchor seiners - have the wheelhouse and accommodation aft and the working deck amidships, thus resembling side trawlers. The seine net is stored and shot from the stern, and they may carry a power block. Anchor seiners have the coiler and winch mounted transversally amidships.
  - Scottish seiners - are basically configured the same as anchor seiners. The only difference is that, whereas the anchor seiner has the coiler and winch mounted transversally amidships, the Scottish seiner has them mounted transversally in the forward part of the vessel.
  - Asian seiners - In Asia the seine netter usually has the wheelhouse forward and the working deck aft, in the manner of a stern trawler. However, in regions where the fishing effort is a labour intensive, low technology approach, they are often undecked and may be powered by outboards motors, or even by sail.

LINE VESSELS

- Longliners - use one or more long heavy fishing lines with a series of hundreds or even thousands of baitedhooks hanging from the main line by means of branch lines called "snoods". Hand operated longlining can be operated from boats of any size. The number of hooks and lines handled depends on the size of vessel, the number of crew, and the level of mechanisation. Large purpose built longliners can be designed for single species fisheries such as tuna. On such larger vessels the bridge is usually placed aft, and the gear is hauled from the bow or from the side with mechanical or hydraulic line haulers. The lines are set over the stern. Automatic or semi-automatic systems are used to bait hooks and shoot and haul lines. These systems include rail rollers, line haulers, hook separators, dehookers and hook cleaners, and storage racks or drums. To avoid incidental catches of seabirds, an outboard setting funnel is used to guide the line from the setting position on the stern down to a depth of one or two metres. Small scale longliners handle the gear by hand. The line is stored into baskets or tubs, perhaps using a hand cranked line drum.

- Bottom longliners -
- Midwaterlongliners - are usually medium sized vessels which operate worldwide, purpose built to catch large pelagics. The line hauler is usually forward starboard, where the fish are hauled through a gate in the rail. The lines are set from the stern where a baiting table and chute are located. These boats need adequate speed to reach distant fishing grounds, enough endurance for continued fishing, adequate freezing storage, suitable mechanisms for shooting and hauling longlines quickly, and proper storage for fishing gears and accessories.
- Freezer longliners - are outfitted with freezing equipment. The holds are insulated and refrigerated. Freezer longliners are medium to large with the same general characteristics of other longliners. Most longliners operating on the high seas are freezer longliners.
- Factory longliners - are generally equipped with processing plant, including mechanical gutting and filleting equipment accompanied by freezing facilities, as well as fish oil, fish meal and sometimes canning plants. These vessels have a large buffer capacity. Thus, caught fish can be stored in refrigerated sea water tanks and piks in the catch can also be used. Freezer longliners are large ships, working the high seas with the same general characteristics of other large longliners.
- Wet-fish longliners - keep the caught fish in the hold in the fresh/wet condition. The fish is stored in boxes and covered with ice, or stored with ice in the fish hold. The fishing time of such vessels is limited, so they operate close to the landing place.

• Pole and line vessels - are used mainly to catch tuna and skipjack. The fishers stand at the railing or on special platforms and fish with poles and lines. The lines have hooks which are baited, preferably with live bait. Caught tuna are swung on board, by two to three fishermen if the tuna is big, or with an automated swinging mechanism. The tuna usually release themselves from the barbless hook when they hit the deck. Tanks with live bait are placed round the decks, and water spray systems are used to attract the fish. The vessels are 15 to 45 metres o/a. On smaller vessels fishers fish from the main deck right around the boat. With larger vessels, there are two different deck styles: the American style and the Japanese style.

  - American style - fishers stand on platforms arranged over the side abaft amidships and around the stern. The vessel moves ahead during fishing operation."Drawing". FAO.

  - Japanese style - fishers stand at the rail in the forepart of the vessel. The vessel drifts during fishing operations."Drawing". FAO.

- Trollers - catch fish by towing astern one of more trolling lines. A trolling line is a fishing line with natural or artificial baitedhooks trailed by a vessel near the surface or at a certain depth. Several lines can be towed at the same time using outriggers to keep the lines apart. The lines can be hauled in manually or by small winches. A length of rubber is often included in each line as a shock absorber. The trolling line is towed at a speed depending on the target species, from 2.3 knots up to at least 7 knots. Trollers range from small open boats to large refrigerated vessels 30 meters long. In many tropical artisanal fisheries, trolling is done with sailing canoes with outriggers for stability. With properly designed vessels, trolling is an economical and efficient way of catching tuna, mackerel and other pelagic fish swimming close to the surface. Purpose built trollers are usually equipped with two or four trolling booms raised and lowered by topping lifts, held in position by adjustable stays. Electrically powered or hydraulic reels can be used to haul in the lines.
- Jiggers - there are two types of jiggers: specialised squid jiggers which work mostly in the southern hemisphere and smaller vessels using jigging techniques in the northern hemisphere mainly for catching cod.
  - Squid jiggers - have single or double drum jigger winches lined along the rails around the vessel. Strong lamps, up to 5000 W each, are used to attract the squid. These are arranged 50–60 centimetres apart, either as one row in the centre of the vessel, or two rows, one on each side. As the squid are caught they are transferred by chutes to the processing plant of the vessel. The jigging motion can be produced mechanically by the shape of the drum or electronically by adjustment to the winch motor. Squid jiggers are often used during the day as midwater trawlers and during the night as jiggers.
  - Cod jiggers - use single jigger machines and do not use lights to attract the fish. The fish are attracted by the jigging motion and artificial bait.

OTHER VESSELS

- Dredgers - use a dredge for collecting molluscs from the seafloor. There are three types of dredges: (a) The dredge can be dragged along the seabed, scooping the shellfish from the ground. These dredges are towed in a manner similar to beam trawlers, and large dredgers can work three or more dredges on each side. (b) Heavy mechanical dredging units are operated by special gallows from the bow of the vessel. (c) The dredger employs a hydraulic dredge which uses a powerful water pump to operates water jets which flush the molluscs from the bottom. Dredgers don't have a typical deck arrangement, the bridge and accommodation can be aft or forward. Derricks and winches may be installed for lowering and lifting the dredge. Echosounders are used for determining depths.

- Gillnetters - On inland waters and inshore, gillnets can be operated from open boats and canoes. In coastal waters, they are operated by small decked vessels which can have their wheelhouse either aft or forward. In coastal waters, gillnetting is often used as a second fishing method by trawlers or beam trawlers, depending on fishing seasons and targeted species. For offshore fishing, or fishing on the high seas, medium sized vessels using drifting gillnets are called drifters, and the bridge is usually located aft. The nets are set and hauled by hand on small open boats. Larger boats use hydraulic or occasionally mechanical net haulers, or net drums. These vessels can be equipped with an echosounder, although locating fish is more a matter of the fishermen's personal knowledge of the fishing grounds rather than depending on special detection equipment.
  - Set netters - also operate gillnets. However, during fishing operations the vessel is not attached to the nets. The size of the vessels varies from open boats to large specialised drifters operating on the high seas. The wheelhouse is usually located aft, and the front deck is used for handling gear. Normally the nets are set at the stern by steaming ahead. Hauling is done over the side at the forepart of the deck, usually using hydraulic driven net haulers. Wet fish is packed in containers chilled with ice. Larger vessels might freeze the catch.
- Lift netters - are equipped to operate lift nets, which are held from the vessel's side and raised and lowered by means of outriggers. Lift netters range from open boats about 10 meters long to larger vessels with open ocean capability. Decked vessels usually have the bridge amidships. Larger vessels are often equipped with winches and derricks for handling the lifting lines, as well as outriggers and light booms. They can be fitted with powerful lights to attract and aggregate the fish to the surface. Open boats are usually unmechanized or use hand operated winches. Electronic equipment, such as fishfinders, sonar and echo sounders are used extensively on larger boats.

- Trap setters - are used to set pots or traps for catching fish, crabs, lobsters, crayfish and other similar species. Trap setters range in size from open boats operating inshore to larger decked vessels, 20 to 50 metres long, operating out to the edge of the continental shelf. Small decked trap setters have the wheelhouse either forward or aft with the fish hold amidships. They use hydraulic or mechanical pot haulers. Larger vessels have the wheelhouse forward, and are equipped with derricks, davits or cranes for hauling pots aboard. Locating fish is often more a matter of the fishermen's knowledge of the fishing grounds rather than the use of special detection equipment. Decked vessels are usually equipped with an echosounder, and large vessels may also have a Loran or GPS.
- Handliners - are normally undecked vessels used for handlining (fishing with a line and hook). Handliners include canoes and other small or medium sized vessels. Traditional handliners are less than 12 metres o/a, and do not have special gear handling, there is no winch or gurdy. Locating fish is left to the fishermen's personal knowledge of fishing grounds rather than the use of special electronic equipment. Non traditionalhandliners can set and haul using electrical or hydraulic powered reels. These mechanised reels are normally fastened to the gunwale or set on stanchions close to or overhanging the gunwale. They operate all over the world, some in shallow waters, some fishing up to 300 meters deep. No typical deck arrangement exists for handliners.
- Multipurpose vessels - are vessels which are designed so they can deploy more than one type of fishing gear without major modifications to the vessels. The fish detection equipment present on board also changes according to which fishing gear is being used.
  - Trawler/Purse seiners - are designed so the deck arrangement and equipment, including a suitable combination winch, can be used for both methods. Rollers, blocks, trawl gallows and purse davits need to be arranged so they control the lead of warps and pursing lines in such a way as to reduce the time needed to convert from one type to the other. Typical fish detection equipment includes a sonar and an echosounder. These vessels are usually designed as trawlers, since the power requirement for trawling is higher.
- Research vessels - a fisheries research vessel (FRV) requires platforms which are capable of towing different types of fishing nets, collecting plankton or water samples from a range of depths, and carrying acoustic fish-finding equipment. Fisheries research vessels are often designed and built along the same lines as a large fishing vessel,

but with space given over to laboratories and equipment storage, as opposed to storage of the catch. An example of a fisheries research vessel is FRV Scotia.

ARTISAN VESSELS

Artisan fishing is small-scale commercial or subsistence fishing, particularly practices involving coastal or island ethnic groups using traditional fishing techniques and traditional boats. This may also include heritage groups involved in customary fishing practices.

According to the FAO, at the end of 2004, the world fishing fleet consisted of about 4 million vessels, of which 2.7 million were undecked (open) boats. While nearly all decked vessels were mechanized, only one-third of the undecked fishing boats were powered, usually with outboard engines. The remaining 1.8 million boats were traditional craft of various types, operated by sail and oars.

These figures for small fishing vessels are probably under reported. The FAO compiles these figures largely from national registers. These records often omit smaller boats where registration is not required or where fishing licences are granted by provincial or municipal authorities.

Artisan fishing boats are usually small traditional fishing boats, appropriately designed for use on their local inland waters or coasts. Many localities around the world have developed their own traditional types of fishing boats, adapted to use local materials suitable for boat building and to the specific requirements of the fisheries and sea conditions in their area. Artisan boats are often open (undecked). Many have sails, but they do not usually use much, or any mechanised or electronic gear.

Large numbers of artisan fishing boats are still in use, particularly in developing countries with long productive marine coastlines. For example, Indonesia has reported about 700,000 fishing boats, 25 percent of which are dugout canoes, and half of which are without motors. The Philippines have reported a similar number of small fishing boats. Many of the boats in this area are double-outrigger craft, consisting of a narrow main hull with two attached outriggers, commonly known as jukung in Indonesia and banca in the Philippines.

ICEBREAKER

An icebreaker is a special-purpose ship or boat designed to move and navigate through ice-covered waters. Although the term usually refers to ice-breaking ships, it may also refer to smaller vessels, such as the icebreaking boats that were once used on the canals of the United Kingdom.

For a ship to be considered an icebreaker, it requires three traits most normal ships lack: a strengthened hull, an ice-clearing shape, and the power to push through sea ice.

Icebreakers clear paths by pushing straight into ice pockets. The bending strength of sea ice is so low that usually the ice breaks without noticeable change in the vessel's trim. In cases of very thick ice, an icebreaker can drive its bow onto the ice to break it under the weight of the ship. Because a buildup of broken ice in front of a ship can slow it down much more than the breaking of the ice itself, icebreakers have a specially designed hull to direct the broken ice around or under the vessel. The external components of the ship's propulsion system (propellers, propeller shafts, etc.) are at even greater risk of damage than the vessel's hull, so the ability of an icebreaker to propel itself onto the ice, break it, and clear the debris from its path successfully is essential for its safety.

HISTORY

Sailing ships in the polar waters

Even in the earliest days of polar exploration, ice-strengthened ships were used. These were originally wooden and based on existing designs, but reinforced, particularly around the waterline with double planking to the hull and strengthening cross members inside the ship. Bands of iron were wrapped around the outside. Sometimes metal sheeting was placed at the bows, stern and along the keel. Such strengthening was designed to help the ship push through ice and also to protect the ship in case it was "nipped" by the ice. Nipping occurs when ice floes around a ship are pushed against the ship, trapping it as if in a vice and causing damage. This vice-like action is caused by the force of winds and tides on ice formations. Although such wind and tidal forces may be exerted many miles away, the ice transmits the force.

The first boats to be used in the polar waters were those of the indigenous Arctic people. Their kayaks are small human-powered boats with a covered deck, and one or more cockpits, each seating one paddler who strokes a single or double-bladed paddle. Such boats, of course, have no icebreaking capabilities, but they are light and well fit to carry over the ice.

In the 9th and 10th centuries, the Viking expansion reached the North Atlantic, and eventually Greenland and Svalbard in the Arctic. Vikings, however, operated their ships in the waters that were ice-free for most of the year, in the conditions of the Medieval Warm Period.

In the 11th century, Russians started settling the coasts of the White Sea, named so for being ice-covered for over half of a year. The ethnic subgroup of Russians that lived on the shores of the Arctic Ocean became known as Pomors ("seaside settlers"). Gradually they developed a special type of small one- or two-mast wooden sailing ships, used for voyages in the ice conditions of the Arctic seas and later on Siberian rivers. These earliest icebreakers were called kochi. Koch's hull was protected by a belt of ice-floe resistant flush skin-planking (made of oak or larch) along the variable water-line, and had a false keel for on-ice portage. If a koch became squeezed by the ice-fields, its rounded bodylines below the water-line would allow for the ship to be pushed up out of the water and onto the ice with no damage.

In the 19th century, similar protective measures were adopted to modern steam-powered icebreakers. Some notable sailing ships in the end of the Age of Sail also featured the egg-shaped form alike that of Pomor boats, for example the famous Fram, used by Fridtjof Nansen and other great NorwegianPolar explorers. Fram is said to be the wooden ship to have sailed farthest north (85°57'N) and farthest south (78°41'S), and perhaps the strongest wooden ship ever built.

Steam-powered icebreakers

An early ship designed to operate in icy conditions was a 51-metre (167 ft) wooden paddle steamer, City Ice Boat No. 1, that was built for the city of Philadelphia by Vandusen&Birelyn in 1837. The ship's wooden paddles, powered by two 250-horsepower steam engines, were reinforced with iron coverings.

With its rounded shape and strong metal hull, the Russian Pilot of 1864 was an important predecessor of modern icebreakers. Built on the orders of merchant and shipbuilder Mikhail Britnev, it had the bow altered to achieve an ice-clearing capability (20° raise from keel line). This allowed the Pilot to push itself on the top of the ice and consequently break it. Britnev fashioned the bow of his ship after the shape of old Pomor boats, which had been navigating icy waters of the White Sea and Barents Sea for centuries. Pilot was used between 1864-1890 for navigation in the Gulf of Finland between Kronstadt and Oranienbaum thus extending the summer navigation season by several weeks. Inspired by the success of the Pilot, Mikhail Britnev built a second similar vessel Boy ("Breakage" in Russian) in 1875 and a third Booy ("Buoy" in Russian) in 1889.

The cold winter of 1870-1871 caused the Elbe River and the port of Hamburg to freeze over, causing a prolonged halt to navigation and huge commercial losses. The Germans purchased the Pilot's design from Britnev to make their own ice-breaker, the Eisbrecher I.

The first true modern sea-going icebreaker was built at the turn of the 20th century. Icebreaker Yermak, was built in 1897 at the Armstrong Whitworth naval yards in England under contract from the Russian Navy. The ship borrowed the main principles from Pilot and applied them to the creation of the first polar icebreaker, which was able to run over and crush pack ice. The ship weighed 5,000 tons, and its' steam-reciprocating engines delivered 10,000 horsepower. The ship was so well built that it was only finally decommissioned and scrapped in 1963, making it one of the longest serving ice-breakers in the world.

At the beginning of the 20th century, several other countries began to operate purpose-built icebreakers. Most were coastal icebreakers, but Russia, and later, the Soviet Union, also built several oceangoing icebreakers of around 10,000 ton displacement.

Diesel-powered icebreakers

The world's first diesel-electric icebreaker was the 4,330-ton Swedish icebreaker Ymer. At 9,000 hp divided between two propellers in the stern and one propeller in the bow, she remained the most powerful Swedish icebreaker until the commissioning of Oden in 1957. Ymer was followed by the Finnish Sisu, the first diesel-electric icebreaker in Finland, in 1939. Both vessels were decommissioned in the 1970s and replaced by much larger icebreakers in both countries, the 1976-built Sisu in Finland and the 1977-built Ymer in Sweden.

In 1941, the United States started building the Wind class. Research in Scandinavia and the Soviet Union led to a design that had a very strongly built short and wide hull, with a cut away forefoot and a rounded bottom. Powerful diesel-electric machinery drove two stern and one auxiliary bow propeller. These features would become the standard for postwar icebreakers until the 1980s.

NUCLEAR ICEBREAKERS

Several technological advances were introduced into icebreaking technology over the years, but it was not until the introduction of nuclear power in the Soviet icebreaker Lenin in 1959 that icebreakers developed to their full potential. NS Lenin was launched in 1957. It was both the world's first nuclear-powered surface ship and the first nuclear-powered civilian vessel. Lenin was put into operation in 1959 and officially decommissioned in 1989.

The second Soviet nuclear icebreaker was NS Arktika, the lead ship of the Arktika class. In service since 1975, she was the first surface ship to reach the North Pole, on August 17, 1977.

In May 2007, sea trials were completed for the nuclear-powered Russian ice-breaker NS50 Let Pobedy. The vessel was put into service by Murmansk Shipping Company, which manages all eight Russian state-owned nuclear icebreakers. The keel was originally laid in 1989 by Baltic Works of Leningrad (now St Petersburg), and the ship was launched in 1993 as the NS Ural. This icebreaker was intended to be the sixth and last of the Arktika class, and currently is the world's largest icebreaker.

FUNCTION OF ICEBREAKERS

Today, most icebreakers are needed to keep trade routes open where there are either seasonal or permanent ice conditions. While the merchant vessels calling ports in these regions are strengthened for navigation in ice, they are usually not powerful enough to manage the ice by themselves. For this reason, in the Baltic Sea, the Great Lakes and the Saint Lawrence Seaway, and along the Northern Sea Route, the main function of icebreakers is to escort convoys of one or more ships safely through ice-infested waters. When a ship becomes immobilized by ice, the icebreaker has to free it by breaking the ice surrounding the ship and, if necessary, open a safe passage through the ice field. In difficult ice conditions, the icebreaker can also tow the weakest ships.

Some icebreakers are also used to support scientific research in the Arctic and Antarctic. In addition to icebreaking capability, the ships need to have reasonably good open water characteristics for transit to and from the polar regions, facilities and accommodation for the scientific personnel, and cargo capacity for supplying research stations on the shore. Countries such as Argentina and South Africa, which do not require icebreakers in domestic waters, have research icebreakers for carrying out studies in the polar regions.

As offshore drilling moves to the Arctic seas, icebreaking vessels are needed to supply cargo and equipment to the drilling sites and protect the drillships and oil platforms from ice by performing ice management, which includes for example breaking drifting ice into smaller floes and steering icebergs away from the protected object. In the past, such operations were carried out primarily in the North America, but today Arctic offshore drilling and oil production is also going on in various parts of the Russian Arctic.

CHARACTERISTICS OF ICEBREAKERS

Ice resistance and hull form

Icebreakers are often described as ships that literally drive their sloping bows onto the ice and break it under the weight of the ship. In reality, this only happens in very thick ice where the icebreaker will proceed at walking pace or may even have to repeatedly back down several ship lengths and ram the ice pack at full power. More commonly the ice, which has a relatively low flexural (bending) strength, is easily broken and submerged under the hull without a noticeable change in the icebreaker's trim while the vessel moves forward at a relatively high and constant speed.

When an icebreaker is designed, one of the main goals is to minimize the forces resulting from crushing and breaking the ice, and submerging the broken floes under the vessel. The average value of the longitudinal components of these instantaneous forces is called the ship's ice resistance. Naval architects who design icebreakers use the so-called h-v-curve to determine the icebreaking capability of the vessel. It shows the speed (v) that the ship is able to achieve as a function of ice thickness. This is done by solving the velocity at which the thrust from the propellers equals to the combined hydrodynamic and ice resistance of the vessel. An alternative means to determine the icebreaking capability of a vessel in different ice conditions such as pressure ridges is to perform model tests in an ice tank. Regardless of the method, the actual performance of new icebreakers is verified in full scale ice trials once the ship has been built.

In order to minimize the icebreaking forces, the hull lines of an icebreaker are usually designed so that the flare at the waterline is as small as possible. As a result, icebreaking ships are characterized by a sloping or rounded stem as well as sloping sides and a short parallel midship to improve maneuverability in ice.

However, the spoon-shaped bow and round hull have poor hydrodynamic efficiency and seakeeping characteristics, and make the icebreaker susceptible to slamming. For this reason, the hull of an icebreaker is often a compromise between minimum ice resistance, maneuverability in ice, low hydrodynamic resistance, and adequate open water characteristics.

Some icebreakers have a hull that is wider in the bow than in the stern. These so-called "reamers" increase the width of the ice channel and thus reduce frictional resistance in the aftship as well as improve the ship's maneuverability in ice.

In addition to low friction paint, some icebreakers utilize an explosion-welded abrasion-resistant stainless steel ice belt that further reduces friction and protects the ship's hull from corrosion. Auxiliary system such as powerful water deluge and air bubbling systems are used to reduce the friction by forming a lubricating layer between the hull and the ice. Pumping water between heeling tanks on both sides of the vessel results in continuous rolling that reduces friction and makes steady progress through the ice easier. Experimental bow designs such as the flat Thyssen-Waas bow and a cylindrical bow have been tried over the years to further reduce the ice resistance and create an ice-free channel behind the vessel.

STRUCTURAL DESIGN

Icebreakers and other ships operating in ice-infested waters require additional structural strengthening against various global and local loads resulting from the contact between the hull of the vessel and the surrounding ice. As ice pressures vary between different regions of the hull, the most reinforced areas in the hull of an icegoing vessel are the bow, which experiences the highest ice loads, and the waterline, where the additional strengthening extend both above and below the waterline to form a continuous ice belt around the ship.

Short and stubby icebreakers are generally built using transverse framing in which the shell plating is stiffened with frames placed about 400 to 1,000 millimetres (1 to 3 ft) apart as opposed to longitudinal framing used in longer ships. Near the waterline, the frames running in vertical direction distribute the local ice loads on the shell plating to longitudinal girders called stringers, which in turn are supported by web frames and bulkheads that carry the global hull loads. While the shell plating, which is in direct contact with the ice, can be up to 50 millimetres (2.0 in) thick in older polar icebreakers, the use of high strength steel with yield strength up to 500 MPa (73,000 psi) in modern icebreakers results in the same structural strength with smaller material thicknesses and lower steel weight.

Regardless of the strength, the steel used in the hull structures of an icebreaker must be capable of resisting brittle fracture in low ambient temperatures and high loading conditions, both of which are typical for operations in ice-infested waters.

If built according to the rules set by a classification society such as American Bureau of Shipping, Det Norske Veritas or Lloyd's Register, icebreakers may be assigned an ice class based on the level of ice strengthening in the ship's hull. It is usually determined by the maximum ice thickness where the ship is expected to operate and other requirements such as possible limitations on ramming.

While the ice class is generally an indication of the level of ice strengthening, not the actual icebreaking capability of an icebreaker, some classification societies such as the Russian Maritime Register of Shipping have operational capability requirements for certain ice classes. Since the 2000s, International Association of Classification Societies (IACS) has proposed adopting an unified system known as the Polar class to replace classification society specific ice class notations.

POWER AND PROPULSION

Before the first diesel-electric icebreakers were built in the 1930s, icebreakers were either coal- or oil-fired steam ships. Reciprocating steam engines were preferred in icebreakers due to their reliability, robustness, good torque characteristics, and ability to reverse the direction of rotation quickly. During the steam era, the most powerful pre-war steam-powered icebreakers had a propulsion power of about 10,000 shaft horsepower (7,500 kW).

Since the Second World War, most icebreakers have been built with diesel-electric propulsion in which diesel engines coupled to generators produce electricity for propulsion motors that turn the fixed pitch propellers. The first diesel-electric icebreakers were built with direct current (DC) generators and propulsion motors, but over the years the technology advanced first to alternating current (AC) generators and finally to frequency-controlled AC-AC systems. In modern diesel-electric icebreakers, the propulsion system is built according to the power plant principle in which the main generators supply electricity for all onboard consumers and no auxiliary engines are needed. Since the mid-1970s, the most powerful diesel-electric icebreakers have been the formerly Soviet and later Russian icebreakers Ermak, Admiral Makarov and Krasin which have nine twelve-cylinder diesel generators producing electricity for three propulsion motors with a combined output of 26,500 kW (35,500 hp). In 2017, they will be surpassed by the new Canadian polar icebreaker, CCGS John G. Diefenbaker, which will have a combined propulsion power of 36,000 kW (48,000 hp).

Although the diesel-electric powertrain is the preferred choice for icebreakers due to the good low speed torque characteristics of the electric propulsion motors, icebreakers have also been built with diesel engines mechanically coupled to reduction gearboxes and controllable pitch propellers. The mechanical powertrain has several advantages over diesel-electric propulsion systems, such as lower weight and better fuel efficiency. However, diesel engines are sensitive to sudden changes in propeller revolutions, and to counter this mechanical powertrains are usually fitted with large flywheels or hydrodynamic couplings to absorb the torque variations resulting from propeller-ice interaction.

The steam-powered icebreakers were resurrected in the late 1950s when the Soviet Union commissioned the first nuclear-powered icebreaker, Lenin, in 1959. It had a nuclear-turbo-electric powertrain in which the nuclear reactor was used to produce steam for turbogenerators, which in turn produced electricity for propulsion motors.

Starting from 1975, the Russians commissioned six Arktika-class nuclear icebreakers of which the last, 2007-built 50 Let Pobedy, is the largest and most powerful icebreaker in the world as of 2013 at 52,800 kW (70,800 hp). In addition, two shallow-draft Taymyr-class nuclear icebreakers were built in Finland for the Soviet Union in the late 1980s. The Soviets also built a nuclear-powered icebreaking cargo ship, Sevmorput, which had a single nuclear reactor and a steam turbine directly coupled to the propeller shaft. Russia, which remains the sole operator of nuclear-powered icebreakar, is currently building a new 60,000 kW (80,000 hp) icebreakers to replace the aging Arktika class. The first vessel of this type is expected to enter service in 2017.

The 1969-built Canadian polar icebreaker CCGS Louis S. St-Laurent was one of the few icebreakers fitted with steam boilers and turbogenerators that produced power for three electric propulsion motors. It was later refitted with five diesel engines, which provide better fuel economy than steam turbines. Later Canadian icebreakers were built with diesel-electric powertrain.

The most powerful conventional (non-nuclear) icebreakers in the world, two Polar-class icebreakers operated by the United States Coast Guard, have a combined diesel-electric and mechanical propulsion system that consists of six diesel engines and three gas turbines. While the diesel engines are coupled to generators that produce power for three propulsion motors, the gas turbines are directly coupled to the propeller shafts driving controllable pitch propellers. The diesel-electric power plant can produce up to 13,000 kW (18,000 hp) while the gas turbines have a continuous combined rating of 45,000 kW (60,000 hp).

The number, type and location of the propellers depends on the power, draft and intended purpose of the vessel. Smaller icebreakers and icebreaking special purpose ships may be able to do with just one propeller while large polar icebreakers typically need up to three large propellers to absorb all power and deliver enough thrust. Some shallow draught river icebreakers have been built with four propellers in the stern.

Nozzles may be used to increase the thrust at lower speeds, but they may become clogged by ice. Until the 1980s, icebreakers operating regularly in ridged ice fields in the Baltic Sea were fitted with first one and later two bow propellers to create a powerful flush along the hull of the vessel. This considerably increased the icebreaking capability of the vessels by reducing the friction between the hull and the ice, and allowed the icebreakers to penetrate thick ice ridges without ramming.

However, the bow propellers are not suitable for polar icebreakers operating in the presence of harder multi-year ice and thus have not been used in the Arctic.

Azimuth thrusters remove the need of traditional propellers and rudders by having the propellers in steerable gondolas that can rotate 360 degrees around a vertical axis. These thrusters improve propulsion efficiency, icebreaking capability and maneuverability.

The use of azimuth thrusters also allows a ship to move astern in ice without losing maneuverability. This has led to the development of double acting ships, vessels with the stern shaped like an icebreaker's bow and the bow designed for open water performance. In this way, the ship remains economical to operate in open water without compromising its ability to operate in difficult ice conditions. Azimuth thrusters have also made it possible to develop new experimental icebreakers that operate sideways to open a wide channel though ice.

MERCHANT SUBMARINE

A merchant submarine is a type of submarine intended for trade, and being without armaments, it is not considered a warship like most other types of submarines. The intended use would be blockade running, or to dive under Arctic ice.

Strictly speaking, only two submarines have so far been purpose-built for non-military merchant shipping use, though standard or partly converted military submarines have been used to transport smaller amounts of important cargo, especially during wartime, and large-scale proposals for modern merchant submarines have been produced by manufacturers.

GERMANY

Only two merchant submarines have historically been built, both in Germany during World War I. They were constructed to slip through the naval blockade of the Entente Powers, mainly enforced by the efforts of Great Britain's Royal Navy. The British blockade had led to great difficulties for German companies in acquiring those raw materials which were not found in quantity within the German sphere of influence, and thus was hindering the German war efforts substantially.

The submarines were built in 1916 by a private shipping company created for the enterprise, the Deutsche Ozean-Reederei, a subsidiary company of the North German Lloyd shipping company (now Hapag-Lloyd) and the Deutsche Bank. They were intended to travel the route from Germany to the neutral U.S., bringing back the required raw materials. As the U.S. would not profit enough from receiving German currency, the ships were to carry trade goods both ways.

Britain soon protested with the U.S. against the use of submarines as merchant ships, arguing that they could not be stopped and inspected for munitions in the same manner as other vessels. The U.S., under diplomatic pressure for supposedly showing favoritism while having declared itselfneutral, rejected the argument. Even submarines, as long as they were unarmed, were to be regarded as merchant vessels and accordingly would be permitted to trade.

Deutschland

The Deutschland had a carrying capacity of 700 tons (much of it outside the pressure hull), and could travel at 15 knots (17.3 mph; 27.8 km/h) on the surface and 7 knots (8.1 mph; 13.0 km/h) while submerged. It had a crew of 29 men and was commanded by Paul König, a former surface merchantman captain.

On its first journey to the US, departing on the 23 June 1916, Deutschland carried 163 tons of highly sought-after chemical dyes, as well as medical drugs and mail. Passing undetected through the English Channel she arrived in Baltimore on the 8 July 1916 and soon re-embarked with 348 tons of rubber, 341 tons of nickel and 93 tons of tin, arriving back in Bremerhaven on 25 August 1916. She had travelled 8,450 nautical miles (9,724 mi; 15,649 km), though only 190 nmi (219 mi; 352 km) of these submerged.

The profit from the journey was 17.5 million Reichsmark, more than four times the building cost, mainly because of the high prices of the patented, highly concentrated dyes, which would have cost 26.9 thousand U.S. dollars per pound once adjusted for inflation. In return, the raw materials brought back covered the specific needs of the German war industry for several months.

A second journey in October-December of the same year was also very successful, again trading chemicals, medicines and gems for rubber, nickel, alloys and tin. However, the Deutschland was lightly damaged during a collision with a tug in New London. Following his return, captain Paul König wrote a book (or possibly had it ghost-written) about the journeys of the Deutschland. The book was heavily publicized, as it was intended to sway public opinion in both Germany and the U.S.

A third journey, planned for January 1917, was however aborted after the U.S. entered the war against Germany. The declaration of war had been partly because of U.S. anger over the actions of German submarines sinking shipping bound for Great Britain, sometimes just outside of American territorial waters. The Deutschland was taken over by the German Imperial Navy and converted into the submarine cruiser (U-kreuzer) U-155 (a type of submarine with added artillery to fight when surfaced). It was successful in three war cruises, sinking 43 ships. After the war it was taken to England as a war trophy in December 1918. Scrapped in 1921, the boat's history ended on a tragic note, with 5 workers dying due to an explosion ripping apart the sub during dismantling.

Bremen

A second merchant submarine, the sister ship of Deutschland, was launched on its first journey in August 1916 under Karl Schwartzkopf, but never arrived in the US. Its fate was never decisively uncovered, though she may have collided with the British armed merchant cruiser HMS Mantua south of Iceland, as was theorized after the war. There are also presumptions that she might have hit a mine off the Orkney Islands.

Other boats

Six further merchant submarines were in the process of being built by the Deutsche Ozean-Reederei when the US entered the war in early 1917. The construction of the merchant submarines was subsequently halted or changed into submarine cruisers, similar to the fate of Deutschland.

In World War II, Germany used milk cow submarines to refuel its hunter u-boats in the Atlantic. As these boats were part of Kriegsmarine (Nazi Germany's navy), did carry light armaments (anti-aircraft guns), and never engaged in trade as such, they do not qualify as merchant submarines. However, they shared the large amounts of cargo space compared to normal submarines of their day.

Germany forcibly acquired five Italian 'merchant submarines' (again having defensive armament and thus not legally merchant ships, though having many of the appropriate characteristics) from a relatively extensive Italian program after the Italian armistice in September 1943.

ITALY

A 12-boat 'R'-class of 2100-ton submarines had been designed in Italy to carry approximately 600 tons of cargo with a surface speed of 13 knots (15.0 mph; 24.1 km/h) and submerged speed of 6 knots (6.9 mph; 11.1 km/h). A 63-man crew would operate a defensive armament of three 20 mm guns. Romolo and Remo were laid down in July 1942 at the Tosi Yard in Taranto with launch scheduled for March 1943. Ten large submarines built for combat service were also scheduled for conversion to merchant service after their designs had been found unsuitable for use against allied convoys. These were the 880-ton Archimede, the 940-ton Barbarigo, the 951-ton ComandanteCappellini, the 1030-ton AlpinoBagnolini and Reginaldo Giuliani, the 1036-ton Leonardo da Vinci and Luigi Torelli, the 1331-ton Enrico Tazzoli and Giuseppe Finzi, and the 1504-ton AmmaraglioCagni.

Conversions were to be accomplished at Bordeaux, with armament limited to defensive machine-guns, while the conversion cargo capacity of 160 tons also reduced reserve buoyancy from 20–25% to 3.5–6%. Several French submarines captured at Bizerta were also scheduled for conversion, being the 974-ton Phoque, Requin, Espadon, and Dauphin.

The ships were used on an eastbound route from Bordeaux to Singapore (then in Japanese, thus Axis, hands) with cargoes of mercury, steel and aluminum bars, welding steel, bomb prototypes, 20 mm guns, blueprints for tanks and bombsights, and up to a dozen passengers. Return trip loadings were 110 to 155 tons of rubber, 44 to 70 tons of zinc, 5 tons of tungsten, 2 tons of quinine, 2 tons of opium, bamboo, rattan and passengers. ComandanteCappellini, Reginaldo Giuliani, and Enrico Tazzoli departed Bordeaux in May, 1943. The first two completed their voyages in July and August, but Enrico Tazzoli was destroyed by allied bombers in the Bay of Biscay. Barbarigo was similarly destroyed during a June departure, but Luigi Torrelli reached Singapore in August.

Following the Italian armistice in September, Giuseppe Finzi and AlpinoBagnolini were seized by Germany while undergoing conversion at Bordeaux, and designated UIT-21 and UIT-22, respectively. Reginaldo Giuliani, CommandanteCappellini, and Luigi Torelli were seized by the Japanese in the East Indies, given to Germany, and designated UIT-23, UIT-24 and UIT-25, respectively. UIT-22 departed Bordeaux for Sumatra in January 1944 and was destroyed by RAF 262 squadron Catalina bombers off South Africa in March. UIT-23 was sunk by the British submarine Tally-Ho in February. UIT-24 departed Sumatra for Bordeaux in February, but returned to Sumatra in March after its refuelling ship was sunk.

Of the other ships, AmmiraglioCagni surrendered at South Africa, Archimede and Leonardo da Vinciwere sunk before conversion to merchant service while Romolo, Remo and the French Phoque were sunk prior to loading. The remaining 'R'-class submarines were not completed and conversion work ceased on the remaining three French submarines.

SOVIET UNION

The Soviet Union had plans to construct cargo submarines both during World War II and in the Cold War, but these plans were never carried out. These would not strictly count as merchant submarines, as they would have been at least lightly armed and used mainly for directly war-related duties, such as supplying troops or delivering military forces to their targets. However, in the post-Cold War period, Soviet designers also proposed purely peaceful applications.

World War II

In World War II, the Soviet Union used submarines (as well as other ships) to supply the besieged Crimean port of Sevastopol. The largest could transfer up to 95 tons of cargo, loading even the torpedo tubes with supplies. Around 4,000 tons were delivered by about 80 runs of 27 submarines, though Sevastopol still eventually fell.

Based on this experience, the Soviet Navy's high command initiated a transport submarine program. A first project (Project 605) envisaged a sub that would be basically a towed barge, connected to a standard sub. This idea was discarded due to difficulties with the towing. Later, a small cargo submarine design (Project 607) with a capacity of 250 to 300 tons of solid cargo and two folding cargo cranes was proposed. No weapons beyond two deck guns were envisaged, and the design borrowed many existing parts from the earlier VI and VI-bis submarine series to simplify construction. However, by 1943 the strategic situation had changed, and the plans were not executed.

Cold War

The Soviet Union envisaged and almost realized various concepts for large cargo submarines during the 1950s and 1960s, though these would not have been counted as merchant ships, being envisaged as navy landing ships to transport troops. They would have been amongst the largest submarines of their day, had they been built.

Post Cold War

In the 1990s, the Malachite design bureau proposed plans for submarines capable of transporting petroleum or freight containers in or through Arctic regions. It was envisaged that these ships would dive under the polar ice cap to travel directly between European and Asian ports, and possibly northern Canada, with the designers noting that:

"Given equal cargo capacity, the efficiency of an underwater container ship is considerably higher, for example, than that of an icebreaker transport ship of the Norilsk type. The underwater tanker is competitive." The tanker and container variants would follow the same design as standard military nuclear submarines, with the tanker variant carrying almost 30,000 tons of petroleum, to be loaded and discharged from surface or underwater terminals. The container carrier was to transport 912 standard (20-foot) freight containers, loaded within 30 hours through hatches, assisted by internal conveyance systems.

However, these plans came to nothing in the hard financial straits following the Soviet Union's dissolution later in the 1990s.

A similar design has been proposed by the Rubin Design Bureau with the 'Submarine Cargo Vessel', a civilian redesign of the famous Typhoon-class submarine of the Cold War.

The ship of a concept of Submarine Freight Transportation System (SFTS) is a new system approach to idea of 'Submarine Cargo Vessel'. This concept was suggested in 1997 by Vladimir Postnikov and present time it is considered as a sea part of Global Intelligent Transportation System concept.

UNITED STATES

Similar to the post-Cold War ideas of the Soviet Union, there have been some concept plans to use atomic-powered submarine oil tankers to exploit Arctic oilfields in Alaska and Siberia. General Dynamics had apparently approached German shipbuilders during the early 1980s about the possible construction of either a US$725 million nuclear-powered or a US$700 million methane-powered version of a liquefied natural gas (LNG) submarine tanker to carry LNG from the Arctic to North America and Europe.

OTHER USES

Another (albeit black market) type of 'trade' usage is the known use of narco submarines or 'drug subs' by drug smugglers. In one case, a Colombiandrug cartel was even interrupted before finishing the construction of a professional-grade, 30 m long, 200 tons carrying-capacity submarine apparently intended for the cocaine trade with the U.S. At the time of the police raid, the submarine was being constructed in segmented parts in a warehouse high in the Andes near Bogotá. However, most drug subs so far are not as sophisticated as professional merchant submarines would be, being mainly intended to run just under the surface, rather than deeply submerged.

NARCO-SUBMARINE

A narco-submarine (also called narco-sub, drug sub and Bigfoot submarine) is a type of custom-made ocean-going self-propelled submersible vessel built by drug traffickers to smuggle drugs. They are especially known to be used by Colombian drug cartel members to export cocaine from

Colombia to Mexico, which is often then transported overland to the United States. The first known vessels, detected in 1993, were semi-submersibles since they could not dive: most of the craft was submerged with little more than the cockpit and the exhaust gas pipes above the water.

Modern narco-submarines are fully submersible, designed specifically to be difficult to detect visually or by radar, sonar and infrared systems.

COCAINE-SMUGGLING SEA VESSEL

During the 1980s, go-fast boats became the drug-smuggling vessel of choice in many parts of the world. These boats can be detected by radar; as radar coverage improved, Colombian drug cartels started using less easily detected semi-submersibles from the 1990s.

The first time the U.S. Coast Guard found one, authorities dubbed it Bigfoot because they had heard rumors that such things existed, but none had actually been seen. It was late 2006 when a Bigfoot was seized 145 kilometers (90 mi; 78 nmi) southwest of Costa Rica carrying several tons of cocaine.

In 2006, US officials say they detected three; in 2008, they were spotting an average of ten per month, but only one out of ten was intercepted. Few were seized as their crews scuttle them upon interception and they sink within a minute or so. By 2009, the U.S.A. detected as many as 60 narco sub events and it was calculated they were moving as much as 330 metric tons (360 short tons; 320 long tons) of cocaine per year. Costing up to two million dollars each to construct, they can move enough cocaine in a single trip to generate more than USD$100 million in illicit proceeds for the traffickers.

After the November 5, 2010 arrest of Harold Mauricio Poveda, a key Mexican-Colombian link, it is suspected that the Revolutionary Armed Forces of Colombia (FARC) is behind the construction of narco-submarines and is collaborating with the Sinaloa Cartel to fund its armed activities.

CONSTRUCTION

Colombia's Pacific coastline, where muddy rivers loop into the ocean, has long been a smugglers' paradise. Behind the jagged cliffs that jut into the ocean is a vast jungle, laced with mangrove-fringed coves and virtually thousands of miles of waterways, apt for clandestine shipyards. A Colombian Navy Commander stated that it is most striking to notice the logistical capacity required of these criminals in order to take all the material into the heart of the jungle, including heavy equipment such as propulsion gear and generators. Sometimes they are put together in pieces and then reassembled in other locations under the jungle canopy, in camps outfitted with sleeping quarters for workers.

The narco-submarines can cost about $2 million USD and take upward of a year to build. Despite the costs, some of the craft are intended for one-time use, being abandoned at sea after a successful delivery. After all, their cargoes carry a street value of up to $400 million. On other seized craft however, officials found zinc bars used as sacrificial anodes, lessening corrosion on metal parts exposed to seawater. As corrosion would not be a concern on a single trip but is a factor influencing long-term durability, this is a clear indication that multiple use was intended. This, in turn, opens up the question of any illicit return cargo, like weapons, that they might carry back to Colombia.

The design and manufacturing techniques employed in their construction have improved over time: the boats have become faster, more seaworthy, and of higher capacity than earlier models. A 60 feet (18.3 m) long narco-submarine can reach speeds of 11 miles per hour (18 km/h; 9.6 kn) and carry up to 10 short tons (8.9 long tons; 9.1 t) of cocaine.

They are typically made of fiberglass, powered by a 300 hp (220 kW)/350 hp (260 kW) diesel engine and manned by a crew of four. They have enough cargo space to carry two to ten tons of cocaine, carry large fuel tanks which give them a range of 2,000 miles (3,200 km; 1,700 nmi), and are equipped with satellite navigation systems. There is no head (toilet), and accommodation is cramped.

Because much of its structure is fiberglass and it travels barely under the surface, the vessel is nearly impossible to detect via sonar or radar, and very difficult to spot visually. The newer models pipe their exhaust along the bottom to cool it before venting it, making the boat even less susceptible to infrared detection.

They are most easily spotted visually from the air, though even that is difficult as they are camouflaged with blue paint and produce almost no wake. They have ballast tanks to alter the vessel's buoyancy so that they ride low in the water.

TYPICAL CHARACTERISTICS

These are the typical characteristics as stated by the U.S. Joint Interagency Task Force South:

- Hull material: wood, fiberglass, or steel
- Length 40 to 80 feet (12.2 to 24.4 m)
- Freeboard 18 inches (45.7 cm)
- Engines: single or twin diesel
- Fuel capacity 1,500 US gallons (1,200 imp gal; 5,700 L)
- Range 2,000 miles (3,200 km; 1,700 nmi)
- Speed 6 knots (11 km/h; 6.9 mph) or more

- Crew: 3
- Capacity 4–12 tonnes (4.4–13 short tons) or 4–12 tonnes (3.9–11.8 long tons) cocaine
- Control: human or remote

TRUE SUBMARINES

Narco-submarines were considered by officials to be an oddity until 2000, when Colombian police discovered a true steel 30-meter (98.4 ft) half-built submarine in a warehouse outside Bogota. The double-hulled steel vessel could have traveled 2,000 nautical miles (3,700 km; 2,300 mi), dived 330 feet (100.6 m) and carried 150 short tons (133.9 long tons; 136.1 t)-200 short tons (178.6 long tons; 181.4 t) of cocaine.

On 3 July 2010, the Ecuadorian authorities seized a fully functional, completely submersible submarine in the jungles bordering Ecuador and Colombia. This diesel electric submarine had a cylindrical fiberglass and Kevlar hull 31 meters (101.7 ft) long, a 3-meter (9.8 ft) conning tower with periscope and air conditioning. The vessel had the capacity for about 10 metric tons (11 short tons; 9.8 long tons) of cargo, a crew of five or six people, the ability to fully submerge down to 65 feet (19.8 m), and capable of long-range underwater operation. Ecuadorean authorities seized the vessel before its maiden voyage.

On 14 February 2011, another submarine was seized by the Colombian navy. The 31 m (101.7 ft)-long fibreglass and Kevlar vessel was found hidden in a jungle area in Timbiqui, in south-western Colombia. It was capable of travelling 9 m (29.5 ft) below water and it could carry four people and up to 8 metric tons (8.8 short tons; 7.9 long tons) of cargo.

NARCO TORPEDO

Semi-submersibles are hard to spot from patrol ships, but are easy to detect from the air. To address this problem, a new concept was adopted by smugglers. Instead of a full-featured self-propelled ship, a "torpedo"-style cargo container is used with a ballast tank (submersion control) to keep it at about 30 m (98 ft 5 in) under water while being towed by a regular fishing boat. If a patrol ship is spotted, the "torpedo" cargo container is released. While still submerged, it automatically releases one buoy concealed as a wooden log and equipped with a location transmitter system for a second support fishing vessel to retrieve it and continue the cocaine delivery. None of these boats do anything suspicious that could reveal their drug smuggling activity.

The buoy contains a mechanism to temporarily raise and then lower its antenna and transmit its coordinates in encrypted form a few times per day. This system was adapted from existing buoys used on tunafishing nets. One of its designers claims a 90% shipment delivery success rate, and stated that the "torpedo" development was heading towards a remote control feature using encrypted signals transmitted via satellite.

ROUTES AND SEIZURES

Experts estimated that 25 to 40 cocaine semi-subs departed from South America in 2007, and expected that figure to double in 2008. The western Colombian shore topography is near ideal for transporting the cocaine produced in clandestine laboratories in nearby Nariño department. About a third of the 600 short tons (535.7 long tons; 544.3 t) of cocaine coming out of Colombia each year leaves via the Pacific coast and a significant amount is being carried in semi-submersibles. The U.S. Homeland Security estimates that drug submarines now account for 32 percent of all maritime cocaine flow between Latin America and the United States.

While the subs are most frequently used from the Pacific coast of Colombia, they are showing up elsewhere as well. The Coast Guard says drug runners have devised a complete logistics system, with fishing boats stationed along the way to warn the crews against patrols and provide them with food and water and resorting to putting refueling vessels far offshore so drug-carrying boats can avoid coastal areas. For traffickers, reaching Mexico is well worth the trouble, as a 10-short-ton (8.9-long-ton; 9.1 t) load can fetch nearly US$200 million wholesale. Fishermen hired specifically for the task are often at the controls, and those who complete the trip successfully are paid about US$3,000.

Smugglers normally unload their cargo onto fast power boats for the final leg to shore and the semi-submersible is scuttled. None have been sighted unloading at North American ports or beaches. In 2006, a 10-meter (32.8 ft) long sub was found abandoned on the northern coast of Spain, where the authorities suspect the crew had unloaded a cargo of cocaine before fleeing. In March 2006, the Calabrianmafia ('Ndrangheta) ordered a shipment of 10 short tons (8.9 long tons; 9.1 t) of cocaine to be transported by a narco-submarine from Colombia to Italy, but the vessel was discovered by the Colombian police while it was still under construction.

During 2007, thirteen of the vessels were seized on Colombian dry land or stopped at sea by Colombian or U.S. patrol boats, more than in the previous fourteen years combined, but arrests are rare. When clandestine shipyards were discovered, workmen escaped into the jungle. In some instances semi-subs are towed behind other vessels and are scuttled if detected. Authorities are investigating reports that some semi-submersibles are unmanned and are operated remotely.

In the first six months of 2008, the U.S. Coast Guard and U.S. Navy detected 42 drug subs heading north towards the United States and off the coast of Central America, but few seizures resulted. The service estimated that 85 individual events would bring in about 600 short tons (535.7 long tons;

544.3 t) of cocaine by the end of 2008. As of 2007, the U.S. Coast Guard was adjusting its underwater acoustic sensors to listen to a narco-submarine's engine over long distances.

On July 16, 2008, the Mexican Navy intercepted a 10 meters (32.8 ft) long narco-submarine travelling about 200 kilometres (120 mi) southwest of Oaxaca. Mexican Navy Special Forces rappelled from a helicopter on to its deck and arrested four smugglers before they could scuttle their vessel. The vessel was found to be loaded with 5.8 short tons (5.2 long tons; 5.3 t) of cocaine and was towed to Huatulco, Oaxaca, by a Mexican Navy patrol boat.

On September 12, 2008, the U.S. Coast Guard captured a semi-submersible about 563 kilometers (350 mi) west of Guatemala; it was carrying 7 short tons (6.3 long tons; 6.4 t) of cocaine. The 18 meters (59.1 ft) long steel and fiberglass craft was detected by a U.S. Navy aircraft as part of Operation Panama Express and was intercepted by Coast Guard Law Enforcement Detachment 402 which was deployed aboard USS McInerney. Five days later, a 60-foot (18.3 m) semi-submersible was seized by the Coast Guard cutter Midgett about 322 kilometers (200 mi) south of Guatemala.

On June 1 and 2, 2009 the Colombian authorities seized three narco-submarines on the shores of the Pacific coast, one of them loaded with 1.5 short tons (1.3 long tons; 1.4 t) of cocaine. The Colombian navy had intercepted or discovered 33 narco-submarines by 2009.

LEGAL SITUATION

When semi-submersibles are stopped at sea, their crews usually scuttle them, sending both the boat and the cocaine to the bottom in a minute or so and leaving no evidence of trafficking. Until 2008, in accordance with maritime law, the crew was rescued and, if there was no physical evidence of wrongdoing, released without criminal charges. To address this legal loophole, the US Drug Trafficking Vessel Interdiction Act was enacted in September, 2008, making it a "felony for those who knowingly or intentionally operate or embark in a self-propelled semi-submersible (SPSS) that is without nationality and that is or has navigated in international waters, with the intent to evade detection." The penalty is a prison term of up to twenty years in the U.S.

The bill does not apply to flagged vessels (i.e., that have been registered with some nation). The bill grants extraterritorial jurisdiction over international waters, and also makes it illegal to lack relevant documents. Instead of an anti-narcotics operation turning into a rescue mission when the submarines are scuttled and sinks, the crew can be arrested and charged.

Some alleged narco-submarine smugglers are now facing criminal charges in the US for operating an unflagged semi-submersible.

Colombia's Congress passed a law in June, 2009, punishing the building of semi-submersible vessels with up to twelve years in prison, and transporting drugs in them with up to fourteen years in prison.

National security issues related to torpedo style cargo containers, semi-submersible vessels, and submarines used for smuggling and/or terrorist activities were reviewed in an August 2012 article in Homeland Security Affairs. Also presented are behaviors indicating shifts in methods of operating by drug traffickers and the corresponding risk to national security.

PIPE-LAYING SHIP

A pipelaying ship is a maritime vessel used in the construction of subsea infrastructure. It serves to connect oil production platforms with refineries on shore. To accomplish this goal a typical pipelaying vessel carries a heavy lift crane, used to install pumps and valves, and equipment to lay pipe between subsea structures.

Lay methods consist of S-lay and J-lay and can be reel-lay or welded length by length. Pipelaying ships make use of dynamic positioning systems or anchor spreads to maintain the correct position and speed while laying pipe.

Recent advances have been made, with pipe being laid in water depths of more than 2,500 metres.

The term "pipelaying vessel" or "pipelayer" refers to all vessels capable of laying pipe on the ocean floor. It can also refer to "dual activity" ships. These vessels are capable of laying pipe on the ocean floor in addition to their primary job. Examples of dual activity pipelayers include barges, modified bulk carriers, modified drillships semi-immersible laying vessels among others.

RESEARCH VESSEL

A research vessel (RV or R/V) is a ship designed and equipped to carry out research at sea. Research vessels carry out a number of roles. Some of these roles can be combined into a single vessel, others require a dedicated vessel. Due to the demanding nature of the work, research vessels are often constructed around an icebreakerhull, allowing them to operate in polar waters.

HISTORY

The research ship had origins in the early voyages of exploration. By the time of James Cook's Endeavour, the essentials of what today we would call a research ship are clearly apparent. In 1766, the Royal Society hired Cook to travel to the Pacific Ocean to observe and record the transit of Venus across the Sun. The Endeavour was a sturdy boat, well designed and equipped for the ordeals she would face, and fitted out with facilities for her "research personnel", Joseph Banks. And, as is common with contemporary research vessels, Endeavour carried out more than one kind of research, including comprehensive hydrographic survey work.

Some other notable early research vessels were HMS Beagle, RV Calypso, HMS Challenger, USFC Albatross, and the Endurance and Terra Nova.

The names of early research vessels have been used to name later research vessels, as well as Space Shuttles.

MODERN TYPES

Hydrographic survey

A hydrographic survey ship is a vessel designed to conduct hydrographic research and survey. Nautical charts are produced from this information to ensure safe navigation by military and civilianshipping.

Hydrographic survey vessels also conduct seismic surveys of the seabed and the underlying geology. Apart from producing the charts, this information is useful for detecting geological features which are likely to bear oil or gas. These vessels usually mount equipment on a towed structure, for example, air cannons, used to generate a high pressureshock wave to sound the strata beneath the seabed, or mounted on the keel, for example, a depth sounder.

In practice, hydrographic survey vessels are often equipped to perform multiple roles. Some function also as oceanographic research ships. Naval hydrographic survey vessels often do naval research, for example, on submarine detection.

Oceanographic research

Oceanographic research vessels carry out research on the physical, chemical and biological characteristics of water, the atmosphere and climate, and to these ends carry equipment for collecting water samples from a range of depths, including the deep seas, as well as equipment for the hydrographic sounding of the seabed, along with numerous other environmental sensors. These vessels often also carry scientific divers and unmanned underwater vehicles. Since the requirements of both oceanographic and hydrographic research are very different from those of fisheries research, these boats often fulfill dual roles. An example of an oceanographic research vessel is NOAAS Ronald H. Brown.

Fisheries research

A fisheries research vessel (FRV) requires platforms which are capable of towing different types of fishing nets, collecting plankton or water samples from a range of depths, and carrying acoustic fish-finding equipment. Fisheries research vessels are often designed and built along the same lines as a large fishing vessel, but with space given over to laboratories and equipment storage, as opposed to storage of the catch. An example of a fisheries research vessel is FRV Scotia.

Naval research

Naval research vessels investigate naval concerns, such as submarine and mine detection, sonar and weapon trialling.

An example of a naval research vessel is the Planet of the German Navy.

Polar research

Polar research vessels are constructed around an icebreakerhull, allowing them to operate in polar waters. These boats usually have dual roles, particularly in the Antarctic where they function also as polar replenishment and supply vessels to the Antarctic research bases.

An example of a polar research vessel is USCGC Polar Star.

Oil exploration

Oil exploration is performed in a number of ways, one of the most common being mobile drilling platforms or ships that are moved from area to area as needed to drill into the seabed to find out what deposits may or may not lie beneath it.

RIVERBOAT

A riverboat is a watercraft designed for inland navigation on lakes, rivers, and artificial waterways. They are generally equipped and outfitted as work boats in one of the carrying trades, for freight or people transport, including luxury units constructed for entertainment enterprises, such as lake or harbourtour boats. As larger water craft, virtually all riverboats are especially designed and constructed, or alternatively, constructed with special purpose features that optimizes them as riverine or lake service craft—such as dredgers, survey boats, fisheries management craft, fireboats and law enforcement patrol craft.

INLAND DESIGN DIFFERENCES

These vessels are usually less sturdy than ships built for the open seas, with limited navigational and rescue equipment, as they do not have to survive the high winds or large waves characteristic to large lakes, seas or oceans. They can thus be built from light composite materials. They are limited in size by width and depth of the river as well as the height of bridges spanning the river. They can be designed with shallow drafts, as were the paddle wheel steamers on the Mississippi River that could operate in water under two metres deep.

While a ferryboat is often used to cross a river, a riverboat is used to travel along the course of the river, while carrying passengers and cargo, or both, for revenue. (Vessels like 'Riverboat casinos' are not considered here as they are essentially stationary).

The significance of riverboats is dependent on the number of navigable rivers and channels as well as the condition of the road and rail network. Generally speaking, riverboats provide slow but cheap transport especially suited for bulk cargo and containers.

HISTORY

As early as 20,000 BC people started fishing in rivers and lakes using rafts and dugouts. Roman sources dated 50 BC mention extensive transportation of goods and people on the river Rhine. Upstream, boats were usually powered by sails or oars. In the Middle Ages, towpaths were built along most waterways to use working animals or people to pull riverboats. In the 19th century, steamboats became common.

The most famous riverboats were on the rivers of the midwestern and central southern United States, on the Mississippi, Ohio and Missouri rivers in the early 19th century. Out west, riverboats were common transportation on the Colorado, Columbia, and Sacramento rivers. These American riverboats were designed to draw very little water, and in fact it was commonly said that they could "navigate on a heavy dew".

Australia has a history of riverboats. Australia's biggest river, the Murray, has an inland port called Echuca. Many large riverboats were working on the Murray, but now a lower water level is stopping them. The Kalgan River in Western Australia is one of the oldest rivers in the world; it has had two main riverboats. The Silver Star, 1918 to 1935, would lower her funnel to get under the low bridge. Today, the Kalgan Queen riverboat takes tourists up the river to taste the local wines. She lowers her roof to get under the same bridge.

It is these early steam-driven river craft that typically come to mind when "steamboat" is mentioned, as these were powered by burning wood, with iron boilers drafted by a pair of tall smokestacks belching smoke and cinders, and twin double-acting pistons driving a large paddlewheel at the stern churning foam. This type of propulsion was an advantage as a rear paddlewheel operates in an area clear of snags, is easily repaired, and is not likely to suffer damage in a grounding. By burning wood, the boat could consume fuel provided by woodcutters along the shore of the river. These early boats carried a brow (a short bridge) on the bow, so they could head in to an unimproved shore for transfer of cargo and passengers.

Modern riverboats are generally screw (propeller) driven, with pairs of diesel engines of several thousand horsepower. The standard reference for the development of the steamboat is Steamboats on Western Rivers: An Economic and Technological History by Louis C. Hunter (1949).

MODERN RIVERBOATS

Many of the riverboats shown below were operating on the Yangtze (Chang Jiang) river.

Luxury tourist transport

Some large riverboats are comparable in accommodation, food service, and entertainment to a modern oceanic cruise ship. Tourist boats provide a scenic and relaxing trip through the segment they operate in.

On the Yangtze River, they typically employ staff for double duties: both as serving staff and as evening-costumed dancing entertainers.

Smaller luxury craft (without entertainment) operate on European waterways - both rivers and canals, with some providing bicycle and van side trips to smaller villages.

HIGH SPEED PASSENGER TRANSPORT

High speed boats such as those shown here had a special advantage in some operations in the free running Yangze. In several locations within the three gorges one way travel was enforced through fast narrows. While less maneuverable and deeper draft vessels were obliged to wait for clearance these high speed boats were free to zip past waiting traffic by running in the shallows.

LOCAL AND LOW COST PASSENGER TRANSPORT

Smaller riverboats are used in urban and suburban areas for sightseeing and public transport. Sightseeing boats can be found in Amsterdam, Paris, and other touristic cities where historical monuments are located near water.

The concept of local waterborn public transport is known as Water taxi in English-speaking countries, vaporetto in Venice, water/river tramway in former Soviet Union and Poland (although sightseeing boats can be called water tramways too). Local waterborn public transport is similar to ferry.

The transport craft shown below is used for short distance carriage of passengers between villages and small cities along the Yangtze, while Larger craft are used for low cost carriage over longer distance, without the fancy food or shows seen on the tourist riverboats. In some cases the traveller must provide their own food.

GOODS TRANSPORT

Multimodal

Roads through this region are inadequate for heavy truck transport and roads along the river are extremely dangerous. As the major rivers are mostly east-west, most railroad transport is typically north-south.

Here, a drive/on drive/off ramp barge is used to transport trucks. In many cases the trucks transported are new and are being delivered to customers or dealers. Perhaps unique to China, the new trucks observed traveling upstream were all blue, while the new trucks traveling downstream were all white.

Bulk cargo

Low value goods are transported on rivers and canals worldwide, since slow speed barge traffic offers the lowest possible cost per ton mile and the capital cost per ton carried is also quite low compared to other modes of transport

HISTORY

Terrace, British Columbia, Canada, celebrates "Riverboat Days" each summer. The Skeena River passes through Terrace and played a crucial role during the age of the steamboat. The first steam-powered vessel to enter the Skeena was the Union in 1864. In 1866 the Mumford attempted to ascend the river but was only able to reach the Kitsumkalum River. It was not until 1891 that the Hudson's Bay Company sternwheeler the Caledonia successfully negotiated through the Kitselas Canyon and reached Hazelton. A number of other steamers were built around the turn of the century, in part due to the growing fish industry and the gold rush.

The WT Preston, a museum ship that was once a specialised river dredge, also called a "snagboat".

SEMI-SUBMERSIBLE

A semi-submersible (semisubmerged ship) is a specialisedmarine vessel used in a number of specific offshore roles such as offshore drilling rigs, safety vessels, oil production platforms, and heavy lift cranes. They are designed with good stability and seakeeping characteristics. Other terms include semisubmersible, semi-sub, or simply semi.

CHARACTERISTICS

Offshore drilling in water depth greater than around 520 meters requires that operations be carried out from a floating vessel, as fixed structures are not practical. Initially in the early 1950s monohull ships were used like CUSS I, but these were found to have significant heave, pitch and yaw motions in large waves, and the industry needed more stable drilling platforms.

A semi-submersible obtains its buoyancy from ballasted, watertight pontoons located below the ocean surface and wave action. The operating deck can be located high above the sea level due to the good stability of the design, and therefore the operating deck is kept well away from the waves. Structural columns connect the pontoons and operating deck.

With its hull structure submerged at a deep draft, the semi-submersible is less affected by wave loadings than a normal ship. With a small water-plane area, however, the semi-submersible is sensitive to load changes, and therefore must be carefully trimmed to maintain stability. Unlike a submarine or submersible, during normal operations, a semi-submersible vessel is never entirely underwater. A semi-submersible vessel is able to transform from a deep to a shallow draft by deballasting (removing ballast water from the hull), and thereby become a surface vessel. The heavy lift vessels use this capability to submerge the majority of their structure, locate beneath another floating vessel, and then deballast to pick up the other vessel as a cargo.

EARLY HISTORY

The semi-submersible design was first developed for offshore drilling activities. Bruce Collipp of Shell is regarded as the inventor. But Edward Robert Armstrong may have paved the way with his idea of "seadrome" landing strips for airplanes in the late 1920s, since his idea involved the same use of columns on ballast tanks below the surface and anchored to the ocean floor by steel cables.

When oil drilling moved into offshore waters, fixed platform rigs and submersible rigs were built, but were limited to shallow waters. When demands for drilling equipment was needed in water depths greater than 100 feet (30 m) in the Gulf of Mexico, the first jackup rigs were built.

The first semisubmersible arrived by accident in 1961. Blue Water Drilling Company owned and operated the four column submersible drilling rigBlue Water Rig No.1 in the Gulf of Mexico for Shell Oil Company. As the pontoons were not sufficiently buoyant to support the weight of the rig and its consumables, it was towed between locations at a draught mid way between the top of the pontoons and the underside of the deck. It was observed that the motions at this draught were very small, and Blue Water Drilling and Shell jointly decided that the rig could be operated in the floating mode.

The first purpose built drilling semi-submersible Ocean Driller was launched in 1963. Since then, many semi-submersibles have been purpose-designed for the drilling industry mobile offshore fleet.

The industry quickly accepted the semi-submersible concept and the fleet increased rapidly to 30 units by 1972.

CLASSIFICATION

Drilling rig construction has historically occurred in boom periods and therefore "batches" of drilling rigs have been built. Offshore drilling rigs have been classified in nominal "generations" depending upon the year built and water depth capability as follows:

Generation	Water Depth		Dates
First	about 600 ft	200 m	Early 1960s
Second	about 1000 ft	300 m	1969–1974
Third	about 1500 ft	500 m	Early 1980s
Fourth	about 3000 ft	1000 m	1990s
Fifth	about 7500 ft	2500 m	1998–2004
Sixth	about 10000 ft	3000 m	2005–2010

APPLICATIONS

Mobile offshore drilling units (MODU)

Semi-submersible rigs make stable platforms for drilling for offshore oil and gas. They can be towed into position by a tugboat and anchored, or moved by and kept in position by their own azimuth thrusters with dynamic positioning.

The IMO MODU Code is an accredited design and operational guideline for Mobile Offshore Drilling Units of the semi-submersible type.

Semi-submersible crane vessels (SSCV)

The advantages of the semi-submersible vessel stability were soon recognized for offshore construction when in 1978 Heerema Marine Contractors constructed the two sister crane vessels called Balder and Hermod. These semi-submersible crane vessels (SSCV) consist of two lower hulls (pontoons), three columns on each pontoon and an upper hull. Shortly after J. Ray McDermott and Saipem also introduced SSCV's, resulting in two new enormous vessels DB-102 (now Thialf) and Saipem 7000, capable of lifting respectively 14,200 and 14,000 tons.

During transit an SSCV will be de-ballasted to a draught where only part of the lower hull is submerged. During lifting operations, the vessel will be ballasted down. This way, the lower hull is well submerged. This reduces the effect of waves and swell. High stability is obtained by placing the columns far apart. The high stability allows them to lift extreme high loads.

OFFSHORE SUPPORT VESSELS (OSV)

Semi-submersibles are particularly suited to a number of offshore support vessel roles because of their good stability, large deck areas, and variable deck load (VDL). Some of the most prominent vessels are;

- Uncle John – Diving/ Construction support vessel, built for Houlder Offshore in 1977
- Seaway Swan – Diving Support Vessel built in 1977
- Tharos – Offshore Safety support vessel, built in 1979 and since converted into a drilling vessel, and rechristened Transocean Marianas.
- Stadive – Diving Support Vessel (DSV) built for Shell in 1982
- Iolair – Offshore safety support vessel, built for BP in 1982, Sedco/ Phillips SS was the first built to Red Adair's recommendations. Iolair followed.
- Safe Karinia – Offshore operations vessel, built in 1982
- Polyconfidence – Offshore accommodation platform, built in 1988.

- Q4000 – Offshore Multiservice Vessel, built for Caldive in 2002
- Ocean Odyssey – Converted semi-submersible drilling rig used as a rocket launch pad.

OFFSHORE PRODUCTION PLATFORMS

When oil fields were first developed in offshore locations, drilling semi-submersibles were converted for use as combined drilling and production platforms. These vessels offered very stable and cost effective platforms. The first semi-submersible floating production platform was the Argyll FPF converted from the Transworld 58 drilling semi-submersible in 1975 for the Hamilton Brothers North Sea Argyll oil field.

As the oil industry has progressed into deeper water and harsh environments, purpose-built production semi-submersible platforms were designed. The first purpose-built semi-submersible production platform was for the Balmoral field, UK North Sea in 1986.

A summary of offshore semi-submersible oil production platforms is given in the following table derived from industry data.

SNAGBOAT

A snagboat is a river boat, resembling a barge with superstructure for crew accommodations, and deck-mounted cranes and hoists for removing snags and other obstructions from rivers and other shallow waterways.

During the American Civil War, when much of the naval fighting was done on rivers and their tributaries, numerous snagboats were in operation. USS Benton, for example, was a commercial snagboat quickly converted by the Union Army to a river gunboat when the American Civil War broke out.

In Canada, many of the rivers of British Columbia were maintained and kept open for navigation by federal Department of Public Works snagboats. On the Fraser River, in southern British Columbia, a series of sternwheelersnagboats named Samson were operated from the early 1880s until the retirement of Samson V in 1980.

In northern British Columbia, Department of Public Works snagboats operated out of Prince Rupert and cleared the waters of the Nass, Ecstall, and Skeena rivers.

The snag-clearance service was mainly important on the Fraser River because of the large amount of marine traffic. Passenger and freight-carrying sternwheelers operated out of New Westminster from 1859 until the early 1920s. These lightly built vessels were vulnerable to the woody debris and drift logs that would wash down the river with every spring freshet. After the 1920s, most of the traffic on the Fraser was tug and barge service along with deep sea shipping in the lower reaches of the river, and a greater portion of the snagboat's assignments was in maintenance of government docks and aids to navigation. In northern British Columbia, a major part of the snagboat service provided by the Canadian federal government was in support of the gillnet fishing industry and the canneries that were built in and around the estuaries of the major rivers. Huge amounts of timber debris would wash down-river every year creating hazards for fishermen and destroying nets.

7

Naval Architecture

Naval architecture is an engineering discipline dealing with the design, construction, maintenance and operation of marine vessels and structures. Naval architecture involves basic and applied research, design, development, design evaluation and calculations during all stages of the life of a marine vehicle.

Preliminary design of the vessel, its detailed design, construction, trials, operation and maintenance, launching and dry-docking are the main activities involved. Ship design calculations are also required for ships being modified (by means of conversion, rebuilding, modernization, or repair). Naval architecture also involves formulation of safety regulations and damage control rules and the approval and certification of ship designs to meet statutory and non-statutory requirements.

MAIN SUBJECTS

The word "vessel" includes every description of watercraft, including non-displacement craft, WIG craft and seaplanes, used or capable of being used as a means of transportation on water. The principal elements of naval architecture are:

HYDROSTATICS

Hydrostatics concerns the conditions to which the vessel is subjected to while at rest in water and its ability to remain afloat. This involves computing buoyancy, (displacement) and other hydrostatic properties. Trim - The measure of the longitudinal inclination of the vessel. Stability - The ability of a vessel to restore itself to an upright position after being inclined by wind, sea, or loading conditions.

HYDRODYNAMICS

Hydrodynamics concerns the flow of water around the ship's hull, bow, stern and over bodies such as propeller blades or rudder, or through thruster tunnels. Resistance - resistance towards motion in water primarily caused due to flow of water around the hull. Powering calculation is done based on this. Propulsion - to move the vessel through water using propellers, thrusters, water jets, sails etc. Engine types are mainly internal combustion. Some vessels are electrically powered using nuclear or solar energy. Ship motions - involves motions of the vessel in seaway and its responses in waves and wind. Controllability (maneuvering) - involves controlling and maintaining position and direction of the vessel

STRUCTURES

Structures involves selection of material of construction, structural analysis of global and local strength of the vessel, vibration of the structural components and structural responses of the vessel during motions in seaway.

ARRANGEMENTS

Arrangements involvesconcept design, layout and access, fire protection, allocation of spaces, ergonomics and capacity.

CONSTRUCTION

Construction depends on the material used. When steel or aluminium is used this involves welding of the plates and profiles after rolling, marking, cutting and bending as per the structural design drawings or models, followed by erection and launching. Other joining techniques are used for other materials like fibre reinforced plastic and glass-reinforced plastic.

SCIENCE AND CRAFT

Traditionally, naval architecture has been more craft than science. The suitability of a vessel's shape was judged by looking at a half-model of a vessel or a prototype. Ungainly shapes or abrupt transitions were frowned on as being flawed.

This included rigging, deck arrangements, and even fixtures. Subjective descriptors such as ungainly, full, and fine were used as a substitute for the more precise terms used today. A vessel was, and still is described as having a 'fair' shape. The term 'fair' is meant to denote not only a smooth transition from fore to aft but also a shape that was 'right.' Determining what is 'right' in a particular situation in the absence of definitive supporting analysis encompasses the art of naval architecture to this day.

Modern low-cost digital computers and dedicated software, combined with extensive research to correlate full-scale, towing tank and computational data, have enabled naval architects to more accurately predict the performance of a marine vehicle. These tools are used for static stability (intact and damaged), dynamic stability, resistance, powering, hull development, structural analysis, green water modelling, and slamming analysis. Data is regularly shared in international conferences sponsored by RINA, Society of

Naval Architects and Marine Engineers (SNAME) and others. Computational Fluid Dynamics is being applied to predict the response of a floating body in a random sea.

THE NAVAL ARCHITECT

Due to the complexity associated with operating in a marine environment, naval architecture is a co-operative effort between groups of technically skilled individuals who are specialists in particular fields, often coordinated by a lead naval architect. This inherent complexity also means that the analytical tools available are much less evolved than those for designing aircraft, cars and even spacecraft. This is due primarily to the paucity of data on the environment the marine vehicle is required to work in and the complexity of the interaction of waves and wind on a marine structure.

A naval architect is an engineer who is responsible for the design, construction, and/or repair of ships, boats, other marine vessels, and offshore structures, both commercial and military, including:

- Merchant ships - oil tankers, gas tankers, cargo ships, bulk carriers, container ships
- Passenger/vehicle ferries, cruise ships
- Warships - frigates, destroyers, aircraft carriers, amphibious ships
- Submarines and underwater vehicles
- Icebreakers
- High speed craft - hovercraft, multi-hull ships, hydrofoil craft
- Workboats - barges, fishing boats, anchor handling tug supply vessels, platform supply vessels, tug boats, pilot vessels, rescue craft
- Yachts, power boats, and other recreational watercraft
- Offshore platforms and subsea developments

Some of these vessels are amongst the largest (such as supertankers), most complex (such as Aircraft carriers), and highly valued movable structures produced by mankind. They are typically the most efficient method of transporting the world's raw materials and products. Modern engineering on this scale is essentially a team activity conducted by specialists in their respective fields and disciplines. Naval architects integrate these activities. This demanding leadership role requires managerial qualities and the ability to bring together the often-conflicting demands of the various design constraints to produce a product which is fit for the purpose.

In addition to this leadership role, a naval architect also has a specialist function in ensuring that a safe, economic, environmentally sound and seaworthy design is produced. To undertake all these tasks, a naval architect must have an understanding of many branches of engineering and must be in the forefront of high technology areas. He or she must be able to effectively utilize the services provided by scientists, lawyers, accountants, and business people of many kinds.

Naval architects typically work for shipyards, ship owners, design firms and consultancies, equipment manufacturers, Classification societies, regulatory bodies (Admiralty law), navies, and governments.

ANGLE OF LOLL

Angle of loll is the state of a ship that is unstable when upright (i.e. has a negative metacentric height, GMt) and therefore takes on an angle of heel to either port or starboard.

When a vessel has negative GM i.e., is in unstable equilibrium, any external force applied to the vessel will cause it to start heeling. As it heels, the moment of inertia of the vessel's waterplane (a plane intersecting the hull at the water's surface) increases, which increases the vessel's BM (distance from the center of buoyancy to the metacenter). Since there is relatively little change in KB (distance from the keel to the center of buoyancy) of the vessel, the KM (distance from keel to the metacenter) of the vessel increases.

At some angle of heel (say 10°), KM will increase sufficiently equal to KG (distance from the keel to the center of gravity), thus making GM of vessel equal to zero.

When this occurs, the vessel goes to neutral equibrium, and the angle of heel at which it happens is called angle of loll, In other words, when an unstable vessel heels over towards a progressively increasing angle of heel, at a certain angle of heel, the center of buoyancy (B) may fall vertically below the center of gravity (G). Note that Angle of List should not be confused with angle of loll. Angle of List is caused by unequal loading on either side of center line of vessel.

Although a vessel at angle of loll does display features of stable equilibrium, this is an extremely dangerous situation, and rapid remedial action is required to prevent the vessel from capsizing.

It is often caused by the influence of a large free surface or the loss of stability due to damaged compartments. It is different from list in that the vessel is not induced to heel to one side or the other by the distribution of weight, it is merely incapable of maintaining a zero heel attitude.

ANGLE OF LIST

The angle of list is the degree to which a vessel heels (leans, or tilts) to either port or starboard.

A listing vessel is stable and at equilibrium, but the distribution of weight aboard causes it to heel to one side or the other.

List refers to a ship leaning to one side under stable conditions, often caused by uneven loading or flooding. By contrast "roll" refers to the dynamic movement from side to side caused by waves. If a listing ship goes beyond the point where a righting moment will keep it afloat, it will capsize and potentially sink.

ANTI-TORPEDO BULGE

The anti-torpedo bulge (also known as an anti-torpedo blister) is a form of passive defence against naval torpedoes that featured in warship construction in the period between the First and Second World Wars.

THEORY AND FORM

Essentially, the bulge is a lateral compartment at the waterline level that is isolated from the ship's internal volume. It is part air-filled, and part free-flooding. In theory, a torpedo strike will rupture and flood the outer air-filled component of the bulge and the inner water-filled part will dissipate the shock and absorb explosive fragments, leaving the ship's main hull structurally intact. Transverse bulkheads within the bulge limit flooding throughout the entirety of the structure.

The bulge was developed by the BritishDirector of Naval Construction, Eustace Tennyson-D'Eyncourt, who had four old Edgar-classprotected cruisers so fitted in 1914. These ships were used for shore bombardment duties, and so were exposed to inshore submarine and torpedo boat attack. Grafton was torpedoed in 1917, and apart from a few minor splinter holes, the damage was confined to the bulge and the ship safely made port. Edgar was hit in 1918, this time damage to the elderly hull was confined to dented plating. The Royal Navy had all new construction fitted with bulges from 1914, beginning with the Revenge-class battleships. Older ships also had bulges incorporated during refits. The Royal Navy had its large monitors fitted with enormous bulges. This was fortuitous for Terror, which survived three torpedoes striking the hull forward, and for her sister Erebus, which survived a direct hit from a remotely-controlled explosive motor boat that ripped off 50 feet (15.25 m) of her bulge.

Later designs of bulges incorporated various combinations of air and water filled compartments and packing of wood and sealed tubes. As bulges increased a ship's beam, they caused a reduction in speed, which is a function of the length-to-beam ratio. Therefore, various combinations of narrow and internal bulges appeared throughout the 1920s and into the 1930s. The bulge had disappeared from construction in the 1930s, being replaced by internal arrangements of compartments with a similar function. Anti-torpedo bulges were still added as retrofits to older ships, such as HMS Renown and USS Arizona.

OBSOLESCENCE

For greater effect, modern torpedoes are designed to explode beneath the hull of the target so they rarely strike the side of the ship directly.

CAMBER (SHIP)

The camber is a measure of lateral main deck curvature in naval architecture. The curve is applied to a deck transversely, measured as the height of deck at centreline above the height of deck at side.

The practice of adding camber to a ship's deck originated in the era of small sailing ships. These vessels were built with the decks curving downwards at the sides in order to allow water that washed onto the deck to spill off. It adds to the ship's longitudinal strength also.

CAPSIZE SCREENING FORMULA

The capsize screening formula (CSF) is a somewhat controversial figure. It is defined for sailboats as:

CSF = Beam/ (Displacement/64.2)

It came into being after the 1979 Fastnet race in England where a storm shredded the race fleet. The Cruising Club of America (CCA) put together a technical committee that analyzed race boat data. They came up with this formula to compare boats based on readily available data. The CCA characterizes the formula as "rough".

A lower value is supposed to indicate a sailboat is less likely to capsize. A value of 2 is taken as a cutoff for acceptable to certain race committees. However this is an arbitrary cutoff based on the performance of boats in the 1979 Fastnet race. The CSF does not consider the hull shape or ballast location.

Any two sailboats will have the same CSF value if their displacement and beam are the same. As an example, one could have a light hull with 50% ballast in a bulb at the bottom of an eight foot fin keel, the other could have a heavy hull with 20% ballast in a 2-foot-deep (0.61 m) full-length keel. The stability characteristics of the two sailboats will be drastically different despite the identical CSF value.

COFFERDAM

A cofferdam (also called a coffer) is a temporary enclosure built within, or in pairs across, a body of water and constructed to allow the enclosed area to be pumped out, creating a dry work environment for the major work to proceed. Enclosed coffers are commonly used for construction and repair of oil platforms, bridge piers and other support structures built within or over water. These cofferdams are usually welded steel structures, with components consisting of sheet piles, wales, and cross braces. Such structures are typically dismantled after the ultimate work is completed.

For dam construction, two cofferdams are usually built, one upstream and one downstream of the proposed dam, after an alternative diversion tunnel or channel has been provided for the river flow to bypass the dam foundation area. These cofferdams are typically a conventional embankment dam of both earth- and rock-fill, but concrete or some sheet piling also may be used. Typically, upon completion of the dam and associated structures, the downstream coffer is removed and the upstream coffer is flooded as the diversion is closed and the reservoir begins to fill. Dependent upon the geography of a dam site, in some applications, a "U"-shaped cofferdam is used in the construction of one half of a dam. When complete, the cofferdam is removed and a similar one is created on the opposite side of the river for the construction of the dam's other half.

The cofferdam is also used on occasion in the shipbuilding and ship repair industry, when it is not practical to put a ship in drydock for repair or alteration. An example of such an application is certain ship lengthening operations. In some cases a ship is actually cut in two while still in the water, and a new section of ship is floated in to lengthen the ship. Torch cutting of the hull is done inside a cofferdam attached directly to the hull of the ship, and is then detached before the hull sections are floated apart. The cofferdam is later replaced while the hull sections are welded together again. As expensive as this may be to accomplish, use of a drydock may be even more expensive.

A 100 ton open caisson that was lowered more than a mile to the sea floor in attempts to stop the flow of oil in the Deepwater Horizon oil spill has been called a cofferdam. It did not work as methane hydrates froze in the upper levels preventing the containment.

NAVAL ARCHITECTURE

A cofferdam may also refer to an insulating space between two watertight bulkheads or decks within a ship. A cofferdam may be a void (empty) space or a ballast space. Cofferdams are usually employed to ensure oil or other chemicals do not leak into machinery spaces.

If two different cargoes that react dangerously with each other are carried on the same vessel, one or more cofferdams are usually required between the cargo spaces.

The division between the tanks and the hull of a double-hulled vessel is not normally called a cofferdam, although it serves this function.

LIMIT OF POSITIVE STABILITY

Limit of Positive Stability or LPS is the angle from the vertical at which a boat will no longer stay upright but will capsize, becoming inverted, or turtled. It is also known as the Angle of Vanishing Stability or AVS. For example, if a boat with an LPS of 120 degrees rolls past this point, i.e. its mast is already at an angle of 30 degrees below the water, it will continue to roll and be completely upside down in the water. Most sailboats have lead or other heavy materials in their keel at the bottom of their hulls to keep them from capsizing.

LPS was a part of the Offshore Racing Rules and is used to measure how stable or seaworthy a sailboat is. The modern offshore racing rules published by the International Sailing Federation may also use the measurement.

NOISE AND VIBRATION ON MARITIME VESSELS

Noise and vibration on maritime vessels are not the same but they have the same origin and come in many forms. The methods to handle the related problems are similar, to a certain level, where most shipboard noise problems are reduced by controlling vibration.

SOURCES

The main producers of mechanically created noise and vibration are the engines, but there are also other sources, like the air conditioning, shaft-line, cargo handling and control equipment and mooring machinery.

DIESEL ENGINES

When looking at diesel driven vessels, the engines induce large accelerations that travel from the foundation of the engine throughout the ship. In most compartments, this type of vibration normally manifests itself as audible noise. The problem with diesels is that, for a given size, there is a fixed amount of power generated per cylinder. To increase power it is necessary to add cylinders but, when cylinders are added, the crankshaft has to be lengthened and after a very limited number of additions, the lengthened crankshaft begins to flex and vibrate all on its own. This results in an increase of vibrations spread all over the ships structure. Crankshaft vibration can be reduced by a harmonic balancer.

TURBINES

Steam turbines and gas turbines, on the other hand, when new and/or in good repair, do not, by themselves generate excessive vibration as long as the turbine blades are in a perfect condition and rotate in a smooth gas flow. But after some time microscopic defects appear and cause small pits to appear in the surface of the intake and the blades which set up eddies in the gas flow, resulting in loss of performance and vibrations. Vibration levels may change with different loading conditions or when doing a manoeuvre.

OTHER SOURCES

Besides mechanical produced vibrations, other sources are caused by the motion of the sea, slamming of the vessel on the waves and water depth to mention just a few. The main problem here is that they are less controllable.

EXPOSURE LIMITS

Exposure to noise and vibrations is regulated and limits for maritime vessels are given in the ISO standard 6954: Guidelines for permissible mechanical vibrations on board seagoing vessels to protect personnel and crew.

Because there are different noise regulations from country to country, the International Maritime Organization (IMO) sets some standards for vessels. The table below gives some comparisons of preferred maximum noise levels on board of vessels and onshore levels.

Area	Noise limit land (dB)	IMO noise limit (dB)
workshop	70	85
kitchen	60	75
control rooms	55	75
offices	55	65
dining rooms	55	65
sleeping area	45	60

NOISE AND VIBRATION CONTROL

Noise generated on board ships and submarines can have far-reaching effects on the ability of the vessel to operate safely and efficiently. Military vessels in particular need to be quiet to avoid detection by sonar, so many methods have been used to limit a vessel's noise signature. Controlling noise is therefore a defense measure, most acutely for submarines.

PREVENTION

At the design table, the naval architect makes the necessary choices concerning the ship's structure to achieve an optimized design towards noise and vibration control. Decisions are made about the engine and shaft, what kind of instruments and material can be used to reduce noise and vibrations throughout the vessel and what is the best way to implement these. Advanced computer technology tries to simulate these vibrations under different ship conditions to provide an overview of weak spots. The generated vibrations are also compared with the natural frequencies of the different parts/sections and adaptions can be done to the structure.

CONTROL AT SOURCE

To control the vibrations at the origin, isolating fittings, elastic mounting of engines, elastic holding of pipes or dampers can be installed. These will absorb a part of the vibrations (and the noise) produced by the machines.

MAINTENANCE

Regular maintenance will have a major influence on the performance of instruments and machines. Lubrication of the joints, tightening of the bolts, good alignment of stern contour of the vessel, adjusting of variables following the weekly and monthly schedule are the most effective routes to noise and vibration control.

PADDED V-HULL

A padded v-hull is a type of high performance watercraft.

VERSIONS

They can come in many different configurations from that of a pure race boat to that of a recreational craft. A padded v-hull is very similar in basic shape to the popular v-hull which simply forms a vee when looking at the back of the watercraft. The difference in design with the padded v-hull is that where the point of the vee would be on the bottom of a plain v-hull there is a flat area ranging from six to ten inches wide. When looking at a padded v-hull from underneath, the front of the hull shows a vee which slowly starts to taper and blend back to the flat pad area.

This back portion of the hull is the pad and it will protrude from the vee surface one-half to one-full inch. The pad more efficiently provides hydrodynamic lift due to very low deadrise planing surface, compared to the vee hull lifting surfaces.

This highly efficient lift helps to unwet the less efficient vee sections hull which reduces drag tremendously. It uses hydrodynamic pressure to ride higher in the water. As the boats speed increases, water pressure builds on the flat surface of the pad causing the boat to ride higher in the water and ultimately the boat will be riding on just the pad area. At low speeds these hulls ride and handle just the same as a regular v-hull of the same size and weight. Once speeds increase the padded hull will out accelerate and have a higher top speed than a plain v-hull since the padded hull has less drag once speeds increase.

DRIVING

Driving a padded v-hull takes practice and patience. At speed the hull is riding on a small area roughly the size of a paper towel. It is a balancing act to keep the hull on the pad and it requires small steering inputs from the driver to keep the hull flying level. Padded v-hulls will want to chine-walk if no steering corrections are used. Chine-walk is when the boat rocks side to side on the rear portion of the hull. As speeds increase, chine walk becomes more of a factor and can become violent and dangerous if the driver does not know how to compensate for it.

PNEUMATIC STABILIZED PLATFORM

A Pneumatic stabilized platform (PSP) is a technology used to float a very large floating structure (VLFS). PSP utilizes indirect displacement, in which a platform rests on trapped air that displaces the water. The primary buoyancy force is provided by air pressure acting on the underside of the deck. The PSP is a distinct type of pneumatic platform, one in which the platform is composed of a number of cylindrical shaped components packed together in a rectangular pattern to form a module.

DEVELOPMENT

The Pneumatically Stabilized Platform was originally proposed for constructing a new floating airport for San Diego in the Pacific Ocean, at least three miles off the tip of Point Loma. However, this proposed design was rejected in October, 2003 due to high cost, the difficulty in accessing such an airport, the difficulty in transporting jet fuel, electricity, water, and gas to the structure, failure to address security concerns such as a bomb blast, inadequate room for high-speed exits and taxiways, and environmental concerns. [1]

PONTOON EFFECT

The pontoon effect refers to the tendency of a vessel whose flotation depends on lateral pontoons to capsize without warning when a lateral force is applied. The effect can be sudden and dramatic because the vessel is stable and self-righting as greater lateral force is applied, up to the point that the pontoon(s) on one side of the vessel are completely submerged. At this point, stability suddenly disappears and the vessel rapidly capsizes.

(The same term can also arise when describing a design in which the attributes of a pontoon are created without using explicit pontoons—when a design effectively incorporates pontoons. This page describes the specific phenomenon described above.)

The pontoon effect is theoretically possible whenever the vessel's entire weight exceeds the buoyancy of the pontoon(s) on either side. However, the pontoon effect is much more likely in vessels with a high center of gravity and low or non-existent displacement other than the pontoons.

A pontoon vessel such as a catamaran floats in a level position when the center of gravity of the entire vessel (including its load) is above the center of buoyancy. This is the opposite of the case in a traditional or displacement hull vessel, which derives positive stability from having its center of buoyancy above the center of gravity. If the pontoon vessel tips, it will remain stable as long as the center of gravity does not move further to the side than the center of buoyancy is moved by the change in the depth (and displacement) of each pontoon. Under these conditions a "righting force" (a turning moment) acts on the vessel to push it back toward the level position.

However if the center of gravity is high relative to the width of the vessel, and the pontoons on one side are unable to bear the vessel's complete weight, the lateral movement of the center of buoyancy will be restricted. Even a relatively small lateral force can move the center of gravity further to the side than the center of buoyancy can go. At this point, the righting force will disappear, replaced by a turning moment in the opposite direction. This can capsize the vessel at the point at which one pontoon is completely submerged.

When using twin lateral pontoons, each pontoon should have enough buoyancy to bear the load of the entire vessel on its own. If the vessel is so heavy that either pontoon is mostly submerged when no lateral force is applied, it will be vulnerable to the pontoon effect. If sufficient lateral force arises (such as wind or shifting load), the vessel can tip enough to submerge one pontoon.

At this point, the sunken pontoon will provide no further buoyancy to right the vessel. As the center of buoyancy cannot move further to that side to match the center of gravity, that pontoon will continue sinking. The tipping angle will increase until the vessel capsizes. This can continue until the vessel inverts completely with the pontoons again floating on the surface but the rest of the vessel underwater. At this point, the upside-down vessel will be highly stable. If, on the other hand, the vessel is designed and loaded so that each pontoon can support the vessel's entire weight (plus any lateral forces that arise like wind), the center of gravity cannot move transversely beyond the center of buoyancy at the most extreme tipping angle, and the pontoon effect cannot occur.

Note, however, that this is not the sole effect to be taken into consideration when assessing the likelihood of capsize. The change in hull windage as the vessel heels is also important. In the case of a trimaran designed for cruising, with solid wing decks (as opposed to racing-type designs with mesh or open wings), those with wide-beam floats able to support the whole weight of the vessel are more likely to capsize than those with narrow-beam floats of lesser buoyancy that can be submerged as the vessel heels. As the wide-beam float comes to take the entire weight of the heeling vessel, the centre hull lifts out of the water; this exposes the entire area of the underside of both wings to the wind, and also increases the turning moment of the wind force on the weather wing.

There is now a considerable overturning force due to the wind and the vessel is very likely to capsize. In contrast, a trimaran with narrow-beam floats will simply submerge the lee float, exposing only the weather wing and that with a lesser moment. In practical sea situations the windage effect is greater than the buoyancy effect and so cruising trimarans with highly buoyant floats are more, not less, likely to capsize than those with less buoyant floats.

A trimaran is best stabilised not by adding buoyancy on the lee float but adding weight to the weather float. This is the basis of the "cool-tubes" stability system invented by Tristan Jones and L. Surtees. A large-diameter pipe closed at the aft end is attached to the keel of each float and fills with water. While it remains submerged buoyancy forces cancel the weight of the trapped water and the weight of the tube is effectively zero. But if the boat heels enough to bring the weather float out of the water, this effect no longer operates and the water provides a heavy ballast weight on the float, creating a righting moment. In the abstract sense, the principles at work govern the stability of all boats and ships including those without lateral pontoons.

RESPONSE AMPLITUDE OPERATOR

In the field of ship design and design of other floating structures, a response amplitude operator (RAO) is an engineering statistic, or set of such statistics, that are used to determine the likely behavior of a ship when operating at sea. Known by the acronym of RAO, response amplitude operators are usually obtained from models of proposed ship designs tested in a model basin, or from running specialized CFD computer programs, often both. RAOs are usually calculated for all ship motions and for all wave headings.

USAGE

RAOs are effectively transfer functions used to determine the effect that a sea state will have upon the motion of a ship through the water, and therefore, for example, whether or not (in the case of cargo vessels) the addition of cargo to the vessel will require measures to be taken to improve stability and prevent the cargo from shifting within the vessel. Generation of extensive RAOs at the design phase allows shipbuilders to determine the modifications to a design that may be required for safety reasons (i.e., to make the design robust and resistant to capsizing or sinking in highly adverse sea conditions) or to improve performance (e.g., improve top speed, fuel consumption, stability in rough seas).

RAOs are computed in tandem with the generation of a hydrodynamic database, which is a model of the effects of water pressure upon the ship's hull under a wide variety of flow conditions. Together, the RAOs and hydrodynamic database provide (inasmuch as this is possible within modelling and engineering constraints) certain assurances about the behavior of a proposed ship design. They also allow the designer to dimension the ship or structure so it will hold up to the most extreme sea states it will likely be subjected to (based on sea state statistics).

RAOS IN SHIP DESIGN

Different modelling and design criteria will affect the nature of the 'ideal' RAO curves (as plotted graphically) being sought for a particular ship: for example, an ocean cruise liner will have a considerable emphasis placed upon minimizing accelerations to ensure the comfort of the passengers, while the stability concerns for a naval warship will be concentrated upon making the ship an effective weapons platform.

1. Finding the forces on the ship when it is restrained from motion and subjected to regular waves. The forces acting on the body are:

- The Froude–Krylov force, which is the pressure in the undisturbed waves integrated over the wetted surface of the ship.
- The Diffraction forces, which are pressures that occur due to the disturbances in the water because of the ship being present.

2. Finding the forces on the ship when it is forced to oscillate in still water conditions. The forces are divided into:
   - Added mass forces due to having to accelerate the water along with the ship.
   - Damping forces due to the oscillations creating outgoing waves which carry energy away from the ship.
   - Restoring forces due to bringing the buoyancy/weight equilibrium out of balance.

In the above "Ship" must be interpreted widely to also include other forms of floating structures. The obvious problem in the above method is the neglection of viscous forces which contribute heavily in modes of motion like surge and roll.

On a computer the above algorithm was first introduced by using strip theory. Today strip theory is still used if the need for fast calculations outweigh the need for precise results and the ship designer knows the limitations of strip theory. More advanced programs that are used today (such as WAMIT, SESAM WADAM, MOSES and ANSYS AQWA) may not use the exact algorithm outlined above and some may also include the effects of viscosity. The insight into the forces that governs the seakeeping behavior of a ship gained from the above are of course still valid.

ARMOURED FLIGHT DECK

An armoured flight deck is an aircraft carrier flight deck that incorporates substantial armour in its design.

Comparison is often made between some of designs of the Royal Navy (RN) and the United States Navy (USN). The two navies followed differing philosophies in the use of armour on carrier flight decks starting with the design of the RN's Illustrious class and ending with the design of the Midway class, when the USN also adopted armoured flight decks. The two classes most easily compared are the RN's Illustrious class and Implacable class and their nearest USN contemporaries, the Yorktown and Essex classes. The Illustrious class followed the Yorktown but preceded the Essex, while the Implacable class design predated the Essex but these ships were completed after the lead ships of the Essex class.

The development of armoured flight deck carriers proceeded during World War Two and before the end of World War Two, both the USN, with USS Midway, and the Imperial Japanese Navy (IJN), with Taiho and Shinano, would also commission armoured flight deck carriers, while all USN fleet aircraft carriers built since 1945 feature armoured flight decks. The remainder of the IJN carrier force during World War II had unarmoured flight decks just like the Yorktown and Essex classes of the USN.

DESIGN

In choosing the best design for their carriers, the British had to consider the advantages and disadvantages of hangar design. There was a choice between open or closed hangar and the position of the armour. The placing of the strongest deck affected the strength of the hull. The further apart the deck and the keel, the stronger the design. If the flight deck was placed above the main deck then it had to be built to allow for movement with expansion sections. A closed hangar design was the strongest structurally and made for a lighter hull and the RN carried this concept one step further and designed the armoured flight deck to also act as the strength deck without any underlying plating, thus achieving an armoured flight deck on the lowest possible displacement.

The carriers that were built with armoured decks fall into two distinct types – those with armour at the flight deck level protecting the hangar and those that only had armour between the hangar deck and the lower levels of the ship. The different thickness of armour, and how they were distributed, are described in the table below.

Armour thickness of some World War II era aircraft carriers			
Class (standard displacement)	**Flight deck**	**Main deck**	**Side belt**
Yorktown class (19,875 tons)	n/a	1.5 in (38 mm)	2.5 – 4 in (64 – 101 mm)
Ark Royal class (22,000 tons)	.75 in (19 mm)	3.5 in (89 mm)	4.5 in (114 mm)
Illustrious class (23,000 tons)	3 in (76 mm)	2 in (51 mm)	4.5 in (114 mm)
Shōkaku class (25,600 tons)	n/a	3.9 in (99 mm) over machinery	1.8 in (46 mm)
Essex class (27,200 tons)	n/a	2.5 in (64 mm)	4.75 in (121 mm)
Taiho (29,770 tons)	3.1 in (80 mm)	1.3 in (32 mm)	2.2 in (56 mm) abreast machinery
Implacable class (23,500 tons)	3 in (76 mm)	2.5 in (64 mm)	4.5 in (114 mm)
Shinano (62,000 tons)	3.1 in (80 mm)	3.9 in (99 mm)	5 in (127 mm)
Midway (45,000 tons)	3.5 in (89 mm)	2 in (51 mm)	7.9 in (200 mm)

THEORY

Armour at the flight deck level would protect the hangar deck and the aircraft stored there from most bombs. The armour of the Illustrious class was intended to protect against 1,000 pound bombs. In the Illustrious class, the armoured flight deck extended for about two-thirds of the length of the ship, bounded by the two aircraft lifts (which were without the armour). The deck was closed by 4.5-inch (110 mm) armoured sides and bulkheads, forming an armoured box. The bulkheads had sliding armoured portals to allow access between the hangar and the aircraft lift. There were 3-inch (76 mm) lateral strakes of main deck armour that extended from the base of the hangar side-wall to the top of the main side belt. The latter protected the machinery, magazines and aircraft fuel and weaponry stores. The RN's closed and armoured hangars were capable of being environmentally sealed for protection against chemical weapon attack. The armoured design meant that it would have to be attacked with Armour Piercing (AP) bombs, which have much less blast effect than higher-capacity General Purpose (GP) bombs carrying about twice the explosive amount. GP bombs also caused severe hull damage if they exploded in the water close to the hull; AP bombs, much less so. The USN open hangar design allowed large numbers of aircraft to be warmed up while inside, theoretically reducing the time required to range and launch a strike, but stowage of fuelled and armed aircraft in an unarmoured hangar was extremely dangerous:

...Captain John S. McCain of the Ranger...actually preferred a relatively small carrier, as long as it could be protected against bombing. Again and again he told the General Board that any U.S. carrier, if her flight and hangar decks were crowded with fuelled and bombed aircraft, was a potential inferno, and that friendly fighters could not guarantee the security of any flight deck...

During the war, the British fitted immersion heaters to the oil tanks of its aircraft so minimal warm-up was required when they reach the flight deck.

US and earlier Japanese carriers had their armour placed at the hangar deck, essentially treating the hangar spaces and flight deck as superstructure – making these areas very vulnerable to the blast from GP bombs and other explosions, which in turn caused massive casualties in comparison to RN designs.

A bomb that struck the flight deck would likely penetrate and explode in the hangar deck, but the armour there could still protect the ship's vitals – including the engine spaces and fuel storage. The flight deck could also possibly fuze light bombs prematurely, which would reduce the chance of them going through the hangar deck. Such a design allowed for larger, open-sided hangar bays (improving ventilation but making the ship very vulnerable to chemical weapon attack) and the installation of deck-edge elevators. USN carriers with hangar deck armour only, usually had wooden decking over thin mild steel flight decks which were easy to repair. The USN moved the structural strength deck to the flight deck, starting with the Forrestal class which had "...an enclosed..." hangar.

Aviation fuel delivery and stowage systems were extremely vulnerable. The Royal Navy stowed aviation fuel in cylindrical tanks, that in turn were surrounded by seawater. RN aviation fuel lines were purged with carbon dioxide when not in use. The USN used a similar system, which was further improved after the two navies began exchanging information in 1940. Pre-war USN and IJN carrier designs used a fuel stowage system which was not as secure as that used by the RN, but allowed for much greater stowage capacity. Several USN and IJN carriers were lost due to aviation gas fume explosions.

DOCTRINE AND DESIGN

The Royal Navy had to be ready to fight a war in the confines of the North Sea and Mediterranean Sea, under the umbrella of land-based enemy air forces. The Royal Navy, with its extensive network of bases and colonies in the Pacific ocean, had also to be ready to fight in the vast expanses of the Pacific, as did the USN and the IJN, but the USN and IJN did not have to worry about operating in the Mediterranean. The differences in construction were determined by doctrine that was largely driven by the different approaches to the same tactical problem: How to destroy the enemy's aircraft carriers while surviving the inevitable counter strike. Prior to WWII the RN and USN both recognised that the dive bomber could disable the flight decks of enemy aircraft carriers:

...From about 1933 on, the Admiralty showed increasing interest in dive-bombing, as the best means of accurate delivery against small and highly manoeuvrable ships. Dive-bombing was also particularly attractive as a means of neutralizing enemy aircraft carriers, which some in the Fleet Air Arm considered their primary targets. British observers seem to have been impressed by US demonstrations...

The RN was thus faced with designing a carrier that would be survivable under the conditions to be expected in the Atlantic, Mediterranean, and Pacific Oceans, and before the development of effective naval Radar; these conflicting demands resulted in the development of aircraft carriers whose decks were armoured against 500 lb Armour Piercing bombs and 1000 lb General Purpose bombs.

The RN considered that an unarmoured carrier would be unlikely to be able fly off more than one deck load of strike aircraft prior to being attacked so the armoured flight deck carriers accepted a reduction in hangar capacity to the equivalent to one deck load of aircraft. USN, IJN some RN Fleet carriers such as Ark Royal had sufficient aircraft capacity to allow for two ranges, each equal to a full deck load of strike aircraft.

The RN and IJN limited their aircraft carrier's aircraft capacity to the capacity of their hangars, and struck down all aircraft between operations. The USN, typically, used a permanent deck park to augment the capacity of their aircraft carrier's hangars. The use of a permanent deck park appeared to give USN carriers a much larger aircraft capacity than contemporary RN armoured flight deck carriers. The flight deck armour also reduced the length of the flight deck, reducing the maximum aircraft capacity of the armoured flight deck carrier, however the largest part of the disparity between RN and USN carriers in aircraft capacity was due to the use of a permanent deck park on USN carriers.

The Royal Navy also had the disadvantage that they entered into WWII with the Royal Navy being pitted against large, land based, air-forces whose aircraft also had superior performance to all existing naval aircraft, while the RAF's increased demand for high performance land based aircraft, after the Fall of France, actually retarded the production and development of Fleet Air Arm aircraft.

On the other hand, the RN rapidly introduced new technologies, such as radar which enhanced the defensive capability of aircraft carriers. The RN thus had to develop new operational doctrines during the war. The USN, in contrast, was able to benefit from technology transfers from the UK and the wartime experiences of the RN, which was freely shared with the USN, prior to its entry into the war, allowing it to anticipate the changes needed to prepare its carriers for the coming conflict with Japan. The USN designed the armoured flight decks of the Midway class carriers based upon an analysis of the effectiveness of RN armoured flight decks. The IJN also benefited from being able to observe the effectiveness of RN aircraft carriers in action, while both the USN and IJN were able to introduce new aircraft types, prior to their entry into WWII.

AIRCRAFT RESTRICTIONS

All RN fleet carriers had 16 ft (4.9 m) hangar heights, except the two Implacable class ships, which had 14 ft (4.3 m) heights, and Indomitable which had a 16 ft (4.9 m) lower hangar and a 14 ft (4.3 m) upper hangar. The Illustrious class had a single 16 ft (4.9 m) high hangar that was 468 ft (143 m) long. Within the confines of ship design, and the Second London Naval Treaty to which they complied, the Indomitable and Implacable-type carriers had to accept a reduction in hangar heights (to keep the metacentric height within acceptable limits) and size, and as a result, had some restriction on aircraft types supplied via Lend-Lease. IJN carriers typically had 16 feet (4.9 m) high hangars, including Taiho and Shinano. The USN Lexington class had 20 ft (6.1 m) hangar heights while the Yorktown, Wasp, Essex, and Midway classes had 17 ft 6 in (5.33 m) hangar heights.

DEFENCES

The British approach of armoured flight decks was an effective form of passive defence from bombs and kamikaze attacks that actually struck their carriers, but the American carriers primarily relied on fighters to prevent the carriers from being hit in the first place. RN carriers such as Ark Royal or Illustrious had far heavier AA outfits than their USN counterparts, up to the introduction of the USN Essex class carriers. Ark Royal, in 1940, carried 16 x 4.5-inch guns, 32 x 40mm "Pom-pom" and 32 x 0.5 inch against 8 x 5", 16 x 28mm and 24 x.5" for Enterprise, in 1940. "In wartime, however, the US Navy found the armoured carriers fascinating. After having examined HMS

Formidable in 1940, the US naval attaché commented that, were he crossing the Pacific, he would prefer her to a Yorktown, the closest US equivalent, on the basis that she might carry fewer aircraft, but she would be much more likely to get there".

Late in the war when the USN operated many carriers together and had improved radar, their fighter and AA defence was reasonably effective, yet both conventional and kamikaze attacks were still able to penetrate USN defences. Bunker Hill and Franklin nearly succumbed in 1945. The larger air groups (80–110 planes, vs. 52–81 for late war British ships) allowed for a more effective combat air patrol (CAP) without reducing strike capability, improving the protection of the whole battle group and lessening the workload of the carrier escorts.

Carrier fighters were able to shoot down far more kamikaze aircraft than any amount of deck armour would have protected against showing the value of absolute numbers, but in the early war period IJN aircraft had little difficulty in penetrating USN CAPs; near the end of the war, veteran American fighter pilots in superior F6F Hellcat and F4U Corsair fighters were able to defeat the young, inexperienced and ill-trained kamikaze pilots with ease and run up huge kill scores but attackers were still able to get through. (In addition to larger aircraft complements, the US Navy had larger fleets and more resources, so they could establish destroyer pickets and develop dedicated AAW ships such as the Atlanta-class antiaircraft cruisers which would have also drawn attention away from the carriers.) On the surface, the record seems balanced.

British naval historian D.K. Brown put the practical difference between American and British design philosophies in no uncertain terms: "More fighters would have been better protection than armour." but that British designs were good for the circumstances in which they were meant to be used. Yet, even the Ark Royal, Britain's newest carrier prior to WW2, never operated close to her theoretical aircraft capacity. Prior to the development of effective Radar and high speed monoplane fighters, a successful fighter defence was extremely unlikely for any navy thus calling into doubt D.K. Brown's conclusions.

The benefits of flight deck armour were intended to counter these issues. Fewer aircraft meant a lower priority to attack than the more heavily armed American carriers and the RN's operational doctrine dictated smaller airgroups, and the armoured hangar carriers had smaller Avgas and ammunition supplies to match. However, RN carriers carried far more aircraft later in the war, making use of the deck park when they adopted USN style operational doctrine.

The 2nd generation RN armoured carriers, Indomitable and the Implacable class which had an additional half length lower hangar, were considerably less outmatched by their USN counterparts in the numbers of aircraft operated. The RN operating in harsher weather protected their aircraft from the elements and did not use a permanent deck park in the earlier part of the war. US carriers and their fighters shot down more than 1,900 suicide aircraft during Operation Kikusui (the last and largest Kamikaze attack in the Okinawa campaign), versus a mere 75 for the British, yet both forces suffered the same number of serious hits (four), on their carriers. However the kamikazes made 173 strikes against other USN targets and the 4 USN carriers suffered a massive death toll, in contrast to the relatively light casualties on the RN carriers.

The kamikaze threat overall was serious, but allied defences neutralised it, and many kamikaze strikes missed the deck armour entirely, or bounced off the decks of both British or American carriers. In some cases, kamikazes either struck glancing blows that did only superficial damage that was fixed within minutes or hours, or missed entirely, due to the poor training and poorer flight experience of their pilots. The majority of kamikazes that did inflict harm caused no more damage than they would have against smaller ships.

After a successful kamikaze hit, the British were able to clear the flight deck and resume flight operations in just hours, while their American counterparts often could do the same, but not always; in some cases repairs took a few days or even months. The USN liaison officer on HMS Indefatigable commented: "When a kamikaze hits a U.S. carrier it means 6 months of repair at Pearl [Harbor]. When a kamikaze hits a Limey carrier it's just a case of "Sweepers, man your brooms.""

American carriers of the Essex class suffered very high casualties from serious kamikaze hits, though they did survive. USS Franklin was struck by two 250 kg(550 lbs) bombs, one semi-armour piercing (SAP) and one general purpose (GP), both of which penetrated into her hangar and set off ammunition, killing 724 personnel. USS Bunker Hill was severely damaged by pair of kamikaze hits which killed 346 men. Each of these USN carriers suffered more casualties than all the British RN armoured carriers combined, illustrating the life saving features of RN carrier design. Illustrious, which had the highest toll, suffered 126 fatal casualties and 84 wounded when hit by six 1100 lb bombs on 10 January 1941. The USN studied the superior defensive qualities of Royal Navy armoured carriers and this analysis is partly revealed in the damage report following the attack on Franklin on 13 March 1945:

As a result of study of damage sustained by various British carriers prior to our entry into the war, two important departures from traditional U.S. Navy carrier design were incorporated in the CVB Class, then still under development. HMS ILLUSTRIOUS in an action off Malta on 1 January 1941 was hit by several bombs, three of which detonated in the hangar space. Large fires swept fore and aft among parked planes thereby demonstrating the desirability of attempting to confine the limits of such explosions and fires by structural sectionalization of the hangar space. On the CVB Class the hangar was therefore divided into five compartments separated by 40 and 50-pound STS division bulkheads extending from the hangar deck to the flight deck, each fitted with a large door suitable for handling aircraft.

It is hoped that this sectionalization, in conjunction with sprinkler and fog foam systems, will effectively prevent fires from spreading throughout the hangar spaces, as occurred on FRANKLIN on 30 October and 19 March. The damage experiences of several British carriers, which unlike our own were fitted with armoured flight decks, demonstrated the effectiveness of such armour in shielding hangar spaces from GP bombs and vital spaces below the hangar deck from SAP bombs. Accordingly, the CVB Class was designed with an armoured flight deck consisting of 3-1/2-inch STS from frames 46 to 175 with a hangar deck consisting of two courses of 40-pound STS between frames 36 and 192. Although none of the CVB Class carriers were completed in time to take part in war operations, the effectiveness of armoured flight decks against Kamikaze attacks was demonstrated by various carriers attached to the British Pacific Fleet.

Reference (k) reports two such interesting cases. The VICTORIOUS was struck by three Kamikaze aircraft, two of which ricocheted off the armoured flight deck and over the side, causing no important damage. The third carried a bomb which detonated at frame 30 starboard at the butt of the 3-inch flight deck armour with 1-1/2-inch "D" quality (equivalent to HTS) steel. It does not appear that the Kamikaze actually struck the ship.

The bomb detonation, however, depressed the 3-inch deck slightly but did not tear it open. On the other hand, the 1-1/2-inch "D" quality deck plating was ripped open over a total area of about 25 square feet. Two days were required for temporary repairs, at the conclusion of which the ship was fully operational. HMS FORMIDABLE was hit by two bombs, the first of which struck and detonated on the flight deck 9 feet to port of the center-line at frame 79, directly over a deep bent and at a juncture of three armoured plates. The armoured deck was depressed over an area 24 feet long and 20 feet wide. Maximum depression was 15 inches.

Adjacent bents spaced 12 feet forward and aft of the point of impact were slightly depressed. A hole 2 square feet in area was blown in the 3-inch deck. Three fragments penetrated downward through the ship into the center boiler room. The damage in this boiler room, which was not described, temporarily reduced speed to 18 knots. The second bomb struck and detonated on the centreline of the flight deck at frame 94. The 3-inch deck and deep bent directly below the point of impact were depressed about 4-1/2 inches and one rivet was knocked out. However, the ship was fully operational within about 5 hours, including flight operations. The only Allied carrier lost to a deck hit was the American Independence-class light carrier, USS Princeton (CVL-23).

Indeed, many light and escort carriers were unarmoured, with no protection on the hangar or flight deck, and thus they fared poorly against deck hits.

POST WAR ANALYSIS

What was not discovered until late in the war was that the kamikaze impacts proved to have a long term effect on the structural integrity of British carriers and their post war life was shortened, as the RN lacked the financial resources to repair the damage, in contrast to the vast resources of the USN which was even able to rebuild carriers such as Franklin that had been completely gutted and the crew decimated by IJN attacks. HMS Formidable (R67) was an excellent example of this; while she weathered a severe kamikaze hit in 1945 which cratered her deck armour, the hit caused severe internal structural damage and permanently warped the hull (damage worsened in a postwar aircraft-handling accident wherein a Vought Corsair rolled off a lift and raked the hangar deck with 20mm cannon fire, causing a severe fire); but plans to rebuild her as per Victorious were abandoned due to budget cuts, not structural damage, and she lingered in reserve until 1956 before being towed off to the breakers. The Royal Navy planned to rebuild most of the armoured carriers in the early post war period:

There seems to have been general agreement that the first ship to be modernized should be an Illustrious. Formidable was laid up and required a long refit in any case, so she was provisionally selected for modernization. Illustrious was a deck landing training and trials carrier, and could not be spared, particularly as she was needed to test the new generation of naval aircraft.

This left HMS Victorious as the only other candidate. In early 1951 the other two ships of the programme were HMS Implacable, followed by HMS Indefatigable, for modernisation, respectively, 1953–55 (to relieve HMS Eagle so that she could refit in 1956 with steam catapults) and 1954–57. HMS Indomitable was scheduled for a more limited modernisation (1957) as the future deck landing training ship. At this time Eagle was scheduled for completion in August 1951 and Ark Royal in 1954, so that the full programme would provide the Royal Navy with five fleet carriers plus a semi-modernised deck landing training ship.

Illustrious suffered a similar battering, especially off of Malta in 1941 when hit by German dive bombers and late in the war was limited to 22 knots (41 km/h) because her centreline shaft was disabled due to accumulated wartime damage; she spent five years as a training and trials carrier (1948–53) and was disposed of in 1954. Indomitable was completely refit to like-new condition, only to suffer a severe gasoline explosion on board, which caused "considerable structural and electrical damage to the ship". Indomitable was refitted between 1948 and 1950 and served as flagship of the Home Fleet then served a tour of duty in the Mediterranean, where she was damaged by the petrol explosion. She was partially repaired before proceeding under her own power to Queen Elizabeth II's 1953 Coronation Review, before being placed in reserve in 1954.

Indomitable was scrapped in 1956. The explosion which occurred on Indomitable's hangar deck, while severe, would also have caused severe casualties and extensive damage to an Essex-class carrier, several of which returned to service after hangar explosions, primarily due to the USN's considerable financial and material resources. The postwar Royal Navy could only afford to rebuild Victorious and had to abandon plans to rebuild four other armoured carriers due to cost, and to provide crews to man the postwar built carriers, such as Ark Royal, due to reductions in manpower.

Another factor is the advantage in resources that the US Navy had over the Royal Navy. The numerous and capacious American yards on the East and West Coasts allowed the US Navy to build and repair carriers at a more leisurely pace and higher quality individually, while producing ships collectively at a furious rate.

The British with their strained facilities were forced to rush repairs (indeed the overloaded British shipyards had forced some vessels to be sent to the US for repairs) and some ships such as Illustrious, were forced into service even though not fully repaired. The RN was in a state of continual contraction after WWII, and simply did not have the resources or inclination to repair ships that it could no longer man.

MIDWAY AND FORRESTAL CLASSES

While flight deck level armour was eventually adopted by the Americans for the Midway design, the strength deck remained on the hangar level. Midway had originally been planned to have a very heavy gun armament (8 in weapons).

The removal of these weapons freed up enough tonnage to add 3 inches (76 mm) of armour at the flight deck level. While this made a great deal of sense from an air group perspective, the Midway ships sat very low in the water for carriers (due to their much greater displacement), certainly much lower than the smaller Essex-class carriers, and had a great deal of difficulty operating in heavy seas. Flight deck armoured ships almost universally (except for the Midway class as completed) possessed a hurricane bow, where the bows were sealed up to the flight deck; wartime experience demonstrated that ships with the hurricane bow configuration (also including the American Lexington class) shipped less water than ships with an open bow.

Late-life refits to Midway to bulge her hull and improve freeboard instead gave her a dangerously sharp roll, and made flight operations difficult even in moderate seas. This was therefore not repeated on Coral Sea (Roosevelt had been decommissioned years earlier). After the war, most of the Essex class ships were modified with a hurricane bow and in the case of Oriskany the wooden flight deck surface was replaced with aluminium for improved resistance against the blast of jet engines, making them appear to have armoured flight decks, but in fact their armour remained at hangar level.

The supercarriers of the postwar era, starting with the Forrestal class — nearly 200 feet (61 m) longer and 40 feet (12 m) wider in the beam than their World War II counterparts – would eventually be forced to move the strength deck up to the flight deck level as a result of their great size; a shallow hull of those dimensions became too impractical to continue. The issue of protection had no influence on the change; the Forrestal class had an armoured flight deck of at least 1.5" thickness.

Some of the follow on classes to the Forrestals also had armoured flight decks although deck armour is of little to no use against modern anti-ship missiles, it may help limit the damage from flight deck explosions. The experience of World War Two caused the USN to change their design policy in favour of armoured flight decks:

The main armor carried on Enterprise is the heavy armored flight deck. This was to prove a significant factor in the catastrophic fire and explosions that occurred on Enterprise's flight deck in 1969. The US Navy learned its lesson the hard way during World War II when all its carriers had only armored hangar decks. All attack carriers built since the Midway class have had armored flight decks.

FLARE (SHIP)

Flare is the angle at which a ship's hull plate or planking departs from the vertical in an outward direction with increasing height. A flared hull typically has a deck area larger than its cross-sectional area at the waterline. Most vessels have some degree of flare above the waterline. Advantages of hull flare can include improvements in stability, splash and wash suppression, and dockside utility.

Tumblehome is the inverse of flare, where the hull becomes narrower with increasing height.

FLOAT-OUT

Float-out is the process in modern shipbuilding that follows the keel laying and precedes the fitting-out process. It is analogous to launching a ship, a specific process that has largely been discontinued in modern shipbuilding.

Both floating-out and launching are the times when the ship leaves dry land and becomes waterborne for the first time, and often take place during ceremonies celebrating and commemorating that event.

LAUNCHING

Prior to the large-scale use of drydocks (building or graving docks) for constructing ships, most vessels were constructed on a slipway, i.e. an inclined building platform sloping toward a body of water into which the ship would be launched.

CONTEMPORARY SHIPBUILDING

The launching of ships has been largely replaced by the "floating" process. After a ship is ordered for construction, its keel is laid in a drydock. Construction of the ship continues in the dock, usually in the form of prefabricated units that are assembled.

After the hull has been substantially completed, sluice gates are opened and the drydock fills with water. The dock gates are then opened and the ship is pulled out by tugboats to a berth where the remaining construction continues. This usually includes further construction of the superstructure, attaching of masts and funnels, and the installation of equipment and furnishings.

The completed ship will usually return to drydock for installation of other equipment, propulsion parts, and the painting of its hull.

The first superliner to be constructed in this manner was the SS United States. But the history of 'floating" ships rather than "launching" goes back more than one hundred years before that vessel's construction. The SS Great Britain designed by Isambard Kingdom Brunel was constructed in drydock and floated on July 19, 1843. She is currently in Bristol, England, United Kingdom.

NAMING CEREMONY

Ships which are launched typically are christened and formally named at their launching ceremonies, even though they are not completed until later. Some recent passenger vessels which were constructed in drydocks were not formally christened when floated out. The naming ceremonies of RMS Queen Mary 2 and MS Freedom of the Seas took place after completion and delivery to their owners, in the case of Freedom of the Seas after her first transatlantic crossing.

FLUSH DECK

In naval architecture, a flush deck refers to when the upper deck of a vessel extends unbroken from stem to stern. There is no raised forecastle or lowered quarterdeck. Ships of this type may be referred to as "flush deckers", although this is often taken as referring to a series of United States Navy destroyers originating from World War I and typified by the Wickes class. For aircraft carriers it means that no "island" superstructure was fitted.

FREE SURFACE EFFECT

The free surface effect is one of several mechanisms which can cause a craft to become unstable and roll over (capsize). It refers to the tendency of liquids — and of aggregates of small solid objects, like seeds, gravel, or crushed ore which can act as liquids — to slosh about: to move in response to changes in the attitude of a craft's cargo holds, decks, or liquid tanks in reaction to operator-induced motions (or sea states caused by waves & wind acting upon the craft). When referring to the free surface effect, the condition of a tank that is not full is described as a "slack tank", while a full tank is "pressed up".

STABILITY AND EQUILIBRIUM

In a normally laden vessel any rolling from perpendicular is countered by a righting moment generated from the increased volume of water displaced by the hull on the lowered side. This assumes the center of gravity of the vessel is relatively constant. If a moving mass inside the vessel moves in the direction of the roll, this counters the righting effect by moving the center of gravity towards the lowered side. The free surface effect can become a problem in a craft with large partially full bulk cargo compartments, fuel or water tanks, (especially if they are spanning the full breadth of the ship), or from accidental flooding, such as has occurred in several accidents involving RORO type ferries.

If a compartment or tank is either empty or full, there is no change in the craft's center of mass as it rolls from side to side (in strong winds, heavy seas, or on sharp motions or turns). However, if the compartment is only partially full, the liquid in the compartment will respond to the vessel's heave, pitch, roll, surge, sway or yaw. For example, as a vessel rolls to port, liquid will displace to the port side of a compartment, and this will move the vessel's center of mass to port. This has the effect of slowing the vessel's return to vertical.

The momentum of large volumes of moving liquids cause significant dynamic forces, which act against the righting effect. When the vessel returns to vertical the roll continues and the effect is repeated on the opposite side. In heavy sea states, this can become a positive feedback loop, causing each roll to become more and more extreme, eventually overcoming the righting effect leading to a capsize. While repeated oscillations of increasing magnitude are commonly associated with the free surface effect, they are not a necessary condition. For example, in the cases of both the SS Normandie and MS al-Salam Boccaccio 98, gradual buildup of water from fire-fighting caused capsizing in a single continuous roll.

MITIGATION

To mitigate this hazard, cargo vessels use multiple smaller bulk compartments or liquid tanks, instead of fewer larger ones, and possibly baffles within bulk compartments or liquid tanks to minimize the free surface effects on the craft as a whole. Keeping individual bulk compartments or liquid tanks either relatively empty or full is another way to minimize the effect and its attendant problems. Tanks or compartments that do not straddle the vessel's centerline are somewhat less prone to destabilising oscillations. Similarly, narrow compartments (aligned bow to stern) and compartments at the extremes away from the centerline, are less prone to cause instability.

HISTORICAL EXAMPLES

Flooding, liquid cargo leakage, or unintended water (from precipitation, waves, or hull damage) in any compartments or on any decks of watercraft, and the resulting free surface effect are often a contributing cause of accidents, capsizes, and casualties e.g. the loss of TEV Wahine (Wellington, New Zealand, April 1968), the MS Herald of Free Enterprise (Zeebrugge, Belgium, March 1987), and the MS Estonia (Baltic Sea, September 1994).

In the case of the RORO ferry al-Salam Boccaccio 98 (Red Sea, February 2006), improper fire-fighting procedures caused flooding leading directly to instability and capsize.

In both the cases of the al-Salam Boccaccio 98 and MS Costa Concordia, severe listing followed immediately after the ship had undergone a hard turn, causing unstable volumes of water (from collision damage in the latter) to surge from one side of the ship to the other.

EFFECTS ON LAND AND AIRCRAFT

The free surface effect can affect any kind of craft, including watercraft (where it is most common), bulk cargo or liquid tanker semi-trailers and trucks (causing either jackknifing or roll-overs), and aircraft (especially fire-fighting water-droppers and refueling tankers where baffles mitigate but do not eliminate the effects).

The term "free surface effect" implies a liquid under the influence of gravity. Slosh dynamics is the overarching field which covers both free surface effects and situations such as space vehicles, where gravity is inconsequential but inertia and momentum interact with complex fluid mechanics to cause vehicle instability.

SHIP RESISTANCE AND PROPULSION

A ship must be designed to move efficiently through the water with a minimum of external force. For thousands of years ship designers and builders of sailing vessels used rules of thumb based on the midship-section area to size the sails for a given vessel. The hull form and sail plan for the clipper ships, for, example evolved from experience, not from theory. It was not until the advent of steam power and the construction of large iron ships in the mid-19th century that it became clear to ship owners and builders that a more rigorous approach was needed.

DEFINITION

Ship resistance is defined as the force required to tow the ship in calm water at a constant velocity.

COMPONENTS OF RESISTANCE

A body in water which is stationary with respect to water, experiences only hydrostatic pressure. Hydrostatic pressure always acts to oppose the weight of the body. If the body is in motion, then there are also hydrodynamic pressures that act on the body.

FROUDE'S EXPERIMENTS

When testing ship models and then comparing the results to actual ships, the models tended to over predict the resistance of the ship.

Froude had observed that when a ship or model was at its so called Hull speed the wave pattern of the transverse waves (the waves along the hull) have a wavelength equal to the length of the waterline. This means that the ship's bow was riding on one wave crest and so was its stern. This is often called hull speed (the theoretical top speed of the ship) is a function of the length of the ship

$$V = 1.34\sqrt{L}$$

Observing this, Froude realized that the ship resistance problem had to be broken into two different parts: residuary resistance (mainly wave making resistance) and frictional resistance. To get the proper residuary resistance, it was necessary to recreate the wave train created by the ship in the model tests. He found for any ship and geometrically similar model towed at the suitable speed that: There is a frictional drag that is given by the shear due to the viscosity. This can result in 50% of the total resistance in fast ship designs and 80% of the total resistance in slower ship designs.

To account for the frictional resistance Froude decided to tow a series of flat plates and measure the resistance of these plates, which were of the same wetted surface area and length as the model ship, and subtract this frictional resistance from the total resistance and get the remainder as the residuary resistance.

FRICTION

In a viscous fluid, a boundary layer is formed. This causes a net drag due to friction. The boundary layer under goes shear at different rates extending from the hull surface until it reaches the field flow of the water.

WAVE-MAKING RESISTANCE

A ship moving over the surface of undisturbed water sets up waves emanating mainly from the bow and stern of the ship. The waves created by the ship consist of divergent and transverse waves. The divergent waves are observed as the wake of a ship with a series of diagonal or oblique crests moving outwardly from the point of disturbance.

These waves were first studied by Lord Kelvin, who found that regardless of the speed of the ship, they were always contained in the 19 degree (each side) symmetric wedge following the ship. The divergent waves do not cause much resistance against the ships forward motion. However, the transverse waves appear as troughs and crests along the length of a ship and constitute the major part of the wave-making resistance of a ship. The energy associated with the transverse wave system travels at one half the phase velocity or the group velocity of the waves.

The prime mover of the vessel must put additional energy into the system in order to overcome this expense of energy. The relationship between the velocity of ships and that of the transverse waves can be found by equating the wave celerity and the ship's velocity.

SIGNIFICANT WAVE HEIGHT

In physical oceanography, the significant wave height (SWH or Hs) is defined traditionally as the mean wave height (trough to crest) of the highest third of the waves (H1/3).

Nowadays it is usually defined as four times the standard deviation of the surface elevation – or equivalently as four times the square root of the zeroth-order moment (area) of the wave spectrum. The symbol Hm0 is usually used for that latter definition. The significant wave height may thus refer to Hm0 or H1/3; the difference in magnitude between the two definitions is only a few percent.

ORIGIN AND DEFINITION

The original definition resulted from work by the oceanographer Walter Munk during World War II.

The significant wave height was intended to mathematically express the height estimated by a "trained observer". It is commonly used as a measure of the height of ocean waves.

STATISTICAL DISTRIBUTION OF THE HEIGHTS OF INDIVIDUAL WAVES

Significant wave height, scientifically represented as Hs or Hsig, is an important parameter for the statistical distribution of ocean waves. The most common waves are less in height than Hs.

This implies that encountering the significant wave is not too frequent. However, statistically, it is possible to encounter a wave that is much higher than the significant wave.

Generally, the statistical distribution of the individual wave heights is well approximated by a Rayleigh distribution. For example, given that Hs is 10 metres (33 feet), statistically:

- 1 in 10 will be larger than 10.7 metres (35 ft)
- 1 in 100 will be larger than 15.1 metres (50 ft)
- 1 in 1000 will be larger than 18.6 metres (61 ft)

This implies that one might encounter a wave that is roughly double the significant wave height. However, in rapidly changing conditions, the disparity between the significant wave height and the largest individual waves might be even larger.

OTHER STATISTICS

Other statistical measures of the wave height are also widely used. The RMS wave height, which is defined as square root of the average of the squares of all wave heights, is approximately equal to Hs divided by 1.4.

For example, according to the Irish Marine Institute:

- "... at midnight on 9/12/2007 a record significant wave height was recorded of 17.2m at with a period of 14 seconds."

MEASUREMENT

Although most measuring devices estimate the significant wave height from a wave spectrum, satellite radar altimeters are unique in measuring directly the significant wave height thanks to the different time of return from wave crests and troughs within the area illuminated by the radar. The maximum ever measured wave height from a satellite is 20.1m during a North Atlantic storm in 2011.

WEATHER FORECASTS

The World Meteorological Organization stipulates that certain countries are responsible for providing weather forecasts for the world's oceans. These respective countries' meteorological offices are called Regional Specialized Meteorological Centers, or RSMCs. In their weather products, they give ocean wave height forecasts in significant wave height. In the United States, NOAA's National Weather Service is the RSMC for a portion of the North Atlantic, and a portion of the North Pacific. The Ocean Prediction Center and the Tropical Prediction Center's Tropical Analysis and Forecast Branch (TAFB) issue these forecasts.

RSMCs use wind-wave models as tools to help predict the sea conditions. In the U.S., NOAA's WAVEWATCH III model is used heavily.

GENERALIZATION TO WAVE SYSTEMS

A significant wave height is also defined similarly, from the wave spectrum, for the different systems that make up the sea. We then have a significant wave height for the wind-sea or for a particular swell.

SLAMMING

Slamming is the impact of the bottom structure of a ship onto the sea surface. It is mainly observed while sailing in waves, when the bow raises from the water and subsequently impacts on it. Slamming induces extremely high loads to ship structures and is taken into consideration when designing ships.

SPRINGING

Springing as a nautical term refers to global vertical resonant hull girder vibration due to oscillating wave loads along the hull of the ship.

The hydrodynamic theory of springing is not yet fully understood due to the complex description of the surface waves and structure interaction. It is, however, well known that larger ships with longer resonant periods are more exposed to this type of vibration. Examples of this include very large crude carriers and bulk carriers, but possibly also container vessels. The container ships are more slender, has higher service speeds and have more pronounced bow flare. These are also known to get significant whipping (transient) vibrations from bow impacts. Whipping may also occur on blunt ships especially in the cases of flat bottom impacts in the bow area. The bottom part of the bow however rarely exits from the water on such ships.

In the extreme cases it may cause severe fatigue cracking of critical structural details, especially in moderate to rough head seas with low peak periods. Vibration in ballast condition is normally more easily excited by waves than cargo condition. The trade may also matter, since some ships experience more head wind and waves in ballast conditions, while other ships may experience more head wind and waves in cargo condition, thereby vibrating less overall.

The first experience with this phenomenon is related to fatigue cracking on Great Lakes bulk carriers (700 feet) during the 1950s. Later 1000 feet Great Lakes bulk carriers experienced the same problems even if the strength requirements became stricter. Ocean-going ships have not had this problem until recently, when high tensile steel was introduced as a common material in the whole ship to reduce the initial costs. This makes the ships less stiff and the nominal stress level higher. Today's ship rules does not account for this effect which may dominate the contribution to fatigue for some vessels. The vibration from whipping may also increase the extreme loading of ships potentially contributing to breaking vessels in two in harsh storms.

SQUAT EFFECT

The squat effect is the hydrodynamic phenomenon by which a vessel moving quickly through shallow water creates an area of lowered pressure that causes the ship to be closer to the seabed than would otherwise be expected. This phenomenon is caused when water that should normally flow under the hull encounters resistance due to the close proximity of the hull to the seabed.

This causes the water to move faster, creating a low-pressure area with lowered water level surface. This squat effect results from a combination of (vertical) sinkage and a change of trim that may cause the vessel to dip towards the stern or towards the bow.

Squat effect is approximately proportional to the square of the speed of the ship. Thus, by reducing speed by half, the squat effect is reduced by a factor of four. Squat effect is usually felt more when the depth/draft ratio is less than four or when sailing close to a bank. It can lead to unexpected groundings and handling difficulties.

It is believed to have been one of the causes of the 7 August 1992 grounding of the Queen Elizabeth 2 (QE2) off Cuttyhunk Island, near Martha's Vineyard. It is also known to have been a factor in the collision of the bulk carriers Tecam Sea and Federal Fuji in the port of Sorel, Quebec, in April 2000.

At the time of the QE2's grounding she was reportedly traveling at 24 knots (12 m/s) and her draft was 32 feet (9.8 m). The rock upon which she grounded was an uncharted shoal later determined to be 34.5 feet (10.5 m), which should have given her room to spare, if not for the "squat effect." U.S. National Transportation Safety Board investigators found that the QE2's officers significantly underestimated the amount the increase in speed would increase the ship's squat.

The officers allowed for 2 feet (0.61 m) of squat in their calculations, but the NTSB concluded that her squat at that speed and depth would have been between 4.5 and 8 feet (1.4 and 2.4 m).

The second largest cruise ship in the world, Oasis of the Seas, used this effect as a contributing factor to pass under the Great Belt bridge, Denmark, 1 November 2009, on her voyage from the shipyard in Turku, Finland to Florida, USA. Without the presence of the squat effect, the ship wouldn't have been able to clear the bridge safely - the margin would have been very slight. However, travelling at 20 knots (37 km/h) in the shallow channel, Oasis experienced a 30 cm squat, allowing sufficient room to clear the bridge safely.

STABILITY CONDITIONS

The Stability conditions of watercraft are the various standard loading configurations to which a ship, boat, or offshore platform may be subjected. They are recognized by classification societies such as Det Norske Veritas, Lloyd's Register and American Bureau of Shipping (ABS). Classification societies follow rules and guidelines laid down by International Convention for the Safety of Life at Sea (SOLAS) conventions, the International Maritime Organization and laws of the country under which the vessel is flagged, such as the Code of Federal Regulations.

Stability is normally broken into two distinct types: Intact and Damaged

INTACT STABILITY

The vessel is in normal operational configuration. The hull is not breached in any compartment. The vessel will be expected to meet various stability criteria such as GMt (metacentric height), area under the GZ (righting lever) curve, range of stability, trim, etc.

LIGHTSHIP OR LIGHT DISPLACEMENT

The vessel is complete and ready for service in every respect, including permanent ballast, spare parts, lubricating oil, and working stores but is without fuel, cargo, drinking or washing water, officers, crew, passengers, their effects, or any other variable load.

FULL LOAD DEPARTURE OR FULL DISPLACEMENT

Along with all the Lightship loads, the vessel has all systems charged meaning that all fresh water, cooling, lubricating, hydraulic and fuel service header tanks, piping and equipment systems are filled with their normal operating fluids. Crew and effects are at their normal values. Consumables (provisions, potable water and fuel) are at 100% capacity. Ammunition and/ or cargo is at maximum capacity. The vessel is at its limiting draft or legal load line.

STANDARD CONDITION

This is only for military vessels. Along with all the Lightship loads, the vessel has all systems charged meaning that all fresh water, cooling, lubricating, hydraulic and fuel service header tanks, piping and equipment systems are filled with their normal operating fluids. Crew and effects are at their normal values. Consumables (provisions, potable water and fuel) are at 50% capacity. Ammunition and/or cargo is at 100% capacity. This condition is normally used for range and speed calculations.

LIGHT ARRIVAL

Along with all the Lightship loads, the vessel has all systems charged meaning that all fresh water, cooling, lubricating, hydraulic and fuel service header tanks, piping and equipment systems are filled with their normal operating fluids. Crew and effects are at their normal values. Consumables (provisions, potable water and fuel) are at 10% full load. Ammunition and/or cargo is at 100% capacity.

DAMAGED STABILITY

The vessel in the assessed "Worst Intact Condition" is analytically damaged by opening various combinations of watertight compartments to the sea.

The number of compartments and their location are dictated by IMO regulations, SOLAS conventions, or other applicable rules. Typically these conditions are identified by the compartment(s) damaged ex: "Hold #3 and Water Ballast Tank 4 Port"

SUBMARINE HULL

A light hull (casing in British usage) of a submarine is the outer non-watertight hull which provides a hydrodynamically efficient shape. The pressure hull is the inner hull of a submarine; this holds the difference between outside and inside pressure.

SUBMARINE HULL

Modern submarines are usually cigar-shaped. This design, already visible on very early submarines is called a "teardrop hull", and was patterned after the bodies of whales. It significantly reduces the hydrodynamic drag on the sub when submerged, but decreases the sea-keeping capabilities and increases the drag while surfaced.

HISTORY

The concept of an outer hydrodynamically streamlined light hull separated from the inner pressure hull was first introduced in the early pioneering submarine Ictineo I in 1859. However, when military submarines entered service in the early 1900s, the limitations of their propulsion systems forced them to operate on the surface most of the time; their hull designs were a compromise, with the outer hulls resembling a ship, allowing for good surface navigation, and a relatively streamlined superstructure to minimize drag under water.

Because of the slow submerged speeds of these submarines, usually well below 10 knots (19 km/h), the increased drag for underwater travel by the conventional ship like outer hull was considered acceptable. Only late in World War II, when technology enhancements allowed faster and longer submerged operations and increased surveillance by enemy aircraft forced submarines to spend most of their times below the surface, did hull designs become teardrop shaped again, to reduce drag and noise.

On modern military submarines the outer hull (and sometimes also the propeller) is covered with a thick layer of special sound-absorbing rubber, or anechoic plating, to make the submarine more difficult to detect by active and passive SONAR.

TYPES

All small modern submarines and submersibles, as well as the oldest ones, have a single hull. However, for large submarines, the approaches have separated. All Soviet heavy submarines are built with a double hull structure, but American submarines usually are single-hulled. They still have light hull sections in bow and stern, which house main ballast tanks and provide hydrodynamically optimized shape, but the main, usually cylindrical, hull section has only a single plating layer.

LIGHT HULL

The double hull of a submarine is different from a ship's double hull. The external hull, which actually forms the shape of submarine, is called the outer hull, casing or light hull. This term is especially appropriate for Russian submarine construction, where the light hull is usually made of steel that is only 2 to 4 millimetres thick, as it has the same pressure on both sides. The light hull can be used to mount equipment, which if attached directly to the pressure hull could cause unnecessary stress.

The double hull approach also saves space inside the pressure hull, as the ring stiffeners and longitudinals can be located between the hulls. These measures help minimise the size of the pressure hull, which is much heavier than the light hull. Also, in case the submarine is damaged, the light hull takes some of the damage and does not compromise the vessel's integrity, as long as the pressure hull is intact.

PRESSURE HULL

Inside the outer hull there is a strong hull, or pressure hull, which actually withstands the outside pressure and has normal atmospheric pressure inside. The pressure hull is generally constructed of thick high-strength steel with a complex structure and high strength reserve, and is separated with watertight bulkheads into several compartments. The pressure and light hulls aren't separated, and form a three-dimensional structure with increased strength. The interhull space is used for some of the equipment which doesn't require constant pressure to operate. The list significantly differs between submarines, and generally includes different water/air tanks. In case of a single-hull submarine, the light hull and the pressure hull are the same except for the bow and stern.

The task of building a pressure hull is very difficult. No matter how large the submarine is, its hull must be constructed with high precision. Inevitable minor deviations are resisted by the stiffener rings, but even a one inch (25 mm) deviation from roundness results in over 30 percent decrease of hydrostatic load. The total pressure force of several million tons must be distributed evenly over the hull and be oriented longitudinally, as no material could resist such force by bending. A submarine hull has to use expensive transversal construction, with the stiffeners rings located more frequently than the longitudinals. All hull parts must be welded without defects, and all joints are checked several times with different methods.

DIVE DEPTH

The dive depth cannot be increased easily. Simply making the hull thicker increases the weight and requires reduction of the weight of onboard equipment, ultimately resulting in a bathyscaphe. This is affordable for civilian research submersibles, but not military submarines, so their dive depth was always bounded by current technology.

The World War One submarines had their hulls built of carbon steel, and usually had test depths of no more than 100 metres (328 feet). During World War Two, high-strength alloyed steel was introduced, allowing for depths up to 200 metres (656 feet), post-war calculations have suggested crush-depths exceeding 300m for late-war German Type VII U-boats. High-strength alloyed steel is still the main material for submarines today, with 250-350 metres (820 to 1,148 feet) depth limit, which cannot be exceeded on a military submarine without sacrificing other characteristics. To exceed that limit, a few submarines were built with titanium hulls. Titanium is stronger and lighter than steel, and is non-magnetic. Titanium submarines were especially favoured by the Soviets, as they had developed specialized high-strength alloys, built an industry for producing titanium with affordable costs, and have several types of titanium submarines. Titanium alloys allow a major increase in depth, but other systems need to be redesigned as well, so test depth was limited to 1000 metres (3,281 feet) for the Soviet submarine Komsomolets, the deepest-diving military submarine. An Alfa-class submarine may have successfully operated at 1300 metres (4,265 feet), though continuous operation at such depths would be an excessive stress for many submarine systems. Despite its benefits, high costs of titanium construction led to abandonment of titanium submarines idea as the Cold War ended.

OTHER TYPES

There are examples of more than two hulls inside a submarine. The light hull of Typhoon-class submarines houses two main pressure hulls, a smaller third pressure hull constituting most of the sail, two other for torpedoes and steering gear, and between the main hulls 20 MIRV SLBMs along with ballast tanks and some other systems. The Royal Netherlands Navy Dolfijn- and Potvis-class submarines housed three main pressure hulls.

TRIBON

Tribon is a naval architecture program originally developed by Kockum Computer Systems (KCS) for designing commercial and naval vessels. KCS was spun off from Kockums shipyards as an independent company, later renamed Tribon Systems, which was in turn acquired by AVEVA in 2004.

Tribon is actually a family of programs that create and refer to a common set of databases containing the design details of the ship. Together, these databases are used to depict a 3D model of the ship, with embedded information for all of the parts of the design, from ship structural elements to pipe segments to equipment. Many common ship design elements, especially equipment, can be downloaded from databases on Tribon.com.

VERY LARGE FLOATING STRUCTURE

Very large floating structures (VLFSs) or, as some literature refers to them, very large floating platforms (VLFPs) can be constructed to create floating airports, bridges, breakwaters, piers and docks, storage facilities (for oil & natural gas), wind and solar power plants, for military purposes, to create industrial space, emergency bases, entertainment facilities (such as casinos), recreation parks, mobile offshore structures and even for habitation. Currently, different concepts have been proposed for building floating cities or huge living complexes.

OVERVIEW

Unlike the top surface of vessels, that of a VLFS is used as the ground, and therefore the floating structure should provide a very large surface area. It can be constructed by joining the necessary number of floating units together.

The design of the floating structure must obey safety and strength requirements, operating conditions, etc. Steel, concrete (prestressed or reinforced hybrid) or steel-concrete composite materials may be used to build the floating structure. The motions of the floating structure must be less than those allowed to ensure the safety of people and facilities on a VLFS. Generally, floating structures shall be moored at the same site for a long time.

CLASSIFICATION

VLFSs may be classified under two broad categories, namely the pontoon-type and the semi-submersible type. The former type is a simple box structure and features high stability, low manufacturing cost and easy maintenance and repair. In open sea, where the wave heights are relatively large, it is necessary to use the semi-submersible VLFS type to minimize the effects of waves while maintaining a constant buoyant force. VLFSs of the semi-submersible type are used for oil and gas exploration in sea and other purposes. They are fixed in place by column tubes, piles, or other bracing systems.

In contrast, the pontoon-type VLFS just floats (lies) on the sea surface. The pontoon-type VLFS is very flexible compared to other kinds of offshore structures, so that the elastic deformations are more important than their rigid body motions. Thus, hydroelastic analysis takes center stage in the analysis of the pontoon-type VLFSs. Together with the motion of the floating structure, the response of the structure to water waves and the impact on the entire fluid domain have to be studied.

VLFS TYPES

Pontoon-type VLFSs are also known in the literature as mat-like VLFSs because of their small draft in relation to the length dimensions. Very large pontoon-type floating structure is often called Mega-Floats. As a rule, the Mega-Float is a floating structure having at least one length dimension greater than 60 meters. Horizontally large floating structures can be from 500 to 5000 meters in length and 100 to 1000 meters in width, while their thickness can be of the order of about 2-10 meters.

Aircushion supported Mega-Floaters are mega floaters that are supported by an air cushion. They were invented by Jan Van Kessel of TU Delft.

WATERCRAFT

The term watercraft covers a range of different vehicles including ships, boats, hovercraft and submarines, and differs from a simple device that merely floats, such as a log raft.

GREAT SHIPS

Seafaring has a large corpus of traditional lore associated with watercrafts, in both its meanings, as the foundation of its heritage and culture in which most seafarers see a significant degree of pride, and which forms their trade and professional identity. This is often reflected in the industry-specific terminology and concepts that have been retained and are now applied for the sake of tradition alone. Aside from small craft used by individuals, maritime tradition identifies a ship as any water vehicle that has, or is capable of carrying three masts within its hull.

Three masted ships at one time were called the Great Ships, and marked transition in European seafaring from shallow coastal waters of the Age of Navigation confined primarily to the European shores and those of North Africa, via the Age of Discovery of other continents in relative proximity of Western Europe, to the "deep sea" oceanic sailing of the Age of Sail. The term 'a great ship' therefore holds a deeper and far more significant meaning to seafarers than 'landlubbers', or those who do not serve on ships or other vessels, and has remained so through the Age of Steam and into the 21st century.

While rigged masts have been discontinued for the vast majority of ships since the late 19th century, a rule of thumb based on the hull having a wooden construction would determine her as a ship. If the length of the watercraft deck prevents the mounting of three masts, it is a boat, while a single-masted hull can be termed a craft. This is paralleled with the degree of difficulty that was required in the past by different trades constructing the hull based on complexity. A ship was always constructed by a shipwright working with a naval surveyor or a naval architect. A boat could be constructed by a ship's carpenter. A watercraft such as a lifeboat, a dinghy, or a runabout could be constructed by any craftsman familiar with woodworking, such as a builder's carpenter or a joiner, or by a qualified marine trades person or shipwright.

USES OF WATER CRAFT

Usually the purposes behind watercraft designs and skills are for seafaring education or leisure activities, fishing and resource extraction, transportation of cargo or passengers, and for conducting combat or salvage operations. In general, the purpose of a water vehicle identifies its utility with a maritime industry sub-sector.

DESIGN

The design from which a water vehicle is created usually seeks to achieve a balance between internal capacity (tonnage), speed and seaworthiness. Tonnage is predominantly a consideration in transport operations, speed is important for warships, and safety is a primary consideration for less experienced or often smaller and less stable training and leisure vehicles. This is due to the great level of regulatory compliance required by the larger watercraft, which ensures very infrequent instances of foundering at sea through application of extensive computer modeling and ship model basin testing before shipyard construction begins.

PROPULSION

Propulsion is the primary application of technology in watercraft. Historically water vehicles have been propelled by poles, paddles or oars, through manipulation of sailing rigs that propel by lifting using the wind, and a variety of engineered machinery that creates subsurface thrust through the process or internal combustion. The technological history of watercraft in the European history can be divided into marine propulsion using the simple paddle craft, oared galleys from the 8th century BCE until 15th century, lateen sail during the Age of Discovery from the early 15th century and into the early 17th century, full rigged ships of the Age of Sail from the 16th to the mid 19th century, the Age of Steam marine steam engine roughly between 1770 and use of the steam turbine until 1914, the internal combustion engines using diesel, petrol and LNG as fuels from the turn of the 20th century, which has been supplemented to some degree with the nuclear marine propulsion since the 1950s. Current technological development seeks to identify cheaper, renewable and less polluting sources of propulsion for watercraft of all shapes and sizes.

CONSTRUCTION

Secondary applications of technology in watercraft have been those of used structural materials, navigation aids, and in the case of warships, weapon systems. The purpose of usage and the physical environment define the materials used in construction which had historically included grasses, leather, timbers, metals combined with timber or without, silicate and plastic derivatives, and others.

NAVIGATION

Navigation aids have varied over time from astronomical observation, to mechanical mechanisms, and more recently analog and digital computer devices that now rely on GPS systems.

WEAPONS

Naval weapon systems have closely followed the development in land weapons, developing from:

- aircraft carriers
- breach-loading rifled guns
- direct enemy hull ramming to use of basic mechanical projectiles
- firing shells
- missiles and remotely piloted devices
- naval mine layers
- smooth-bore cannonball firing guns
- torpedo-armed submarines
- warships armed with fire control directed weapons

Until development of steam propulsion was coupled with rapid firing breach-loading guns, naval combat was often concluded by a boarding combat between the opposing crews. Since the early 20th century, there has been a substantial development in technologies which allow force projection from a naval task force to a land objective using marine infantry.

WAVE-MAKING RESISTANCE

Wave-making resistance is a form of drag that affects surface watercraft, such as boats and ships, and reflects the energy required to push the water out of the way of the hull. This energy goes into creating the wave.

PHYSICS

For small displacement hulls, such as sailboats or rowboats, wave-making resistance is the major source of the marine vessel drag. A salient property of water waves is dispersiveness, i.e. the longer the wave, the faster it moves.

Waves generated by a ship are affected by her geometry and speed, and most of the energy given by the ship for making waves is transferred to water through the bow and stern parts. Simply speaking, these two wave systems, i.e. bow and stern waves interact with each other, and the resulting waves are responsible for the resistance.

E.g., the phase speed of deepwater waves is proportional to the square root of the wavelength of the generated waves, and the length of a ship causes the difference in phases of waves generated by bow and stern parts. Thus, there is a direct relationship between the waterline length (and thus wave propagation speed) and the magnitude of the wave-making resistance.

A simple way of considering wave-making resistance is to look at the hull in relation to bow and stern waves. If the length of a ship is half the waves generated, the resulting wave will be very small due to cancellation, and if the length is the same as the wavelength, the wave will be large due to enhancement.

The phase speed C of waves is given by the following formula:

$$c = \sqrt{\frac{g}{2\pi} l}$$

where l is the length of the wave and g the gravitational acceleration. Substituting in the appropriate value for g yields the equation:

$$\text{c in knots} \approx 1.341 \times \sqrt{\text{length in ft}} \approx \frac{4}{3} \times \sqrt{\text{length in ft}}$$

Or, in metric units:

$$\text{c in knots} \approx 2.429 \times \sqrt{\text{length in m}} \approx \sqrt{6 \times \text{length in m}} \approx 2.5 \times \sqrt{\text{length in m}}$$

These values, 1.34, 2.5 and very easy 6, are often used in the hull speed rule of thumb used to compare potential speeds of displacement hulls, and this relationship is also fundamental to the Froude number, used in the comparison of different scales of watercraft.

When the vessel exceeds a "speed–length ratio" (speed in knots divided by square root of length in feet) of 0.94, it starts to outrun most of its bow wave, the hull actually settles slightly in the water as it is now only supported by two wave peaks. As the vessel exceeds a speed-length ratio of 1.34, the hull speed, the wavelength is now longer than the hull, and the stern is no longer supported by the wake, causing the stern to squat, and the bow rise. The hull is now starting to climb its own bow wave, and resistance begins to increase at a very high rate. While it is possible to drive a displacement hull faster than a speed-length ratio of 1.34, it is prohibitively expensive to do so. Most large vessels operate at speed-length ratios well below that level, at speed-length ratios of under 1.0.

WAYS OF REDUCING WAVE-MAKING RESISTANCE

Since wave-making resistance is based on the energy required to push the water out of the way of the hull, there are a number of ways that this can be minimized.

Reduced displacement

Reducing the displacement of the craft, by eliminating excess weight, is the most straightforward way to reduce the wave making drag. Another way is to shape the hull so as to generate lift as it moves through the water. Semi-displacement hulls and planing hulls do this, and they are able to break through the hull speed barrier and transition into a realm where drag increases at a much lower rate. The disadvantage of this is that planing is only practical on smaller vessels, with high power-to-weight ratios, such as motorboats. It is not a practical solution for a large vessel such as a supertanker.

Fine entry

A hull with a blunt bow has to push the water away very quickly to pass through, and this high acceleration requires large amounts of energy. By using a fine bow, with a sharper angle that pushes the water out of the way more gradually, the amount of energy required to displace the water will be less, even though the same total amount of water will be displaced. A modern variation is the wave-piercing design.

Bulbous bow

A special type of bow, called a bulbous bow, is often used on large motor vessels to reduce wave making drag. The bulb alters the waves generated by the hull, but due to its very limited range of effect, is only useful on large motor vessels operating at constant speeds.

SEMI-DISPLACEMENT AND PLANING HULLS

Since semi-displacement and planing hulls generate a significant amount of lift in operation, they are capable of breaking the barrier of the wave propagation speed and operating in realms of much lower drag, but to do this they must be capable of first pushing past that speed, which requires significant power. Once the hull gets over the hump of the bow wave, the rate of increase of the wave drag will start to reduce significantly.

A qualitative interpretation of the wave resistance plot is that a displacement hull resonates with a wave that has a crest near its bow and a trough near its stern, because the water is pushed away at the bow and pulled back at the stern. A planing hull simply pushed down on the water under it, so it resonates with a wave that has a trough under it, which has about twice the length and therefore four times the speed.

WAVE-PIERCING HULL

A wave-piercing boat hull has a very fine bow, with reduced buoyancy in the forward portions.

When a wave is encountered, the lack of buoyancy means the hull pierces through the water rather than riding over the top - resulting in a smoother ride than traditional designs, and in diminished stress on the vessel and crew. It also reduces a boat's wave making resistance.

Design theory calls for very long thin hulls, so in practice most are multi-hulls such as catamarans.

The main current usage areas are passenger ferries and military craft.

The reduced buoyancy can be problematic in rough sea, because the ship isn't lifted above the wave as much.

8

Shipbuilding

Shipbuilding is the construction of ships and floating vessels. It normally takes place in a specialized facility known as a shipyard. Shipbuilders, also called shipwrights, follow a specialized occupation that traces its roots to before recorded history.

Shipbuilding and ship repairs, both commercial and military, are referred to as "naval engineering". The construction of boats is a similar activity called boat building. The dismantling of ships is called ship breaking.

HISTORY

PREHISTORY

Archaeological evidence indicates that humans arrived on Borneo at least 120,000 years ago, probably by sea from the Asian mainland during an ice age period when the sea was lower and distances between islands shorter. The ancestors of Australian Aborigines and New Guineans also went across the Lombok Strait to Sahul by boat over 50,000 years ago.

4th Millennium BC

Evidence from Ancient Egypt shows that the early Egyptians knew how to assemble planks of wood into a ship hull as early as 3000 BC. The Archaeological Institute of America reports that some of the oldest ships yet unearthed are known as the Abydos boats. These are a group of 14 discovered ships in Abydos that were constructed of wooden planks which were "sewn" together.

Discovered by Egyptologist David O'Connor of New York University, woven straps were found to have been used to lash the planks together, and reeds or grass stuffed between the planks helped to seal the seams. Because the ships are all buried together and near a mortuary belonging to Pharaoh Khasekhemwy, originally they were all thought to have belonged to him, but one of the 14 ships dates to 3000 BC, and the associated pottery jars buried with the vessels also suggest earlier dating. The ship dating to 3000 BC was about 25 m, 75 feet long and is now thought to perhaps have belonged to an earlier pharaoh. According to professor O'Connor, the 5,000-year-old ship may have even belonged to Pharaoh Aha.

3rd Millennium BC

Early Egyptians also knew how to assemble planks of wood with treenails to fasten them together, using pitch for caulking the seams. The "Khufu ship", a 43.6-meter vessel sealed into a pit in the Giza pyramid complex at the foot of the Great Pyramid of Giza in the Fourth Dynasty around 2500 BC, is a full-size surviving example which may have fulfilled the symbolic function of a solar barque. Early Egyptians also knew how to fasten the planks of this ship together with mortise and tenon joints.

The oldest known tidal dock in the world was built around 2500 BC during the Harappan civilisation at Lothal near the present day Mangrol harbour on the Gujarat coast in India. Other ports were probably at Balakot and Dwarka.

However, it is probable that many small-scale ports, and not massive ports, were used for the Harappan maritime trade. Ships from the harbour at these ancient port cities established trade with Mesopotamia. Shipbuilding and boatmaking may have been prosperous industries in ancient India. Native labourers may have manufactured the flotilla of boats used by Alexander the Great to navigate across the Hydaspes and even the Indus, under Nearchos. The Indians also exported teak for shipbuilding to ancient Persia. Other references to Indian timber used for shipbuilding is noted in the works of Ibn Jubayr.

2nd millennium BC

The ships of Ancient Egypt's Eighteenth Dynasty were typically about 25 meters (80 ft) in length, and had a single mast, sometimes consisting of two poles lashed together at the top making an "A" shape. They mounted a single square sail on a yard, with an additional spar along the bottom of the sail.

These ships could also be oar propelled. The ocean and sea going ships of Ancient Egypt were constructed with cedar wood, most likely hailing from Lebanon.

The ships of Phoenicia seem to have been of a similar design. The Greeks and probably others introduced the use of multiple banks of oars for additional speed, and the ships were of a light construction for speed and so they could be carried ashore.

1st millennium BC

The naval history of China stems back to the Spring and Autumn Period (722 BC–481 BC) of the ancient Chinese Zhou Dynasty. The Chinese built large rectangular barges known as "castle ships", which were essentially floating fortresses complete with multiple decks with guarded ramparts.

Early 1st millennium AD

The ancient Chinese also built ramming vessels as in the Greco-Roman tradition of the trireme, although oar-steered ships in China lost favor very early on since it was in the 1st century China that the stern-mounted rudder was first developed. This was dually met with the introduction of the Han Dynasty junk ship design in the same century.

Archeological investigations done at Portus near Rome have revealed inscriptions indicating the existence of a 'guild of shipbuilders' during the time of Hadrian.

MEDIEVAL EUROPE, SONG CHINA, ABBASID CALIPHATE, PACIFIC ISLANDERS

Viking longships developed from an alternate tradition of clinker-built hulls fastened with leather thongs. Sometime around the 12th century, northern European ships began to be built with a straight sternpost, enabling the mounting of a rudder, which was much more durable than a steering oar held over the side. Development in the Middle Ages favored "round ships", with a broad beam and heavily curved at both ends. Another important ship type was the galley which was constructed with both sails and oars.

An insight into ship building in the North Sea/Baltic areas of the early medieval period was found at Sutton Hoo, England, where a ship was buried with a chieftain. the ship was 26 metres (85 ft) long and, 4.3 metres (14 ft) wide. Upward from the keel, the hull was made by overlapping nine planks on either side with rivets fastening the oaken planks together. It could hold upwards of thirty men.

The first extant treatise on shipbuilding was written ca. 1436 by Michael of Rhodes, a man who began his career as an oarsman on a Venetian galley in 1401 and worked his way up into officer positions. He wrote and illustrated a book that contains a treatise on ship building, a treatise on mathematics, much material on astrology, and other materials. His treatise on shipbuilding treats three kinds of galleys and two kinds of round ships.

Outside Medieval Europe, great advances were being made in shipbuilding. The shipbuilding industry in Imperial China reached its height during the Song Dynasty, Yuan Dynasty, and early Ming Dynasty, building commercial vessels that by the end of this period were to reach a size and sophistication far exceeding that of contemporary Europe. The mainstay of China's merchant and naval fleets was the junk, which had existed for centuries, but it was at this time that the large ships based on this design were built.

During the Sung period (960–1279 AD), the establishment of China's first official standing navy in 1132 AD and the enormous increase in maritime trade abroad (from Heian Japan to Fatimid Egypt) allowed the shipbuilding industry in provinces like Fujian to thrive as never before. The largest seaports in the world were in China and included Guangzhou, Quanzhou, and Xiamen.

In the Islamic world, shipbuilding thrived at Basra and Alexandria, the dhow, felucca, baghlah and the sambuk, became symbols of successful maritime trade around the Indian Ocean; from the ports of East Africa to Southeast Asia and the ports of Sindh and Hind (India) during the Abbasid period.

At this time islands spread over vast distances across the Pacific Ocean were being colonised by the Melenesians and Polynesians, who built giant canoes and progressed to great catamarans.

EARLY MODERN

With the development of the carrack, the west moved into a new era of ship construction by building the first regular ocean going vessels. In a relatively short time, these ships grew to an unprecedented size, complexity and cost.

Shipyards became large industrial complexes and the ships built were financed by consortia of investors These considerations led to the documentation of design and construction practices in what had previously been a secretive trade run by master shipwrights, and ultimately led to the field of naval architecture, where professional designers and draughtsmen played an increasingly important role. Even so, construction techniques changed only very gradually. The ships of the Napoleonic Wars were still built more or less to the same basic plan as those of the Spanish Armada of two centuries earlier but there had been numerous subtle improvements in ship design and construction throughout this period. For instance, the introduction of tumblehome; adjustments to the shapes of sails and hulls; the introduction of the wheel; the introduction of hardened copper fastenings below the waterline; the introduction of copper sheathing as a deterrent to shipworm and fouling; etc.

INDUSTRIAL REVOLUTION

The industrial revolution made possible the use of new materials and designs that radically altered shipbuilding. Other than its widespread use in fastenings, Iron was gradually adopted in ship construction, initially in discrete areas in a wooden hull needing greater strength, (e.g. as deck knees, hanging knees, knee riders and the like).

Then, in the form of plates rivetted together and made watertight, it was used to form the hull itself. Initially copying wooden construction traditions with a frame over which the hull was fastened, Isambard Kingdom Brunel's Great Britain of 1843 was the first radical new design, being built entirely of wrought iron. Despite her success, and the great savings in cost and space provided by the iron hull, compared to a copper sheathed counterpart, there remained problems with fouling due to the adherence of weeds and barnacles. As a result composite construction remained the dominant approach where fast ships were required, with wooden timbers laid over an iron frame (the Cutty Sark is a famous example). Later Great Britain's iron hull was sheathed in wood to enable it to carry a copper-based sheathing.

Brunel's Great Eastern represented the next great development in shipbuilding. Built in association with John Scott Russell, it used longitudinal stringers for strength, inner and outer hulls, and bulkheads to form multiple watertight compartments. Steel also supplanted wrought iron when it became readily available in the latter half of the 19th century, providing great savings when compared with iron in cost and weight. Wood continued to be favored for the decks.

WORLDWIDE SHIPBUILDING INDUSTRY

After the Second World War, shipbuilding (which encompasses the shipyards, the marine equipment manufacturers, and many related service and knowledge providers) grew as an important and strategic industry in a number of countries around the world. This importance stems from:

- The large number of skilled workers required directly by the shipyard, along with supporting industries such as steel mills, railroads and engine manufacturers; and
- A nation's need to manufacture and repair its own navy and vessels that support its primary industries

Historically, the industry has suffered from the absence of global rules and a tendency towards (state-supported) over-investment due to the fact that shipyards offer a wide range of technologies, employ a significant number of workers, and generate income as the shipbuilding market is global.

Shipbuilding is therefore an attractive industry for developing nations. Japan used shipbuilding in the 1950s and 1960s to rebuild its industrial structure; South Korea started to make shipbuilding a strategic industry in the 1970s, and China is now in the process of repeating these models with large state-supported investments in this industry. Conversely, Croatia is privatising its shipbuilding industry.

As a result, the world shipbuilding market suffers from over-capacities, depressed prices (although the industry experienced a price increase in the period 2003–2005 due to strong demand for new ships which was in excess of actual cost increases), low profit margins, trade distortions and widespread subsidisation. All efforts to address the problems in the OECD have so far failed, with the 1994 international shipbuilding agreement never entering into force and the 2003–2005 round of negotiations being paused in September 2005 after no agreement was possible.

After numerous efforts to restart the negotiations these were formally terminated in December 2010. The OECD's Council Working Party on Shipbuilding (WP6) will continue its efforts to identify and progressively reduce factors that distort the shipbuilding market.

Where state subsidies have been removed and domestic industrial policies do not provide support, in high-cost nations shipbuilding has usually gone into steady, if not rapid, decline. The British shipbuilding industry is a prime example of this.

From a position in the early 1970s where British yards could still build the largest types of sophisticated merchant ships, British shipbuilders today have been reduced to a handful specialising in defence contracts and repair work. In the U.S.A., the Jones Act (which places restrictions on the ships that can be used for moving domestic cargoes) has meant that merchant shipbuilding has continued, but such protection has failed to penalise shipbuilding inefficiencies. The consequence of this is contract prices that are far higher than those of any other nation building oceangoing ships.

PRESENT DAY SHIPBUILDING

China is an emerging shipbuilder overtook South Korea during the 2008-2010 global financial crisis as they won new orders for medium and small-sized container ships. China is now firmly the world's largest shipbuilder with 45% of the world's total orders, and its quality and technology have improved very much.

Today, South Korea is the world's second largest shipbuilding country with a global market share of 29% in 2012. South Korea leads in the production of large vessels such as cruise liners, super tankers, LNG carriers, drill ships, and large container ships. In the 3rd quarter of 2011, South Korea won all 18 orders for LNG carriers, 3 out of 5 drill ships and 5 out of 7 large container ships. Japan had been the dominant ship building country from the 1960s through to the end of 1990s but gradually lost its competitive advantage to the emerging industry in South Korea which had the advantages of much cheaper wages, strong government backing and a cheaper currency. South Korean production overtook Japan's in 2003 and Japanese market share has since fallen sharply.

The market share of European ship builders began to decline in the 1960s as they lost work to the Japanese in the same way as Japanese builders have lost work to South Koreans more recently; Europe's production is now a tenth of South Korea's and is primarily military, although cruise liners and some cargo ships are still built in Italy, Finland, France, Germany and Denmark. The output of the United States also underwent a similar change.

South Korea's shipyards are highly efficient, with the world's largest shipyard in Ulsan operated by Hyundai Heavy Industries slipping a newly built, $80 million vessel into the water every four working days. South Korea's "big three" shipbuilders, Hyundai Heavy Industries, Samsung Heavy Industries, and Daewoo Shipbuilding & Marine Engineering, dominate global shipbuilding, with STX Shipbuilding, Hyundai Samho Heavy Industries, Hanjin Heavy Industries, and Sungdong Shipbuilding & Marine Engineering also ranking among the top ten shipbuilders in the world. In 2007, STX Shipbuilding further strengthened South Korea's leading position in the industry by acquiring Aker Yards, the largest shipbuilding group in Europe. (The former Aker Yards was renamed STX Europe in 2008). In the first half of 2011, South Korean shipbuilders won new orders to build 25 LNG carriers, out of the total 29 orders placed worldwide during the period.

World shipbuilding market share by countries (2012)

Rank	Country	Combined GT	%
1	China	67,000,000	45%
2	South Korea	53,000,000	29%
3	Japan	28,000,000	18%
4	European Union	4,500,000	1%
	Rest of the world	11,000,000	7%

MODERN SHIPBUILDING MANUFACTURING TECHNIQUES

Modern shipbuilding makes considerable use of prefabricated sections. Entire multi-deck segments of the hull or superstructure will be built elsewhere in the yard, transported to the building dock or slipway, then lifted into place. This is known as "block construction". The most modern shipyards pre-install equipment, pipes, electrical cables, and any other components within the blocks, to minimize the effort needed to assemble or install components deep within the hull once it is welded together.

Ship design work, also called naval architecture, may be conducted using a ship model basin. Modern ships, since roughly 1940, have been produced almost exclusively of welded steel. Early welded steel ships used steels with inadequate fracture toughness, which resulted in some ships suffering catastrophic brittle fracture structural cracks. Since roughly 1950, specialized steels such as ABS Steels with good properties for ship construction have been used. Although it is commonly accepted that modern steel has eliminated brittle fracture in ships, some controversy still exists. Brittle fracture of modern vessels continues to occur from time to time because grade A and grade B steel of unknown toughness or fracture appearance transition temperature (FATT) in ships' side shells can be less than adequate for all ambient conditions.

SHIP REPAIR INDUSTRY

All ships need maintenance and repairs. A part of these jobs must be carried out under the supervision of the Classification Society. A lot of maintenance is carried out while at sea or in port by ship's staff. However a large number of repair and maintenance works can only be carried out while the ship is out of commercial operation, in a Shiprepair Yard. Prior to undergoing repairs, tankers must dock at a Deballasting Station for completing the tank cleaning operations and pumping ashore its slops (dirty cleaning water and hydrocarbon residues).

Index

P

R

S

T

U

V